Finding the Synoptic Gospels' Construction Process

# Linguistic Biblical Studies

*Series Editors*

Stanley E. Porter
Jesús Peláez
Jonathan M. Watt

VOLUME 26

This series, Linguistic Biblical Studies, is dedicated to the development and promotion of linguistically informed study of the Bible in its original languages. Biblical studies has greatly benefited from modern theoretical and applied linguistics, but stands poised to benefit from further integration of the two fields of study. Most linguistics has studied contemporary languages, and attempts to apply linguistic methods to study of ancient languages requires systematic re-assessment of their approaches. This series is designed to address such challenges, by providing a venue for linguistically based analysis of the languages of the Bible. As a result, monograph-length studies and collections of essays in the major areas of linguistics, such as syntax, semantics, pragmatics, discourse analysis and text linguistics, corpus linguistics, cognitive linguistics, comparative linguistics, and the like, will be encouraged, and any theoretical linguistic approach will be considered, both formal and functional. Primary consideration is given to the Greek of the New and Old Testaments and of other relevant ancient authors, but studies in Hebrew, Coptic, and other related languages will be entertained as appropriate.

The titles published in this series are listed at *brill.com/lbs*

# Finding the Synoptic Gospels' Construction Process

*A Comparative-Linguistic Analysis of the Eucharist and Its Co-texts*

By

Hojoon J. Ahn

BRILL

LEIDEN | BOSTON

Library of Congress Cataloging-in-Publication Data

Names: Ahn, Hojoon J., author.
Title: Finding Synoptic Gospels' Construction Process : a
   Comparative-Linguistic Analysis of the Eucharist and Its Co-texts / by
   Hojoon J. Ahn.
Description: Leiden ; Boston : Brill, 2024 | Series: Linguistic biblical
   studies, 1877-7554 ; vol. 26 | Includes bibliographical references and
   index. | Summary: "This study critically examines the current state of
   Synoptic Gospel studies, particularly many scholars' reliance on the
   literary-dependence hypothesis, and endeavors to advance a more balanced
   approach. The author attempts to deduce the Synoptic Gospels'
   construction process by meticulously examining the Eucharist and its
   co-text within these Gospels, by employing a model of Mode Register
   Analysis based on Systemic Functional Linguistics. This study uncovers
   the probability that each designated text in the Synoptic Gospels was
   constructed based on oral Gospel tradition(s) under the influence of
   each constructor's identity"—Provided by publisher.
Identifiers: LCCN 2024014504 (print) | LCCN 2024014505 (ebook) | ISBN
   9789004696327 (hardback) | ISBN 9789004696372 (ebook)
Subjects: LCSH: Lord's Supper. | Bible. Gospels—Criticism, interpretation,
   etc.
Classification: LCC BV825.3 .A43 2024 (print) | LCC BV825.3 (ebook) | DDC
   234/.163—dc23/eng/20240520
LC record available at https://lccn.loc.gov/2024014504
LC ebook record available at https://lccn.loc.gov/2024014505

Typeface for the Latin, Greek, and Cyrillic scripts: "Brill". See and download: brill.com/brill-typeface.

ISSN 1877-7554
ISBN 978-90-04-69632-7 (hardback)
ISBN 978-90-04-69637-2 (e-book)
DOI 10.1163/9789004696372

Copyright 2024 by Hojoon J. Ahn. Published by Koninklijke Brill BV, Leiden, The Netherlands.
Koninklijke Brill BV incorporates the imprints Brill, Brill Nijhoff, Brill Schöningh, Brill Fink, Brill mentis,
Brill Wageningen Academic, Vandenhoeck & Ruprecht, Böhlau and V&R unipress.
Koninklijke Brill BV reserves the right to protect this publication against unauthorized use. Requests for
re-use and/or translations must be addressed to Koninklijke Brill BV via brill.com or copyright.com.

This book is printed on acid-free paper and produced in a sustainable manner.

# Contents

Preface VII
Acknowledgments VIII
List of Figures and Tables X
Abbreviations XIII

Introduction 1

### 1 A Survey of Studies on the Synoptic Problem 7
1 Introduction 7
2 A Brief History of the Studies Related to the Synoptic Problem 8
3 Four Major Views 30
4 Analysis and Evaluation of the Literary Dependence Hypothesis 40
5 A Complementing Approach to Resolve the Synoptic Problem 44
6 The Synoptic Gospels' Authorship and Its Implication for This Study 46
7 The Position of This Study 52
8 Conclusion 52

### 2 Methodology—Mode Register Analysis 54
1 Foundational Concepts for Methodology 54
2 Mode Register Analysis Based on SFL 58
3 Systemic Functional Linguistics 59
4 Register Analysis Based on SFL for Analyzing Ancient Greek Texts 63
5 Mode: Textual Meaning 67
6 Procedure 90

### 3 Mode Register Analysis of Matthew 26:14–35 91
1 Thematization 91
2 Cohesion 97
3 Orality and Textuality 119
4 Verbal Aspect 121
5 Conclusion 123

### 4 Mode Register Analysis of Mark 14:10–31 125
1 Thematization 125
2 Cohesion 131
3 Orality and Textuality 151

# VI
CONTENTS

    4   Verbal Aspect   153
    5   Conclusion   155

## 5 Mode Register Analysis of Luke 22:3–23, 31–34   156
    1   Scope of the Text for Analysis   156
    2   Thematization   156
    3   Cohesion   163
    4   Orality and Textuality   181
    5   Verbal Aspect   184
    6   Conclusion   186

## 6 Comparison and Implications   187
    1   Thematization   187
    2   Cohesion   188
    3   Orality and Textuality   200
    4   Verbal Aspect   201
    5   Summary   203

## 7 Conclusion and Further Research   205
    1   Conclusions   205
    2   Further Possible Research   210

## *Appendices*

Appendix 1: Prime and Subsequent Analysis of Matthew 26:14–35   217
Appendix 2: Prime and Subsequent Analysis of Mark 14:10–31   220
Appendix 3: Prime and Subsequent Analysis of Luke 22:3–23, 31–34   223
Appendix 4: Prime and Subsequent Analysis of Luke 22:24–30   226
Appendix 5: Theme and Rheme Analysis of Matthew 26:14–35   227
Appendix 6: Theme and Rheme Analysis of Mark 14:10–31   235
Appendix 7: Theme and Rheme Analysis of Luke 22:3–23, 31–34   242
Appendix 8: Theme and Rheme Analysis of Luke 22:24–30   249
Appendix 9: Translation of Matthew 26:14–35 Based on Conjunction and
   Verbal Aspect Analysis   251
Appendix 10: Translation of Mark 14:10–31 Based on Conjunction and
   Verbal Aspect Analysis   254
Appendix 11: Translation of Luke 22:3–23, 31–34 Based on Conjunction
   and Verbal Aspect Analysis   256
Bibliography   258
Index of Modern Authors   272
Index of Biblical References   275

# Preface

During my time as a part-time porter, one of the challenging tasks was folding aprons. After washing and drying dozens of aprons, their straps would become entangled with each other, forming a complex web which resembled tangled hair. Untangling these apron straps required a considerable amount of patience. Initially, I tried to untangle them forcefully, but that only exacerbated the situation, tightening the knots further. The approach I found was to take one strap at a time, carefully untangle the entwined sections, and gradually work my way through. With time and effort, gaps would form between the straps, and they would eventually unravel. This process reminds me of what I encountered while dealing with the so-called "Synoptic Problem" in this monograph. This subject matter was so intricately interwoven, much like the tangled apron straps. Thus, my goal was not to resolve the broad issue but to focus on identifying and untangling a single strand, creating a small opening that may allow the release of subsequent strands.

This study attempts to analyze the Eucharist in the Synoptic Gospels including their co-texts (Matt 26:14–35; Mark 14:10–31; Luke 22:3–23, 31–34), via a Mode Register Analysis based on Systemic Functional Linguistics. The purpose of this study is threefold: (1) to model a linguistic methodology and to apply it to each text of the Eucharist and its co-texts in the Synoptic Gospels, (2) to find meaningful linguistic characteristics of each designated text via a comparative analysis based on the preceding study, and finally (3) to suggest a balanced and plausible hypothesis which may offer convincing explanations of the Synoptic Gospels' construction process. The thesis of this study is as follows: in the Synoptic Gospels' construction process, each constructor reflected the oral Gospel tradition(s) significantly, as the one who had formed/contributed the tradition (probably Matthew), or the one who delivered it (probably Mark), or the one who preserved it (probably Luke), though there is also the possibility that each of them made use of written sources including the other Gospel(s).

# Acknowledgments

This monograph is a revision of my doctoral dissertation at McMaster Divinity College (2023). I am grateful to those who provided support and assistance throughout the writing of this monograph.

First and foremost, I extend my profound gratitude to my doctoral advisor, Dr. Stanley E. Porter. Stan has read and commented insightfully on the papers I wrote during his courses (especially, "History of Biblical Interpretation," "Synoptic Gospels," and "Advanced Grammar and Linguistics"), which formed the foundation of this volume. Throughout the process in writing my dissertation, he provided thoughtful suggestions that greatly aided the progression of this monograph. Most importantly, his encouragement and support from the inception to the completion of this seemingly daunting project enabled me to run and finally finish the race. I deeply appreciate his dedication and care. I also extend deep gratitude to my second supervisor, Dr. Cynthia L. Westfall. From the proposal to the final draft, Cindy offered meticulous feedback and posed challenging questions, significantly enhancing the balance and comprehensiveness of this monograph. I am thankful for her efforts and insights. Along with Stan and Cindy, I extend my sincere gratitude to the external examiner, Dr. Todd R. Chipman, whose role was invaluable. His insightful questions and suggestions during the defense contributed to the refinement of this monograph.

During my academic endeavors, I faced challenging periods, yet my six-year tenure as a chapel assistant at MDC's Chapel provided me the strength and comfort, derived from divine guidance. I express my sincere gratitude to Dr. Wendy J. Porter for giving me the opportunity and supporting me throughout. To Dong-jin Park, Ji-hoe Kim, Zachary K. Dawson, and many other fellow students, who have been my companions and provided support and encouragement throughout my doctoral journey, I am truly thankful. I am also grateful to all who prayed for and supported me throughout the doctoral process. Particularly, I express my gratitude to my parents, Chang-uk Ahn and Jin-sun Choi, and to my parents-in-law, Yong-eui Yang and Hyun-ja Park, who have shown me unwavering love and support in various ways. In particular, Yang provided invaluable insights and comments that greatly enhanced the balance and credibility of this monograph. Also, I extend my gratitude to So-ra Ahn, Hee-seok Choi, Chul-gil Hong, Seung-myeon Hu, Geun-sin Kang, Hyun-woo Kim, Mi-neo Kim, In-chul Lim, and the members of Bo-kwang Church and Se-dong-nea Church for their spiritual and financial support. Furthermore, I extend my gratitude to my dedicated friend, Kyle Hicks, who not only served

ACKNOWLEDGMENTS

as a reader of my papers but also offered invaluable support as an English tutor, aiding me in managing the academic workload. I am also deeply grateful to Pieter Vandermeer, whose sincere support provided my family with a beautiful house beyond our means.

Most of all, I am immensely grateful to my three children, Yerang, Yejoon, and Yebon, for their understanding and being a source of joy through this entire journey, though I could not dedicate enough time for them. Finally, I wish to convey my deepest gratitude to my beloved wife, Kyungjin Yang. Throughout the extensive doctoral journey, she has remained my closest friend, diligently reviewing all my papers and engaging in insightful discussions. Her unwavering support was integral to the completion of this entire process. I dedicate this monograph to my lifelong love and partner, Kyungjin.

# Figures and Tables

## Figures

1.1   The Two Source Hypothesis  30
1.2   Evans's Two Source Hypothesis  32
1.3   The Farrer Hypothesis  33
1.4   The Griesbach Hypothesis  34
1.5   Peabody's Two Gospel Hypothesis  35
1.6   Riesner's Orality and Memory Hypothesis  39
2.1   Hypothetical system network  62
2.2   Halliday's stratification  62
2.3   The relationship between the situation and the text (Halliday)  66
3.1   Participant-referent chains in Matt 26:14–16  104
3.2   Participant-referent chains in Matt 26:17–19  105
3.3   Participant-referent chains in Matt 26:20–25  106
3.4   Participant-referent chains in Matt 26:26–30  107
3.5   Participant-referent chains in Matt 26:31–35  108
3.6   Lexical cohesion chains in Matt 26:14–35  117
4.1   Participant-referent chains in Mark 14:10–11  139
4.2   Participant-referent chains in Mark 14:12–16  140
4.3   Participant-referent chains in Mark 14:17–26  141
4.4   Participant-referent chains in Mark 14:27–31  142
4.5   Lexical cohesion chains in Mark 14:10–31  150
5.1   Participant-referent chains in Luke 22:3–6  170
5.2   Participant-referent chains in Luke 22:7–13  171
5.3   Participant-referent chains in Luke 22:14–23  172
5.4   Participant-referent chains in Luke 22:31–34  173
5.5   Lexical cohesion chains in Luke 22:3–23, 31–34  180

## Tables

1.1   Literary dependence or independence  29
1.2   Attitudes towards oral tradition  30
1.3   Two types of the four major views on the Synoptic Problem  40
1.4   Arguments in pairs of the Literary Dependence Hypotheses  41
1.5   Distinct arguments in the Literary Dependence Hypotheses  41
1.6   Textual usages of the three proponents  42

# FIGURES AND TABLES

XI

1.7 Three different interpretations of Matt 26:68 and Luke 22:64 43

2.1 Levels of thematization suggested by Porter and O'Donnell 73

2.2 Rearrangement of Porter's three verbal aspects 89

3.1 Prime-subsequent examples in Matt 26:14–35 91

3.2 Thematic participants and processes in Matt 26:14–35 95

3.3 Paragraph division & topics of UBS[5] and this study 96

3.4 Conjunctions and asyndeton in the narratives and direct speeches of Matt 26:14–35 98

3.5 Semantic domains of the lexemes in Matt 26:14–16 110

3.6 Semantic domains of the lexemes in Matt 26:17–19 111

3.7 Semantic domains of the lexemes in Matt 26:20–25 113

3.8 Semantic domains of the lexemes in Matt 26:26–30 114

3.9 Semantic domains of the lexemes in Matt 26:31–35 116

3.10 Lexical density of Matt 26:14–35 119

3.11 Lexical density of the direct speech and narrative in Matt 26:14–35 120

3.12 Grammatical intricacy of Matt 26:14–35 121

3.13 Analysis of verbs in Matt 26:14–35 focusing on verbal aspect 122

4.1 Prime-subsequent examples in Mark 14:10–31 125

4.2 Thematic participants and processes in Mark 14:10–31 129

4.3 Paragraph division & topics of UBS[5] and this study 130

4.4 Conjunctions and asyndeton in the narratives and direct speeches of Mark 14:10–31 131

4.5 Semantic domains of the lexemes in Mark 14:10–11 143

4.6 Semantic domains of the lexemes in Mark 14:12–16 144

4.7 Semantic domains of the lexemes in Mark 14:17–26 145

4.8 Semantic domains of the lexemes in Mark 14:27–31 148

4.9 Lexical density of Mark 14:10–31 151

4.10 Lexical density of the direct speech and narrative in Mark 14:10–31 152

4.11 Grammatical intricacy of Mark 14:10–31 152

4.12 Analysis of verbs in Mark 14:10–31 focusing on verbal aspect 154

5.1 Prime-subsequent examples in Luke 22:3–23, 31–34 156

5.2 Thematic participants and processes in Luke 22:3–23, 31–34 (including 2:24–30) 160

5.3 Paragraph division & topics of UBS[5] and this study 162

5.4 Conjunctions and asyndeton in the narrative and direct speech of Luke 22:3–23, 31–34 163

5.5 Semantic domains of the lexemes in Luke 22:3–6 175

5.6 Semantic domains of the lexemes in Luke 22:7–13 176

5.7 Semantic domains of the lexemes in Luke 22:14–23 177

5.8 Semantic domains of the lexemes in Luke 22:31–34 179

| | | |
|---|---|---|
| 5.9 | Lexical density of Luke 22:3–23, 31–34 | 182 |

5.9 Lexical density of Luke 22:3–23, 31–34    182

5.10 Lexical density of the speech and narrative in Luke 22:3–23, 31–34    182

5.11 Grammatical intricacy of Luke 22:3–23, 31–34    183

5.12 Analysis of verbs in Luke 22:3–23, 31–34 focusing on verbal aspect    185

6.1 Thematization comparison between Matt 26:14–35, Mark 14:10–31, and Luke 22:3–23, 31–34    187

6.2 References to Jesus in Matt 26:14–35, Mark 14:10–31, Luke 22:3–23, 31–34    190

6.3 Substitution and ellipsis comparison between Matt 26:14–35, Mark 14:10–31, and Luke 22:3–23, 31–34    194

6.4 Comparison between four texts on the substitution of ποτήριον    196

6.5 Comparative lexical cohesion analysis between Matt 26:14–35, Mark 14:10–31, and Luke 22:3–23, 31–34    198

6.6 Lexical density and grammatical intricacy comparison between Matt 26:14–35, Mark 14:10–31, and Luke 22:3–23, 31–34    200

6.7 Lexical density of direct speech and narrative parts in Matt 26:14–35, Mark 14:10–3, and Luke 22:3–23, 31–34    200

6.8 Stative aspects in the designated texts    202

# Abbreviations

| | |
|---|---|
| ACNT | Augsburg Commentary on the New Testament |
| ANTC | Abingdon New Testament Commentaries |
| *AJ* | *Africanus Journal* |
| *AJT* | *American Journal of Theology* |
| AMS | Africanus Monograph Series |
| *BAGL* | *Biblical Ancient Greek Linguistics* |
| BECNT | Baker Exegetical Commentary on the New Testament |
| BJS | Brown Judaic Studies |
| BLG | Biblical Languages Greek |
| BNTC | Black's New Testament Commentaries |
| BTCB | Brazos Theological Commentary on the Bible |
| BZNW | Beihefte zur Zeitschrift für die neutestamentliche Wissenschaft |
| *CBR* | *Currents in Biblical Research* |
| CBC | Collegeville Bible Commentary |
| *Chu* | *Churchman* |
| CTL | Cambridge Textbooks in Linguistics |
| ELS | Explorations in Language Study |
| *ExpT* | *Expository Times* |
| FBPC | Fortress Biblical Preaching Commentaries |
| *HistH* | *History of Humanities* |
| ICC | International Critical Commentary |
| *JGRChJ* | *Journal of Greco-Roman Christianity and Judaism* |
| *JLIABG* | *Journal of the Linguistics Institute for Ancient and Biblical Greek* |
| JSNT | Journal for the Study of the New Testament |
| JSNTSup | Journal for the Study of the New Testament Supplement Series |
| JSOTSup | Journal for the Study of the Old Testament Supplement Series |
| *JTS* | *Journal of Theological Studies* |
| LBS | Linguistic Biblical Studies |
| LENT | Linguistic Exegesis of the New Testament |
| LNTG | Library of New Testament Greek |
| LNTS | Library of New Testament Studies |
| NCBC | New Cambridge Bible Commentary |
| NCC | New Covenant Commentary |
| NICNT | New International Commentary on the New Testament |
| NIGTC | New International Greek Testament Commentary |
| *NovT* | *Novum Testamentum* |
| NTM | New Testament Monographs |

| | |
|---|---|
| *NTS* | *New Testament Studies* |
| PBCS | Performance Biblical Criticism Series |
| *PM* | *Psychological Monographs* |
| PNTC | Pillar New Testament Commentary |
| SBG | Studies in Biblical Greek |
| SBL | Society of Biblical Literature |
| SNTSMS | Society for New Testament Studies Monograph Series |
| SPS | Sacra Pagina Series |
| TCSG | T&T Clark Study Guides |
| *ThStK* | *Theologische Studien und Kritiken* |
| WBC | Word Biblical Commentary |
| WUNT | Wissenschaftliche Untersuchungen zum Neuen Testament |
| ZECNT | Zondervan Exegetical Commentary Series on the New Testament |
| *ZNW* | *Zeitschrift für die neutestamentliche Wissenschaft und die Kunde der älteren Kirche* |

# Introduction

Over the past two centuries, various arguments have been ardently presented concerning the issue of the so-called "Synoptic Problem,"[1] although the construction process and relationship between Synoptic Gospels had been discussed since Papias.[2] The major position regarding the Synoptic Gospels throughout early church history was that Matthew was written first, and Mark and Luke were written later, without mentions on literary dependence between the three.[3] However, since the eighteenth century, scholars have suggested many kinds of hypotheses on the issue of the Synoptic Problem,[4] and now the overwhelming scholarly consensus is literary dependence on Mark and Q: the Two Source Hypothesis.[5] Besides this, positions such as the Two

---

1  It has been regarded as a "problem" due to its enigmatic character in terms of finding a solution to several questions: "What is the first written Gospel? Were Gospels dependent on one another or independent?" According to Stanley E. Porter and Bryan R. Dyer, the very term "Synoptic Problem" seems problematic since, the moment we define this as a "problem," we get an image that there is something wrong with it—especially in terms of how the Synoptic Gospels are relating to one another—and it can create an illusion that there is *a* solution. See Stanley E. Porter and Bryan R. Dyer, "Synoptic Problem: An Introduction to Its Key Terms, Concepts, Figures, and Hypotheses," in *The Synoptic Problem: Four Views*, ed. Stanley E. Porter and Bryan R. Dyer (Grand Rapids: Baker Academic, 2016), 13. Bruce Chilton also has this type of opinion: "The Synoptic Problem ... is also the banner of a perspective, which sees that relationship as *a problem*, a complicated interaction of sources which can ultimately be named and described according to their place in the process of documentary cause and effect which produced the Gospels." (italics are mine). See Bruce Chilton, *Profiles of a Rabbi: Synoptic Opportunities in Reading About Jesus* (BJS 177; Atlanta: Scholars, 1989), 3. Withholding these concerns, this study will use the term "Synoptic Problem" limitedly just for convenience's sake.
2  Eusebius, *Hist. eccl.* 3.39.15. More details on this will be covered in chapter 1 of this volume.
3  Eusebius, *Hist. eccl.* 3.24.6–7; Augustine, *Cons.* 1.2.3. (trans. S. D. F. Salmond; Bolton: Aeterna, 2014); cf. Panayiotis Tzamalikos, *Origen: New Fragments from the Commentary on Matthew* (Leiden: Brill, 2020), 2.
4  It will be covered in chapter 1, the literature review.
5  In the nineteenth century, Markan priority started to be magnified by Karl Lachman (1793–1851) and Heinrich J. Holtzmann (1832–1910), even though it seems that Markan priority was originally initiated by Gottlob C. Storr (1746–1805). After that, in 1924, influenced by the work of William Sanday (1843–1920), Burnett H. Streeter (1874–1937) contended that Mark's Gospel was written first, then Matthew and Luke constructed their Gospels based on Mark, "Q" (*Quelle*; source), with a source used by Matthew (M) and a source used by Luke (L). Streeter argues that Proto-Luke, which was formed by Q and L, influenced the construction of the Gospel of Luke along with Mark's Gospel. See Burnett H. Streeter, *The Four Gospels: A Study of Origins* (London: Macmillan, 1924), 150. This hypothesis is called "the Two Source Hypothesis" (or Four Source Hypothesis), and in a considerable time this hypothesis had

---

© HOJOON J. AHN, 2024 | DOI:10.1163/9789004696372_002

Gospel Hypothesis[6] and the Farrer Hypothesis,[7] which all belong to the literary dependence hypothesis, have also been accepted by considerable scholars. The comparative analysis of the arguments of three representative scholars in the literary dependent positions (the Two Source Hypothesis of Craig A. Evans, the Farrer Hypothesis of Mark Goodacre, and the Two Gospel Hypothesis of David B. Peabody)[8] in chapter 1 will show us the following aspects: (1) the utilized texts of the Synoptic Gospels by the three scholars to support each of their own positions barely overlap each other; (2) when the texts are overlapping,

---

become dominant in the academic field of the Synoptic Problem. Representative advocates of this position are Werner G. Kümmel, Christopher M. Tuckett, and Craig A. Evans.

6  In the eighteenth century, based on several scholars' suggestions, a critical study of the relationship among the Synoptic Gospels was pursued by Johann J. Griesbach (1745–1812). See Stanley E. Porter, "The Synoptic Problem: The State of the Question," *JGRChJ* 12 (2016): 75. Griesbach asserted that the Gospel of Matthew was written first, then Luke's Gospel was written via reliance on Matthew, then lastly, Mark's Gospel was written by relying on Matthew and Luke (Griesbach Hypothesis). See Johann J. Griesbach, "A Demonstration that Mark Was Written after Matthew and Luke," in *J. J. Griesbach: Synoptic and Text-Critical Studies 1776–1976*, eds. Bernard Orchard and Thomas R. W. Longstaff (trans. Bernard Orchard; SNTSMS 34; Cambridge: Cambridge University Press, 1978), 106. After the dominant period of the Two Source Hypothesis, in 1964, William R. Farmer (1921–2000) revived the Griesbach Hypothesis via his monograph on the Synoptic Problem, which argues Matthean priority and the reliance on Matthew of Luke and Mark (also Mark's use of Luke), along with the influence of oral tradition; this was called "the Two Gospel Hypothesis." In *The Synoptic Problem: A Critical Analysis*, after analyzing the problem of the Two Source Hypothesis supporters' assertion (48–198), Farmer reveals the evidence of the Two Gospel Hypothesis by presenting sixteen steps (199–232) along with the evidence of Mark's redaction (233–83). See William R. Farmer, *The Synoptic Problem: A Critical Analysis* (New York: Macmillan, 1964). A representative proponent of the Two Gospel Hypothesis is David B. Peabody.

7  Before Farmer's assertion, in 1955, another position supporting Markan priority was attempted by Austin Farrer (1904–68). He objected to the existence of Q in his article, and it was called "the Farrer Hypothesis." See Austin Farrer, "Dispensing with Q," in *Studies in the Gospels: Essays in Memory of R. H. Lightfoot* (ed. Dennis E. Nineham; Oxford: Blackwell, 1955), 55–88. A representative advocate for the Farrer Hypothesis is Michael D. Goulder and Mark Goodacre. Especially, Goulder tried to extend Farrer's work via the "lectionary theory." See Cynthia L. Westfall, "Goulder, Michael D. (1927–)," in *Dictionary of Biblical Criticism and Interpretation*, ed. Stanley E. Porter (New York: Routledge, 2007), 136. In addition, Andris Abakuks supports the Farrer Hypothesis by investigating the Synoptic Gospels statistically. See Andris Abakuks, *The Synoptic Problem and Statistics* (Boca Raton, FL: CRC, 2015), 179–81.

8  For a more detailed explanation of each position, see Craig A. Evans, "The Two Source Hypothesis," in *The Synoptic Problem: Four Views* (eds. Stanley E. Porter and Bryan R. Dyer; Grand Rapids: Baker Academic, 2016), 27–45; Mark Goodacre, "The Farrer Hypothesis," in *The Synoptic Problem: Four Views* (ed. Stanley E. Porter and Bryan R. Dyer; Grand Rapids: Baker Academic, 2016), 47–66; David B. Peabody, "The Two Gospel Hypothesis," in *The Synoptic Problem: Four Views*, eds. Stanley E. Porter and Bryan R. Dyer (Grand Rapids: Baker Academic, 2016), 67–88.

INTRODUCTION

they interpret the same texts differently and find different evidence(s) which support each of their positions, and particularly, they interpret the Double Tradition (the common parts of Matthew and Luke) very differently.[9] Even though each interpretation contradicts the other interpretation(s), it does not mean that all the interpretations are wrong; logically speaking, one of them still could be right. As a matter of fact, we cannot deny that each position has strong grounds in its arguments. Nevertheless, neither can we deny that each position has clear limitations as well.[10] In such a situation, we may need to consider another approach from a different angle, which may resolve the limitations of the literary dependence hypotheses.

The scholars supporting the Oral Tradition Hypothesis[11] presume that the formative process of the Gospels was considerably complex and that various elements were involved in the process.[12] Scholars, such as B. F. Westcott (1825–1901),[13] Rudolf Bultmann (1884–1976),[14] Birger Gehardsson (1926–2013),[15]

---

9    A representative example can be shown in the different interpretations of Matt 26:68; Luke 22:64 (cf. Mark 14:65). Chapter 1 reveals how the three advocates in the Dependence Hypothesis (Evans, Goodacre, Peabody) differently interpret the same passages according to each of their positions (Evans, "Two Source Hypothesis," 31; Goodacre, "Farrer Hypothesis," 56; Peabody, "Two Gospel Hypothesis," 81).

10   Several limitations of each position within the literary dependence hypothesis will be shown in chapter 1.

11   This position focuses on the role of oral tradition in the process of construction of the Synoptic Gospels. For a brief history of the oral tradition studies focusing on the "modal unidirectionality from oral into written tradition," see Lee Sang-Il, *Jesus and Gospel Traditions in Bilingual Context: A Study in the Interdirectionality of Language* (BZNW 186; Berlin: de Gruyter, 2012), 20–36.

12   Regarding the complexity of the formation of the Gospels based on the various portraits of Jesus circulated among the followers and observers of early Christian society, see Keith, Chris et al., "Introduction," in *The Reception of Jesus in the First Three Centuries*, ed. Helen K. Bond (London: T&T Clark, 2020), 1:xv–xxvii.

13   Influenced by Johann K. L. Gieseler's (1792–1854) understanding of oral Ur-Gospel. See A. D. Baum, "Synoptic Problem," in *Dictionary of Jesus and the Gospels*, ed. Joel B. Green, et al. (2nd ed.; Nottingham: InterVarsity, 2013), 914. B. F. Westcott asserts that there has been a common oral tradition regarding Jesus' ministry and teaching, and they affected each Synoptic Gospel separately. See B. F. Westcott, *Introduction to the Study of the Gospels* (3rd ed.; London: Macmillan, 1867), 152–95.

14   After Westcott, Rudolf Bultmann contends that the formulation of the Gospels was influenced by the Synoptic tradition of the early Christian community. See Rudolf Bultmann, *History of the Synoptic Tradition* (trans. John Marsh; New York: Harper & Row, 1963), 368.

15   Based on the critique of Form Criticism, Birger Gerhardsson attempted to study the origins of the Gospel source and its transmission historically. See Birger Gerhardsson, *The Origins of the Gospel Traditions* (trans. Gene J. Lund; Philadelphia: Fortress, 1979), 8–9. Here, Gerhardsson criticizes Form Criticism that "their work is not sufficiently *historical*." In particular, he focuses on the oral and written transmission of the early Church

Samuel Byrskog,[16] Richard Bauckham,[17] Rainer Riesner, Werner H. Kelber,[18] David Wenham,[19] and others[20] have focused on the oral tradition's influence on the Gospels.[21] Based on their studies, the Orality and Memory Hypothesis has been developed in detail as one type of the Oral Tradition Hypothesis.

One of the scholars of the Orality and Memory Hypothesis is Riesner.[22] His model is particularly notable in terms of the Synoptic Gospels' construction

---

community compared to Rabbinic Judaism in his scheme of memory theory. See Birger Gerhardsson, *Memory and Manuscript: Oral Tradition and Written Transmission in Rabbinic Judaism and Early Christianity* (trans. Eric J. Sharpe; Grand Rapids: Eerdmans, 1998), x–xvi.

16    Via the analysis based on the modern discipline of oral history, Samuel Byrskog contends that the Gospel narrative should be regarded as "a story as history" and, at the same time, "a history as a story" since its tradition "originated and developed in a constant process of re-oralization." See Samuel Byrskog, *Story as History-History as Story: The Gospel Tradition in the Context of Ancient Oral History* (WUNT 123; Tübingen: Mohr Siebeck, 2000), 305.

17    With confidence that the Gospels contain historical and theological aspects, Richard Bauckham focuses on eyewitnesses' reliable "testimony" in the Gospels since "the Gospels were written within living memory of the events they recount." See Richard Bauckham, *Jesus and the Eyewitnesses: The Gospels as Eyewitness Testimony* (2nd ed.; Grand Rapids: Eerdmans, 2017), 5–7.

18    Werner H. Kelber, *Imprints, Voiceprints, and Footprints of Memory* (Atlanta: Society of Biblical Literature, 2013); "Mark and Oral Tradition," *Semeia* 16 (1979): 7–55, *The Oral Tradition and the Written Gospel: The Hermeneutics of Speaking and Writing in the Synoptic Tradition, Mark, Paul, and Q* (Bloomington: Indiana University Press, 1983).

19    David Wenham, *From Good News to Gospels: What Did the First Christians Say about Jesus?* (Grand Rapids: Eerdmans, 2018).

20    E.g., David Rhoads, Joanna Dewey, and Donald Michie argue that the Gospel of Mark was told for the audiences of that time as an oral performance by heart. See David Rhoads et al., *Mark as Story: An Introduction to the Narrative of a Gospel* (3rd ed.; Minneapolis: Fortress, 2012), xi–xii. Their observation shows us the memorable ability of people of that era. In addition, an extended or revised form of the Orality and Memory Hypothesis is "Media Criticism," which deals with four parts: (1) orality studies, (2) social memory theory, (3) performance criticism, and (4) the reception of the Bible in modern media. See Nicholas A. Elder, "New Testament Media Criticism," *CBR* 15 (2017): 315.

21    When this study refers to "oral tradition," it means "oral Gospel tradition," except the "oral tradition" section of chapter 2 where we deal with the general meaning of oral traditions.

22    Rainer Riesner's methodological approach and applications were dealt with in my paper "Rainer Riesner: A Synthetic-Historical Researcher on the Historical Jesus and Gospel Tradition Studies," which was a research project with Porter in 2017 (it has been revised/edited for publication). Concerning the process of Gospel formation, Riesner takes four steps as follows: (1) background: Jewish elementary education; (2) origin: Jesus as a teacher; (3) transmission: pre-Synoptic traditions (which assumes a previous sort of half-step of preservation by Jesus' immediate disciples); and (4) publication: the Synoptic Gospels ("Messianic Teacher," 409–43). For more detailed elements of Riesner's hypothesis, see Rainer Riesner, "The Orality and Memory Hypothesis," in *The Synoptic Problem: Four Views*, eds. Stanley E. Porter and Bryan R. Dyer (Grand Rapids: Baker Academic, 2016), 107.

INTRODUCTION

process in which it considers the plausible situation of Jesus' era. He argues that the Synoptic Gospels significantly contain Jesus' teachings and stories about him which were preserved in the early Christian Communities' traditions based on memory and mediums at hand (e.g., note-taking).[23] In this sense, he asserts that the Synoptic Gospels were possibly written in a literary-independent way.[24] However, this position also has limitations, particularly, in that it does not consider the identity of each Gospel's constructor[25] enough.

In order to find the construction process of Synoptic Gospels, in light of oral tradition(s) and the constructor's identity, this study attempts to analyze the Eucharistic passages in the Synoptic Gospels including their co-texts (Matt 26:14–35; Mark 14:10–31; Luke 22:3–23, 31–34)[26] via a mode Register Analysis (hereafter RA) model based on Systemic Functional Linguistics (hereafter SFL). The designated texts can be regarded as an effective test case for this study since they show us clear differences as well as remarkable similarities between the three versions of the same "context of situation."[27] Furthermore, the study of these texts seems meaningful in that they have not yet been linguistically dealt with adequately.[28] The purpose of this study is threefold:

---

23   Thus, Riesner argues that "the tradition preserved in the Synoptic Gospels" has the value of a historical source. See Rainer Riesner, *Jesus als Lehrer: Eine Untersuchung zum Ursprung der Evangelien-Überlieferung* (WUNT 2/7; 3rd ed.; Tübingen: Mohr Siebeck, 1988), 1–2.

24   Riesner, "Orality and Memory," 107.

25   This study uses the term "constructor" to refer to each one who published each Gospel since it seems hard to regard each constructor as an author—in a typical sense—when we consider the existence of several factors (e.g., oral tradition[s], each constructors' identity, etc.). For more detailed information on it, see Hojoon J. Ahn, "Exploration of the Appropriateness of the Expression 'Author' and 'Author's Intention' in the Synoptic Gospels" *KNTS* 31 (2024): 1–34.

26   This study deals with the Eucharistic passages and the surrounding co-texts in the Synoptic Gospels: Matt 26:14–35, Mark 14:10–31, and Luke 22:3–23, 31–34. Luke 22:1–2 and 22:24–30 are omitted here, since they do not have direct parallels in Matthew and Mark. Furthermore, by omitting them, the text amount is similar to each amount of the other two text, which may help the comparative analysis between the three texts. A linguistic analysis of the Gospel according to Luke, however, will be done with the omitted parts in mind, and they will be referred to and analyzed when it is deemed necessary. Other relevant Eucharistic texts (1 Cor 11:17–34; cf. John 6:51–58; 19:34, etc.) are not the direct objects of this study since its main focus is on the Synoptic texts related to the issue of the Synoptic Problem. Nevertheless, a part of 1 Cor 11:17–34 (1 Cor 11:25b) will be comparatively dealt with in chapter 6.

27   Some parallel passages of the Synoptic Gospels are debatable whether they took place in a single context (e.g., Matt 5:1–7:29; Luke 6:20–49). However, the designated texts of this study appear to have happened in one context without dispute. In this respect, the designated texts meet the aim of this study effectively, which is searching for the construction processes of the three versions of a single historical event.

28   There have been many studies regarding Jesus' Eucharistic words, and a literature review on the representative writings regarding the Eucharist is attempted in Hojoon J. Ahn,

(1) to model a linguistic methodology and to apply it to each text of the Eucharist and its co-texts in the Synoptic Gospels, (2) to find meaningful linguistic characteristics of each designated text via a comparative analysis based on the preceding study, and finally (3) to suggest a balanced and plausible hypothesis which may offer convincing explanations of the Synoptic Gospel's constructions process.

---

*History of Interpretation of the Eucharist and Joachim Jeremias* (2023, kindle edition). The above monograph observes the history of interpretation of the Eucharist via analyzing scholars in this area. Many scholars' major focus in terms of methodology is liturgical, systematic (or dogmatic), and historical. Among the scholars, this monograph deals with Joachim Jeremias's work on the Eucharist in detail by analyzing his diverse methodology and its application to the Eucharistic texts. However, his linguistic analysis seems insufficient due to his lack of knowledge of modern linguistic theories.

CHAPTER 1

# A Survey of Studies on the Synoptic Problem

## 1    Introduction

The field of the Synoptic Gospel studies is vast. The major topics regarding the Synoptic studies can be classified into threefold categories: "Genre," "the Synoptic Problem," and "the Historical Jesus." First, the genre study on the Synoptic Gospels is about the Gospel texts' distinct types such as "history," "biography," "folk literature," etc.[1] The identification of the genre of the Gospel is crucial because the way of interpreting the Gospels may be affected according to its genre.[2] Second, the study on "Synoptic Problem" is concerned with studying the interrelationship among the Synoptic Gospels which share similar (or identical) features along with different features.[3] Numerous scholars have attempted to settle this issue,[4] but it is not yet fully settled.[5] Third, the Historical Jesus research has generally addressed the issue of the real aspect

---

1   The views on the Gospels' genre can be historically arranged as follows: (1) to the Reformers, the Gospels were understood as "history," or sometimes as "biography"; (2) to the Form-critical scholars (Karl L. Schmidt, Bultmann), in which the Gospels were identified as "popular folk literature"; (3) to the Redaction-critical scholars (G. Bornkamm, Hans Conzelmann), in which the Gospels were regarded as "community document"; and (4) to the Literary-critical scholars, in which the Gospels were considered as "first century literature." See Richard A. Burridge, "Gospel: Genre" in *Dictionary of Jesus and the Gospels* (eds. Joel B. Green, et al.; 2nd ed.; Nottingham: InterVarsity, 2013), 336–37. Richard A. Burridge argues that the Gospels were written as an ancient biography focusing on one person, Jesus of Nazareth. See Richard A. Burridge, *What Are the Gospels? A Comparison with Graeco-Roman Biography* (2nd ed.; Grand Rapids: Eerdmans, 2004), 39.
2   Richard A. Burridge, "Gospel: Genre" in *Dictionary of Biblical Criticism and Interpretation* (ed. Stanley E. Porter; London: Routledge, 2007), 129.
3   Baum, "Synoptic Problem," 911.
4   According to Porter and Dyer, the four major hypotheses have been suggested in terms of the Synoptic Problem: "the Two Gospels Hypothesis," "the Two Source Hypothesis," "the Oral Tradition and Memory Hypothesis," and "the Farrer Hypothesis." See Stanley E. Porter and Bryan R. Dyer, "The Synoptic Problem: An Introduction to Its Key Terms, Concepts, Figures, and Hypotheses," in *The Synoptic Problem: Four Views*, eds. Stanley E. Porter and Bryan R. Dyer (Grand Rapids: Baker Academic, 2016), 14–23.
5   Robert H. Stein refers to the long journey on this theme as follows: "it may well be that more time and effort has been spent on this 'Synoptic Problem' than on any other biblical issue." See Robert H. Stein, *Studying the Synoptic Gospels: Origin and Interpretation* (2nd ed.; Grand Rapids: Baker Academic, 2001), 18.

© HOJOON J. AHN, 2024 | DOI:10.1163/9789004696372_003

of Jesus' life and teaching.[6] This research tends to be related to the Synoptic Problem, since not a few scholars regard differences in the synoptic parallels as indicating their untrustworthiness. They usually focus on the issues of priority and authenticity of the Gospels.[7]

In the broad area of Synoptic Gospel studies, this chapter aims to review a brief history[8] of the Synoptic Problem studies. In addition, we will analyze four major hypotheses (the Two Source Hypothesis, the Farrer Hypothesis, the Two Gospel Hypothesis, and the Orality and Memory Hypothesis) which are borrowed from *The Synoptic Problem: Four Views*.[9] This analysis in the end will lead us to propose a balanced position on the Synoptic Gospels.

## 2      A Brief History of the Studies Related to the Synoptic Problem

### 2.1      *Papias to Spinoza*

The first mention regarding the constructing process and the characteristics of the Synoptic Gospels in church history is found in Papias's utterance. Papias (75–140) was a bishop of Hierapolis, a city in Asia Minor, and was one of the third-generation Christians who had been taught the Christian tradition by a community that followed Jesus.[10] According to records of Irenaeus (115–200), Papias was the "hearer" of John who preached Jesus' words.[11] In his book, *Exegeses of the Lord's Sayings*, Papias comments about Mark and Matthew as follows (the following is Jeremy M. Schott's translation):

---

6      Craig A. Evans, ed., *The Historical Jesus: Critical Concepts in Religious Studies* (vol. 1; London: Routledge, 2004), 1–3.

7      Many scholars have approached this issue with the Aramaic language hypothesis; e.g., Joachim Jeremias, *The Eucharistic Words of Jesus* (trans. Norman Perrin; Philadelphia: Fortress, 1981), 160–203. However, Porter suggests Jesus' possible use of Greek to provide a new criterion for authenticity via linguistic analysis. See Stanley E. Porter, *The Criteria for Authenticity in Historical-Jesus Research: Previous Discussion and New Proposals* (JSNTSup 191; Sheffield: Sheffield Academic, 2000), 22–25.

8      In the part dealing with the history of the studies concerned with the Synoptic Problem, I will discuss about those who played an important role from the early church to modern times.

9      Porter and Dyer, eds., *Synoptic Problem*. It seems meaningful to arrange the recent trend of the Synoptic Problem studies according to this book since the four contributors (Evans, Goodacre, Peabody, and Riesner) to the book can be rightly regarded as the recent representative proponents of the four major positions of the Synoptic Problem.

10      A. C. Perumalil, "Papias," *ExpT* 85 (1974): 361.

11      Eusebius, *Hist. eccl.* 3.39.1; for the original source, see Irenaeus, *Haer.* 5.33.4.

# A SURVEY OF STUDIES ON THE SYNOPTIC PROBLEM

> And the presbyter used to say this: that Mark was Peter's translator, and he wrote down accurately, though not in order, what he remembered [hearing] about what the Lord had said and done. For he had not heard the Lord or been his followers, but later, as I said, was Peter's. Peter used to teach using short examples, but he did not compose an ordered account of the Lord's sayings, with the result that Mark did not err in writing the particulars he remembered. For he took forethought for one thing, not to falsify or omit anything of what he had heard in the accounts he wrote ... Matthew composed the sayings in the Hebrew language, and each translated them as well as he could.[12]

As regards Papias's comments on Mark, while Schott translates ἑρμηνευτής as "translator," G. A. Williamson translates it as "interpreter."[13] In principle, both translations are possible.[14] If we translate it as "interpreter," it can be understood as a person who tries to explain the meaning of Peter's words according to one's own thoughts rather than writing them down as they are. However, in Papias's comments, Mark is portrayed as a person who writes down Peter's words accurately and constructs the Gospel accordingly. The other possible translation, "translator," could be understood as implying Mark's role in translating Peter's Aramaic/Hebrew wordings into Greek. As regards Papias's comment on Matthew, we note that Matthew is portrayed as a person who translated Jesus' Semitic words into Greek.[15] From the discussions above, we can conclude that Papias regards Mark and Matthew as responsible preservers of "what the Lord had said and done," even though it is still debatable whether Jesus taught in Aramaic/Hebrew or Greek.[16] We can also affirm that, in Papias's

---

12    Eusebius, *Hist. eccl.* 3.39.15–16 (Schott); the original source is from the fragment of Papias's *Exegeses of the Lord's Sayings*.

13    Eusebius, *Hist. eccl.* 3.39.15 (Williamson).

14    According to J. H. Thayer and G. Abbott-Smith, ἑρμηνευτής means "interpreter," and it also has the possibility to be rendered as "translator." See J. H. Thayer, *A Greek-English Lexicon of the New Testament Being Grimm's Wilke's Clavis Novi Testamenti* (Grand Rapids: Baker, 1977), 250; G. Abbott-Smith, *A Manual Greek Lexicon of the New Testament* (New York: Charles Scribner's Sons, 1922), 180. W. D. Mounce suggests translating this word primarily into a translator. See W. D. Mounce, *Greek-Dictionary*, http://www.bill mounce.com/greek-dictionary /hermeneutes.

15    In fact, every word of Papias's comment on Matthew is notoriously ambiguous. Nevertheless, the above understanding could be arguably drawn out. See R. T. France, *Matthew: Evangelist and Teacher* (Downers Grove: InterVarsity, 1998), 53–60.

16    In such a situation, it can be inferred that the Gospels written in Greek may have been in Aramaic or Hebrew at an earlier stage—although there is also a possibility that the Gospels were originally written in Greek based on Jesus' teachings in Greek and

comments, there is no mention of how the Gospels of Matthew and Mark influenced each other. In other words, the concept of literary dependence between the Synoptic Gospels is not found in Papias.

Justin Martyr (100–165) was a non-Jewish philosopher, theologian, apologist, exegete, and Christian martyr.[17] He regards the Gospels as "memoirs" of the Apostles: "The Apostles in their memoirs, which are called Gospels, have handed down what Jesus ordered them to do."[18] This expression of Justin significantly reveals the possibility that the words given by Jesus already existed as an oral tradition by the apostles' memory before the written Gospels. The approach he took to interpret the Gospels was, in a sense, harmonization.[19] Criticizing the inconsistency and contradictions in Greek's myth and philosophy, he pursued to harmonize the Gospels in his writings.[20] According to David L. Dungan, the reason was: "Far from being meant to replace the Christian Gospels, his harmonized quotations were ... intended to keep the Christian message as clear as possible."[21] A reliance on Matthew is found when Justin tries harmonization—in an interpretative point of view—, which seems to have been due to his valuing of Matthew's tendency to represent Christ in fulfilment of the OT, rather than pursuing a Matthean priority.[22] Justin makes no reference on one Gospel's priority or literary dependence on one another.

Tatian (110–180), Justin's student, took his teacher's approach and created a harmonized Gospel called Diatessaron (or the *Euangellion da-Mehallete*; Gospel of the Mixed), "a gospel harmony combining the four 'canonical' Gospels with one or more Jewish-Christian gospel(s)."[23] By doing this, Tatian tried to make a "single seamless narrative."[24] This combined text was widespread in eastern countries—as far as China.[25] It seems that Tatian's purpose

---

his disciples' testimony in Greek. For more detailed information, see Hojoon J. Ahn, *Fundamental Foundations for the New Testament Gospel Studies* (2023, kindle edition).

17  Sara Parvis and Paul Foster, eds., *Justin Martyr and His Worlds* (Minneapolis: Fortress, 2007), 1.

18  Justin, *1 Apol.* 66.

19  Winrich Löhr, "Justin Martyr," in *The Reception of Jesus in the First Three Centuries. Vol. 2: From Thomas to Tertullian: Christian Literary Receptions of Jesus in the Second and Third Centuries CE*, eds. Jens Schröter and Christine Jacobi (London: T&T Clark, 2020), 439.

20  David L. Dungan, *A History of the Synoptic Problem: The Canon, the Text, the Composition, and the Interpretation of the Gospels* (New York: Doubleday, 1999), 38.

21  Dungan, *Synoptic Problem*, 39.

22  Dungan, *Synoptic Problem*, 39; Wolf-Dietrich Köhler, *Die Rezeption des Matthäusevangeliums in der Zeit vor Irenäus* (Tübingen: Mohr Siebeck, 1987).

23  Emily J. Hunt, *Christianity in the Second Century: The Case of Tatian* (London: Routledge, 2003), 56.

24  Dungan, *Synoptic Problem*, 41.

25  Hunt, *Christianity*, 145.

A SURVEY OF STUDIES ON THE SYNOPTIC PROBLEM

in creating this text—like Justin—was to pursue the consistency of the Gospels while criticizing the inconsistency of Greek philosophy at the time. In other words, he tried to construct a combined gospel for "catechetical and/or apologetic functions."[26] In Tatian, there is again no reference to an idea of the priority of any Gospel or the literary dependence between the Gospels.

Marcion of Sinope (85–160) does not admit the OT—the canon of the Jews—as a true scripture and rejected any attempt to portray Jesus Christ as the king and the Messiah of the Jews.[27] He even says that Jesus was neither born nor crucified but only "appeared out of the blue": thus, he only admits Jesus' divinity.[28] The only Gospel he admits is the Gospel of Luke, except for chapters 1 and 2—the accounts of Jesus' birth and youth. He does not admit any Jewish elements even in that Gospel.[29] As regards the Synoptic Problem, it seems that he tried to solve this problem by excluding all the Gospels other than the Gospel of Luke and regarding it as the only true Gospel.

Celsus, a philosopher, criticized Christianity by publishing a book called *On the True Doctrine* in the era of Marcus Aurelius.[30] He can be seen as the first philosopher to attack Christianity in earnest. Although his data are mostly lost, his views are revealed in the refutation made by Origen.[31] Basically, Celsus regards Christianity as a religion derived from Stoicism and Plato's philosophy. His position on the Gospels as revealed by Origen is as follows. "Some believers as though from a drinking bout go so far as to oppose themselves and alter the original text of the gospel three or four or several times over, and they change its character to enable them to deny difficulties in the face of criticism."[32] According to Henry Chadwick, "Celsus's meaning is uncertain. He may mean the different gospels, *three or four* being a reference to the canonical four (it is just conceivable that the phrase shows knowledge of those who rejected St. John), and *several* to the apocryphal gospels."[33] Considering Chadwick's

---

26    Nicholas Perrin, "Diatessaron," in *The Reception of Jesus in the First Three Centuries. Vol. 2: From Thomas to Tertullian: Christian Literary Receptions of Jesus in the Second and Third Centuries CE*, eds. Jens Schröter and Christine Jacobi (London: T&T Clark, 2020), 145.

27    Paul Foster, "Marcion: His Life, Works, Beliefs, and Impact," *ExpT* 121 (2010): 273.

28    Dungan, *Synoptic Problem*, 48.

29    Marcion, *The Gospel of the Lord: An Early Version Which Was Circulated by Marcion of Sinope as the Original Gospel* (trans. James H. Hill; New York: Guernsey, 1891), i–viii.

30    Coleman M. Ford, "Able to Convince Only the Foolish: Anti-Christian Polemic as Social Scrutiny in Celsus's *On the True Doctrine*," *Chu* 133 (2019): 21.

31    Dungan, *Synoptic Problem*, 59.

32    Origen, *Cels.* 2.27.

33    Origen, *Contra Celsum* (ed. and trans. Henry Chadwick; Cambridge: Cambridge University Press, 1965), 90. It is written by Chadwick, the editor and translator of this volume, as a footnote.

comment, we need to pay attention to Celsus's statement that "Some believers ... alter the original text of the gospel three or four or several times over," which hints that he believed in the existence of an original gospel with priority. Celsus argues that the original gospel text was altered by Christians for their own purposes; thus, he claims a literary dependence between the original one and the subsequent ones. In this sense, Celsus could be regarded as a pioneer of the concepts of Gospel priority and literary dependence. Also, through his argument, he has made the church recognize the interrelationship between the Gospels as *a problem*, which scholars later called the "Synoptic Problem," as a task to be solved.

Origen (185–253) can be considered as the first Christian scholar to organize the so-called Synoptic Problem logically and systematically.[34] He addresses one of the key issues in the Synoptic Problem by asking what consists a reliable and authentic text about Jesus.[35] Origen views the Gospel of Matthew as the first authentic Gospel to be written, and he mentions that the rest of the Gospels were written in the order of Matthew, Mark, Luke, and John.

> About the four gospels, which alone are unopposed in the church of God under heaven, I have learned by tradition that the first to have been written was the one according to him who was then a tax-collector, but later an apostle of Jesus Christ—*Matthew*—which he put out for the believers from Judaism, and was composed in Hebrew letters. And that the second is that *According to Mark*, who produced it with Peter's guidance, and whom Peter declares a "son" in the general letter where he says, "Your fellow elect in Babylon and Mark, my son, greet you." And the third is that *According to Luke*, who produced for those from the Gentiles the gospel praised by Paul, and last of all that *According to John*.[36]

Origen seems to demonstrate the traditional order of formation of the four Gospels. Though he clearly talks about the order of formation, however, he does not refer to the interrelationship between the Gospels. Origen rather views the diversity of the Gospels as evidence of the Holy Spirit's accommodation to

---

34     Dungan, *Synoptic Problem*, 66.

35     Regarding the relationship between the Gospels, Origen had the following questions: "Which Gospels are the authentic records of the life and ministry of Jesus Christ?; Which texts of the authentic Gospels must be used?; How were these authentic Gospels composed, and how were they originally related to one another?; How should they be rightly interpreted?" See Dungan, *Synoptic Problem*, 69.

36     Eusebius, *Hist. eccl.* 6.25.4–6. Italics are mine.

A SURVEY OF STUDIES ON THE SYNOPTIC PROBLEM                    13

human's different needs and capacities.[37] In Origen's remarks concerning the second Gospel's construction process, "Peter's guidance" can be considered as verbally given by Peter to Mark. This may possibly infer that Origen was aware of the existence of oral testimony about Jesus.

Porphyry of Tyre (234–305) attempted to refute Christianity in detail after reading the entire Bible, the canon of Christianity.[38] He has been called the most notorious/dangerous enemy among the church's adversaries,[39] though someone may call him a constructive critic.[40] His writings were mostly destroyed by Constantine the Great and can only be found indirectly through the writings of those who wrote against him.

In Porphyry's writing, it is mentioned: "The saying in John 6:54 about eating his flesh and drinking his blood is worse than the cannibals in its savagery. The first three Gospel writers probably omitted it because it was so repulsive."[41] Porphyry tried to find seemingly inordinate or contradictory words of Jesus and, by doing this, tried to reveal the falsehoods in and problems of the Christian faith. From his wordings, we can at least recognize his perspective and premise on the Gospels, that the authors of the Synoptic Gospels deliberately omitted the words of Jesus in the Gospel of John due to inappropriateness, despite their knowledge. Porphyry's understanding of the Gospels presumes that the Gospels were written according to the personal judgments and intentions of the Gospel authors.

What Porphyry says below is more directly related to the Synoptic Problem: the problem of data inconsistency.

> There are numerous discrepancies in the four accounts of the crucifixion of Jesus. Mark says someone offered Jesus vinegar, and he uttered the cry "My God, My God," etc. Matthew says it was wine mixed with gall which he tasted and refused. John says they gave him vinegar with hyssop, which he took and said, "It is finished," and died. Luke says the great cry was "Father into thy hands," etc. These discrepancies show that the Gospels are not historically reliable.[42]

---

37    Dungan, *Synoptic Problem*, 111.
38    Dungan, *Synoptic Problem*, 90.
39    Cf. Eusebius, *Hist. eccl.* 6.19.2.
40    According to George Karamanolis, Porphyry criticized Christians' "simple" trust in their own faith without critical examination. See George Karamanolis, *The Philosophy of Early Christianity* (2nd ed.; London: Routledge, 2021), 3.
41    Quotation from Dungan, *Synoptic Problem*, 94.
42    Quotation from Dungan, *Synoptic Problem*, 95.

Porphyry, however, approaches the so-called Synoptic Problem too simply by merely enumerating divergent data from the Gospels, and treats such diversity in the Gospels as historically unreliable. In short, Porphyry claims that the authors of each Gospel have changed the text of the previous Gospel(s) according to their own purposes, which resulted in the diversity of the Gospels; his view in the end shares a similar concept with the literary dependence hypothesis.

Eusebius of Caesarea (260–340), a historian and theologian, countered Porphyry's argument and attempted to reveal that the inconsistencies in the Gospels can be sufficiently explained harmoniously. His position on the Synoptic Problem is shown in his explanation on the Gospel texts that seem like discrepancies. For example, the following shows how Eusebius deals with the divergencies between Luke and Matthew concerning the childhood of Jesus: "After Jesus was born, he was circumcised in the temple and taken to Nazareth (Luke), but two years later, Joseph and Mary went to Bethlehem again, whence they fled to Egypt (Matthew)."[43] We can recognize from these references that Eusebius tried to explain the problem of the Synoptic Gospels in the manner of harmonization to defend the authority of the Gospels against his contemporary opponents. Nevertheless, Eusebius did not deal with this issue in physical harmonization but in a way that respects the "original literal diversity" of each Gospel and empathized the massive, shared materials among the Gospels.[44] He surely recognized the presence of oral tradition, which played a role in the construction process of the second Gospel.[45]

Augustine of Hippo (354–430) is a philosopher and theologian who was once involved in Manichaeism. Manichaeans regarded inconsistencies between the Gospels as creating contradictions and called Christianity "muddle-headed."[46] Augustine wrote *On the Harmony of the Gospels* to defend against these attacks on Christianity by revealing each Gospel's value and authority. His approach to the Gospels is divided into two parts: (1) from the beginning to the Eucharist, he compares and analyzes the four Gospels, centering on Matthew; (2) from the Eucharist to the end (resurrection), he constructs a harmonized version of the four Gospels.[47] In book 1, chapter 1 of *The Harmony of the Gospels*, Augustine

---

43    Timothy D. Barnes, *Constantine and Eusebius* (Cambridge, MA: Harvard University Press, 1981), 123.

44    Dungan, *Synoptic Problem*, 111. David L. Dungan praises Eusebius's approach as "a brilliant solution to an exceedingly thorny problem."

45    Eusebius, *Hist. eccl.* 2.15.1.

46    Dungan, *Synoptic Problem*, 113.

47    Dungan addresses that Augustine constitutes a synthesis of the four Gospels and a "literally true super-narrative" since the Titan (*Synoptic Problem*, 118); however, this assessment seems somewhat excessive. It seems better to say: *Augustine attempted partial harmonization.*

A SURVEY OF STUDIES ON THE SYNOPTIC PROBLEM

deals with the authority of the Gospels, first presenting Matthew and John as direct witnesses to Jesus, and then presenting Mark and Luke as indirect experiencers.[48] Augustine also identifies the order in which the four Gospels were written as follows: Matthew, Mark, Luke, and John.[49] Here Augustine addresses that Mark and Luke were supported by Matthew and John; however, Augustine addresses that the authority of all four Gospels can be accepted as divine because all these processes took place through the agency of the Holy Spirit.[50] His basic presupposition is that each evangelist was fully aware of their "predecessor(s)"[51] and did not exclude or ignore what the predecessor(s) had done, but nevertheless constructed each Gospel under the guidance of the Holy Spirit, while restraining "any superfluous conjoint compositions."[52] Since Augustine argues that the Gospel of Mark was constructed by using the Gospel of Matthew,[53] Augustine's position, in this sense, can be regarded as a "literary dependence hypothesis."[54] Augustinian Hypothesis ended previous debates by other religions (e.g., the Manichaeans, the Porphyrians)[55] and became a concrete position of the Christian church for more than 1000 years.[56]

Now, we will focus on the era of the Protestant Reformers. It is well known that Martin Luther (1483–1546), a pioneer of Protestantism, placed Paul's writings, not the Gospels, at the center of his hermeneutics, especially Romans and Galatians. He placed particular importance on the Gospel of John compared to other canonical Gospels.[57] Of course, he had no doubts regarding their canonical status; he did not deny the authority of the three Gospels. However, he was particularly interested in the Gospel of John. Such a tendency he held was probably due to his view on Jesus: a savior rather than a lawgiver. To borrow Dungan's words, Luther only had a slight interest in the Synoptic Gospels because "he refused to use the teachings of Christ in the Gospels as a guide to Christian holiness."[58] In his monograph, *Sermons on the Gospel of St. John,*

---

48 Augustine, *Cons.* 1.1.1–2.
49 Augustine, *Cons.* 1.2.3.
50 Augustine, *Cons.* 1.1.2.
51 Dungan, *Synoptic Problem*, 136.
52 Augustine, *Cons.* 1.2.4.
53 Augustine, *Cons.* 1.2.4. Cf. Griesbach, "Demonstration," 104. Here Griesbach says, "Augustine was, as we know, the first to state that Mark followed Matthew as a sort of abbreviator and close imitator."
54 Michael Strickland, "Evangelicals and the Synoptic Problem" (PhD diss., University of Birmingham, 2011), 10.
55 Dungan, *Synoptic Problem*, 140.
56 Dungan, *Synoptic Problem*, 140.
57 Martin Luther, *Luther's Works: Sermons on the Gospel of St. John Chapter 1–4* (ed. Jaroslav Pelikan; vol. 22; Saint Louis: Concordia, 1957), ix.
58 Dungan, *Synoptic Problem*, 178.

16  CHAPTER 1

Luther compared the Gospel of John with other Gospels and dealt with the differences[59] in an Augustinian harmonistic stance.[60]

John Calvin (1509–64), a Protestant theologian and reformer, considers the Gospels as "four histories" in which the gospel of God—God's great work for salvation through Jesus' birth, death, and resurrection—was revealed through the inspiration of the Holy Spirit.[61] Calvin addresses that each evangelist's role was not decisive in terms of the construction of each Gospel.[62] In his commentary on Mark, for instance, Calvin says, "it is of little importance to us, provided only we believe that he (Mark) is a properly qualified and divinely appointed witness, who committed nothing to writing, but as the Holy Spirit directed him and guided his pen."[63] Calvin's following words reveal his position supporting the independent formation of the Gospels: "he [Mark] had not seen Matthew's book when he wrote his own."[64] Calvin also begins his account of Luke by saying: "as they [the three Evangelists] intended to give an honest narrative of what they knew to be certain and undoubted, each followed that method which he reckoned best."[65] In describing the commonalities and differences in the Synoptic Gospels, Calvin regards each evangelist as providing an "honest narrative" based on what they firmly knew and were guided by the Holy Spirit. He concludes that the Gospels constitute "astonishing harmony."[66] Thus, for Calvin, the similarities and differences between the Gospels did not matter, and if we are to ask the reason for the Gospels' such characteristics, he would say that they came from the Holy Spirit who played the most crucial role in the construction of the Gospels.[67]

Baruch Spinoza (1632–77), a philosopher of Jewish origin, asserts that the biblical text is "a product of human history and evolution," and therefore, that the Bible should be interpreted thoroughly in the light of natural history and "the natural light of reason."[68] As regards the Gospels, he believes that the

---

59  Luther, *Gospel of St. John*, 160, 218.

60  Dungan, *Synoptic Problem*, 179.

61  John Calvin, *Commentary on a Harmony of the Evangelists, Matthew, Mark, and Luke* (trans. William Pringle; 3 vols.; Edinburgh: Calvin Translation Society, 1845), 14–15.

62  Calvin, *Harmony*, 15.

63  Calvin, *Harmony*, 15.

64  Calvin, *Harmony*, 15.

65  Calvin, *Harmony*, 15.

66  Calvin, *Harmony*, 15.

67  Cf. Strickland, "Synoptic Problem," 23. Here Michael Strickland says, "Calvin argued ... that the Holy Spirit was the source of their agreements as well as their differences."

68  Mark S. Gignilliat, *Old Testament Criticism: From Benedict Spinoza to Brevard Childs* (Grand Rapids: Zondervan, 2012), 15. Baruch Spinoza addresses that the Bible is not the word of God, the word of God is rather in our hearts; thus, the truth regarding God is

# A SURVEY OF STUDIES ON THE SYNOPTIC PROBLEM

evangelists were not prophets and were not inspired by the Holy Spirit; he regards the Gospels as books written by humans. Spinoza compactly reveals his understanding of the construction and relationship between the Gospels as follows: "Each Evangelist preached his message in a different place, and each wrote down in simple style what he had preached with a view to telling clearly the story of Christ, and not with a view to explaining the other Evangelists."[69] Through this, we can derive two conclusions on Spinoza's understanding of the Gospels: (1) the construction of the Gospels was done by four evangelists based on their message and style; (2) each Gospel was written independently without any influence from other Gospels.

## 2.2 *Lessing to Dunn*

Spinoza's historical-critical approach was developed by later scholars. Gotthold E. Lessing (1729–81), a pioneer in the area of religion, aesthetics, and poetry,[70] attempts a historical-critical approach to the Synoptic Problem. In his article, Lessing argues that Matthew, Mark, and Luke are three separate translated versions based on the original Gospel, that is, the Hebrew or Syriac-Chaldaic Gospel of Nazarenes (cf. Acts 24:5), a hypothetical Gospel based on oral tradition retained by the Apostles.[71] In other words, he claims that variants emerged in the process of translating the original Gospel by each evangelist. Lessing asserts that Matthew made the first translated version of the original Gospel faithfully and cautiously.[72] He also addresses that Luke had the original Gospel, translated most of it, but changed the order and refined the

---

attainable from outside the Bible. See Baruch Spinoza, *Theological-Political Treatise*, trans. Samuel Shirley (2nd ed.; Indianapolis: Hackett, 2001), 145; Dungan, *Synoptic Problem*, 244. According to Dungan, Spinoza began the historical criticism, and as a result, an academic atmosphere that focused on the history of the text itself rather than the referent of the Bible (e.g., God's activity, Jesus Christ). See Dungan, *Synoptic Problem*, 172. Dungan (*Synoptic Problem*, 259) also says that all of these approaches were carefully calculated and intended, and caution should be taken with these destructive intents.

69 Spinoza, *Treatise*, 150.

70 Helen Zimmern, *Gotthold Ephraim Lessing: His Life and His Works* (London: Longmans, 1878), v.

71 Gotthold E. Lessing, "New Hypothesis on the Evangelists as Merely Human Historians," in *Philosophical and Theological Writings*, ed. Hugh B. Nisbet (Cambridge: Cambridge University Press, 2012), 156; cf. Farmer, *Synoptic Problem*, 4. Later, scholars named it "an Aramaic Proto-Gospel." See Bo Reicke, "Griesbach's Answer to the Synoptic Question," in *J. J. Griesbach: Synoptic and Text-Critical Studies 1776–1976*, eds. Bernard Orchard and Thomas R. W. Longstaff (SNTSMS 34; Cambridge: Cambridge University Press, 1978), 52.

72 Lessing, "New Hypothesis," 156, 161. Gotthold E. Lessing infers that for this reason, the original Gospel was also called "the Gospel of Matthew." See "New Hypothesis," 153.

18                                                                                                    CHAPTER 1

language.[73] Regarding Mark, Lessing proposes that he had the original Gospel but composed its abstract version because he had a less complete copy.[74] In short, Lessing's position is that each Gospel is dependent on the original Gospel but independent from each other.

Johann J. Griesbach (1745–1812) is a scholar who contributed to the study of New Testament by constructing his critical volumes of the Greek text, synopsis,[75] and Synoptic theory. In particular, he theorizes a specific model for the Synoptic Problem by arguing for the literary relationships between the Gospels with a source-critical and historical-critical theory.[76] Griesbach's position can be considered as a modification of Augustine's theory. In his publication in 1783, "Inquiritur in fontes, unde evangelistae suas de resurrectione Domini narrationes hauserint," Griesbach tries to defend the historicity of Jesus' resurrection, opposing Hermann S. Reimarus's argument, and argues that the Gospel of Mark was a *compendium* of Matthew's and Luke's Gospels.[77] In his other publication in 1789, "Commentatio qua Marci evangelium totum e Matthaei et Lucae commentariis decerptum esse monstratur,"[78] he asserts that the most original Gospel was written by Matthew, Luke constructed his Gospel based on Matthew, and the Gospel of Mark was formed based on the two previous Gospels, along with oral tradition occasionally, in a shorter version.[79] Thus, Griesbach follows Augustine's Matthean priority but does not follow the rest of Augustine's argument about Luke's reliance on Mark.[80]

Gottlob C. Storr (1746–1805) presents one type of literary-dependence theory through another source-critical approach, arguing Markan priority. In

---

73    Lessing, "New Hypothesis," 167.

74    Lessing, "New Hypothesis," 167.

75    Griesbach was the first to arrange the Gospel texts in parallel columns, which was called "synopsis" (it comes from the Greek word σύνοψις, which means "seeing all together" or "survey"), in 1774. See Bo Reicke, *The Roots of the Synoptic Gospels* (Philadelphia: Fortress, 1986), 1.

76    Reicke, "Griesbach's Answer," 50.

77    Johann J. Griesbach, "Inquiritur in fontes, unde evangelistae suas de resurrectione Domini narrationes hauserint," in *Opuscula academica*, ed. J. P. Gabler (vol. 2; Jena: Fr. Frommanni, 1825).

78    This thesis was written in Latin and was translated into English by Bernard Orchard; the translated title is "A Demonstration that Mark was written after Matthew and Luke."

79    Johann J. Griesbach, "Commentatio qua Marci evangelium totum e Matthaei et Lucae commentariis decerptum esse monstratur." In *Opuscula academica*, ed. J. P. Gabler (vol. 2; Jena: Fr. Frommanni, 1825); Reicke, "Griesbach's Answer," 50–51; Werner G. Kümmel, *The New Testament: The History of the Investigation of Its Problems* (Nashville: Abingdon, 1972), 75.

80    According to Kümmel, "[i]n the course of the initial literary investigation of the 'synoptic question,' a question that had become a 'problem,' several other attempts at a solution were independently advanced." See Kümmel, *New Testament*, 75.

A SURVEY OF STUDIES ON THE SYNOPTIC PROBLEM

his monograph, *Über den Zweck der evangelischen Geschichte, und der Briefe Johannes* (1789), Storr asserts that the earliest Gospel is constructed by Mark[81]—under Peter's superintendence[82]—on which Matthew and Luke were formed respectively.[83] Storr, along with Carl C. Flatt, explains three possible reasons for the plausibility that the Gospel of Mark was written first: (1) the coincidence of Mark with Matthew and Luke is considerably prominent; (2) if the Gospel of Mark was written last, it is difficult to explain why so much of what appears in Matthew and Luke is taken away; and (3) Mark has something that Matthew and Luke do not have, but very little.[84] Storr addresses that Matthew and John had apostolic authority and that Mark and Luke also had divine authority because they were constructed under the apostolic authority of Peter and Paul, respectively.[85] Storr appears to have been the first to claim Markan priority.

Johann G. Eichhorn (1752–1827), a theologian, philosopher, and orientalist, argues that since biblical texts were developed prior to the development of modern culture and thinking, they must be approached with "their own type of thinking" in order to be understood properly.[86] Regarding the Gospel studies, in the first volume of *Einleitung in das Neue Testament* (1820), he accepts Lessing's hypothesis almost verbatim, arguing that the Aramaic Ur-Gospel was first formed, and the Gospels of Matthew, Mark, Luke, and other Gospels were also formed based on this; in particular, he proposes that the original Gospel was formed in AD 35 by a disciple of an apostle.[87] He argues that the Synoptic Gospels were independently constructed in the later second century, by using the Aramaic Gospel which did not include the miracle accounts.[88]

Johann G. von Herder (1744–1803) was a German theologian, philosopher, and poet who criticized and warned against the negative aspects of

---

81  Gottlob C. Storr and Carl C. Flatt, *An Elementary Course of Biblical Theology* (2nd ed.; trans. Samuel S. Schmucker; New York: Gould and Newman, 1836), 98.

82  Storr and Flatt, *Biblical Theology*, 146.

83  Gottlob C. Storr, *Über den Zweck der evangelischen Geschichte, und der Briefe Johannes* (Tübingen: Jacob Friedrich Heerbrandt, 1789), 375–76.

84  Storr and Flatt, *Biblical Theology*, 98.

85  Storr and Flatt, *Biblical Theology*, 146–47.

86  John Sandys-Wunsch, "Eichhorn, J(ohann) G(ottefried) (1752–1827)," in *Dictionary of Major Biblical Interpreters*, ed. Donald K. McKim (Downers Grove: InterVarsity, 2007), 400–401.

87  Johann G. Eichhorn, *Einleitung in das Neue Testament* (vol. 1.; Leipzig: Weidmannischen Buchhandlung, 1820), 6–84

88  Sandys-Wunsch, "Eichhorn," 402. Johann G. Eichhorn is criticized for being insufficient in providing evidence for his claims. See Eta Linnemann, *Is There a Synoptic Problem?: Rethinking the Literary Dependence of the First Three Gospels* (trans. Robert W. Yarbrough; Grand Rapids: Baker, 1992), 29; Sandys-Wunsch, "Eichhorn," 403.

Enlightenment.[89] In his monograph, *Eine Metakritik zur Kritik der reinen Vernunft* (published in 1799; translated by Marcia Bunge titled *Against Pure Reason*), Herder emphasizes that the Gospels are neither biography nor history but are written with a completely different character.[90] Herder opposes the presence of Ur-Gospel, which is not found in the writings of the Fathers, and argues that Mark was first written based on oral tradition.[91] According to Herder, the Gospel of Mark has a dramatic nuance and is well-suited for oral reading to the congregation.[92] Furthermore, he asserts that Matthew and Luke were constructed independently after Mark without dependent interrelation.[93] As can be seen from the following quotation, Herder tries to reveal the unique value and meaning of each Gospel, while excluding any Gospel's priority or literary dependence between them: "No evangelist wanted to build over the others or to overpower them. On the contrary, each set down *his* narration for his own sake. Perhaps not one of the evangelists saw the gospel of another; if he did, then he did not use it as he wrote his own."[94] Nevertheless, despite his assertion, Herder is interestingly regarded as preparing the grounds for recognizing the priority of Mark and developing the Two Document Hypothesis.[95]

Johann L. Hug (1765–1846) re-emphasizes the Matthean priority, but his arguments differ from Griesbach's. In his two-volume book, *Einleitung in die Schriften des Neuen Testaments*, Hug basically perceives the Gospels as a type of biography via a generic point of view.[96] He asserts that it is appropriate to view Matthew as the oldest Gospel according to church history, and that the order of writing is Matthew, Mark, and Luke.[97] Hug addresses that Matthew

---

89  Johann G. von Herder, *Against Pure Reason: Writings on Religion, Language, and History* (ed. and trans. Marcia Bunge; Minneapolis: Fortress, 1993), 1–2. Johann G. von Herder pursued the proper use of reason against the spirit of the time, which focused on pure reason. However, his writings have not been translated much into English; that is why he is often mistakenly perceived as an anti-rationalist by the English-American scholars. See Herder, *Against Pure Reason*, 4.

90  Herder, *Against Pure Reason*, 176.

91  Herder, *Against Pure Reason*, 179.

92  Herder, *Against Pure Reason*, 186–87.

93  Herder, *Against Pure Reason*, 183; cf. Kümmel, *New Testament*, 79–83. Not only for the Synoptic Gospels, Herder emphasizes the individuality of each New Testament text by default. See Herder, *Against Pure Reason*, 29.

94  Herder, *Against Pure Reason*, 183.

95  Kümmel, *New Testament*, 82.

96  Johann L. Hug, *Hug's Introduction to the New Testament* (trans. David Fosdick Jr.; Andover: Gould & Newman, 1836), 311–13. In addition, Johann L. Hug emphasizes the historical aspect of the Gospels constructed by Mark and Luke by referring to them as "historians." See Hug, *Introduction*, 313.

97  Hug, *Introduction*, 311.

# A SURVEY OF STUDIES ON THE SYNOPTIC PROBLEM

composed his Gospel for Jews, Mark and Luke for Gentiles, and he explains that the differences between the Gospels were fundamentally influenced by the differences between their readers.[98] Regarding the relationship between the Gospels, he argues that the Gospel of Mark was written based on the Gospel of Matthew[99] and that the Gospel of Luke was formed under the influence of these two Gospels.[100]

In his monograph, *Historisch-kritischer Versuch über die Entstehung und die frühesten Schicksale der schriftlichen Evangelien* (1818), Johann K. L. Gieseler (1792–1854) agrees to a degree with Lessing and Eichhorn on the Ur-Gospel, but he takes the possibility that the Ur-Gospel existed and was passed down in oral form for a considerable time—in this sense, Herder's argument for an oral Gospel was revived in Gieseler.[101] He asserts that the oral gospel, transmitted first in Aramaic and later in Greek, became the source for the canonical Gospels.[102] Thus, Gieseler addresses that these Synoptic Gospels share a Hebraic-Greek language characteristic.[103] Gieseler's monograph does not have any reference to the relationship between Matthew, Mark, and Luke, but it only asserts that oral Ur-Gospel influenced these Gospels.[104]

Friedrich Schleiermacher (1768–1834), a German biblical scholar and philosopher, asserts that numerous written fragments of gospel narratives existed and influenced the formation of the Gospels of Matthew, Mark, and Luke. In his monograph, *A Critical Essay on the Gospel of St. Luke* (1825),[105] he argues against Eichhorn's claim that the life of Jesus was woven into a *single*-original narrative, and asserts that the material of Jesus' words existed as a collection of fragments.[106] He may have played a preliminary role for Q. Schleiermacher also claims that each Gospel was constructed according to its author's perspective

---

98    Hug, *Introduction*, 311–312.

99    Hug, *Introduction*, 355.

100   Hug, *Introduction*, 398. Here Hug states that Luke was influenced by both Matthew and Mark, but was more adherent to the earliest written text, Matthew.

101   Johann K. L. Gieseler, *Historisch-kritischer Versuch über die Entstehung und die frühesten Schicksale der schriftlichen Evangelien* (Leipzig: Wilhelm Engelmann, 1818), 53. In this monograph, Gieseler takes a careful and humble attitude toward the study of the origin of the written Gospels. He mentions that nobody can reach complete certainty in terms of dealing with the origin of the ancient documents but only pursue the probability (Wahrscheinlichkeit). See Gieseler, *Historisch-kritischer Versuch*, 1.

102   Gieseler, *Historisch-kritischer Versuch*, 87–92.

103   Gieseler, *Historisch-kritischer Versuch*, 4.

104   Linnemann, *Synoptic Problem*, 31.

105   Frederick Schleiermacher, *A Critical Essay on the Gospel of St. Luke* (London: John Taylor, 1825), 14–15. Frederick Schleiermacher opposes pursuing a specific original Gospel before the written Gospels. See Schleiermacher, *Gospel of St. Luke*, 1–18.

106   Schleiermacher, *Gospel of St. Luke*, 10.

22                                                                                    CHAPTER 1

based on the reliable materials from eyewitnesses.[107] From a religious point of view, he regarded John as the most important, but from a historical view, he saw Luke as the most important and Mark as the most historically unreliable text.[108] In Schleiermacher's arguments, however, it is hard to find the idea of literary dependence between the Gospels.

Karl Lachmann (1793–1851), who published textual editions of classics and biblical texts,[109] researched the narrative sequence of the Synoptic Gospels.[110] In his article, "De ordine narrationum in evangeliis synopticis" (1935), he attempts to study the Synoptic Problem with regard to the order of the narratives.[111] He did not regard this issue as a matter of tradition but as a literary problem.[112] Concerning the order of the Synoptic Gospels, although he could not confirm the historical order of the narratives, he is quite confident that it is at least possible to infer which Gospel is earlier and which evangelist follows or changes the order of the earlier Gospel.[113] He points out that the order of the narratives of all Synoptic Gospels agrees only when Matthew and Luke agree with the order of Mark, but Matthew and Luke do not agree with one another's order when they depart from the order of Mark. He further asserts that Matthew's deviations from Mark's order can be explained by Matthew's addition of other material into Markan order.[114] In this way, he supports Markan Priority.

Christian G. Wilke (1788–1854), a Saxon pastor and scholar, also offers a detailed study on the relationship between the Synoptic Gospels in his monograph, *Der Urevangelist oder exegetisch kritische Untersuchung über das Verwandtschaftsverhältniß der drei ersten Evangelien*, published in 1838. He argues that the presupposition of an original oral gospel or primal fragments is not plausible,[115] and also argues that it is rather reasonable to regard

---

107    D. DeVries, "Schleiermacher, Friedrich Daniel Ernst (*1768–1834*)," in *Dictionary of Major Biblical Interpreters* (ed. Donald K. McKim; Downers Grove: InterVarsity, 2007), 889.

108    DeVries, "Schleiermacher," 889.

109    Glenn W. Most, "Karl Lachmann (1793–1851): Reconstructing the Transmission of a Classical Latin Author," *HistH* 4 (2019): 269.

110    Kümmel, *New Testament*, 147–48.

111    Karl Lachmann, "De ordine narrationum in evangeliis synopticis," *ThStK* 8 (1935): 574. Karl Lachmann is considered to be the earliest to study the Synoptic Problem focusing on the order of the narratives.

112    Lachmann, "De ordine narrationum," 573–74.

113    Lachmann, "De ordine narrationum," 583–84.

114    Lachmann, "De ordine narrationum," 574. Cf. Kümmel, *New Testament*, 147.

115    Christian G. Wilke, *Der Urevangelist oder exegetisch kritische Untersuchung über das Verwandtschaftsverhältniß der drei ersten Evangelien* (Dresden: Gerhard Fleischer, 1838), 684. Here Christian G. Wilke asserts that "this work (Mark's) is not a copy of an original oral Gospels, but an artificial composition." This translation and the words in bracket are mine.

A SURVEY OF STUDIES ON THE SYNOPTIC PROBLEM

Mark as the earliest evangelist because Mark's work lies under the other two Gospels (Matthew and Luke).[116] He claims that Mark influenced both Luke and Matthew, and that Matthew was influenced by the Gospel of Luke,[117] which is precisely contrary to what Griesbach asserted.

Christian H. Weiße (1801–66) can be considered a pioneer of the Two-Document hypothesis. In his two-volume monograph, *Die evangelische Geschichte, kritisch und philosophisch bearbeitet*, published in 1838, he claims that the material of the words of Jesus—a document related to the double tradition in Matthew and Luke—pre-existed along with the Gospel of Mark, the oldest Gospel, and that Matthew and Luke were formed under the influence of them.[118] Weiße argues that Mark composed a text in a form/genre that never existed before; thus, the awkwardness and clumsiness were derived from the constructor's unfamiliarity with the literary form.[119] Weiße thus affirms the priority of Mark along with the literary dependence of Matthew and Luke on Mark and the Jesus' sayings material.

Ferdinand C. Baur (1792–1860), who is regarded as a founder of the Tübingen School, in his monograph *Kritische Untersuchungen über die kanonische Evangelien*, published in 1848, argues for Matthean priority and the existence of Ur-Luke.[120] In other words, he asserts that the Gospel of Jewish Matthew and Pauline proto-Luke were pre-existing, that the Gospel of Luke was formed under their influence, and that the Gospel of Mark was constructed under the influence of these two Gospels, Matthew, and Luke.[121]

Bernhard Weiß (1827–1918) formulates a hypothesis about Aramaic Ur-Matthew based on source criticism. He argues that the original Ur-Matthew was later translated into Greek Ur-Matthew and that the Gospels of Matthew, Mark, and Luke were composed around it. According to Weiß, the oral tradition given by Peter directly influenced Mark, and after Mark was formed, Matthew and Luke were influenced by Mark.[122] He seems to have tried to find a middle ground between Matthean and Markan priority throughout his argument.[123]

---

116 Wilke, *Urevangelist*, 684; cf. Kümmel, *New Testament*, 148.

117 Wilke, *Urevangelist*, 685. For reference, he agrees that all the canonical Gospels are constructed in the Hebrew type. See *Urevangelist*, 3.

118 Christian H. Weiße, *Die evangelische Geschichte, kritisch und philosophisch bearbeitet* (2 vols.; Leipzig: Breitkopf und Härtel, 1838); Theodor Zahn, *Introduction to the New Testament* (trans. John M. Trout, et al.; New York: Charles Scribner's Sons, 1909), 2:414–15.

119 Weiße, *Die evangelische Geschichte*.

120 Ferdinand C. Baur, *Kritische Untersuchungen über die kanonische Evangelien* (Tübingen: Fues, 1847).

121 Zahn, *Introduction*, 2:412–14.

122 Weiß presumes additional sources were also involved in the formation of Luke's Gospel (see Zahn, *Introduction*, 2:417–18).

123 Linnemann, *Synoptic Problem*, 34.

Heinrich J. Holtzmann (1832–1910) shares Weiße's position but in a slightly modified form. In his monograph, *Die synoptischen Evangelien: Ihr Ursprung und ihr geschichtlicher Charakter* (1863), Holtzmann asserts Markan priority based on Ur-Mark.[124] He also argues that Matthew and Luke were respectively formed under the influence of Matthew's collection of Jesus' sayings, as well as under the influence of Mark.[125] In this regard, Holzmann, along with Weiße, is probably considered as one who laid the foundation for the Two Document theory—although Holzmann's position seems closer to the Four Document theory.[126]

Westcott (1825–1901), a British biblical scholar, in his monograph, *Introduction to the Study of the Gospels* (1862), claims that there was a common oral tradition regarding Jesus' ministry and teaching, which influenced each Synoptic Gospel separately.[127] Westcott explains the constructive process of the Gospels as follows: "the successive remoulding of the oral Gospel according to the peculiar requirements of different classes of hearers, furnishes a natural explanation of the general similarity in form and substance between the several Gospels, combined with peculiarities and differences in arrangement and contents."[128] Unfortunately, Westcott has been neglected by later scholars, despite his contribution to the oral tradition and many other studies.[129]

William Sanday (1843–1920), a British scholar and Anglican priest, in his article titled "The Conditions under which the Gospels Were Written, in Their Bearing upon Some Difficulties of the Synoptic Problem," supports the Two-Document Hypothesis by assuming that the similarity among the Synoptic Gospels is resulted by the presence of common documents.[130] He assumes that the common documents are the Gospel of Mark and a collection including the main discourses of Jesus.[131]

Julius Wellhausen (1844–1918), a German biblical scholar, mainly contributed to the Old Testament textual studies and the reconstruction of Israel's

---

124 Zahn, *Introduction*, 415.

125 Kümmel, *New Testament*, 151.

126 Kümmel, *New Testament*, 151–52.

127 Westcott, *Gospels*, 152–95. He was influenced by Gieseler's view of the oral Ur-Gospel (see Baum, "Synoptic Problem," 914).

128 Westcott, *Gospels*, 193.

129 Stanley E. Porter, "The Legacy of B. F. Westcott and Oral Gospel Tradition," in *Earliest Christianity within the Boundaries of Judaism: Essays in Honor of Bruce Chilton*, eds. Alan J. Avery-Peck, et al. (Leiden: Brill, 2016), 334–40.

130 William Sanday, "The Conditions under which the Gospels Were Written, in Their Bearing upon Some Difficulties of the Synoptic Problem," in *Studies in the Synoptic Problem: By Members of the University of Oxford*, ed. William Sanday (Oxford: Clarendon, 1911), 3.

131 Sanday, "Synoptic Problem," 3.

A SURVEY OF STUDIES ON THE SYNOPTIC PROBLEM

history, but he also made a meaningful contribution to the Synoptic Gospels study.[132] In his monograph, *Einleitung in die drei ersten Evangelien* (1905), he assumes that Jesus' words and stories about him were formed in Aramaic, and the oral tradition also existed in Aramaic, which was later translated into Greek and influenced Matthew, Mark, and Luke.[133] On the issue of the interrelationship between the Gospels, he supports Markan priority and assumes a common material for Matthew and Luke, the so-called "Q,"[134] both of which influence on the construction of Matthew and Luke.[135]

Burnett H. Streeter (1874–1937) asserts Markan priority by arguing that Mark was the basis of Matthew and Luke. In his monograph, *The Four Gospels: A Study of Origins* (1924), Streeter regards Matthew as an "enlarged edition of Mark" and Luke as an "independent work incorporating considerable portions of Mark."[136] He assumes a hypothetical material, "Q,"[137] and the special source of Matthew (M) and that of Luke (L), in oral or written forms.[138] Streeter contends that Mark's Gospel was written first, then Matthew and Luke constructed their Gospels based on Mark, Q, and their special materials (M or L).[139] In this sense, his position is called the "Four Document Hypothesis."[140] Streeter also argues that Proto-Luke, which was formed by Q and L, influenced the

---

132  R. E. Clements, "Wellhausen, Julius," in *Dictionary of Major Biblical Interpreters* (ed. Donald K. McKim; Downers Grove: InterVarsity, 2007), 1030–31.

133  Julius Wellhausen, *Einleitung in die drei ersten Evangelien* (Berlin: Georg Reimer, 1905), 14. However, his assertion had changed via his later works as Nils A. Dahl mentions: "(Wellhausen) started with the assumption that at least the original form of Mark and the sayings common to Matthew and Luke had been written in Aramaic (1895 and 1896) but gradually modified his claims (compare 1905:35–38, 57, 68 with 1911:26f., 48, 60). He became increasingly skeptical about conjectural mistranslations and translation variants even though he retained some examples which he found convincing (1911:25–28). At the end, he mainly drew attention to syntactical constructions which were common in Aramaic but unusual, if not impossible, in Greek (1911:11–25)." See Nils A. Dahl, "Wellhausen on the New Testament," *Semeia* 25 (1983): 92.

134  The expression "Q" (Quelle; source) was coined by Johannes Weiss, even though Wellhausen already mentioned the common material between Matthew and Luke. See Johannes Weiss, *Paul and Jesus* (trans. H. J. Chaytor; London: Harper and Brothers, 1909), 21.

135  Clements, "Wellhausen," 1033. However, Bultmann notes that Wellhausen has not reached a definitive and detailed conclusion about the Gospel formation process. See Bultmann, *Synoptic Tradition*, 2.

136  Streeter, *Four Gospels*, 151.

137  Streeter, *Four Gospels*, 153.

138  Streeter, *Four Gospels*, 183–84.

139  Streeter, *Four Gospels*, 150.

140  Streeter, *Four Gospels*, 223–70. Streeter contents that Four Document Hypothesis can simply explain the issue that Two Document Hypothesis cannot solve in a satisfiable way, and it can also reflect the Early Church's situation, even though it has limits in terms of

construction of Luke, along with Mark.[141] He further assumes the influence of oral tradition in constructing some parts of the Synoptic Gospels.[142]

Bultmann (1884–1976), a German Lutheran scholar, is famous for introducing existential interpretation and a demythologizing program to the New Testament study and contributed significantly to the study of the formation process of Synoptic Gospels.[143] He claims that the Gospels are not biographical documents; nevertheless, he asserts that they give reliable information regarding Jesus' sayings and doings.[144] In particular, in his monograph, *Die Geschichte der synoptischen Tradition* (published in 1921; translated by John Marsh, titled *History of the Synoptic Tradition*), he asserts that the early Christian community's Synoptic tradition affected the construction of Gospels in mainly five types of different forms: apothegms, dominical sayings, miracle stories, historical stories, and legends.[145] He agrees with Markan Priority, the existence of Q, and the formation of Matthew and Luke under the influence of Mark, Q, and traditional materials.[146]

Austin M. Farrer (1904–1968), an English biblical scholar, supports Markan priority but objects to the existence of Q; it has been called "the Farrer Hypothesis." In his article, "On Dispensing with Q" (1955), he asserts that Q is not required if we contemplate Luke's knowledge of Matthew.[147] To be more specific, Farrer argues that Matthew could be an "amplified version" of Mark, with some influence of oral material, and Luke formed his Gospel by using Mark and Matthew.[148] Thus, Farrer provides a more straightforward proposal than the previous positions assuming Q.[149]

---

      making a "tidy scheme" in explaining the exact source of each Gospel's specific parts. See Streeter, *Four Gospels*, 269.

141    Streeter, *Four Gospels*, 150.

142    Streeter, *Four Gospels*, xvii.

143    D. Fergusson, "Bultmann, Rudolf," in *Dictionary of Major Biblical Interpreters* (ed. Donald K. McKim; Downers Grove: InterVarsity, 2007), 261.

144    Fergusson, "Bultmann," 263.

145    Bultmann, *Synoptic Tradition*, 11–317.

146    Bultmann, *Synoptic Tradition*, 337–74.

147    Farrer, "Dispensing with Q," 55–88.

148    Farrer, "Dispensing with Q," 85. In this sense, Farrer asserts that Matthew and Luke did not independently construct their Gospels influenced by Mark and Q—unlike the Two Document Hypothesis, but that Matthew constructed his Gospel under the influence of Mark, and Luke created a new type of Gospel under the influence of Matthew as well as Mark.

149    Farrer, "Dispensing with Q," 85.

A SURVEY OF STUDIES ON THE SYNOPTIC PROBLEM

Birger Gerhardsson (1926–2013), a Swedish New Testament scholar, endeavored to explore the origin of the Gospel tradition and its oral transmission, in light of the previous form-critical works of Debelius and Bultmann.[150] In *Memory and Manuscript: Oral Tradition and Written Transmission in Rabbinic Judaism and Early Christianity* (1961), he analyzes the technique of oral and written transmission in Rabbinic Judaism and applies that to the early Church community via a framework of memory theory.[151] The conclusion of his study is as follows: (1) Jesus was the Christ, Messiah, and Son of God, but at the same time, he was a Jewish teacher who taught the Messianic Torah as a fulfiller of the pre-Messianic Torah; (2) through Jesus, their teacher, the disciples formed and kept the oral tradition of their teacher's oral Torah based on memory (and other written traditions); (3) each evangelist constructed each Gospel based on the distinct tradition(s) about, and from Jesus.[152]

William R. Farmer (1921–2000), an American New Testament scholar, raises the Griesbach Hypothesis to the surface via his monograph, *The Synoptic Problem: A Critical Review of the Problem of the Literary Relationships between Matthew, Mark, and Luke*, published in 1964. Originally, Farmer was a supporter of the Markan priority because he learned from his teachers who had taught the Markan priority as an "unquestioned tradition"; later, he called it a "false consensus."[153] In his monograph, he argues Matthean priority and Luke and Mark's use of Matthew, as well as Mark's use of Matthew and Luke,[154] and it has been called "the Two Gospel Hypothesis." Thus, he follows Griesbach's theory, by proposing Mark's redaction based on Matthew and Luke.[155] He also agrees that oral tradition and other written sources may have had an influence in constructing the Synoptic Gospels.[156]

Pierre Benoit (1906–87) and Marie-Emile Boismard's (1916–2004) scholarly inquiry, as delineated in their collaborative work *Synopse des quatres*

---

150   Gerhardsson, *Origins*, 8–9.

151   Gerhardsson, *Memory & Manuscript*, x–xvi.

152   Gerhardsson, *Memory & Manuscript*, 324–35.

153   Farmer, *Synoptic Problem*, viii, ix. Farmer was introduced to B. C. Butler by his student H. Ernst, and read Butler's *The Originality of St. Matthew*. With this book, after reading C. F. Burney's *The Poetry of Our Lord*, he gets to a point where he cannot simply put a priority on either Mark or Matthew. Then he went through Farrer Hypothesis, Augustinian Hypothesis, and finally the Griesbach Hypothesis. For more information on this process, see David B. Peabody, "Farmer, William Reuben," in *Dictionary of Major Biblical Interpreters*, ed. Donald K. McKim (Downers Grove: InterVarsity, 2007), 433–34.

154   Farmer, *Synoptic Problem*, 201–2.

155   Farmer, *Synoptic Problem*, 234.

156   Farmer, *Synoptic Problem*, 199.

*Évangiles en français* (1972), delves into the intricate processes underlying the construction of the Synoptic Gospels and the Gospel of John.[157] The ensuing discussion will concentrate on the formative aspects of the Synoptic Gospels, omitting Boismard's postulation regarding the genesis of the Gospel of John. Subsequent to Benoit's introductory remarks, Boismard expounds upon a nuanced and intricate theoretical framework. Within the initial phase, he posits the existence of four distinct documents, denoted as A, B, C, and Q, each exerting divergent influences upon the intermediate manuscripts of Matthew, Mark, and Luke.[158] Specifically, Mt.-interm is asserted to be molded by the confluence of Q and A, Mc.-interm by A, B, C, and Proto-Lc by Q, B, C, and Mt.-interm. Boismard contends that the ultimate configuration of the Gospel of Matthew is the result of the amalgamation of Mt.-interm and Mc.-interm, while the definitive structure of the Gospel of Mark is derived from the interplay of Mt.-interm, Mc.-interm, and Proto-Lc.[159] Concerning the Gospel of Luke, Boismard proposes its formation through Mc.-interm and Proto-Lc.[160] Notably, Boismard's perspective refrains from explicitly affirming direct literary dependence among the final compositions of the Gospels. Moreover, the discernment of references to the influence of oral tradition within his discourse proves to be a challenging endeavor.

Bo Reicke (1914–87), a Swedish biblical scholar, conducted an in-depth study on the influence of tradition on the formation of New Testament texts, primarily based on historical criticism.[161] In his monograph, *The Roots of the Synoptic Gospels* (1986), he examined all the pericope units of the Synoptic Gospels and found that only oral traditions can account for both the overarching parallels and persistent divergencies in syntax and vocabulary within the common Synoptic material.[162]

James D. G. Dunn (1939–2020), a British New Testament scholar, asserts that the Gospels were written under the influence of oral traditions kept as memories by people and that the main subject of oral tradition was Jesus' words and ministries, not emphasizing verbal precision or historical details.[163] Dunn's perception of memory related to Gospel tradition is described in his monograph

---

157    Pierre Benoit and Marie-Emile Boismard, *Synopse des quatres Évangiles en français* (Tome II; Paris: Les Éditions du Cerf, 1972), 15–59.

158    Benoit and Boismard, *Synopse*, 17.

159    Benoit and Boismard, *Synopse*, 17.

160    Benoit and Boismard, *Synopse*, 17.

161    D. P. Moessner, "Reicke, Bo," in *Dictionary of Major Biblical Interpreters*, ed. Donald K. McKim (Downers Grove: InterVarsity, 2007), 853.

162    Moessner, "Reicke," 855; Reicke, *Roots*, 45–149.

163    James D. G. Dunn, *The Living Word* (2nd ed.; Philadelphia: Fortress, 2009), 35.

A SURVEY OF STUDIES ON THE SYNOPTIC PROBLEM

*The Evidence for Jesus: The Impact of Scholarship on Our Understanding of How Christianity Began* (1985). In this work, he asserts that people's memories from which the Gospels were composed were much better than ours: "In societies where the *spoken* word was the chief means of communication, and where a large portion of education consisted in rote-learning, memories were better trained and almost certainly a good deal more retentive."[164] He also argues that the Synoptic Gospels share a common source of a Greek translation of Jesus' Aramaic words.[165] Furthermore, Dunn says that the evangelist of each Gospel should be viewed as editors rather than simply recorders of tradition and that differences emerge because they edited the Jesus tradition in different ways.[166]

Although this section does not cover all scholars associated with the so-called Synoptic Problem, we have looked at some major Church Fathers and scholars in this field. The positions of the scholars shown above can be grouped according to the following issues: (1) literary dependence or literary independence/no mention of literary dependence between the Synoptic Gospels;[167] (2) source of the Synoptic Gospels: oral tradition(s) and/or written documents. Based on these issues, the scholars can be classified as shown in Tables 1.1 and 1.2.

TABLE 1.1    Literary dependence or independence

| Advocacy for literary dependence | Non-advocacy/no mention of literary dependence |
|---|---|
| Augustine, Luther, Griesbach, Storr, Hug, Lachmann, Wilke, Weiße, Baur, Weiß, Holtzmann, Sanday, Wellhausen, Streeter, Bultmann, Farrer, Farmer | Papias, Justin Martyr, Tatian, Marcion, Celsus, Origen, Porphyry, Eusebius, Calvin, Spinoza, Lessing, Eichhorn, Herder, Gieseler, Schleiermacher, Westcott, Gehardsson, Boismard, Reicke, Dunn |

---

164    James D. G. Dunn, *The Evidence for Jesus: The Impact of Scholarship on Our Understanding of How Christianity Began* (London: SCM, 1985), 2.

165    Dunn, *Evidence for Jesus*, 3. Here James D. G. Dunn suggests that the commonalities between Matthew, Mark, and Luke may be due to a common source or from literary dependence on each other. See Dunn, *Evidence for Jesus*, 7.

166    Dunn, *Evidence for Jesus*, 8.

167    This study defines "literary dependence" as the dependence of the Gospels on each other, not the dependence of each Gospel on previous materials.

TABLE 1.2   Attitudes towards oral tradition

| Scholars who support/refer to/imply oral tradition(s) | Scholars who give no mention/attention to oral tradition(s) |
|---|---|
| Papias, Justin Martyr, Origen, Eusebius, Lessing, Herder, Gieseler, Weiß, Westcott, Wellhausen, Streeter, Bultmann, Reicke, Farrer, Gerhardsson, Farmer, Dunn | Tatian, Marcion, Celsus, Porphyry, Augustine, Luther, Calvin, Spinoza, Griesbach, Storr, Eichhorn, Hug, Schleiermacher, Lachmann, Wilke, Weiße, Baur, Weiß, Holtzmann, Sanday, Boismard |

These tables have the following implications: (1) for a long time in the church history, the literary dependence on or the existence of written material was not mentioned or discussed, and this tendency has survived throughout the early church history and also has remained in several medieval and modern scholars; (2) Augustine began the literal dependence discussion, and since the idea was first introduced, it has exerted a great influence on many scholars; and (3) attention to oral tradition has been made by considerable scholars since Papias, although many scholars have overlooked it. Four views stand out as being representative of the numerous views regarding the Synoptic Problem surveyed above.

## 3   Four Major Views

### 3.1   *The Two Source Hypothesis*

The Two Source Hypothesis asserts that Mark's Gospel was formed first, and Matthew and Luke separately wrote their Gospels with reference to Mark along with a non-Markan source called Q. It can be shown in Figure 1.1.

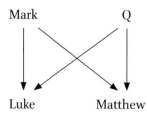

FIGURE 1.1
The Two Source Hypothesis
Porter and Dyer, "Synoptic Problem," 16.

A SURVEY OF STUDIES ON THE SYNOPTIC PROBLEM                    31

The major assumptions in the Two Source Hypothesis, which is a currently dominant position,[168] are "Markan Priority"[169] and the existence of "Q." As a representative proponent of this position, Craig A. Evans contends that, although "no theory of the relationships of the Synoptic Gospels is free from difficulty," the Two Source Hypothesis is "the best explanation of the data."[170] According to Evans, there are three reasons for supporting Markan Priority. First, in terms of style and word selection in the Synoptic Gospels, Evans observes several unnatural usages in Mark; for instance, ἐκβάλλω (Mark 1:12) and παίω (Mark 14:47). If Mark was able to see more suitable words in the parallel texts of Matthew (ἀνάγω in 4:1; πατάσσω in 26:51) and Luke (ἄγω in 4:1, πατάσσω in 22:50), it would have been unlikely for Mark to use such awkward expressions.[171] Second, unlike Matthew and Luke, Mark expresses Jesus' and the disciple's figures as undignified (Mark 4:35–41; 6:47–52; 7:24–30; 8:14–21);[172] it is not easy to imagine that Mark intentionally used these expressions if he had access to Matthew and Luke's Gospels. Third, much more frequent interpretations of Matthew and Luke compared with Mark, can be regarded as the evidence of their redaction based on Mark. In addition, Mark's inclusion of some unique material (Mark 1:1; 2:27; 3:20–21; 4:26–29; 7:2–4, 32–37; 8:22–26; 9:29, 48–49; 13:33–37; 14:51–52) and the omission of many important teachings of Jesus (e.g., the Beatitudes, the Lord's Prayer, the Golden Rule) are hard to explain when we assume Mark's reliance on Matthew and Luke.[173] By presenting these evidences, Evans argues that Markan Priority is a more comprehensive hypothesis than the Matthean Priority of the Two Gospels Hypothesis.

Then, what is the evidence for the existence of Q? The Two Source Hypothesis contends that the common material of Matthew and Luke, unlike Mark, probably came from another source, the so-called Q.[174] Here Evans suggests

---

168  Many scholars/commentators try to find Matthew and Luke's intentions or theologies based on the Two Source Hypothesis. For instance, see O. Wesley. Allen, *Reading the Synoptic Gospels: Basic Methods for Interpreting Matthew, Mark, and Luke* (Saint Louis: Chalice, 2000), 75–101; Darrell L Bock, *Luke 1:1–9:50* (BECNT 3; Grand Rapids: Baker Academic, 1994), 7–14; John Nolland, *Luke 1:1–9:20* (WBC 35A; Grand Rapids: Zondervan, 2000), xxviii–xxxi.

169  The foundation of Markan priority and the dependent construction of Matthew and Luke based on Mark was set by Lachmann and Holtzmann. For more detailed information, see Heinlich J. Holtzmann, *Die synoptischen Evangelien: Ihr Ursprung und geschichtlicher Charakter* (Leipzig: Wilhelm Engelmann, 1863).

170  Evans, "Two Source Hypothesis," 28.

171  Evans, "Two Source Hypothesis," 28–31.

172  Evans, "Two Source Hypothesis," 31–34.

173  Evans, "Two Source Hypothesis," 34–35.

174  Evans, "Two Source Hypothesis," 36.

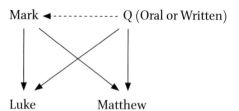

FIGURE 1.2
Evans's Two Source Hypothesis

that Q can include oral or written sources.[175] The figure of the Two Source Hypothesis suggested by Evans can be described as in Figure 1.2.

These are evidences supporting the above argument. First, considering the Greek educational features such as "chreia,"[176] a body of Jesus' teaching (Q) probably existed already and influenced the construction of the Gospels.[177] Second, the non-Markan sources in Matthew and Luke can probably be regarded as one distinctive source (Q), which was *separately* used by Matthew and Luke, since it seems difficult to see that Luke has "disassembled Matthew's well-structured discourses,"[178] as both the Two Gospel Hypothesis and the Farrer Hypothesis suggest. Third, Matthew's and Luke's independent use of the non-Mark material (Q) may lead us to "greater exegetical precision,"[179] as shown by several exegetical examples (e.g., Matt 8:5–13//Luke 7:1–10; Luke 13:28–30; cf. Matt 10:16–23; 28:19–20).[180]

### 3.2 *The Farrer Hypothesis*

The Farrer Hypothesis agrees with the Two Source Hypothesis in terms of Markan Priority. It attempts, however, to solve the phenomenon of the common source between Matthew and Luke by arguing for Luke's reliance on Matthew without Q. It can be shown as in Figure 1.3.

---

175   Evans, "Two Source Hypothesis," 36. In this sense, Evans's argument contains the aspect of Oral Tradition.
176   By "chreia" which means "useful anecdote," students in Greek education could memorize "small units of a master's teaching and learns how to adapt and apply them in various settings" (Evans, "Two Source Hypothesis," 37).
177   Evans ("Two Source Hypothesis," 38) points out the possible influence of Q on Mark as follows: "Stories and sayings are quoted or alluded to in Paul's Letters and the Letter of James. The Gospel of Mark, in whatever way it may have been linked to Peter, contains a large chunk of dominical tradition, comprising deeds and sayings, including elements of Q." However, if we accept this explanation, it is probably difficult to use the term "non-Markan material."
178   Evans, "Two Source Hypothesis," 39.
179   Evans, "Two Source Hypothesis," 40.
180   Evans, "Two Source Hypothesis," 40.

A SURVEY OF STUDIES ON THE SYNOPTIC PROBLEM    33

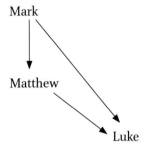

FIGURE 1.3
The Farrer Hypothesis
Cf. Goodacre, "Farrer Hypothesis," 48. The figure is based on Goodacre's version, but the place of Luke is changed into the lower position to reflect its chronological order.

The representative scholar who supports this position is Goodacre. The evidences of the Farrer Hypothesis revealed by Goodacre in terms of the Markan Priority are as follows. First, it seems hard to assume that Mark omitted Matthew's and Luke's intrinsic materials such as the Lord's Prayer and Sermon on the Mount/Plain.[181] Second, in terms of Mark's unique materials, such as "the healing of the deaf-mute" (Mark 7:33–36), it seems natural to regard that, after seeing Mark, Matthew and Luke omitted those materials, not vice versa.[182] The third evidence is about "editorial fatigue," whereby "an author inadvertently betrays his use of a source by making characteristic changes at the beginning of a passage and then reverting to the source's wording later in the same passage."[183] We can find its representative examples in Matthew 14:1–12//Mark 6:14–29 and Mark 6:30–44//Luke 9:10–17. The examples of Matthew's editorial fatigue are as follows: first, unlike Mark's use of "king" for referring to Herod, Matthew aptly depicts him as "tetrarch," but after that, he comes back to Mark's expression, "king" (Matt 14:9); second, Matthew adds his comment regarding Herod's grief regarding John's death although it seems a bit unnatural in terms of its narrative flow.[184] One example of Luke's editorial fatigue is that Luke changes the place of "the feeding of the five thousand" from his initial expression "a city called Bethsaida" (Luke 9:10) to Mark's expression "a desert place" (Luke 9:12), though the connection of the two is unnatural.[185]

The second part of the Farrer Hypothesis is the denial of Q. The critical issue on the existence or nonexistence of Q is concerned with the origin of "the Double Tradition," that is, the common material in Matthew and Luke but not in Mark.[186] Goodacre argues that it is more natural to see that the Double

---

181  Goodacre, "Farrer Hypothesis," 50.
182  Goodacre, "Farrer Hypothesis," 50. The first and second evidences are overlapped with Evans's explanation.
183  Goodacre, "Farrer Hypothesis," 50.
184  Goodacre, "Farrer Hypothesis," 51.
185  Goodacre, "Farrer Hypothesis," 51.
186  Goodacre, "Farrer Hypothesis," 51.

Tradition came from Luke's copy of Matthew, not from a hypothetical material (Q). The main reasons for Luke's literary dependence on Matthew are as follows: (1) Matthew and Luke share the same structure (birth narrative → fulfilling prophecy → John's preaching → commissioning of the disciples → resurrection), unlike Mark (John's preaching → empty tomb);[187] (2) the added same (or almost same) materials (Matt 3:12//Luke 3:17; Matt 26:67b//Luke 22:64b) in the parallel texts (Matt 3:11–12//Mark 1:7–8//Luke 3:15–17; Matt 26:67–68//Mark 14:65//Luke 22:63–64) are from the literary dependency between Matthew and Luke, not from Q;[188] and (3) Luke's editorial fatigue on Matthew is found in Luke's coming back to Matthew after his change (Matt 25:14–30//Luke 19:11–27; three servants → ten servants → three servants).[189] The Farrer Hypothesis argues that Luke's literary dependence on Matthew is a more reasonable way to explain the Double Tradition than Luke's relying on Q, which has no ancient evidence regarding its existence.[190]

### 3.3  *The Two Gospel Hypothesis*

The Two Gospel Hypothesis claims Matthean Priority, based on the traditional understanding of early Christianity. It contends that Luke wrote his Gospel by referring to Matthew, and Mark constructed the abbreviated Gospel based on Matthew and Luke. In fact, this view is the same as the Griesbach Hypothesis, as shown in Figure 1.4.

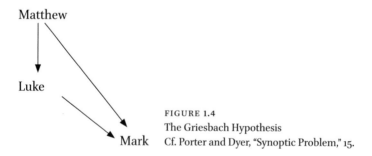

FIGURE 1.4
The Griesbach Hypothesis
Cf. Porter and Dyer, "Synoptic Problem," 15.

---

187  Goodacre, "Farrer Hypothesis," 53.
188  Goodacre, "Farrer Hypothesis," 54–56. According to Goodacre, considering that Q does not include the Passion narrative, the added sharing part in Matt 26:68b, and Luke 22:64b ("Who is it that struck you?") cannot come from Q (Goodacre, "Farrer Hypothesis," 56).
189  Goodacre, "Farrer Hypothesis," 57.
190  Goodacre, "Farrer Hypothesis," 59. Some scholars have identified Q with *the Gospel of Thomas*, but Goodacre objects to this, since, unlike Q proponents' assertion that Q is a pure material of Jesus' saying, we can find "a narrative sequence" in Thomas's Gospel. See Mark Goodacre, *The Case Against Q: Studies in Markan Priority and the Synoptic Problem* (Harrisburg, PA: Trinity Press International, 2002), 171.

The Two Gospel Hypothesis is an expanded form of the Griesbach Hypothesis. The representative scholar who supports this view is Peabody. According to him, the Two Gospel Hypothesis has a more complex scheme than the Griesbach Hypothesis in the following sense: (1) the Gospel of Matthew was written first by using a variety of original source materials; (2) Luke wrote his Gospel by utilizing Matthew's Gospel and "a considerable amount of non-Matthean source material"; and (3) Mark used both Matthew and Luke along with "very little other source material."[191] The Two Gospel Hypothesis emphatically posits a "Markan Overlay," considering Mark's linguistic features. A representative example can be found in Mark's unique use of πάλιν, which is used seventeen times[192] as "a retrospective manner to unite two or more literary contexts in his Gospel."[193]

The Two Gospel Hypothesis argued by Peabody can be described as in Figure 1.5.

Peabody supports the Two Gospel Hypothesis by revealing internal and external evidences. First, six internal evidences are given: (1) verbatim agreements among the Gospels (e.g., Matt 3:7b–10//Luke 3:7b–9) show their "direct literary dependency";[194] (2) analysis of each isolating linguistic feature of the Gospels (suggested by Eduard Zeller) shows Luke's and Mark's dependence on Matthew;[195] (3) Mark's reliance on Matthew and Luke has revealed Mark's conflation of the two Gospels in terms of the order of the pericopae and the word

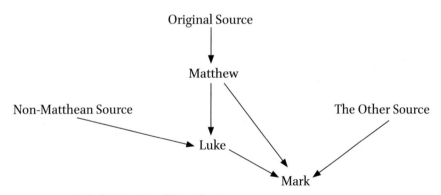

FIGURE 1.5    Peabody's Two Gospel Hypothesis

---

191    Peabody, "Two Gospel Hypothesis," 67.
192    Mark 2:1, 13–14; 3:1, 20; 4:1–2; 5:21; 7:14, 31; 8:1, 13; 10:1, 10, 32; 11:27 (Peabody, "Two Gospel Hypothesis," 68).
193    Peabody, "Two Gospel Hypothesis," 68.
194    Peabody, "Two Gospel Hypothesis," 68.
195    Peabody, "Two Gospel Hypothesis," 70–72.

changing in each pericope;[196] (4) Mark's inclusion of a few whole pericopae seems unlikely to be brought from Matthew's and Luke's Gospel;[197] (5) Mark's literary unity shown by Markan Overlay, including Mark's unique linguistic features, reveals its reliance on Matthew and Luke;[198] and (6) so-called "minor agreements" between Matthew and Luke against Mark (positive: changes, addition; negative: omission) can be regarded as the evidence for the Two Gospel Hypothesis, not for the Two Source Hypothesis or Farrer Hypothesis (e.g., Matt 26:68// Luke 22:64; cf. Mark 14:53–65).[199]

In terms of the external evidence supporting the Two Gospel Hypothesis, Peabody reveals several historical arguments: (1) before the 18th century, no one suggested Markan priority;[200] (2) it was the united tradition of the order of Gospels in the early Church that Matthew's Gospel is the first and the last one is the Gospel of John;[201] (3) several Latin canons regarded the four Gospels' order as "Matthew, John, Luke, and Mark";[202] (4) although Origen considered Mark's Gospel as the second, affected by the general canonical sequence, Matthean priority was still evident;[203] (5) Papias's testimony in *The Church History*, written by Eusebius, was that Matthew wrote Jesus' sayings as an eyewitness, but Mark wrote his Gospel according to Peter's recall;[204] (6) Clement testified that the Gospels of Matthew and Luke were written before other Gospels;[205] and (7) although sometimes his view on the Gospels' order changed, Augustine's major assertion was that Mark's Gospel was written in reliance on Matthew and Luke.[206]

### 3.4 *The Orality and Memory Hypothesis*

The Orality and Memory Hypothesis focuses on the influence of ancient oral/written traditions on the formation of the Gospels in early Christianity.

---

196  Peabody, "Two Gospel Hypothesis," 72–76.
197  Peabody, "Two Gospel Hypothesis," 79.
198  Peabody, "Two Gospel Hypothesis," 79–80.
199  Peabody, "Two Gospel Hypothesis," 81. In his analysis of the parallel texts, Peabody argues that the common part of Matthew and Luke ("Who is it that struck you?") can be considered as the original one, and Mark probably omitted it due to "the somewhat contrasting contexts within their parallel periscopae," which is against the claim of the Two Source Hypothesis ("Two Gospel Hypothesis," 81).
200  Peabody, "Two Gospel Hypothesis," 82.
201  Peabody, "Two Gospel Hypothesis," 82.
202  Peabody, "Two Gospel Hypothesis," 82.
203  Peabody, "Two Gospel Hypothesis," 82–83.
204  Peabody, "Two Gospel Hypothesis," 83–84.
205  Peabody, "Two Gospel Hypothesis," 84.
206  Peabody, "Two Gospel Hypothesis," 84–87.

# A SURVEY OF STUDIES ON THE SYNOPTIC PROBLEM

The emphasis of this position is that various sources in an oral or written form, especially the oral traditions could be preserved by Jesus' disciples and transmitted by the early Church members, before the Gospels existed. It argues that, in the constructing process of the Gospels, there have probably been much more complex steps than the previous three Hypotheses assume. As a representative proponent of the Orality and Memory Hypothesis, Riesner contends that Jesus' teaching was accurately handed down to his disciples by heart along with note-taking, as such an educational feature was common in Jesus' era.[207] He contends that we should understand the function of the oral tradition and ancient eyewitness' memory, and if so, "rather than being dependent upon one another, the three Synoptic Gospel writers each partially used the same intermediary sources, both oral and written."[208] In this sense, the Orality and Memory Hypothesis is clearly differentiated from the previous three Hypotheses, which argue the literary reliance among the Gospels.

According to Riesner, the evidence regarding the ancient memory training can be found in Hellenistic-Roman education (testified by Quintilian, Ovid, Plato, and Philo), Second Temple Judaism (e.g., *hasidim*'s Torah education via "repetition"), and the New Testament (e.g., in Acts 22:3, Paul could quote long Old Testament passages by heart).[209] Especially, in the evidence of the NT, an instance can be found in Paul's unique wording in 1 Corinthians 15:1–3, that is, παρελάβετε ("you received"; indicative aorist active of παραλαμβάνω), παρέδωκα ("I handed down"; indicative aorist active of παραδίδωμι), and παρέλαβον ("I received"; indicative aorist active of παραλαμβάνω).[210] In terms of the usage of these words, Riesner explains that "the nearest philological parallel to the Greek words *paralambanō* (to receive) and *paradidōmi* (to hand down) are the Hebrew technical terms *qibbel* and *masar*, denoting a cultivated oral tradition (*m. Abot* 1:1)."[211]

Another primary evidence of the Orality and Memory Hypothesis is concerned with Jesus' character as a teacher. Jesus was called *rabbi* (Matt 26:25, 49; Mark 9:5; John 1:49), which is the Hebrew/Aramaic title,[212] and from this, we

---

207 Riesner, "Orality and Memory," 89.

208 Riesner, "Orality and Memory," 90.

209 Riesner, "Orality and Memory," 94–96. For a more detailed explanation of Jewish elementary education based on the mnemonic system, see Rainer Riesner, "From the Messianic Teacher to the Gospels of Jesus Christ," in *Handbook for the Study of the Historical Jesus. Vol. 1: How to Study the Historical Jesus*, eds. Tom Holmén and Stanley E. Porter (Leiden: Brill, 2011), 410–14.

210 Riesner, "Orality and Memory," 97–98.

211 Riesner, "Orality and Memory," 98.

212 Riesner, "Orality and Memory," 99.

38                                                                      CHAPTER 1

can assume that "Jesus preached in the synagogues, entered into discussions with the scribes, and assembled a circle of disciples like other contemporaneous Jewish teachers"[213] who used the method of memory and repetition.[214] In addition, Jesus used many devices to make his words memorable: raising his voice, the request to listen, the introductory formula, parallelism, rhetoric features, and using parables.[215] According to Jesus' teaching as a memorable form, eyewitnesses probably played a crucial role as "the tradition bearers" for forming the Gospels.[216] In this process, disciples' written notes that could help memorize Jesus' words were probably used.[217]

Riesner's Hypothesis based on the above observations can be shown as in Figure 1.6.

The major processes of Riesner's model are as follows. Jesus orally taught his disciples. Peter, the major eyewitness of Jesus, and the other disciples preserved Jesus' teaching along with his ministry and passion narrative in oral form.[218] Mark constructed a document by relying on the three oral traditions of Peter, and it can be called "Proto-Mark." Based on Proto-Mark, Jewish-Christian and Gentile-Christian communities formed their own written tradition, and with them, Mark constructed his Gospel in Rome. Relying on the written tradition of a Jewish-Christian community, the Hellenist Jewish-Christians' written tradition, and an independent Galilean memory, Matthew formed his Gospel. Luke wrote his Gospel based on the Hellenist Jewish-Christians' written tradition, the Gentile-Christian Communities' written tradition, and the Lukan special written tradition. In Riesner's Hypothesis, the three Gospel authors independently constructed their Gospels without editorial contributions.[219]

---

213   Riesner, "Orality and Memory," 99.
214   Riesner, "Orality and Memory," 99.
215   Riesner, "Orality and Memory," 99–101; cf. "Messianic Teacher," 418–19.
216   Riesner, "Orality and Memory," 102–4.
217   Riesner, "Orality and Memory," 104–5.
218   Martin Hengel mentions Peter's role in terms of making narrations as follows: "the narration of Jesus' teaching and healing, his death and the appearances of the risen Christ, was much more at the centre of the missionary preaching of direct disciples of Jesus, and above all of Peter himself." See Martin Hengel, *The Four Gospels and the One Gospel of Jesus Christ: An Investigation of the Collection and Origin of the Canonical Gospels* (trans. John Bowden; Harrisburg: Trinity Press International, 2000), 153.
219   According to Riesner, the most important factor of the Synoptic variations is not editorial changes but the influence of special traditions, considering the following: (1) minor agreements, (2) agreement with the non-Synoptic sources such as John's Gospel or Paul's letters, (3) contrast with the editorial tendencies of the Evangelist, (4) lack of a plausible editorial explanation in variations, (5) unusual language usage, (6) Matthean and Lucan stylistic deterioration compared to Mark, (7) Semitism beyond the texts, (8) possible

# A SURVEY OF STUDIES ON THE SYNOPTIC PROBLEM

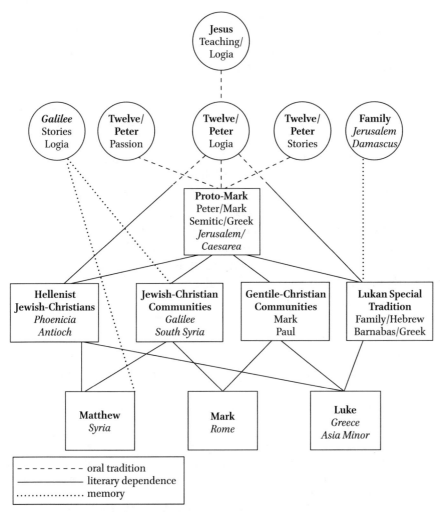

FIGURE 1.6  Riesner's Orality and Memory Hypothesis
Riesner, "Orality and Memory," 107. There is a more detailed diagram including the Gospel of John in Riesner's article "Messianic Teacher" (438).

Riesner's arguments can be summarized as follows. First, he argues that preserving and transmitting Jesus' teachings and stories about him in the early church were very stable. In other words, he claims that, since Jesus' disciples remembered the teachings and stories exactly, the post-Easter Gospel tradition

---

translation variants, (9) stronger Palestinian coloring in the parallels, and (10) greater proximity to mnemotechnical forms of oral transmission (*Jesus als Lehrer*, 5).

was formed without a decisive difference from the pre-Easter Gospel tradition. Second, Riesner argues that the final Synoptic Gospels were published independently, by using different traditions as well as overlapping ones.[220] Thus, this model rejects literary dependence between the Gospels.[221]

## 4 Analysis and Evaluation of the Literary Dependence Hypothesis

The four major views on the Synoptic Problem, which we discussed above, can be divided into two types, as shown in Table 1.3.

The Two Source Hypothesis, the Two Gospel Hypothesis, and the Farrer Hypothesis share a common characteristic, that is, the literary dependence among the Gospels. Only the Orality and Memory Hypothesis argues literary independence between the Gospels. This section will evaluate the dependence hypotheses as presented by Evans, Peabody, and Goodacre. The three Hypotheses arguing for literary dependence share common arguments in pairs, as shown in Table 1.4.

TABLE 1.3   Two types of the four major views on the Synoptic Problem[a]

| Literary Dependence Hypothesis | Literary Independence Hypothesis |
| --- | --- |
| Two Source Hypothesis, Farrer Hypothesis, Two Gospel Hypothesis | Orality and Memory Hypothesis |

a  I used the two terms "the Dependence Hypothesis" (or literary dependence hypothesis) and "the Independence Hypothesis" only in terms of the relationship of the Synoptic Gospels because the Orality and Memory Hypothesis argued by Riesner also has the aspect of "literary dependence" in the formative process of the Gospels. According to Riesner, "there were only literary connections at the pre-Synoptic stage." See Riesner, "Preacher and Teacher," 187. Riesner denies the possibility of the direct dependence among the Gospels; thus, it was presented as "the Independence Hypothesis."

---

220   Riesner explains the independent publications of the Synoptic Gospels affected by the communities' Gospel traditions ("Messianic Teacher," 436–42).

221   For the more detailed explanations of Riesner regarding the forming process of Synoptic Gospels, see Riesner, "Messianic Teacher," 405–46; "Orality and Memory," 89–111; cf. Riesner, *Jesus als Lehrer*, 18–502; Rainer Riesner, "Jesus as Preacher and Teacher," in *Jesus and the Oral Gospel Tradition*, ed. Henry Wansbrough (JSNTSup 64; Sheffield: Sheffield Academic, 1991), 185–210; cf. Hojoon J. Ahn, "Rainer Riesner: A Synthetic-Historical Researcher on the Historical Jesus and Gospel Tradition Studies," in *Pillars in the History of Biblical Interpretation*, ed. Stanley E. Porter and Zachary K. Dawson (Vol. 5; Eugene, OR: Wipf & Stock, forthcoming).

A SURVEY OF STUDIES ON THE SYNOPTIC PROBLEM                    41

TABLE 1.4    Arguments in pairs of the Literary Dependence Hypotheses

| Markan priority | Denial of Q | Luke's reliance on Matthew |
| --- | --- | --- |
| Two Source Hypothesis | Two Gospel Hypothesis | Two Gospel Hypothesis |
| Farrer Hypothesis | Farrer Hypothesis | Farrer Hypothesis |

TABLE 1.5    Distinct arguments in the Literary Dependence Hypotheses

| Support for Q | Matthean priority | Independence between Matthew and Luke |
| --- | --- | --- |
| Two Source Hypothesis | Two Gospel Hypothesis | Two Source Hypothesis |

In terms of three common arguments in pairs of the Literary Dependence Hypotheses, the Farrer Hypothesis contains three common arguments with others (Markan priority, denial to Q, and Luke's reliance on Matthew), while there is no common argument in pairs between the Two Source Hypothesis and the Two Gospel Hypothesis.

In addition, there are three distinct arguments of their own in the Literary Dependence Hypotheses, as shown in Table 1.5.

The Two Source Hypothesis has two distinct arguments: (1) support for Q; (2) independence between Matthew and Luke. The Two Gospel Hypothesis has one distinct argument: Matthean priority. The Farrer Hypothesis, however, does not have its own distinct argument.[222]

To evaluate the Literary Dependence Hypotheses' arguments, we need to observe the textual evidence in the Synoptic Gospels suggested by three proponents of the Literary Dependent Hypothesis. The texts they use to support each of their hypotheses barely overlap. Table 1.6 shows us the passages utilized by the three proponents of each hypothesis.

Except for the evidences regarding the common passages in pairs of the Literary Dependence Hypothesis, most of the evidences suggested by them do not overlap with each other. Only two passages (Matt 26:68; Luke 22:64) were commonly used in the arguments of all three proponents.

The other point is that there are very different interpretations of the Double Tradition, that is, the common parts of Matthew and Luke. A representative

---

222    In this sense, the Farrer Hypothesis may have tried to combine these two hypotheses' merits.

# 42

TABLE 1.6 Textual usages of the three proponents[a]

| Evans (Two Source Hypothesis) | Goodacre (Farrer Hypothesis) | Peabody (Two Gospel Hypothesis) |
|---|---|---|
| Matt **4:1**; **6:9–13**, 30; 7:22; **8:5–13** (8:10, 11–12, 13), 16, 23–27 (8:25, 26), 31; 9:33; 10:1, 5b–6, 8, 16–23, 32; **12:24**, 26, 27, 28; 14:24–33 (**14:28–31**), 33; 15:21–28 (15:22, 24, 25, 26, 27, 28); 16:5–12 (16:6, 8, 8b–9a, 12); 17:19, 20; 20:1–16 (20:4, 13); 21:12, 39; 22:13; 23:34; **25:30**, 31–46; 26:51, *68*; 28:19–20. | Matt 1:1–2:23 (2:1–12); 3:1–12 (3:7–10, 11–12,), 13–17; **4:1–11**; 5:3, 33–37; 6:6–13 (**6:9–13**), 16–18, 25–34; 7:7–11, 33–36; **8:5–13**, 22–26; 9:1–8 (9:6); 12:22–30 (**12:24**); 13:31–32; 14:1–12 (14:9), 22–32, **28–31**; 16:16–19, 22–23; 25:14–30 (25:20, 21, 23, 28, 30); 26:26–29, 67–68; 27:19; 28:1–20 (28:9–20, **19–20**). | Matt 3:7–10 (3:8, 9,10); 5:14–16; 8:16–17; 11:10; 13:55–56; 26:67–68. |
| Mark 1:1, 1:12, 34, 39, 43; 3:15, 20–21, 22, 23; **4:26–29**, 35–41, 38, 40; 5:40; 6:13, 47–52, 49–50; 7:2–4, 24–30 (25, 26, 27, 28, 29), *32–37*; 8:1–21 (15, 17–18, 21), *8:22–26*; 9:18, 28, 38; 9:47, 48–49; 10:47–48; 11:15; 12:8; 13:33–37; 14:47, 51–52; *16:9–20*. | Mark 1:4–8 (1:7–8), 9–11, 12–13; 2:1–12 (2:10–11); 3:20–27 (**3:20–21**); 4:1–34 (**4:26–29**), 30–32, 33–34; 6:14–29 (19–20, 26), 30–44 (35–36), 45–52; 8:32–33; 11:20–25; 14:22–25, 65; 16:1–8, | Mark 3:7–12; 6:3; *7:32–37*; *8:22–26*; 14:53–65 (14:65); *16:9–20*. |
| Luke **4:1**, 29; **7:1–10** (7:10); 8:22–25 (8:24, 25); 9:40, 49; 10:30–37; **11:2b–4, 14, 15, 18, 19**, 20, 49; 12:1, 8, 28; 13:22–30 (27, 28, 29, 30), 32; 14:12–14, 15–24; **16:19–31**; 19:45; 20:12, 15; 22:**64**; 23:47; 24:37. | Luke 1–2 (1:52–53, 62–63); 3:1–20 (3:7–9, 15–17), 21–22; **4:1–13**, 18; 5:17–26 (5:24); 6:24; **7:1–10**; 8:4–18; 9:10–17 (9:12); 11:1–13 (11:1–2a, **2b–4**, 5–8, 9–13), 14–23 (**14, 15, 18, 19**, 20); 12:13–21, 22, 31, 32–34; 13:18–19; 15:8; **16:19–31**; 17:11–19; 19:11–27 (19:16, 17, 18, 19, 20, 24); 22:14–20, 31–32, 63–64; 24:9–53 (24:13–34). | Luke 3:7–9; 4:40–41; 22:63–64. |

---

a  This table is constructed by observing the passages used in the three Dependence Hypotheses (Evans, "Two Source Hypothesis," 27–45; Goodacre, "Farrer Hypothesis," 47–66; Peabody, "Two Gospel Hypothesis," 67–88). For this, the index of Scripture (Porter and Dyer, eds., *Synoptic Problem*, 187–91) is utilized. The common passages between the Two Source and Farrer Hypothesis are highlighted in boldface. The common passages between the Farrer and Two Gospel Hypothesis are underlined. The common passages between the Two Source and Two Gospel Hypothesis are highlighted in italic. The common passages shared by all Dependence Hypotheses are highlighted in boldface and italic.

# A SURVEY OF STUDIES ON THE SYNOPTIC PROBLEM

TABLE 1.7    Three different interpretations of Matt 26:68 and Luke 22:64 (cf. Mark 14:65)

| Evans | Goodacre | Peabody |
|---|---|---|
| "In light of the usage of these verbs, it is not surprising that both Matthew and Luke replace Mark's less suitable *paiō* with the more suitable *patassō* (Matthew and Luke do use *paiō* elsewhere, in the sense of 'beat' with fists or clubs, in Matt. 26:68; Luke 22:64). If Mark wrote last and had Matthew and Luke before him, it is not easy to explain why he would replace the suitable *patassō*, which would have been in both of his sources, for the somewhat less suitable *paiō*." | "At the same point in the narrative, Matthew and Luke insert five identical Greek words, here translated by 'Who is it that struck you?' Since Q, according to its advocates, did not have a Passion Narrative, this kind of agreement cannot have derived from Q. It is a mystery, therefore, how Matthew and Luke could have independently added this identical sentence to their Markan source. The standard answer given by Q advocates is that there must have been some kind of textual corruption, but since the wording is in every known witness of both Matthew and Luke, this answer is weak." | "Advocates of the Two Gospel Hypothesis would argue that, in this literary context, Luke inferred from Matthew's Gospel that Jesus was blindfolded at the time of the mockery and added this detail to his text. Thus, perhaps, Luke made the context of this taunting question more understandable in his Gospel. Mark, however, accepted the detail of the blindfold from Luke 22:64 (cf. Mark 14:65) but omitted the question (Matt. 26//Luke 22:64), which may have motivated Luke to add the detail of the blindfold in the first place. Mark may have then made the significant omission of this question from the Gospels of Matthew and Luke because of the somewhat contrasting contexts within their parallel pericopae, in which Jesus is blindfolded in one and not the other." |

example can be shown in the different interpretations of Matthew 26:68; Luke 22:64 (cf. Mark 14:65). Table 1.7 shows us how the three advocates in the Dependence Hypothesis differently interpret the same passages according to their positions.

This comparison shows us that the different approaches to the same text can draw various conclusions. Evans utilizes Matthew 26:68 and Luke 22:64 to prove Markan Priority via the linguistic approach. By pointing out that Q cannot include the passion narrative, Goodacre uses the two texts to refute the

Two Source hypothesis. By explaining that Mark omitted the question ("Who is it that struck you?") after seeing Luke's expression "blindfold" in 22:24, Peabody utilizes these texts to confirm Mark's reliance on Luke along with the Markan Posteriority.

It may not be, of course, fair to regard the phenomenon that most of the texts used by the three scholars do not overlap as a problem. It may not also be fair to abandon all three hypotheses just because their interpretations of the same text are conflicting each other. Since at least one of the three interpretations could be correct. Nevertheless, each of these three hypotheses has critical limitations as follows.[223] As regards the Two Source Hypothesis, two insoluble problems still persist. First, it is difficult to explain the so-called "minor agreement" persuasively enough. Second, it does not seem to offer compelling explanations for the overwhelming support for the Matthean Priority by the majority of the church fathers.[224] The Two Gospel Hypothesis above all does not really seem to offer persuasive answers to whether it is possible to go from Matthew's sophisticated style to Mark's rather rough style. The critical weakness of the Farrer Hypothesis is that it is not possible to identify the origin of the so-called "distinctive dominical traditions" that appear in Matthew and Luke,[225] and that, like the Two Source Hypothesis, it does not seem to offer compelling explanations for the overwhelming support for the Matthean Priority by the majority of the Church Fathers.[226] These limitations raise the need for another approach that could resolve the problems from a different perspective that they could not.

## 5    A Complementing Approach to Resolve the Synoptic Problem

The previous section explored the discrepancies and limitations of the literary dependence hypotheses. This study shows that another complementing approach to the Synoptic Problem is still waited for. Now, we may need to consider Riesner's Orality and Memory Hypothesis, a model of the Literary Independence Hypothesis. Concerning the need for the Oral Tradition study, Terence C. Mournet's wording seems valuable:

---

223    For more information regarding their limitations, see Porter and Dyer eds., *Synoptic Problem*, 113–63.

224    David B. Peabody, "Two Gospel Hypothesis Response," in *The Synoptic Problem: Four Views*, eds. Stanley E. Porter and Bryan R. Dyer (Grand Rapids: Baker Academic, 2016), 142.

225    Craig A. Evans, "Two Source Hypothesis Response," in *The Synoptic Problem: Four Views* (eds. Stanley E. Porter and Bryan R. Dyer; Grand Rapids: Baker Academic, 2016), 119.

226    Peabody, "Two Gospel Hypothesis Response," 142.

A SURVEY OF STUDIES ON THE SYNOPTIC PROBLEM

Despite the understandable desire to reconstruct an elegant model of Gospel interrelationships, which a strictly literary paradigm enables one to do, we must begin a shift away from an exclusively literary model of Synoptic interrelationships towards an understanding of the Jesus tradition that is able to take account of highly oral milieu that existed during the time of Gospel composition. This, of course, might require a significant revision of the historical-critical method that has driven NT scholarship for more than one hundred years. The model that results from such a process might not prove as straightforward or as elegant as one would desire, but arguably it will be more faithful to the character of the Jesus tradition and to the historical context within which it was initially performed and subsequently transmitted.[227]

As Mournet mentions, "the desire to reconstruct an elegant model of Gospel interrelationships" is understandable, and we cannot deny that the resulted models so far are in many respects beneficial to the studies of the Synoptic Gospel. Nevertheless, oral tradition study is also highly needed to complement the various limitations of the literary dependence hypotheses. The oral tradition study is especially essential in investigating the Jesus tradition, which had significant influences on the formation of the Gospels in the Gospels' formation. Concerning the character of oral tradition, Stanley E. Porter comments that, in the four proponents' arguments, "oral tradition was an integral part of the equation from the start, then it appears that more needs to be done to consider what role oral tradition might play in attempting to answer the question of the origins of the Synoptic Gospels."[228] Although there is skepticism regarding oral tradition study,[229] it seems significant to pay proper attention to the oral tradition in relation to the origin of the Synoptic Gospels for several reasons.

First, it is not easy to deny the existence of the oral/written traditions before the written Gospels.[230] As mentioned above, Evans states the possible influence of oral/written traditions on the Gospels[231] as well as Riesner. In the era of the early church, the eyewitnesses were still alive and were orally conveying

---

227 Terence C. Mournet, *Oral Tradition and Literary Dependency: Variability and Stability in the Synoptic Tradition and Q* (WUNT 195; Tübingen: Mohr Siebeck, 2005), 293.

228 Porter, "Synoptic Problem," 94.

229 Barry W. Henaut is skeptical regarding the oral tradition study due to the following reason: "The Oral phase of the Jesus tradition is now forever lost. The spoken word is transitory by nature and exists for but a moment." Barry W. Henaut, *Oral Tradition and the Gospels: The Problem of Mark 4* (JSNTSup 82; Sheffield: Sheffield Academic, 1993), 295.

230 R. Delbert Burkett, *An Introduction to the New Testament and the Origins of Christianity* (2nd ed.; Cambridge: Cambridge University Press, 2019), 128.

231 Evans is a proponent of the Dependence Hypothesis, who carefully admits the possibility of the oral traditions' influence on Mark.

46

CHAPTER 1

the words of Jesus and the stories about him; thus, there may not have been a need for written texts right away. In addition, considering the Jewish and Hellenistic education systems relying on memory (along with note-taking), Jesus' teachings and the stories about him (ministry and passion narratives) were probably orally preserved well by his disciples.

Second, due to the situation mentioned above, the formation of the written Gospels was probably not simple.[232] According to Riesner, Jesus' teachings were probably preserved in oral traditions, which may have been formed via eyewitnesses' memory[233] (including some note-takings), and a written text was formed on the basis of those oral traditions, and in light of the written text, the early Church communities may have made their own traditions regarding Jesus' teachings and stories about him, which may have affected the formation of the Gospels. Riesner's suggestion leads us to infer that the Gospels were formed through a complicated process.

However, despite the meaningful aspects of this hypothesis, the Orality and Memory Hypothesis seems to reduce the role of the final constructor in the formation of each Gospel. The identity of each constructor, however, should be seen as one of the main factors that may have influenced the construction process of each Gospel; in that case, the constructor's role in the forming of each Gospel should not be overlooked. It seems, therefore, necessary to discuss the Synoptic Gospels' authorship briefly.

## 6      The Synoptic Gospels' Authorship and Its Implication for This Study

This section contains a brief discussion of the identities of the constructor of each Gospel and its implication on the construction process.[234]

---

232      The complex aspect of the formation of the Gospels was admitted by many scholars; e.g., James D. G. Dunn, *The Oral Gospel Tradition* (Grand Rapids: Eerdmans, 2013), 41–79; Willi Marxsen, *Mark the Evangelist* (trans. Roy A. Harrisville; Nashville: Abingdon, 1969), 26–27; Harald Riesenfeld, *The Gospel Tradition* (Philadelphia: Fortress, 1970), 1–29.

233      There are many suggestions concerning the influence of memory on the preservation of oral tradition. Among them, Alan Kirk's argument is notable: "tradition is a product of cultural practices of commemoration; more precisely, that tradition is a media-based artifact that not only emerges but is also transmitted at the interface of the cognitive, social, and cultural operations of memory." See Alan Kirk, "The Memory-Tradition Nexus in the Synoptic Tradition: Memory, Media, and Symbolic Representation," in *Memory and Identity*, ed. Tom Thatcher (Atlanta: SBL, 2014), 132.

234      This study will use both external and internal data to deduce the authorship of each Gospel. In the case of external materials, the texts of the early Church Fathers who

# A SURVEY OF STUDIES ON THE SYNOPTIC PROBLEM

## 6.1 Constructor of the Gospel according to Matthew

The first Gospel itself does not include the information of its constructor, so it could be regarded as anonymous;[235] however, the constructor of the Gospel according to Matthew has long been known as Matthew, the tax-collector, who was one of Jesus' twelve disciples (Matt 9:9; 10:3).[236] Matthew's authorship is mentioned in the writings of Papias and the other early Church Fathers; as a matter of fact, no other person's name has ever been mentioned as its author.[237] The tradition regarding Matthew as the constructor of the first Gospel also can be seen in the heading τὸ εὐαγγέλιον κατὰ Ματθαῖον, which appears in the late second or early third century manuscripts.[238] The issue of authorship of Matthew has been critically addressed among scholars.[239]

---

mentioned the authors of the Gospels and manuscripts that mentioned the Gospel titles will be dealt with. In the case of internal materials, some of references to each Gospel author within the New Testament will be used.

235 Francis W. Beare, *The Gospel according to Matthew: Translation, Introduction and Commentary* (New York: Harper & Row, 1981), 7; Beare, *The Earliest Records of Jesus: A Companion to the Synopsis of the First Three Gospels by Albert Huck* (New York: Abingdon, 1962), 13.

236 Mark L. Strauss, *Four Portraits, One Jesus: An Introduction to Jesus and the Gospels* (Grand Rapids: Zondervan, 2007), 475.

237 R. T. France, *The Gospel of Matthew* (NICNT 1; Grand Rapids: Eerdmans, 2007), 15.

238 Simon Gathercole, "The Earliest Manuscript Title of Matthew's Gospel (BnF Suppl. gr. 1120 ii 3 / Π⁴)," *NT* 54 (2012): 209–35. Although the anonymity of the Gospel constructors has been addressed to some extent earlier, it is necessary to think carefully about the meaning of "anonymity." It does not mean that the authors of the Gospels are not known, but that the author is not specified in the text itself (unlike Pauline epistles). Thus, it is necessary to think carefully the reason why it is mentioned not "Matthew's Gospel" but "the Gospel *according to* (*kata*) Matthew." For the related discussions, see Simon Gathercole, "The Alleged Anonymity of the Canonical Gospels," *JTS* 69 (2018): 447–76.

239 Beare, *Matthew*, 7; cf. Harry Y. Gamble, *Books and Readers in the Early Church: A History of Early Christian Texts* (New Haven: Yale University Press, 1995), 153–54. Francis W. Beare denies Matthew's authorship, saying that it is difficult to see the constructor of the first Gospel as a work of "any immediate disciple of Jesus" due to the "dependence of the book upon documentary sources" (his argument reveals that it may be challenging to insist on the authorship of Matthew within the theory of Markan priority). Nevertheless, in the discussion of the constructor of the Gospel according to Matthew, some scholars have argued the authorship of the apostle Matthew (e.g., Theodor Zahn, A. Wikenhauser, E. J. Goodspeed, N. B. Stonehouse, W. F. Albright, C. S. Mann, and Robert H. Gundry), though many scholars have argued that the constructor of it may have been an anonymous Jewish Christian (e.g., Holtzmann, B. Weiss, O. Pfleiderer, Johannes Weiss, A. Plummer, J. Moffatt, C. G. Montefiore, E. von Dobschütz, T. H. Robinson, B. W. Bacon, F. C. Grant, G. D. Kilpatrick, M. Alberts, W. Michaelis, K. Stendahl, F. V. Filson, E. P. Blair, P. Gaechter, R. Hummel, G. Bornkamm, D. R. A. Hare, W. Grundmann, A. Kretzer, H. A. Guy, E. Lohse, Kümmel, P. F. Ellis, M. D. Goulder, H. Merkel, H. B. Green, L. Cope, J. D. Kingsbury, E. Schweizer, F. Beare, D. A. Hagner, U. Luz) or an anonymous Gentile Christian (e.g., K. W. Clark, P. Nepper-Christensen, W. Trilling, G. Strecker, R. Walker, S. van Tilborg,

48                                                                                          CHAPTER 1

However, it seems difficult to see any of critical arguments incontrovertibly overturn the unanimous surviving patristic witnesses attributing the first Gospel to Matthew.[240] Of course, none of us can confirm the authorship of this Gospel; however, considering strong patristic testimonies seriously, it seems still most likely to conclude that the first Gospel was constructed by Matthew or at least by "someone like the apostle Matthew."[241]

This study, therefore, regards the constructor of the first Gospel as the apostle Matthew, one of the twelve disciples of Jesus. He was an eyewitness and may have contributed to forming oral tradition(s), and these identities may have influenced the first Gospel's construction process.[242]

### 6.2    *Constructor of the Gospel according to Mark*

As in the case of Matthew, Mark is not mentioned as the constructor in the second Gospel itself; thus, this Gospel could also be considered anonymous.[243] This Gospel, however, traditionally has been attributed to John Mark, as mentioned in the writings of Papias[244] and other Church Fathers.[245] There have been critics on Mark's authorship of the second Gospel;[246] however, it

---

         W. Pesch, H. Frankemölle, J. P. Meier, Schuyler Brown, M. J. Cook). For an analysis of the topography of these scholars, see W. D. Davies and Dale C. Allison, *The Gospel according to Saint Matthew* (ICC; Edinburgh: T&T Clark, 1988), 1:10–11.

240     Scholars taking the traditional view are as follows: Case-Winters, *Matthew*, 2; Craig A. Evans, *Matthew* (NCBC; Cambridge: Cambridge University Press, 2012), 1–4; France, *Matthew*, 15; Gibbs, *Matthew 1:1–11:1*, 59–60; Stewart Petrie, "The Authorship of 'The Gospel according to Matthew': A Reconsideration of His External Evidence," *NTS* 14 (1967): 15–32.

241     France, *Matthew*, 15.

242     Matthew may have used other oral and/or written sources when constructing what he did not experience.

243     Gamble, *Books and Readers*, 153; Beare, *Earliest Records*, 13. Regarding this anonymity of the Gospels, according to Stein, we can deduce that "there was no need for the authors to identify themselves" and "Mark and other Gospel writers did not think that what they wrote was 'their Gospel.'" See Robert H. Stein, *Mark* (BECNT; Grand Rapids: Baker, 2008), 1–2; R. T. France, *The Gospel of Mark* (NIGTC 2; Grand Rapids: Eerdmans, 2002), 7; William L. Lane, *The Gospel According to Mark: The English Text with Introduction, Exposition and Notes* (NICNT 2; Grand Rapids: Eerdmans, 1974), 21–25; Philip van Linden, *The Gospel according to Mark* (CBC 2; Collegeville: Liturgical, 1983), 10, 12.

244     Eusebius, *Hist. eccl.* 3.39.15. Here, Eusebius reveals that Papias got this information through John the Elder and Aristion.

245     References to Mark's authorship of the second Gospel are found in the Church Fathers, such as Justin Martyr, Irenaeus, Clement of Alexandria, Origen, Tertullian, Eusebius, and Jerome. See Stein, *Mark*, 3–4.

246     Kurt Niederwimmer, "Johannes Markus und die Frage nach dem Verfasser des zweiten Evangeliums," *ZNW* 58 (1967): 172–88; Pierson Parker, "The Posteriority of Mark," in *New Synoptic Studies: The Cambridge Gospel Conference and Beyond*, ed. William R. Farmer (Macon, GA: Mercer University Press, 1983), 68–70, 73–75.

# A SURVEY OF STUDIES ON THE SYNOPTIC PROBLEM

seems once again difficult to regard any of critical arguments incontrovertibly overturn the strong patristic testimonies attributing the second Gospel to Mark. Like the other Gospels, the heading of this Gospel (τὸ εὐαγγέλιον κατὰ Μᾶρκον)[247] is a crucial pointer to Mark's authorship.[248] It is suggested that Mark was a Christian who was in Rome with Peter during the persecution of Christians by Emperor Nero (cf. 1 Peter 5:13).[249] Based on the several evidences in the New Testament (Acts 12:12, 25; 13:4; 15:36–41; Col 4:10; 2 Tim 4:11; Phlm 24; 1 Peter 5:13), we can deduce that Mark has some special relationship with Peter, Paul, and Barnabas.[250] Particularly, these biblical witnesses may confirm that Mark had a significant role in the early church since he shared close fellowship with Peter.[251] It gives weight to the possibility that Mark constructed the second Gospel based on Peter's oral testimony/tradition.[252]

This study, therefore, considers the constructor of the second Gospel as Mark the preserver and deliverer of the oral testimony/tradition from the apostle Peter who was one of the twelve disciples of Jesus. Peter was an eyewitness and may have contributed to forming oral tradition(s). In this sense, both Mark's and Peter's identities may have influenced the second Gospel's construction process.[253]

---

247   R. T. France suggests that the more appropriate translation of this heading is "the [one] gospel in Mark's version" rather than "the gospel[-book] by Mark." See France, *Mark*, 5.

248   Martin Hengel, *Studies in the Gospel of Mark* (Philadelphia: Fortress, 1985), 64–84. According to Adela Y. Collins, "even if the author did not give his work a title, it is likely that whoever copied it and circulated it to other communities in other geographical locations gave it a title that mentioned Mark." See Adela Y. Collins, *Mark: A Commentary* (Hermeneia; Minneapolis: Fortress, 2007), 2.

249   Lane, *Mark*, 21.

250   Lane, *Mark*, 21–22.

251   Considering the construction process of the second Gospel, the identity of Peter, who is probably the Gospel's original source, also seems important. Peter was a fisherman; he was called by Jesus and became his disciple (Matt 4:18–20; Mark 1:16–18; Luke 5:1–11). His original name was "Simon" (Σίμων), but he was given the name "Peter" (Πέτρος) by Jesus (cf. Matt 16:18). In the Gospels and Acts, he appears as a representative of the twelve apostles (Matt 16:18; Acts 1:15–22; 2:14, 37, 38). For more detailed information on Peter's life and identity, see F. B. Meyer, *Peter: Fisherman, Disciple, Apostle* (London: Morgan & Scott, 1919); Markus Bockmuehl, *Simon Peter in Scripture and Memory: The New Testament Apostle in the Early Church* (Grand Rapids: Baker Academic, 2012).

252   The meaning of "Peter's testimony/tradition" is as follows. Considering the position Peter had in the early church, his testimony may have had a public function. In this study, thus, we regard Peter's testimony as an apostolic/public testimony, which may have been closely related to the oral tradition that he may have contributed.

253   Peter, like Matthew, also may not have testified about what he had not experienced; in that case, Mark may have constructed the Gospel based on other oral traditions or written sources.

## 6.3    *Constructor of the Gospel according to Luke*

The third Gospel could also be regarded as anonymous.[254] Although there is some uncertainty concerning the issue of authorship of this Gospel,[255] the constructor of this Gospel has traditionally been regarded as Luke.[256] Like the other Gospels, the heading of this Gospel in the early manuscripts assumes Luke to be its constructor.[257] References to Luke's authorship of the third Gospel also appear in the writings of the early Church Fathers.[258] Luke has been commonly understood to be the physician, who traveled with the apostle Paul on the missionary journeys as a coworker (e.g., Col 4:14; 2 Tim 4:11; Phlm 24).[259] According to François Bovon, Luke probably belonged to the second or third generation Christians, who was originally Greek, later turned to Judaism, and became a Christian after hearing the gospel.[260] The issue of Luke's authorship is not "clear-cut," but there are "no decisive arguments against it,"[261] and the traditional view, therefore, still remains predominant.

The heading of Luke (1:1–4) clarifies notable elements of the identity of the constructor and the construction process of the third Gospel. First of all, considering Luke 1:3 where the masculine singular participle (παρηκολουθηκότι) appears, we can recognize that the constructor of this Gospel is *a man*.[262] Also, as found in Luke 1:2–4, Luke (κἀμοί) orderly (καθεξῆς) constructed his Gospel "just as they had been handed down" (καθὼς παρέδοσαν) through "eyewitnesses

---

254    Beare, *Earliest Records*, 13; cf. Christopher M. Tuckett, *Luke* (TCSG; London: T&T Clark, 1996), 15. However, John Nolland asserts that the third Gospel is not anonymous since ancient works with dedications, such as Luke 1:1–4, are not anonymous. See Nolland, *Luke 1:1–9:20*, xxxiv.

255    Diane G. Chen, *Luke: A New Covenant Commentary* (NCC; Eugene: Cascade, 2017), 4.

256    Bock, *Luke 1:1–9:50*, 4–7; David E. Garland, *Luke* (ZECNT 3; Grand Rapids: Zondervan, 2011), 21–24; I. Howard Marshall, *The Gospel of Luke* (NIGTC 3; Grand Rapids: Eerdmans, 1978), 33; Nolland, *Luke 1:1–9:20*, xxxiv–xxxvii; David L. Tiede, *Luke* (ACNT; Minneapolis: Augsburg, 1988), 18; cf. Joseph A. Fitzmyer, *Luke the Theologian: Aspects of His Teaching* (Eugene, OR: Wipf & Stock, 1989), 35; Joel B. Green, *The Gospel of Luke* (NICNT; Grand Rapids: Eerdmans, 1997), 21.

257    The heading "τὸ εὐαγγέλιον κατὰ Λουκᾶν" is found at P75, believed to be AD 175–225.

258    E.g., by Tertullian, Luke is mentioned as the author of this Gospel. See Nolland, *Luke 1:1–9:20*, xxxv. For the original source, see Tertullian, *Adversus Marcionem* 4.2.2; 4.2.4; 4.5.3.

259    Chen, *Luke*, 2. The Muratorian Canon, which is estimated to date from AD 170 to about the 4th century AD, also identifies Luke, who was Paul's companion and physician, as the author of this Gospel. See Nolland, *Luke 1:1–9:20*, xxxv.

260    François Bovon, *Luke 1: A Commentary on the Gospel of Luke 1:1–9:50* (Hermeneia; Minneapolis: Fortress, 2002), 8. Considering Luke 1:2–4, the constructor of the third Gospel was not an "eyewitness," and he rather consulted the eyewitnesses. See David L. Jeffrey, *Luke* (BTCB; Grand Rapids: Brazos, 2012), 1.

261    Nolland, *Luke 1:1–9:20*, xxxvii.

262    Bovon, *Luke*, 8.

A SURVEY OF STUDIES ON THE SYNOPTIC PROBLEM                                    51

and servants of the word" (αὐτόπται καὶ ὑπηρέται γενόμενοι τοῦ λόγου),[263] by
investigating everything carefully (ἀκριβῶς), so that the reader may know "the
certainty (τὴν ἀσφάλειαν) of the things." Particularly, two adverbs in Luke 1:3
seem notable in terms of the construction process of Luke: ἀκριβῶς and καθεξῆς. Ἀκριβῶς shows that Luke carefully investigated and preserved oral traditions as well as written sources. Καθεξῆς shows Luke's way of constructing the
third Gospel by using the sources: it was done orderly.[264] From these observations, we can regard Luke as a thorough "preserver" of the oral tradition, not
excluding the possibility of using written sources (Luke 1:1),[265] and a constructor who formed the third Gospel to be a "reliable, accurate history."[266]

In addition, Luke 1:1–4 and Acts 1:1 show Luke to be a constructor of the two
sequel volumes: the third Gospel and the Acts of the Apostles. Considering the
"we-passages" in Acts, Luke may be an eyewitness to some events which he
describes in Acts.[267] Luke 1:1–2, however, reveals that Luke was certainly not an
eyewitness to the events described in the third Gospel.[268]

---

263  According to Darrell L. Bock, the author of the third Gospel "has *relied* on his study of
     *traditions*, which *came from* 'eyewitnesses and servants of the Word'" (italics are mine).
     See Bock, *Luke 1:1–9:50*, 4.
264  The meaning of "order" here could be temporal, logical, or literary. As for the possible
     meanings of καθεξῆς, see Bock, *Luke 1:1–9:50*, 62. An interesting study of καθεξῆς in Luke's
     Gospel was undertaken by Benjamin W. W. Fung. See Benjamin W. W. Fung, *A Defense
     for the Chronological Order of Luke's Gospel: The Meaning of "Orderly" (καθεξῆς) Account
     in Luke 1:3* (AMS 3; Eugene, OR: Wipe & Stock, 2019). Here "Fung argues that καθεξῆς
     in Luke 1:3b 'most likely refers to chronological order' on the basis of four methods:—
     1. an analysis of Luke's two prefaces; 2. a word study of καθεξῆς; 3. an analysis of the
     narrative sequence of Luke; and 4. a comparison between the writing approaches of
     Greco-Roman/Jewish histories and Luke." In Fung's monograph, however, "there remains
     a debate over the genre of Luke (e.g., history, biography, historiography, or ancient
     document) and the chronological issue between Luke 4:16–30, Matthew 13:54–58, and
     Mark 6:1–6a." See Hojoon J. Ahn, review of *A Defense for the Chronological Order of Luke's
     Gospel: The Meaning of 'Orderly' (καθεξῆς) Account in Luke 1:3*, by Benjamin W. W. Fung, *AJ*
     13 (2021): 57–58.
265  Cf. Luke T. Johnson, *The Gospel of Luke* (SPS 3; Collegeville: Liturgical, 1991), 2–6. For
     more full discussions of Luke 1:1, see Loveday Alexander, *The Preface to Luke's Gospel:
     Literary Convention and Social Context in Luke 1.1–4 and Acts 1.1.* (SNTSMS 78; Cambridge:
     Cambridge University Press, 1993), 108–16.
266  France, *Luke*, 6. Here, France suggests that τὴν ἀσφάλειαν in Luke 1:4 can be translated as
     "certainty," which can carry the meaning of being "firmly founded and cannot be moved."
     If we accept this suggestion, we can deduce that Luke attempted to record a "reliable,
     accurate history."
267  France, *Luke*, 2.
268  Tuckett, *Luke*, 15–17.

52 CHAPTER 1

This study, therefore, regards the third Gospel's constructor as Luke, a companion of the apostle Paul. He was not an eyewitness nor a contributor of oral traditions, but in Luke 1:1–4, especially two adverbs (ἀκριβῶς, καθεξῆς) in the passage reveal his cautious manner of constructing the third Gospel. The discussions above suggest that Luke may have orderly constructed the third Gospel faithfully based on oral traditions and written sources.

## 7     The Position of This Study

From the investigations so far, the position of this study can be summed up as follows. First, the words of Jesus and the stories about him have been preserved in oral traditions by eyewitnesses. Second, Matthew was an eyewitness and a contributor to oral tradition(s), and this identity may have influenced the construction process of the first Gospel. Third, Mark constructed the second Gospel as the preserver and deliverer of the oral testimony/tradition from the apostle Peter, who was an eyewitness and may have contributed to forming oral tradition(s); thus, both Mark and Peter's identities may have influenced the construction process of the second Gospel. Fourth, Luke was not an eyewitness nor a contributor to oral traditions, but in Luke 1:1–4, he reveals himself as a cautious preserver of oral traditions and written sources. Fifth, the commonalities and differences in the Synoptic Gospels can be explained by the above assumptions.

This position can be summarized as follows: each volume of the Synoptic Gospels was formed on the basis of oral traditions and written sources. This, however, does not exclusively mean the literary independence between the Synoptic Gospels; this study is open to the possibility of the literary dependence between the three Gospels, though it does not lean to any of the three Hypotheses surveyed above. This approach can be called "Oral Tradition(s) and Constructor's Identity Hypothesis." This study is based on this position and, in the course of the study, the validity of this position will be ascertained.

## 8     Conclusion

This chapter has briefly surveyed the history of the studies related to the Synoptic Problem (from Papias to Dunn) and analyzed the four major positions (the Two Source Hypothesis, the Farrer Hypothesis, the Two Gospel Hypothesis, and the Orality and Memory Hypothesis) by examining representative upholders' arguments. By dividing these hypotheses into the literary dependence position and the literary independence position, this chapter analyzed each position and found that both positions have their own plausibility and limitations. From these analyses, it is necessary to pursue another approach based on a balanced thorough understanding of the situation of Jesus' era, oral tradition, and each Gospel constructor's identity. Thus, this chapter suggests a position, "Oral Tradition(s) and Constructor's Identity Hypothesis," and it will be the starting point and the final goal of this study.

CHAPTER 2

# Methodology—Mode Register Analysis

A model of mode Resister Analysis (RA) based on Systemic Functional Linguistics (SFL) is the methodology of this study. Before discussing this methodology, it seems necessary to consider some of the related issues when the methodology is applied to the Synoptic Gospels. They are genre and oral tradition.

## 1 Foundational Concepts for Methodology

### 1.1 *Genre*

Since an understanding of genre[1] is an essential element for studying the Synoptic Gospels and is also related to the issue of "finding the construction process of a text," it will be discussed briefly before dealing with the methodology.

The genre of the Gospels has long been studied, and the following scholars have contributed to the field of the gospel genre: Ernest Renan, Clyde W. Votaw, Karl L. Schmidt, Martin Dibelius, Bultmann, Charles H. Talbert, Philip L. Schuler, David E. Aune, Richard A. Burridge, Zachary K. Dawson, Craig S. Keener. Renan views the Gospel accounts regarding Jesus as a "biography."[2] For him, the Gospels are "the documents which claim to be biographies of the founder of Christianity and must naturally take the place of honour in a Life of Jesus."[3] However, he considers the Gospels as not just ordinary biographies but historically inaccurate "legendary biographies."[4]

Votaw asserts that the Gospels may or may not be viewed as biography, depending on the definition of biography.[5] He agrees that it is not a historical biography but rather a more general theorem of practical, hortatory characters.[6]

Schmidt argues that the Gospels were naturally woven through oral gospel traditions in the early church—not by the author's intention.[7] He also acknowledges that the Gospel of Luke has a historiographical aspect and the Gospels

---

1   This study defines genre as a literary category or a type of writing that the Synoptic Gospels belong to.
2   Ernest Renan, *Life of Jesus* (New York: Howard Wilford Bell, 1904), 339, 368, 393.
3   Renan, *Life of Jesus*, 339.
4   Renan, *Life of Jesus*, 367.
5   Clyde W. Votaw, "The Gospels and Contemporary Biographies," *AJT* 19 (1915): 49.
6   Votaw, "Gospel and Contemporary Biographies," 49.
7   Karl L. Schmidt, *The Place of the Gospels in the General History of Literature* (trans. Byron R. McCane; Columbia: University of South California Press, 2002), 5, 27.

© HOJOON J. AHN, 2024 | DOI:10.1163/9789004696372_004

INTRODUCTION TO MODE REGISTER ANALYSIS

of Matthew and Mark share this character of Luke, but he warns against the understanding of the Gospels as "historiography" because such an understanding may lead to identifying the constructors of the Gospels as historiographers such as Polybius or Eusebius.[8] He claims that the Gospels "do not belong to any specific strand in the history of literature."[9]

Dibelius does not identify a specific genre of the Gospels, rather, he tries to identify the "forms" within the Gospels, which could be called "sub-genre." He seeks not only to find the origin of the Jesus tradition through a methodology of "form criticism" (Formgeschichte) but also to find some intention of the earliest tradition's construction.[10] He thinks that the Gospels were basically written faithfully to the Jesus tradition, and one cannot rule out whether or not the author's character may be reflected in this process, but it may not have been written by the author's literary intention.[11]

Bultmann shares Dibelius's interest and tries to interpret the Gospels from a form-critical point of view, focusing on the process of forming the Gospels that would have been more complicated.[12] He claims that the Gospels cannot be regarded as an ancient biography due to their mythical, cultic, and world-negating nature.

Talbert opposes Bultmann's view and argues that despite the unique nature of the Gospels, they can be viewed as an ancient biography through comparative analysis with other ancient biographies.[13]

Schuler raises doubts about Schmidt and Dibelius's positions regarding the Gospels as "folk" literature, written without each author's specific intent.[14] He thinks that at least the authors' aims, decisions, and skills were involved in the process of forming the Gospels, and through comparison with other literature, he regards the Gospels' genre as an "encomium" biography.[15]

Aune argues that the Gospels adopted some sort of "Greco-Roman biographical conventions" in order to carry the story of Jesus, even though each Gospel has its own theological agenda.[16]

---

8    Schmidt, *Place of the Gospels*, 5.

9    Schmidt, *Place of the Gospels*, 27.

10   Martin Dibelius, *From Tradition to Gospel* (trans. Bertram L. Woolf; 2nd ed.; London: Ivor Nicholson & Watson, 1934), 7.

11   Dibelius, *From Tradition to Gospel*, 1.

12   Bultmann, *Synoptic Tradition*, 6.

13   Charles H. Talbert, *What Is a Gospel? The Genre of the Canonical Gospels* (Philadelphia: Fortress, 1977), 6, 135.

14   Philip L. Schuler, *A Genre for the Gospels: The Biographical Character of Matthew* (Philadelphia: Fortress, 1982).

15   Schuler, *Genre*, 32.

16   David E. Aune, "Greco-Roman Biography," in *Greco-Roman Literature and the New Testament: Selected Forms and Genres*, ed. David E. Aune (Atlanta: Scholars, 1988), 125.

Burridge claims that the Gospels were constructed as an "ancient biography" focusing on Jesus of Nazareth through his comparative analyses of the Greco-Roman literature based on his genre theory model.[17] This theory of Burridge has been regarded as a consensus in New Testament academia, almost as an orthodox view.[18]

Dawson, however, criticizes that Burridge's view retains the limitations of the modern genre theory and, in particular, this view does not help to understand the purpose of the Gospels in connection with the social situation that may have occurred in the process of forming the Gospels.[19] In the meantime, he attempts to establish a Gospel genre that reveals the social function and purpose of the Gospel by a genre theory model based on SFL.[20]

Keener defines the Gospels as unique documents, which have similar characteristics to other biographies; they are organized on the basis of living memory, and have historical authenticity.[21] Such understanding is evident in his naming the Gospels "Christobiography."[22]

Thus, central issues of the Gospel genre debate are naturally related to the uniqueness of the Gospels among the current literature and the commonalities of them with other current literature. If we focus on their uniqueness, we may claim that it is difficult to view them as a specific literature genre. However, if we focus on the commonality between the Gospels and other literature which are apparent as Burridge points out, we may regard the Gospels as a biography with similar features of history, memoir, etc. In terms of memoir, on the one hand, as Schmidt and Bultmann contend, there may have been a preservation of oral tradition(s) in the process of the Gospels' construction. In terms of history, on the other hand, as Keener pointed out, the Gospels may have historical authenticity. In addition, each constructor of the Gospels would have had the purpose of constructing them. To achieve his purpose, he may have selected some out of many sources in his hands, and may have arranged these selected materials, and in that process, the constructor's own linguistic style may have been reflected.[23]

---

17  Burridge, *Gospels*, 339.

18  Steve Walton, "What Are the Gospels? Richard Burridge's Impact on Scholarly Understanding of the Genre of the Gospels," *CBR* 14 (2015): 81.

19  Zachary K. Dawson, "The Problem of Gospel: Unmasking a Flawed Consensus and Providing a Fresh Way Forward with Systemic Functional Linguistics Genre Theory," *BAGL* 8 (2019): 35.

20  Dawson, "Gospel Genres," 53–70.

21  Craig S. Keener, *Christobiography: Memory, History, and the Reliability of the Gospels* (Grand Rapids: Eerdmans, 2019), 497.

22  Keener, *Christobiography*, 1.

23  Cf. When Philip L. Schuler talks about the authorial intention, it makes sense to say that it is difficult not to take into account the intention, if it is any minimal intention the author

INTRODUCTION TO MODE REGISTER ANALYSIS

Thus, in this study, I define the Synoptic Gospels in terms of genre as "biographical texts based on oral traditions with historical authenticity."

### 1.2 Oral Tradition

This section discusses the influence of oral tradition on the Synoptic Gospels. In the course of applying the mode RA to the designated texts of the Synoptic Gospels, the issues of orality and textuality will be involved. It seems, therefore, necessary to review the concept of oral tradition briefly at this stage. In reviewing this special attention is paid to the possibility that the Synoptic Gospels were constructed on the basis of oral traditions regarding Jesus' words and life. What is "oral traditions"? According to Jan Vansina, oral traditions mean "all oral testimonies concerning the past which are transmitted from one person to another"[24] and "historical sources of a special nature," which "derives from the fact that they are 'unwritten' sources couched in a form suitable for oral transmission, and that their preservation depends on the powers of memory of successive generations of human beings."[25]

Then, how can we confirm the existence of oral tradition in the Gospels? First, we need to look at the internal evidence. When we see Paul's expression, "For I received from the Lord what I also handed on to you" (Ἐγὼ γὰρ παρέλαβον ἀπὸ τοῦ κυρίου, ὃ καὶ παρέδωκα ὑμῖν) in 1 Corinthians 11:23, we can deduce that Jesus' Eucharistic words are based on an oral tradition.[26] In Luke 1:1–4, we can also recognize that Luke—and possibly other Gospel constructors too—constructed the Gospels on the basis of the oral testimonies/traditions of "eyewitnesses and servants of the word" (αὐτόπται καὶ ὑπηρέται γενόμενοι τοῦ λόγου). In addition, as the external evidence, the testimonies of Fathers such as Irenaeus, Eusebius, Tertullian, Origen, Clement of Alexandria, and Jerome witness the existence of these oral traditions.[27] It seems natural to assume that the testimonies on Jesus may have been preserved in some

---

might have, without ignoring oral tradition or other previous processes. See Schuler, *A Genre for the Gospels*, 32. It seems that the organizers of the Gospels at least had the intention to properly and accurately organize the contents of the traditions on Jesus (cf. Luke 1:1–3).

24  Jan Vansina, *Oral Tradition: A Study in Historical Methodology* (trans. H. M. Wright; Chicago: Aldine, 1965), xvii.

25  Vansina, *Oral Tradition*, 1.

26  Gordon D. Fee, *The First Epistle to the Corinthians* (rev. ed.; Grand Rapids: Eerdmans, 2014), 548–49; Anthony C. Thiselton, *1 Corinthians: A Shorter Exegetical & Pastoral Commentary* (Grand Rapids: Eerdmans, 2006), 183.

27  For a related discussion, see T. M. Derico, *Oral Tradition and Synoptic Verbal Agreement: Evaluating the Empirical Evidence for Literary Dependence* (Eugene, OR: Pickwick, 2016), 1–3.

form of oral tradition for several decades. If it is assumed that the canonical Gospels were written during the second half of the 1st century, those oral traditions may have undoubtedly influenced on the process of constructing the Gospels.[28] When this study refers to the term "oral tradition," it means an oral collection of Jesus' words and the stories related to him that the early church members (Jesus' disciples and other eyewitnesses) may have formed and preserved.[29]

## 2　Mode Register Analysis Based on SFL[30]

We are now in a position to discuss the methodology of this study, that is, a model of mode Register Analysis based on SFL. We may first need to consider a complicated aspect of a linguistic framework in applying the mode RA based on SFL to the Greek text. Modern linguistics deals with the characteristics of the "language" which is used in the modern world, and the principle according to which the language is operating. The present study, however, applies this modern theory representing the modern language to the ancient texts which are using the first century Greek. Nevertheless, linguistics also deals with the universal features of the language which are common to all languages used by all humans regardless of age. It is then necessary to point out that M. A. K. Halliday's (1925–2018) SFL based on English probably cannot be applied as it is to the Greek text, even though there are linguistic features in all languages—like meta-functional hypothesis—which can be regarded as "universal."[31] It seems, therefore, crucial to pay attention to the difference between English and ancient Greek and consider this difference in building up the methodological framework.[32]

---

28　Cf. Henaut, *Oral Tradition*, 15.

29　Burkett, *Origins*, 128.

30　When I use the term "register" in this study, it will carry the distinctive register of each constructor and audience/recipient of the Synoptic Gospels. In other words, it means the register in the process of each text composition, not a register in the initial occurrence situation.

31　M. A. K. Halliday, *An Introduction to Functional Grammar* (London: Edward Arnold, 1985), xxxiv.

32　Porter contends the need for re-modeling M. A. K. Halliday's SFL to use it in the field of the Greek New Testament study. See Stanley E. Porter, "Systemic Functional Linguistics and the Greek Language: The Need for Further Modeling," in *Modeling Biblical Language: Selected Papers from the McMaster Divinity College Linguistics Circle*, eds. Stanley E. Porter, et al. (LBS 13; Leiden: Brill, 2016), 10.

INTRODUCTION TO MODE REGISTER ANALYSIS 59

## 3 Systemic Functional Linguistics

Before we discuss the mode RA, we may need to relate SFL briefly on which the mode RA is based. According to Porter, SFL can be summarized as follows.

> SFL is a system-based functional linguistic model that connects socially grounded meanings with instances of language usage. As a result, SFL relies upon defining and examining various theoretical strata that connect context to expression. Each of these strata—context of culture and context of situation (which are non-linguistic), semantics and lexicogrammar (content), and phonology/graphology (expression)—is system driven, and SFL models meaning potential as system networks, in which meaning choices are realized as systems. SFL also utilizes a rank scale to differentiate levels of structure (syntagmatic relations) of language (there has been less work in formalizing context than there has been of the semantics and lexicogrammar).[33]

SFL contains two crucial concepts of language utterance: system and function. Every language entity has its own systemic formation in a specific social background (context of culture and context of situation),[34] and it is used by persons within a given society as a functional tool.[35] Such functional linguistics seems to stem from some scholars in the Prague School (e.g., Vilém Mathesius [1882–1945], Roman Jacobson [1896–1982], *etc.*) and was developed in a systemic way by John R. Firth (1890–1960).[36] However, Halliday is regarded as a pioneer who completed the scheme of SFL.[37] As a basis of SFL, he states that language is "a product of social process."

> Language arises in the life of the individual through an ongoing exchange of meanings with significant others. A child creates, first his child tongue, then his mother tongue, in interaction with that little coterie of people who constitute his meaning group. In this sense, language is a product of social process.[38]

---

33  Stanley E. Porter, *The Letter to the Romans: A Linguistic and Literary Commentary* (NTM 37; Sheffield: Sheffield Phoenix, 2015), 24.

34  Halliday, *Functional Grammar*, xvii.

35  Halliday, *Functional Grammar*, xiii.

36  Cf. Halliday, *Functional Grammar*, xxvi–xxvii.

37  For a detailed survey of the history of SFL, see Porter, "Systemic Functional Linguistics," 2–10.

38  M. A. K. Halliday, *Language as Social Semiotic: The Social Interpretation of Language and Meaning* (Baltimore: University Park Press, 1978), 1.

60                                                                                                    CHAPTER 2

Unlike Cognitive Linguistics, which focuses on the mind or psychological aspect of human beings, SFL regards language as "social semiotic," which is formed in a context of society (systemic dimension) and is used for exchanging meanings in the society by choice in a particular context (functional dimension). Thus, the keywords of SFL can be summarized as follows: (1) function, (2) meaning, (3) context, and (4) choice.[39] In the area of SFL, many scholars have been influenced by Halliday and developed their own paradigms; among them. J. R. Martin and R. P. Fawcett are noteworthy. Martin attempts to model Halliday's grammatical scheme for "discourse semantics."[40] For a more thorough discourse analysis (hereafter DA) based on SFL, Martin deals with several contextual elements in terms of genre and register as a model to overcome Hallidayan SFL's tendency to stay at the clause level.[41] Apart from Martin, Fawcett tries to remodel Halliday's SFL in a more simplified form with several extended elements in order to fulfill twofold practical goals: (1) to have a descriptive framework for text analysis and (2) to get an appropriate sentence model for computer language.[42] Unlike the five elements of a clause in Halliday's SFL (subject, finite, predicator, complement, adjunct), Fawcett suggests six elements (subject, operator, main verb, auxiliaries, complement, and adjunct).[43] Besides, various branches of SFL are still being developed by many scholars. Basically, the object of SFL can be any sort of oral/written material. SFL analyzes a text based on its own linguistic approach which contains pivotal elements such as cohesion, thematization, transitivity, mood system, *etc.*

Even though Halliday's linguistic approach is focused on a language, English, he admits that his linguistic model could be used for other languages as well: "This is not to deny that features may be universal; but those features that are being explicitly claimed as universal are built into the theory. An example of this is the 'metafunctional' hypothesis: it is postulated that in all languages; the content systems are organized into ideational, interpersonal, and textual components."[44] As he said, SFL's metafunctional aspect is embodied in all languages, and he describes this metafunction as "a universal feature of language."[45] Here we will look at some of the key concepts contained within

---

39    Cf. Suzanne Eggins, *An Introduction to Systemic Functional Linguistics* (London: Pinter, 1994), 1–24.

40    J. R. Martin, *English Text: System and Structure* (Philadelphia: Benjamins, 1992).

41    For J. R. Martin, "register" and "genre" are the alternative terms to Halliday's "context."

42    R. P. Fawcett, *Invitation to Systemic Functional Linguistics through the Cardiff Grammar: An Extension and Simplification of Halliday's Systemic Functional Grammar* (3rd ed.; London: Equinox, 2008).

43    In addition, R. P. Fawcett denies the "verbal group" of Halliday's SFL scheme because of the exceptional cases.

44    Halliday, *Functional Grammar*, xxxiv.

45    Halliday, *Functional Grammar*, xxxiv.

Halliday's SFL and consider how to apply these concepts to the New Testament Greek. Let us, then, take a closer look at the two key concepts represented by Halliday's SFL: system and function.[46]

### 3.1 *System*

Halliday explains the adjective "systemic" of Systemic Functional Linguistics as a concept distinct from "systematic" and says that it is deeply connected with the grammar in language. For Halliday, a system is "a set of options with an entry condition: that is to say, a set of things of which one must be chosen, together with a statement of the conditions under which the choice is available."[47] A system often remains and functions in the language in the form of grammar and is mainly connected with the problem of "choice" (or option) in language use.[48] Figure 2.1 shows how a system works through choice to form a language and the meaning of language.

Observing Figure 2.1, there is a "point of origin" on the very left. It is where the first instantaneous choice takes place. The curved bracket in the figure shows the branch of that immediate selection. As a result of choice, it is moved to the lower system of the name of "subnetwork." When selecting a, b, c, or d, the language figure is divided into a-e, a-f, b, c-g, c-h, and d. From these choices, linguistic diversity emerges. It would be an example of a system based on the act of choice.

The other crucial concept in SFL is stratification, and the basic concept Halliday introduces is as follows: "stratification refers to the way a language is organized as a hierarchy of strata, or levels of realization: phonetic, phonological, lexicogrammatical and semantic ... Then, above the semantic, we may add a further stratum of 'context'; this is outside language."[49] According to this basic concept, stratification is shown in a diagram as seen in Figure 2.2.[50]

---

46    Cynthia L. Westfall gives us a succinct understanding on the two core elements of SFL: "SFL studies how language is used to communicate in social interaction (the functional element), and treats language as a network of systems, or interrelated sets of options for making meaning." See Cynthia L. Westfall, "Mapping the Text: How Discourse Analysis Helps Reveal the Way through James," in *The Epistle of James: Linguistic Exegesis of an Early Christian Letter*, eds. James D. Dvorak and Zachary K. Dawson (LENT 1; Eugene, OR: Wipf and Stock, 2019), 13.

47    M. A. K. Halliday, *Halliday: System and Function in Language* (ed. Gunther R. Kress; Oxford: Oxford University Press, 1976), 3.

48    Halliday, *Social Semiotic*, 149.

49    M. A. K. Halliday, "The Gloosy Ganoderm: Systemic Functional Linguistics and Translation," in *Halliday in the 21st Century*, ed. Jonathan J. Webster (Collected Works of M. A. K. Halliday 11; London: Bloomsbury, 2013), 107.

50    M. A. K. Halliday, *Halliday's Introduction to Functional Grammar* (rev. Christian M. I. M. Matthiessen; 4th ed.; Abingdon: Routledge, 2014), 26.

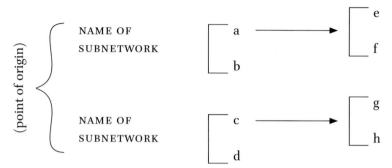

FIGURE 2.1  Hypothetical system network
Butler, *Systemic Linguistics*, 42.

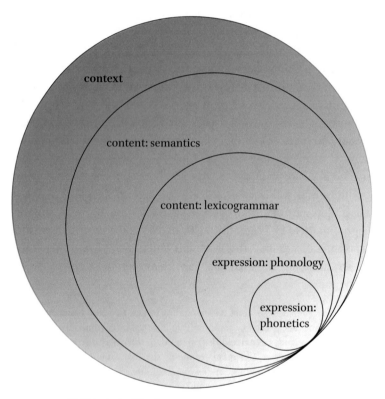

FIGURE 2.2  Halliday's stratification

INTRODUCTION TO MODE REGISTER ANALYSIS

Although scholars' definitions and compositions of stratification related to SFL vary,[51] this study follows the above arrangement. This study also shares the following scheme constructed by David I. Yoon: "This study is interested in how the components within the semantic stratum, realized by components within the lexicogrammar stratum, realize the components within the context stratum."[52]

### 3.2 *Function*

Function is realized by a system through the use of a specific language. Regarding "functional," an essential concept in his linguistic scheme, Halliday says: "It is functional in the sense that it is designed to account for how the language is used."[53] In fact, the functional components of a language are to communicate and understand. He calls these functional components "metafunctions." The composition of metafunctions is basically divided into ideational and interpersonal functions. For Halliday, the ideational function is concerned with understanding the environment of a speech, and the interpersonal function is related to how people behave in relation to other people in the environment.[54] The third metafunction formed by combining the above two metafunctions is textual function. The concept and relationship of these three metafunctions will be dealt with in more detail later in the following part of RA. Next, this study focuses on RA based on SFL.

## 4 Register Analysis Based on SFL for Analyzing Ancient Greek Texts

Throughout history, all human beings have used various oral/written languages to communicate within innumerable societies and social situations. For this reason, language itself fundamentally has a social feature. Regarding the social characteristic of language, Halliday says, "A significant fact about the behaviour of human beings in relation to their social environment is that a large part of it is linguistic behaviour."[55] Such a linguistic

---

51 For instance, unlike the depiction in Figure 2.2, Martin expresses "register" instead of "context" and adds "genre" and "ideology" as higher concepts in his stratification form. See Martin, *English Text*, 496.

52 David I. Yoon, *A Discourse Analysis of Galatians and the New Perspective on Paul* (LBS 17; Leiden: Brill, 2019), 72.

53 Halliday, *Functional Grammar*, xiii.

54 Halliday, *Functional Grammar*, xiii.

55 Halliday, *Functions of Language*, 48.

64                                                                                                    CHAPTER 2

system is "a part of the social system,"[56] and thus, all languages can be called social languages.

The variety existing in languages is usually classified into two levels: dialect and register. According to Halliday, "The variety according to user is a DIALECT; the variety according to use is a REGISTER."[57] In other words, one person's inherited language variety is "dialect," and "register" is associated with language variety when she/he actually uses the language in a situation.

What then is the core concept of "register"? Although the concept of register seems shadowy,[58] we can gain an important understanding through the explanation of Halliday on "register" and "types of linguistic situation" as follows:

> Types of linguistic situation differ from one another, broadly speaking, in three respects: first, what is actually taking place; secondly, who is taking part; and thirdly, what part the language is playing. These three variables, taken together, determine the range within which meanings are selected and the forms which are used for their expression. In other words, they determine the "register."[59]

Here Halliday refers to three types of "linguistic situation." They are concerned with the following three questions: what is happening now; who is involved; what is the point where language functions? According to Halliday, the three linguistic-situational types determine the "range" and "forms" of a text, and he labels these elements (range/forms) as the "register" of a text. Thus, Halliday says that the goal of the register theory is "to uncover the general principles which govern this variation, so that we can begin to understand *what* situation factors determine *what* linguistic features."[60] Based on Halliday's definition, this study defines register as *a linguistic type (range/forms) in a distinct type of situation.*[61]

---

56    M. A. K. Halliday, *Learning How to Mean: Explorations in the Development of Language* (ELS 2; London: Edward Arnold, 1975), 120.

57    M. A. K. Halliday et al., *The Linguistic Sciences and Language Teaching* (Bloomington: Indiana University Press, 1964), 77.

58    R. de Beaugrande. "'Register' in Discourse Studies: A Concept in Search of a Theory," in *Register Analysis: Theory and Practice*, ed. Mohsen Ghadessy (London: Pinter, 1993), 7.

59    Halliday, *Social Semiotic*, 31.

60    Halliday, *Social Semiotic*, 32. Italics are Halliday's. Concerning Halliday's explanation of the aim of the register theory, Helen Leckie-Tarry says the purpose of register analysis is "to propose relationships between language function, determined by situational or social factors, and language form." See Helen Leckie-Tarry, *Language and Context: A Functional Linguistic Theory of Register*, ed. David Birch (London: Pinter, 1995), 6.

61    Cf. Douglas Biber and Susan Conrad, *Register, Genre, and Style* (CTL; Cambridge: Cambridge University Press, 2009), 6. Here Douglas Biber and Susan Conrad define a register as "a variety associated with a particular situation of use (including particular

It is evident that there is always a *context* before forming a language *text*.[62] According to Halliday, a context of a text can be divided into two levels: "context of situation" (immediate environment of the text) and "context of culture" (total cultural background).[63] Here we will focus on the aspect of "context of situation" in terms of the semantic area.[64] If a context of situation determines the range and form of a text, the analysis of a text's language type should include the analysis of the situational elements.

Let us consider the relationship between text and context in more detail. A *text* means a spoken or written "instance of language" in a *context* (context of situation).[65] In other words, a text, which is constructed by words and sentences, is formed differently depending on a different context.[66] Thus, in order to understand a text, we have to know its context. Halliday posits that information of "a context of situation" is encoded in a text; therefore, by analyzing the text linguistically, we can know the context of situation of the text.[67] Unlike the concept of a *historical* context of situation, in SFL, *context* is regarded as "socio-semiotic constructs."[68] Thus, it is possible to say that "the context of situation emerges 'out of' the text."[69]

---

communicative purposes)." Westfall also succinctly defines register as "the specialized language that is used in a certain situation." See Cynthia L. Westfall, *A Discourse Analysis of the Letter to the Hebrews: The Relationship between Form and Meaning* (LNTS 297; London: T&T Clark, 2005), 84.

62    According to John C. Catford, language itself is already "a type of patterned human behavior." Thus, when we talk about "language type" in the Gospel text, it means each text's (or constructor's) sub-language type under the upper-language type of Greek. See John C. Catford, *A Linguistic Theory of Translation* (London: Oxford University Press, 1965), 1.

63    M. A. K. Halliday and Ruqaiya Hasan, *Language, Context, and Text: Aspects of Language in a Social-semiotic Perspective* (2nd ed.; Oxford: Oxford University Press, 1989), 6.

64    This term was coined by Bronislaw Malinowski in his anthropological scheme. See Bronislaw Malinowski, *Coral Gardens and Their Magic: A Study of the Methods of Tilling the Soil and of Agricultural Rites in the Trobriand Islands* (vol. 1; London: Routledge, 2002), 258.

65    Halliday, *Halliday's Introduction*, 3.

66    Cf. Cynthia L. Westfall, "A Moral Dilemma? The Epistolary Body of 2 Timothy," in *Paul and the Ancient Letter Form*, eds. Stanley E. Porter and Sean A. Adams (Leiden: Brill, 2010), 218.

67    According to Westfall, "(t)he linguistic study of the New Testament must be textually based as a starting point—the text is our direct access into the context, ..., since the specific cultural and historic contexts that would shed light on the text have been lost and can only be inferred from the text." See Westfall, *Hebrews*, 18.

68    Halliday and Hasan refer to the origin of the concept of "semiotics" as follows: it "derives initially from the concept of the sign; and the modern word harks back to the terms *semainon, semainomenon* ('signifier, signified') used in ancient Greek linguistics by the Stoic philosophers." See Halliday and Hasan, *Language, Context, and Text*, 3.

69    Christopher D. Land, *The Integrity of 2 Corinthians and Paul's Aggravating Absence* (NTM 36; Sheffield: Sheffield Phoenix, 2015), 51.

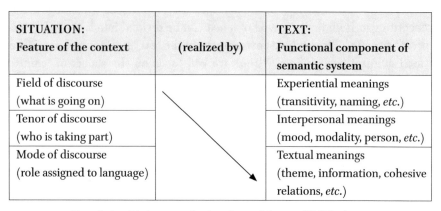

FIGURE 2.3 The relationship between the situation and the text (Halliday)

How, then, can we analyze such a context of situation encoded in a text? In the scheme of Halliday's linguistic approach, there are three metafunctions (ideational [experiential], interpersonal, textual) of register analysis, and through these metafunctions, the three features of the context (field, tenor, mode) can be realized, although others talk about even more elements of the texts.[70] The relation between the situation and the text can be revealed as in Figure 2.3.[71]

Since a textual function in a text is formed by a certain situation, we can assume that we can reach the context of situation by analyzing the textual function. Now, among the meta-functions by which to know the features of the context (field, tenor, mode), we focus on the mode-oriented methodology, since this methodology is most closely related to the study of analyzing the designated texts of the Synoptic Gospels. In relation to the purpose of this study, a mode-oriented analysis is most fruitful; therefore this volume focuses on mode.

---

70  According to Geoffrey Finch, register elements can be summarized as follows. "A good deal of work has been done by linguists interested in stylistics on identifying the various features which determine the particular register we choose to adopt in a given situation. The principal variables are FIELD or subject matter; MEDIUM (speech or writing); MODE, the particular genre (e.g., conversation, sermon, narrative, etc.); CHANNEL, the technical means (e.g., telephone, radio, face to face); TENOR, the relationship between the participants; and CONTEXT, the situation, social, cultural or institutional." See Geoffrey Finch, *Key Concepts in Language and Linguistics* (New York: Palgrave Macmillan, 2005), 228. Thus, as Finch argues, there are many kinds of situational factors in addition to tenor, mode, and field. Among them, Halliday sees these three as the core factors.

71  Halliday and Hasan, *Language, Context, and Text*, 26.

## 5 Mode: Textual Meaning

Halliday explains the mode of discourse as referring to "what part the language is playing, what it is that the participants are expecting the language to do for them in that situation."[72] There are three major textual factors of mode: theme (thematization),[73] cohesion, and information structure (information flow).[74] This study, therefore, deals with thematization, cohesion, oral & written texture, along with verbal aspect.

### 5.1 *Thematization*

First, thematization is a necessary part of analyzing the textual metafunction in the RA model based on SFL.[75] It also has a history in Prague School (hereafter PS) linguistics.[76] This section employs Mathesius of PS, who is the pioneer of the thematization, Halliday (1925–2018) who revises Mathesius's scheme for English, and Porter and Matthew B. O'Donnell who develop their thematization theories for Greek. Considering the various levels in a text (e.g., clause, sentence [including complex clauses], and paragraph[s]), this section engages with the above scholars to present the definitions and functions of "theme," "rheme," and the subordinate concepts of thematization—"prime," "subsequent," "topic," and "comment."

---

72    Halliday and Hasan, *Language, Context, and Text*, 12.

73    According to Porter, "Theme is indicated in Greek by grammatically explicit subjects, which establish those persons and items that create the primary information flow." See Stanley E. Porter, "Dialect and Register in the Greek of the New Testament: Theory," in *Rethinking Contexts, Rereading Texts: Contributions from the Social Sciences to Biblical Interpretation*, ed. M. D. Carroll R. (JSOTSup 299; Sheffield: Sheffield Academic, 2000), 201.

74    Porter explains that information flow is associated with "how these elements (in terms of lexical patterning) are distributed within a discourse, usually in terms of sub-units" ("Dialect and Register," 201). The words in brackets are added.

75    James D. Dvorak, "Thematization, Topic, and Information Flow," *JLIABG* 1 (2008): 19; cf. Perfetti and Goldman, "Discourse Functions of Thematization," 257. David Yoon's definition on "thematization" seems compact and clear: "thematization is about how writers structure their texts in order to convey thematic elements at the different ranks of clause, clause complex, and discourse." See Yoon, *Galatians*, 161.

76    The more detailed contents regarding the history and theoretical frameworks of thematization were dealt with in Hojoon J. Ahn, "Thematization in Luke 4: A Discourse-Thematic Analysis of Luke 4 in Light of the Models of V. Mathesius, M. A. K. Halliday, and S. E. Porter & M. B. O'Donnell," in *The Literary-Linguistic Analysis of the Bible: The Enduring Legacy of Russian Formalism and the Prague Linguistic Circle*, ed. Stanley E. Porter, et al. (Leiden: Brill, forthcoming). Some of this section was brought from this article verbatim.

68                                                        CHAPTER 2

5.1.1        A Background of Thematization: Mathesius and Halliday
Mathesius, the founder of the PS[77] (a linguistic group being mainly interested
in phonological, syntactic, and semantic language studies),[78] made a crucial
contribution to the formation of functional linguistics, textological research,[79]
and speech analysis.[80] Mathesius's explanation that the significance of word
order with the notions of basis (theme) and nucleus (rheme) is a fundamental principle for understanding language formation.[81] Essentially, the order of
theme and rheme is not fixed. For Mathesius, rheme following theme (objective order) is a non-emphatic order, whereas theme following rheme (subjective order) is an emphatic construction.

Mathesius's theory of theme and rheme structure is significant for the foundation of Functional Sentence Perspective (hereafter FSP), and it initiates a
new type of structural/functional/thematic analysis. Mathesius's work, however, needs to be updated in three points, especially in order to apply it to the
following analysis of Gospel texts.

First, though the framework was also applied and developed for English,
Mathesius's model for theme and rheme was designed for his mother tongue
Czech. Although theme generally precedes rheme, Czech (being an inflected
language) has greater flexibility when ordering clause components (subject,
verb, object, etc.) than English[82]—which more often marks grammatical relations with word order. For example, an English sentence *Pavel killed Peter*
could be expressed in Czech with: *Pavel zabil Petra* (S + V + O); *Petra zabil Pavel*
(O + V + S); or *Pavel Petra zabil* (S + O + V).[83] Due to this difference, although
there have been attempts to apply this aspect of Czech to English in a passive

---

77    Vachek, "Mathesius," 69.
78    Cf. Robins, *Linguistics*, 229. For Vilém Mathesius's study on the phonological system of
      Czech in comparison to German based on synchrony, see Vilém Mathesius, "La Structure
      Phonologique du Lexique du Tchéque Moderne," in *A Prague School Reader in Linguistics*,
      ed. Josef Vachek (Bloomington: Indiana University Press, 1964), 156–76. For Mathesius's
      quantitative phonological analysis on the frequency of "a" and "e" sounds in several lan-
      guages (English, Czech, Russian, and Croatian), see Vilém Mathesius, "Zum Problem der
      Belastungs—und Kombinations—fähigkeit der Phoneme?" in *A Prague School Reader in
      Linguistics*, ed. Josef Vachek (Bloomington: Indiana University Press, 1964), 177–82.
79    Vachek, "One of the Forerunners," 69–70. According to Vachek, Mathesius's analyzed
      theme and rheme structure at the paragraph/chapter level as well as clause/sentence level.
80    Daneš, "Prague Functional Approach," 58. Mathesius focuses on the two functions of
      speech, that is, "expressive" and "communicative" functions. For a detailed explanation
      on it, see Vilém Mathesius, "*Řeč a sloh*," in *Čtení o jazyce a poezii*, eds. B. Havránek and
      J. Mukařovský (Prague: Melantrich, 1942).
81    G. Sampson, *Schools of Linguistics* (Stanford: Stanford University Press, 1980), 104.
82    Sampson, *Linguistics*, 105.
83    Naughton, *Czech*, 216. The initials "S," "V," and "O" indicate "subject," "verb," and "object."
      The only coherent English translation of the three sentences is "Pavel killed Petr." In

INTRODUCTION TO MODE REGISTER ANALYSIS

form (e.g., Peter was killed by Pavel),[84] it is not simply applied directly or simply to English without considerable modifications. Although Mathesius says, "every language displays a tendency for this functional sentence perspective, whether the order is objective or subjective,"[85] one may wonder how well it fits in English and other languages as much as Czech.

Second, Mathesius places "sentence"—a combination of words ending in a period (".") which contains one or more clauses—at the center of theme and rheme analysis and argues that word organization at the sentence level gives further meaning to words. Mathesius tried to extend his model beyond sentence level (paragraph or chapter); it is hard to find useful criteria in these higher levels of linguistic analysis in his works. Of course, sentence analysis is the basis of text analysis; however, it seems necessary for additional theoretical development in order to apply theme and rheme to the thematic structure at the paragraph/discourse level.

Third, in Mathesius's model, the predicate functions as a "transitional rheme" within the rheme of a sentence and its remaining rhematic parts.[86] According to Eva Hajičová, "[i]n Mathesius' views, the predicate is a part of the nucleus but on its edge rather than in its center and represents a transition (*přechod*) between the two parts of the utterance."[87] Understanding the predicate as a "transition" into rheme should probably be reconsidered when considering other languages. In particular, when applying Mathesius's model to New Testament Greek, which conveys the point of view of a speaker or author via tense-form,[88] modification is inevitable.

---

English, to change the positions of subject and object, we have to change the verbal form from active to passive, but Czech can change its position without any change in verbs.

84 Sampson, *Linguistics*, 105.

85 Vilém Mathesius, "Functional Linguistics," in *Praguiana: Some Basic and Less Known Aspects of the Prague Linguistic School*, eds. and trans. Josef Vachek and Libuše Dušková (Amsterdam: John Benjamins, 1983), 127. For example, although Mathesius admits the distinctive characteristics of English, he tries to apply his theme-rheme structure of FSP to English as well; thus, he states that there can be two types of order (objective order [rheme follows theme] and subjective order [theme follows rheme]) in English text according to the order of theme and rheme. See Vilém Mathesius, *A Functional Analysis of Present Day English on a General Linguistic Basis* (trans. Libuše Dušková; Paris: Mouton, 1975), 156.

86 Hajičová, "Mathesius," 51.

87 Hajičová, *Syntax-Semantics Interface*, 42.

88 According to Porter, the Greek tense-form does not indicate temporal meaning, instead aspectual meaning (perfective aspect, imperfective aspect, and stative aspect); and a selection of particular tense-form by a New Testament author presents a perspective on the verbal action. He elucidates three verbal aspects according to the extent of their markedness: the stative aspect is the most weighted, the next is imperfective aspect, and the least weighted is the perfective aspect. See Stanley E. Porter, *Idioms of the Greek*

70                                                                                              CHAPTER 2

Although Mathesius's linguistic modeling requires some modification, his methodology has nonetheless proven to be influential.[89] Halliday modified Mathesius's concepts in some respects for his linguistic theory. Halliday argues that the thematic structure of a text is integral to the textual metafunction of language. He furthermore states that the clause is the basic unit of thematic structure study, which possesses an embedded message.[90] Thematization in SFL (as an integral part of the textual metafunction) describes a text's information flow—how the text is organized by means of staging (theme) and developing (rheme).[91] As mentioned above, since Mathesius originally studied thematization in Czech, even though he extended the model to English, Halliday alters the notions of theme and rheme for the study of English thematization.[92] Unlike Mathesius's usage of theme (basis) and rheme (nucleus; cf. new) as the movable elements of sentence for conveying importance and prominence, Halliday uses these terms to denote the ordered elements of a

---

New Testament (2nd ed.; BLG 2; Sheffield: Sheffield Academic, 1994), 22; Stanley E. Porter, Verbal Aspect in the Greek of the New Testament, with Reference to Tense and Mood (SBG 1; New York: Peter Lang, 1989), xi. In fact, Czech has a verbal aspect system, but its function differs from New Testament Greek. Mathesius presents three major functions of verbal aspect in Czech as "alternation of the stem consonant," "derivation which often brings about a change in conjugation," and "set phrases (phraseologically)." See Mathesius, Functional Analysis, 70.

89    Jan Firbas comments that "Mathesius' concepts of known and unknown information point partly to the concept of communicative dynamism, partly to the concepts of contextual dependence and contextual applicability." See Jan Firbas, "On Defining the Theme in Functional Sentence Analysis," in Travaux Linguistiques de Prague 1 (ed. Josef Vachek; Tuscaloosa: University of Alabama Press, 1966), 276. He argues that Mathesius's analysis would bring to "full light the importance of his studies for the inquiry into the laws not only of Czech but of Indo-European word order in general." See Firbas, "Defining the Theme," 276. Based on Mathesius's FSP, Firbas develops his own model of FSP and "Communicative Dynamics" (CD), as "a phenomenon constantly displayed by linguistic elements in the act of communication." See Firbas, Functional Sentence Perspective, 7.

90    Cf. Halliday, Halliday's Introduction, 88.

91    Cf. The term "staging" was used by Peter Cotterell and Max Turner: "Discourse is characterized by staging, the orderly progression in a necessarily linear sequence." Peter Cotterell and Max Turner, Linguistics and Biblical Interpretation (Downers Grove: InterVarsity, 1989), 241; cf. Gillian Brown and George Yule, Discourse Analysis (CTL; Cambridge: Cambridge University Press, 1983), 134.

92    When it comes to studying the thematic development and composition of text in a very different language compared to Czech, that is, English, it is probably clear that the approach is bound to change. Although we do not find a direct comparison between Czech and English in Halliday's utterances, we can probably find a related case between Japanese ("there is a special postposition -wa, which signifies that whatever immediately precedes it is thematic") and English ("the theme is indicated only by position in the clause") in terms of thematic structure, as suggested by Halliday. See Halliday, Functional Grammar, 88.

# INTRODUCTION TO MODE REGISTER ANALYSIS

clause. In other words, for Halliday, theme is a word or word group located at the beginning of a clause; and rheme follows. Halliday explains this phenomenon happens when a writer or speaker chooses their "desired [t]heme,"[93] and markedness is expressed where "[t]heme is anything other than that which is most expected" or by intonation.[94] To sum up, Halliday remodels Mathesius's theme and rheme structure into the analysis of ordered elements within a clause. Halliday's analysis of English, which conveys syntax through the location of words, can be regarded as a well-suited development of Mathesius's work on Czech and English.

Halliday regards the theme and rheme structure within the clause level as "thematic structure," and regards the theme and rheme structure above the clause level as "information-structure." Of course, they are closely connected. In Halliday's information-structure (or information flow), two concepts are important—given (or known) and new (or unknown).[95] However, for Halliday, "given and new thus differ from theme and rheme, though both are textual function, in that 'given' means 'here is a point of contact with what you know' (and thus is not tied to elements in clause structure), whereas 'theme' means 'here is the heading to what I am saying.'"[96] Thus, Halliday's concept of theme and rheme and Mathesius's differ in this respect. Mathesius understands the concept of theme and rheme as given and new, whereas Halliday differentiates between the two. Through the differentiation between theme and rheme and given and new, Halliday finds not only the linguistic significance in word order at the clause level but also the system of information beyond the clause.[97]

### 5.1.2 Porter and O'Donnell's Thematization

Although Halliday modifies Mathesius's linguistic theory, even Halliday's analysis is not sufficiently specified for discourse or paragraph analysis. Furthermore, his model is for the analysis of English. In such a situation, Porter and O'Donnell refine Halliday's work in order to use it for discourse or paragraph analysis applicable especially to New Testament Greek literature.[98]

---

93  Halliday, *Functional Grammar*, 90.

94  Halliday, *Functional Grammar*, 90.

95  M. A. K. Halliday, "Language Structure and Language Function," in *New Horizons in Linguistics*, ed. John Lyons (Harmondsworth: Penguin, 1970), 162.

96  Halliday, "Language Structure," 163. According to Halliday, "[Theme] is put first is being instated by the speaker as the theme of the coming message: it is the setting for the information that follows." See M. A. K. Halliday, "Grammar and Daily Life: Concurrence and Complementarity," in *On Grammar*, ed. Jonathan J. Webster (Collected Works of M. A. K. Halliday 1; London: Continuum, 2002), 371.

97  Halliday, *Functional Grammar*, 114–15.

98  Porter and O'Donnell explain (or define, in a sense) clauses in Greek as follows: "Clauses in Greek can consist of a single group (and hence of a single word), either a nominal or a

Since Mathesius's work on theme and rheme is principally for Czech and also for English, and Halliday's work is for English, some modifications may be necessary for applying their ideas to New Testament Greek. At first sight, New Testament Greek seems to share more linguistic features with Czech than English[99]—like inflection,[100] so it seems reasonable to use Mathesius's model for Czech to analyze New Testament Greek thematization. However, some features of New Testament Greek are different from those of Czech. Furthermore, as mentioned above, Matheisus's model is concerned with analyzing features at or within the sentence and is positioned to view the predicate as a transitional; therefore, it is not suitable for a discourse or paragraph analysis.

Porter and O'Donnell's adaptation of Mathesius and Halliday's work on thematization is, thus, helpful enough for the study of New Testament Greek. While they utilize Mathesius and Halliday's research, Porter and O'Donnell offer a New Testament Greek-optimized model, address theme at various linguistic levels within a single text, and develop a method for modeling thematization by reflecting each step (clause, clause-complex/sentence, and paragraph/discourse). In Porter and O'Donnell's *Discourse Analysis*, they base their approach to thematization primarily upon Halliday's clause-centric concept of theme and rheme, revising it for multiple levels of language—clause, clause-complex, and paragraph/text(discourse) as shown in Table 2.1.[101]

---

verbal group. More usual is to have a clause consisting of at least one complex group with a number of words, such as a verbal group with a verb and its modifiers. More complex clauses may consist of numerous groups, such as nominal groups and verbal groups functioning as subjects, predicates, and complements, as well as adjunctions." Citation taken from a draft version of Stanley E. Porter and Matthew B. O'Donnell. *Discourse Analysis and the Greek New Testament: Text-Generating Resources* (LNTG 2; London: T&T Clark, 2024), 83.

99 Porter et al., *Fundamentals*, 21; Porter, *Idioms*, 286. Though New Testament Greek is more flexible in word order than other languages such as English, it is difficult to consider New Testament Greek as a free word-order language. We find well-structured patterns of word order in New Testament Greek—the position of article and several pronoun and modifier types. See Stanley E. Porter, "Word Order and Clause Structure in New Testament Greek: An Unexplored Area of Greek Linguistics Using Philippians as a Test Case," *Filologia Neotestamentaria* 6 (1993): 181–86; cf. Pitts, "Greek Clause Structure," 340–43.

100 Cf. Westfall, *Hebrews*, 39. As an inflected language, it is a fact that Czech shares several characteristics with Greek. One of them is that Czech also has a grammatical subject within a verb form in terms of verb system. For instance, the Czech sentence "Psal mi." means "He wrote to me," so the verb "psal" includes the pronoun "he" (Mathesius, *Functional Analysis*, 19). However, there are many different elements between Czech and Greek (especially New Testament Greek) in terms of their word-order system, verbal aspect system, etc.

101 Porter and O'Donnell, *Discourse Analysis*, 104.

INTRODUCTION TO MODE REGISTER ANALYSIS

TABLE 2.1    Levels of thematization suggested by Porter and O'Donnell

| Level | Function | Realized through | | Definition |
|---|---|---|---|---|
| **Text & paragraph** | Topic | Semantic shift | Semantic Boundaries | Establishment of a new semantic environment for the discourse |
| | Comment | Semantic continuity | | Support information for the current topic |
| **Clause-complex** | Theme | Change of subject | Participant Involvement | The change of participant as actor of process chain |
| | Rheme | Additional verbal elements | | Additional process information for current actor (extension of process chain) |
| **Clause** | Prime | First group element | Group Order | Who or what the clause is focused upon |
| | Subsequent | Remaining group elements | | Development of the prime |

When humans speak or write, all their sayings and writings are listed sequentially—in chronological order. The resulting speech or text consists of the words that are presented first and then added. This is the fundamental nature of language of speech and writing that is caused by language behavior. When it comes to writing, which is the main concern in this study of the New Testament text, an author writes with a certain message(s) in his/her mind; the sentences cannot be given all at one time but are always presented in a linear form. The important thing is that human language habits tend to present things regarding theme first. The thematic phenomena are accumulated and continued from a clause unit to clause-complex, paragraph, and discourse. Thus, Porter and O'Donnell argue that it is possible to grasp the thematic structure in a text by analyzing the several levels (morpheme, word, clause, clause-complex, paragraph/discourse) through their linguistic model on thematization.[102] This can also be expressed as a sort of hierarchical system in a linearly constructed text.[103] The methodology of thematization suggested by Porter and O'Donnell

---

102    Porter and O'Donnell, *Discourse Analysis*, 105.

103    Porter and O'Donnell, *Discourse Analysis*, 97.

74                                                                                              CHAPTER 2

could be regarded as a significant attempt to overcome the limitations in previous linguists' models in terms of two aspects: (1) systemic enlargement of Halliday's thematic models from clause/cluster of clauses to discourse and (2) remodeling of Halliday's thematic model for the New Testament Greek text by considering the distinctive linguistic features of New Testament Greek. This study, then, attempts to find a thematic structure of each designated text according to Porter and O'Donnell's DA model. The following is a summary of Porter and O'Donnell's thematization DA model, which analyzes the thematic structure by clause, clause-complex, and paragraph(s) unit in turn.

### 5.1.3     Prime and Subsequent

For thematic structure within the clause, Porter and O'Donnell suggest using prime and subsequent in place of theme and rheme.[104] For in Halliday's understanding of theme and rheme, there are tenuous overlapping notions between the clause and clause complex levels.[105] They define prime as *"who or what the clause is focused upon,* realized by the first clausal component in the clause" and subsequent as *"the development of the prime."*[106] Porter and O'Donnell argue that for New Testament Greek, the analysis of clause and clause complex should be separate from English-based analysis, in which the subject usually comes first.[107] Noting that prime can occur without subsequent (Luke 7:40),[108] conjunction and temporal deictic indicators are not included in the prime and subsequent discussion as they are cohesive devices in the context of contextual analysis,[109] and an author often uses prime as a "focus" on the author's concerns.[110] For example, in the clause of ὁ διδάσκαλος λέγει (Matt 26:18d), the prime is ὁ διδάσκαλος, and the subsequent is λέγει.

### 5.1.4     Theme and Rheme

After replacing Halliday's concepts of "theme and rheme" with "prime and subsequent,"[111] Porter and O'Donnell suggest applying the terms of theme and rheme to clause complex units rather than clause units. Although this may seem confusing in the light of traditional usage, they explain the need for this change:

---

104    Porter and O'Donnell, *Discourse Analysis*, 105.
105    Porter and O'Donnell, *Discourse Analysis*, 105.
106    Porter and O'Donnell, *Discourse Analysis*, 105. The italics are Porter and O'Donnell's.
107    Porter and O'Donnell, *Discourse Analysis*, 106.
108    Porter and O'Donnell, *Discourse Analysis*, 107.
109    Porter and O'Donnell, *Discourse Analysis*, 107.
110    Porter and O'Donnell, *Discourse Analysis*, 107.
111    Porter and O'Donnell, *Discourse Analysis*, 105.

INTRODUCTION TO MODE REGISTER ANALYSIS

In place of the terms "given" and "new," we propose to use "theme" and "rheme" for the purpose of identifying thematic elements at the clause-complex level within the paragraph. We realize that this is a potentially confusing choice of terminology, as theme and rheme have a long history of application at the clause level, associated with word order. However, in our analysis the terms seem to fit better at the clause-complex level and not at the clause level realized by clause component position.[112]

Here, the authors focus on the participant(s) at the clause complex level, focusing on the participant-centered questions—who the actor as the subject of the clause complex among its various participants is, and how many clause complexes center on that actor. Based on this, the authors define "theme" as *"the fully grammaticalized participant as the actor in a process chain"* and "rheme" as *"additional process information for the current actor."*[113] When a new participant appears in a text in the form of an explicit subject (e.g., proper noun, pronoun), we can call it a "theme." It can also be called a "thematic actor" in a "thematic unit."[114] Rheme is the remaining part except for theme.

According to James D. Dvorak and Ryder D. Walton, the qualification to be a thematic actor is concerned with the following two elements—the thematic actor must be an explicit subject, meaning that "the actor cannot merely be implied from a verb" and "the thematic participant must be in a primary clause."[115] As an example of theme and rheme, in Mark 14:29, ὁ δὲ Πέτρος ἔφη αὐτῷ· εἰ καὶ πάντες σκανδαλισθήσονται, ἀλλ᾽ οὐκ ἐγώ, the theme is ὁ Πέτρος, and the rheme is ἔφη αὐτῷ· εἰ καὶ πάντες σκανδαλισθήσονται, ἀλλ᾽ οὐκ ἐγώ. Porter and O'Donnell's model notes that there can be multiple clauses and clause complexes containing an actor[116] and that a thematic actor can be located in prime or subsequent. When the thematic actor is located in prime, it is regarded as the most marked actor.[117] In Mark 14:29, for instance, ὁ Πέτρος is the theme and the prime as well in the thematic unit, so it is the most marked actor. This study defines theme and rheme based on Porter and O'Donnell's definition

---

112      Porter and O'Donnell, *Discourse Analysis*, 110. The italics are Porter and O'Donnell's.

113      Porter and O'Donnell, *Discourse Analysis*, 110. The italics are Porter and O'Donnell's. Here, a process chain means "a string of two or more verbal groups with the same actor (subject)."

114      When this study refers to a "thematic unit," it does not mean a unit, which holds one subject, but a unit having a "theme," a new participant/actor in the form of an explicit subject.

115      James D. Dvorak and Ryder D. Walton, "Clause as Message: Theme, Topic, and Information Flow in Mark 2:1–12 and Jude," *BAGL* 3 (2014): 46–47. Cf. Porter and O'Donnell, *Discourse Analysis*, 110–11.

116      Porter and O'Donnell, *Discourse Analysis*, 110.

117      Porter and O'Donnell, *Discourse Analysis*, 110.

76                                                                                          CHAPTER 2

as follows: (1) theme is the actor in an explicit subject in a process chain, and
(2) rheme is the subsequent part after a theme, before the other theme. The
theme rheme analysis will be utilized to find (1) thematic actors, (2) thematic
units, and (3) the marked actor revealed through overlapping position of prime
and theme. While using this methodology, we will attempt to infer the relationship between the entity designated as the most marked actor in each Gospel
and the overall construction of each Gospel.

### 5.1.5    Topic and Comment

Porter and O'Donnell use the terms "topic" and "comment" with regard to
thematization at paragraph and discourse levels. They define "topic" as an
*"establishment of a new semantic environment for the text"* and "comment" as
*"supporting information for the current topic."*[118] With this definition, we may
suppose that they try to show how a text is like a clause.[119]

Before dealing with thematization within a paragraph, it is necessary to
consider what a paragraph is and what the criteria point to paragraph divisions
(especially within a New Testament Greek text). Porter and O'Donnell propose
that there are divisions around discourse markers, which may include tem-
poral/spatial deixis, a switch of participants, key conjunctions, and changes
in lexical cohesion chains.[120] However, the following formal and functional
elements for paragraph demarcation, which Porter suggests, seem to be more
systematic: (1) conjunctions, particles (initial and final), temporal and spatial
references, (2) cohesion and segmentation, (3) participants, full reference,
pronouns, and anaphora, (4) word order and referential distance, (5) topic,
(6) theme, and (7) literary text types.[121]

Porter's criteria reviewed above are optimized for discourse analysis, but
since this study targets a smaller body of text, new modeling for paragraph
division seems necessary. The following will be the elements for paragraph
division: (1) one or more thematic units and thematic participants;[122] (2) tem-
poral/spatial deixis; (3) transition of topic; (4) lexical cohesion.

---

118    Porter and O'Donnell, *Discourse Analysis*, 116. The italics are Porter and O'Donnell's.
119    Cf. M. A. K. Halliday, "Text Semantics and Clause Grammar," in *On Grammar*, ed.
        Jonathan J. Webster (Collected Works of M. A. K. Halliday 1; London: Continuum, 2002),
        227–28. Cf. J. R. Martin and David Rose, *Working with Discourse: Meaning Beyond the
        Clause* (2nd ed.; London: Continuum, 2007), 192.
120    Porter and O'Donnell, *Discourse Analysis*, 117.
121    Stanley E. Porter, "Pericope Markers and the Paragraph," in *The Impact of Unit Delimita-
        tion on Exegesis*, eds. Raymond de Hoop, et al. (Leiden: Brill, 2008), 180–82.
122    This study assumes that to be a paragraph, it should include one or more thematic units
        (and thematic participants) in its *undivided* form.

INTRODUCTION TO MODE REGISTER ANALYSIS

This study utilizes Porter and O'Donnell's thematic approach to analyze the process of thematization, paragraph divisions, and the topic of each paragraph in the Eucharist and its co-texts in Synoptic Gospels.

## 5.2 *Cohesion*

The second part of mode analysis in this study is cohesion. Halliday and Ruqaiya Hasan explain that cohesive relatiónships are "relations between two or more elements in a text that are independent of the structure."[123] Based on this understanding, they define "cohesion" as follows: "The concept of cohesion is a semantic one; it refers to relations of meaning that exist within the text, and that define it as a text."[124] In other words, in order to be called "a text," it has to contain cohesive relationships among the inner elements of the text because cohesion is "the formal links within a text or passage that make it 'hang together' internally and with its immediate co-text."[125] Thus, cohesion reveals how one part of a text is related to another part of the text, and in this regard, we may be able to find the structure of a text via cohesion study. This study attempts a new perspective of cohesion approach along with the general approach of cohesion applied to biblical texts.[126] In other words, we analyze not only the aspect where the cohesiveness of a text is apparent but also the aspect where the degree of cohesiveness of a text tends relatively low, so as to deduce the construction process of each Gospel.

In this study, "cohesiveness" is related to *written texts*. Usually, an author of a text constructs the subsequent part in consideration of the previous one, and thus the text's systematicity can vary depending on the author's role. This study assumes that the degree of cohesiveness varies depending on how systematically the author organizes the text. In general, a text formed by one author can be regarded as having basic cohesiveness, but its degree could vary. For example, it can be considered that the degree of cohesiveness of a text is increased when an author effectively places the position of a character in a

---

123  M. A. K. Halliday and Ruqaiya Hasan, *Cohesion in English* (London: Routledge, 1976), vii.

124  Halliday and Hasan, *Cohesion*, 4.

125  Cynthia L. Westfall, "The Relationship Between the Resurrection, the Proclamation to the Spirits in Prison and Baptismal Regeneration: 1 Peter 3.19–22," in *Resurrection*, eds. Stanley E. Porter, et al., 106–35 (JSNTSup 186; Sheffield: Sheffield Academic, 1999), 107. Her original source are as follows: Halliday and Hasan, *Cohesion*, 4–5; Halliday and Hasan, *Language, Context and Text*, 48.

126  E.g., Land, *2 Corinthians*; Jeffrey T. Reed, *A Discourse Analysis of Philippians: Method and Rhetoric in the Debate over Literary Integrity* (JSNTSup 136; Sheffield: Sheffield Academic, 1997).

78                                                                                           CHAPTER 2

paragraph in the form of a proper noun in consideration of the previous part and the overall organization.

According to Halliday and Hasan, there are five types of "grammatical cohesive devices"[127] which create cohesive ties: (1) reference, (2) substitution, (3) ellipsis, (4) conjunction, and (5) lexical cohesion.[128] Porter and O'Donnell, however, point out that in Hellenistic Greek, "*reference* is the fundamental kind of cohesive relation, and *substitution* and *ellipsis* are specific examples of reference."[129] Although these three concepts are linked, each will be described separately.

### 5.2.1      Reference

First, reference is a type of linguistic element to "make reference to something else for their interpretation."[130] Halliday explains this concept as follows: "In the case of reference, the information to be retrieved is the referential meaning, the identity of the particular thing or class of things that is being referred to; and the cohesion lies in the continuity of reference, whereby the same thing enters into the discourse a second time."[131] In many cases, reference is made through pronouns; however, the New Testament Greek system contains a pronoun as a subject in a verb; thus, some features need to be applied differently from the English system. According to Halliday and Hassan, there are three types of reference: personal reference ("reference by means of function in the speech situation, through the category of PERSON"), demonstrative reference ("reference by means of location, on a scale of PROXIMITY"), and comparative reference ("indirect reference by means of IDENTITY of SIMILARITY").[132] The examples in Hellenistic Greek of these are as follows: 1. personal reference (e.g., αὐτός, ὁ), 2. demonstrative reference (e.g., τοῦτο, ὧδε, νῦν), and 3. comparative reference (e.g., μείζων, μικρότερον).[133] This study will focus on the personal references in the designated texts by following Porter and O'Donnell's threefold concept of reference: exophoric, anaphoric, and cataphoric reference.[134]

---

127   Porter and O'Donnell, *Discourse Analysis*, 198.
128   Halliday and Hasan, *Cohesion*, 4. As a slight expended expression, Porter says cohesion "is concerned with such nonstructural semantic features as reference, substitution and ellipsis, conjunction and lexical cohesion such as reiteration and collocation." See Porter, "Dialect and Register," 201.
129   Porter and O'Donnell, *Discourse Analysis*, 202.
130   Halliday and Hasan, *Cohesion*, 31.
131   Halliday and Hasan, *Cohesion*, 31.
132   Halliday and Hasan, *Cohesion*, 37.
133   Yoon, *Galatians*, 114.
134   Porter and O'Donnell, *Discourse Analysis*, 202. Here, Porter and O'Donnell assert that "Reference is simply when one linguistic item requires reference to another ... for its interpretation."

INTRODUCTION TO MODE REGISTER ANALYSIS

Distinguishing the levels of references (grammaticalized reference, reduced reference, and implied reference) is also helpful in recognizing the degrees of "cohesiveness in referential ties."[135] For instance, if a reduced reference (pronoun) appears where it seems natural to include a grammaticalized reference, it can be viewed as a factor that lowers the degree of cohesiveness of a text. This study will assess the degree of cohesiveness of the designated texts by examining the "participant-referent chains."[136]

### 5.2.2 Substitution

Second, substitution is "the replacement of one item by another"[137] as an "endophoric" cohesive device.[138] This concept is similar to "reference." According to Halliday and Hasan, however, substitution is related to the lexicogrammatical level as a relation between linguistic items, whereas reference is a concept at the semantic level as a relation between meaning.[139] In the case of reference, we have to go back to the previous context to find a semantic object. In the case of substitution, however, we do not need this process because readers can obtain newly added information through substitution, even though it refers to a previous object.[140] There are three types of substitution: nominal, verbal, and clausal substitution; these are functions in a text as a noun, a verb, and a clause, respectively.[141]

### 5.2.3 Ellipsis

Third, an ellipsis is "the omission of an item."[142] This concept is linked to substitution, as it relates to what was previously within a text.[143] However, an ellipsis relates to the former as subtracting rather than adding, so it can be said as "a form of substitution where one item is replaced with nothing."[144] It could be related to a kind of presupposition[145] because sometimes the author and

---

135  Porter and O'Donnell, *Discourse Analysis*, 208–9.
136  Porter and O'Donnell, *Discourse Analysis*, 209–10. The form of participant-referent chain is similar to that of Westfall's concept of "identity chain" (Westfall, *Hebrews*, 50–52). Here, Westfall reveals that the study of identity chain can be used to construct "sections" within a text. In this respect, identity chains can be also used as a useful basis to show the cohesion of one section/unit.
137  Halliday and Hasan, *Cohesion*, 88.
138  Porter and O'Donnell, *Discourse Analysis*, 205.
139  Halliday and Hasan, *Cohesion*, 89.
140  Porter and O'Donnell, *Discourse Analysis*, 205.
141  Halliday and Hasan, *Cohesion*, 90.
142  Halliday and Hasan, *Cohesion*, 88.
143  Halliday and Hasan, *Cohesion*, 144.
144  Porter and O'Donnell, *Discourse Analysis*, 206.
145  Halliday and Hasan, *Cohesion*, 144.

80                                                                                          CHAPTER 2

reader already know about what has already been said or something needs to be conveyed by not saying it. Ellipsis can be also used to avoid repeating what has been said previously, but sometimes as a device to keep semantic possibilities open by omitting certain information. Ellipsis has three following layers: (1) nominal, (2) verbal, and (3) clausal.[146]

### 5.2.4    Conjunction

Fourth, conjunction elements "express certain meanings that presuppose other components' presence in the discourse."[147] Halliday and Hasan say in this regard: "Conjunctive elements are cohesive not in themselves but indirectly, by virtue of their specific meanings; they are not primarily devices for reaching out into the preceding (or following) text, but they express certain meanings which presuppose the presence of other components in the discourse."[148] Halliday and Hasan classify conjunctive relations into four types: additive, adversative, causal, and temporal.[149] Conjunction basically has the function of connecting grammatical units such as phrases or clauses, and plays a fundamental role in securing cohesion of a text.[150] According to Porter, the New Testament Greek conjunctions, as a part of particles, can be extended and classified according to the semantic levels as follows: adversative, causal, comparative, conditional, connective, consecutive, emphatic, explanatory, inferential, and temporal.[151]

Among the conjunctions in the New Testament Greek texts, the designated texts include the following: ἀλλά (but/indeed), γάρ (for/therefore), δέ (but/and/indeed ...), καί (and/so/if ...),[152] ἐάν (if), εἰ (if), ἕως (until), πρίν

---

146    Porter and O'Donnell, *Discourse Analysis*, 206.
147    Halliday and Hasan, *Cohesion*, 227.
148    Halliday and Hasan, *Cohesion*, 226.
149    Halliday and Hasan, *Cohesion*, 242–43.
150    Porter, *Idioms*, 204; David Holton et al., *Greek: An Essential Grammar* (2nd ed.; New York: Routledge, 2016), 193–95.
151    Porter, *Idioms*, 205. Cf. Denniston, *Greek Particles*; F. Blass and A. Debrunner, *A Greek Grammar of the New Testament and Other Early Christian Literature* (Trans. Robert W. Funk; Chicago: University of Chicago Press, 1961), 225.
152    It is difficult to distinguish all the subtle differences between the meanings of δέ and καί. However, it can be said that καί leans to continuity, whereas δέ leans to adversative even if it includes continuity. See David L. Mathewson and Elodie B. Emig, *Intermediate Greek Grammar: Syntax for Students of the New Testament* (Grand Rapids: Baker Academic, 2016), 262–63. In that sense, Porter's naming of καί as a connective, adversative, or emphatic conjunction and δέ as an adversative, connective, or emphatic conjunction is thought to be a cautious expression. See Porter, *Idioms*, 208, 211.

# INTRODUCTION TO MODE REGISTER ANALYSIS

(before),[153] ἵνα (in order to), καθώς (like), μέν (indeed/on the one hand), ὅταν (when), ὅτε (when), ὅτι (that), ὅπου (where), πλήν (but), τότε (then/at that time), ὡς (so/as).[154] There are also some cases of synthetic forms: κἀγώ, (Matt 26:15), κἄν (Matt 26:35; καί [*and, also*] and ἐάν [*if*]).

These conjunctions can be divided into relatively broad (having three or more meanings) or narrow (two or fewer meanings) meaning potentials: (1) conjunctions with broad meaning potential: καί, δέ; (2) conjunctions with narrow meaning potential: ἀλλά, γάρ, ἐάν, εἰ, ἕως, πρίν, ἵνα, καθώς, μέν, ὅταν, ὅτε, ὅτι, ὅπου, πλήν, τότε, ὡς. By analyzing the conjunctions used in a text, there may be a possibility of inferring the linguistic tendency of the person who constructed the text or the construction process of the text.

One more thing we need to think of is asyndeton, which means the vacancy of conjunction.[155] The analysis of asyndeton in the designated texts is included in the conjunction analysis since "it represents an option that alternates with other conjunctive choices."[156]

---

153    It is used in Mark 14:30 with ἤ and has the meaning of "before." Since ἤ is used in coordination with πρίν, having no separate meaning, it is excluded from the list.

154    The meanings of each conjunction are constructed by referring to Porter, *Idioms*, 205–17. The conceptual division of conjunctions is modified on the basis of Stephanie L. Black's monograph: Stephanie L. Black, *Sentence Conjunctions in the Gospel of Matthew: καί, δέ, τότε, γάρ, οὖν and Asyndeton in Narrative Discourse* (JSNTSup 216; Sheffield: Sheffield Academic, 2002). Each conjunction has a meaning potential, and the meaning will be applied according to the context of each designated text. For a more detailed categorization of conjunctions in the New Testament texts, see Richard A. Young, *Intermediate New Testament Greek: A Linguistic and Exegetical Approach* (Nashville: Broadman & Homan, 1994), 180–92. For a detailed analysis of particles, including conjunctions, see A. T. Robertson, *A Grammar of the Greek New Testament in the Light of Historical Research* (4th ed.; Nashville: Broadman, 1923), 1142–93. For a more classical classification and interpretation of conjunctions, see G. B. Winer, *A Treatise on the Grammar of New Testament Greek, Regarded as a Sure Basis for New Testament Exegesis* (trans. W. F. Moulton; 3rd ed.; Edinburgh: T&T Clark, 1882), 541–78.

155    A. T. Robertson and W. H. Davis, *A New Short Grammar of the Greek Testament: For Students Familiar with the Elements of Greek* (10th ed.; Grand Rapids: Baker, 1977), 315; Stephen H. Levinsohn, *Discourse Features of New Testament Greek: A Coursebook on the Information Structure of New Testament Greek* (2nd ed.; Dallas: SIL International, 2000), 69; Black, *Conjunctions*, 18; cf. Steven E. Runge, *Discourse Grammar of the Greek New Testament: A Practical Introduction for Teaching and Exegesis* (Peabody: Hendrickson, 2010), 20. Here, Steven E. Runge defines asyndeton as "the linking of clauses or clause components without the use of a conjunction." He uses the symbol ∅ to reveal asyndeton (Runge, *Discourse Grammar*, 20), but originally this symbol was used in Levinsohn, *Discourse Features*, 70; thus, Runge should mark that this symbol is from Stephen H. Levinsohn. This study will share this symbol for analysis.

156    Black, *Conjunctions*, 18.

82                                                                                                                       CHAPTER 2

This study assesses each conjunction's appropriateness in terms of its usage in each context.[157] Conjunction analysis will be done based on the divided table of the narrative and direct speech/quotation[158] parts since such a scheme seems helpful in analyzing the conjunctions and asyndeton of the designated text.

### 5.2.5    Lexical Cohesion

Fifth, lexical cohesion makes cohesive effects by selecting vocabulary, unlike the previous grammatical elements (reference, substitution, ellipsis, and conjunction).[159] Halliday and Hasan suggest two types of lexical cohesion: reiteration and collocation.[160] They set sub-sections of reiteration as follows: repetition, synonym, superordinate, and general words.[161] Yoon asserts that only repetition and synonym are "actually characteristic of reiteration," and their examples can be found in Matthew 5:3–6 (the repeated part of μακάριοι [blessed]) and 1 John 1:9 (usage of ἀδικίας [sins] as a synonym of ἁμαρτίας [unrighteousness]).[162] This study basically follows Yoon's view but deals with the case of superordinate when it occurs. Collocation usually means two or more words that often co-occur in similar situations. Halliday and Hasan state that "[i]n general, any two lexical items having similar patterns of collocation— that is, tending to appear in similar contexts—will generate a cohesive force if they occur in adjacent sentences."[163] A meaningful example can be found in Romans, that is, the collocational usage of two Greek words, δίκαιος and θεοῦ (almost 16× in Romans).[164]

This study examines the cohesiveness of the designated texts by analyzing "semantic-lexical ties."[165] For this, we utilize J. P. Louw and E. A. Nida's *Greek-English Lexicon of the New Testament Based on Semantic Domains*[166] to

---

157    There might be doubts about whether it is appropriate to evaluate the form of a text with a framework and whether such a way is in line with the principle of SFL; however, this study takes an approach to less common cases, centering on more general usage.

158    "Direct speech/quotation" will be expressed as "direct speech" in short throughout this study.

159    Halliday and Hasan, *Cohesion*, 274.

160    Halliday and Hasan, *Cohesion*, 288.

161    Halliday and Hasan, *Cohesion*, 288.

162    Yoon, *Galatians*, 117.

163    Halliday and Hasan, *Cohesion*, 286.

164    Yoon, *Galatians*, 117.

165    This study defines "semantic-lexical tie" as the case where lexemes in the semantic domain have a semantic connection *within* a paragraph.

166    Regarding the usefulness of this lexicon in terms of the concept of cohesion and semantic domain, see Cynthia L. Westfall, "Blessed Be the Ties that Bind: Semantic Domains and

INTRODUCTION TO MODE REGISTER ANALYSIS

group the lexemes in each paragraph of the texts by their semantic domains. Next, by analyzing the ratio of the lexemes[167] that can be formed into semantic-lexical ties per the number of content lexemes (excluding functional words [pronouns, prepositions, articles, conjunctions, etc.], proper nouns,[168] and verbs in the narrative speech margin[169]), this study attempts to determine the lexical cohesion of each paragraph. This study also analyzes the semantic-lexical chain of the whole designated texts[170] by observing the conceptual flow of core lexemes to identify their cohesiveness.

Therefore, the cohesion analysis of this study will deal with the usages of cohesive elements in the designated texts to observe their degrees of cohesiveness.

### 5.3 Orality and Textuality

The third part of mode analysis in this study is orality and textuality. A linguistic formula regarding oral and written aspects of a text needs to be included in mode analysis. The key is to work out a convincing methodology that leads us *from texts to tradition*. In other words, this section aims to provide a convincing methodology for approaching the tradition that the texts may contain. This section attempts to model an analysis tool for measuring the orality and textuality of a text by which the tradition (particularly oral tradition) could be discerned from the text.

---

Cohesive Chains in Hebrews 1.1–2.4 and 12.5–8," *JGRChJ* 6 (2009): 199–208. However, it also has limitations. For example, it does not "utilize the concept of collocation in its domain classifications" (Porter and O'Donnell, *Discourse Analysis*, 217). Considering this, in the process of analysis, lexemes that are not classified into the same semantic domain but can be connected will be marked separately.

167    The ratio regarding semantic-lexical ties aims to show how strong the cohesiveness is in a target paragraph. Though there is no objective standard to evaluate it, near to or over 50% may well represent strong cohesiveness of the paragraph.

168    Proper nouns are excluded from this analysis since, in the case of proper nouns, cohesiveness is grasped not by semantic-lexical ties but in relation to other references (e.g., personal proper noun, implied subject in verbs). However, the category of content lexemes in orality and textuality analysis below includes proper nouns.

169    The verbs which belong to the narrative speech margins in this study are λέγω and φημί. It is difficult to find specific semantic-lexical ties in each paragraph by the verbs in the narrative speech margins since they mainly function as a link between the narratives and the direct speeches. Thus, we will not include them in content lexemes here (λέγω and φημί will be dealt with when they appear other than this way), but the category of content lexemes in orality and textuality analysis includes them.

170    The term "semantic-lexical chain" means a chain formed by lexemes that can be semantically connected in the text. This includes the expansion or contraction of meaning in the process of semantic flow.

84                                                                                    CHAPTER 2

5.3.1        Studies of Orality and Textuality
The study of oral and written language has a considerably long history. One
who initiated this discussion linguistically is probably Ferdinand de Saussure
(1857–1913). He placed the fundamental properties of oral language as the basis
of his linguistic system, and the following words illustrate his emphasis.

> A language and its written form constitute two separate systems of signs.
> The sole reason for the existence of the latter is to represent the former.
> The object of study in linguistics is not a combination of the written word
> and the spoken word. The spoken word alone constitutes that object. But
> the written word is so intimately connected with the spoken word it rep-
> resents that it manages to usurp the principal role. As much or even more
> importance is given to this representation of the vocal sign as to the vocal
> sign itself. It is rather as if people believed that in order to find out what
> a person looks like it is better to study his photograph than his face.[171]

Saussure firmly reveals his emphasis on oral language by asserting that the
subject of linguistics is not written language but oral language. Even though he
reveals how closely written language is related to oral language, for Saussure,
all languages are derived from oral language to written language; thus, oral language is the main analysis object of linguistics.

After that, Walter J. Ong laid the linguistic foundation for the textual features of orality and literacy. His seminal work, *Orality and Literacy*, delves into
the conceptual framework and intricate relationship between orality and literacy, with a particular emphasis on their divergent characteristics.[172] According
to Ong, the oral realm represents an ancient phenomenon deeply intertwined
with human language and culture, where memory serves as the bedrock of
societal foundations.[173] In contrast, the advent of literacy signifies a transfor-
mative process that culminated in the transcription of oral traditions into written texts, transcending reliance on memory and engendering a novel cognitive
mode.[174] In this regard, Ong underscores the profound influence of oral and
written mediums in shaping the human mind.[175]

---

171   Ferdinand de Saussure, *Course in General Linguistics* (trans. Roy Harris; London: Blooms-
      bury, 1983); Schleiermacher, *Gospel of St. Luke*; Schmidt, *Place of the Gospels*, 28.
172   Walter J. Ong, *Orality and Literacy: The Technologizing of the Word* (3rd ed.; London:
      Routledge, 2012), 13.
173   Ong, *Orality and Literacy*, 31–76.
174   Ong, *Orality and Literacy*, 115–35.
175   Ong, *Orality and Literacy*, 174–76.

INTRODUCTION TO MODE REGISTER ANALYSIS

Halliday then makes a distinctive contribution in the area of spoken and written language. His noteworthy work, *Spoken and Written Language*, elucidates the fundamental interconnectedness of these two linguistic dimensions within specific social contexts, simultaneously illuminating the avenues for discerning their disparities.[176] Halliday's contribution extends further through the provision of a linguistic framework, encompassing metrics like lexical density and grammatical intricacy, to gauge the degrees of orality and textuality within a given textual corpus.[177]

Building upon Halliday's theoretical underpinnings, Porter endeavors to investigate orality and textuality within the Greek NT. Porter acknowledges the inherent symbiosis between spoken and written language, as postulated by Halliday, with particular emphasis on the pivotal role of written texts as the foundation of textuality within the New Testament context.[178] Despite inherent limitations, Porter undertakes a modest endeavor to explore the manifestations of orality and textuality within various forms of New Testament writings, including the Gospels, Acts, and Epistles, by conscientiously considering their linguistic attributes in Greek and leveraging Halliday's linguistic concepts.[179]

Ji Hoe Kim employs Halliday and Porter's theoretical frameworks to yield meaningful insights regarding orality and textuality in Gospel studies. Kim's methodology and analysis overall draw upon Porter's linguistic framework, employing techniques proposed by Porter based on Halliday's work, such as lexical density and grammatical intricacy.[180] Nevertheless, Kim's research assumes significance as a pioneering effort that applies Porter's methodology, particularly in the comparative examination of parallel passages in the Gospels.

5.3.2    Continuity and Discontinuity of Oral and Written Language

Then, fundamentally, we can ask a question in terms of orality and textuality: can we distinguish the oral and written modes in a text? In order to answer this question, we need to think about the essence of language in terms of its medium. In human society, oral language had been around for a long time before writing.[181] Through verbal communication, people are able to communicate

---

176    M. A. K. Halliday, *Spoken and Written Language* (2nd ed.; Oxford: Oxford University Press, 1989), xv–xvi.

177    Halliday, *Spoken and Written Language*, 61–91.

178    Stanley E. Porter, "Orality and Textuality and Implications for Description of the Greek New Testament from a Systemic Function Linguistics Perspective" (Forthcoming), 2.

179    Porter, "Orality and Textuality," 4–14.

180    Ji Hoe Kim, "A Hallidayan Approach to Orality and Textuality and Some Implications for Synoptic Gospel Studies," *BAGL* 8 (2019): 122–26.

181    Ong, *Orality and Literacy*, 82–83.

and share their thoughts. At some point, however, after the necessity of writing came into existence, people devised a character according to the pitch of the speech and created written text systems. In the oral language medium, words are spoken by mouth and heard by ear, but written language medium is constructed by hands and read by eyes. Thus, we may say there is a fundamental difference in the way of creation and communication between the two systems. However, the oral language medium may have an influence on the creation of the written medium because the basic language system, including grammar and syntax, is shared in the two mediums. In this respect, written language could be regarded as an extension of verbal language. Thus, continuity and discontinuity (similarities and differences) may coexist between oral and written languages, and in fact, it does not seem easy to classify them. With this difficulty in mind, Kim's model for uncovering oral aspects in a text will be introduced.[182] Relying on Halliday's functional perspective, Kim describes the relationship between spoken and written language as follows.

> So then, what is the most appropriate way to describe the relationship between spoken and written language? In the history of linguistics, some have treated the two as totally distinct media whereas others have seen them as identical. From a functional point of view, however, they serve different purposes in different contexts, even though they do similar things (such as describing the outer world, enacting social interactions, and the like). Since they perform similar functions in different ways, one variety is never totally distinct from the other. Moreover, their coexistence is evidence for their different roles. In the end, it is best to place spoken and written language on a continuum.[183]

Thus, based on Kim's observation, we try to measure the degree of orality in the designated texts, keeping in mind the intimate relationship between oral and written language.

### 5.3.3 Lexical Density and Grammatical Intricacy

Before entering the two main terms, "lexical density" and "grammatical intricacy," we need to understand the two basic concepts, "lexical" and "grammatical." The following explanation of Halliday seems useful for understanding the concepts.

---

182   Ji Hoe Kim's methodological model relies heavily on Porter.
183   Kim, "Orality and Textuality," 120.

INTRODUCTION TO MODE REGISTER ANALYSIS

Lexical items are often called 'content words.' Technically, they are ITEMS (i.e., constituents of variable length) rather than words in the usual sense, because they may consist of more than one word: for example, *stand up*, *take over*, *call of*, and other phrasal verbs all function as single lexical items. They are LEXICAL because they function in lexical sets not grammatical systems: that is to say, they enter into open not closed contrasts.

A grammatical item enters into a closed system. For example, the personal pronoun *him* contrasts on one dimension with *he, his*; on another dimension with *me, you, her, it, us, them, one*; but that is all. There are no more items in these classes and we cannot add any. With a lexical item, however, we cannot close off its class membership; it enters into an open set, which is indefinitely extendable.[184]

According to Halliday, written language tends to have a high lexical density,[185] and oral language is characterized by a high grammatical intricacy.[186] Based on these ideas, Porter made his model in an SFL framework for the orality or textuality of the New Testament Greek text. According to him, "All ancient texts from the ancient world—even those purporting to represent speech, including the documentary papyri as well—are transcriptions that have been transformed into the written medium and taken on characteristics of writing, even if some of the characteristics of spoken language are retained."[187]

In order to calculate lexical density and grammatical intricacy, the following elements need to be considered: (1) lexical density: non-embedded clauses, content words, grammatical words; (2) grammatical intricacy: non-embedded clauses, clause complex.[188] Lexical density is calculated by the content words

---

184   Halliday, *Spoken and Written Language*, 63.
185   According to Halliday, "written language displays a much higher ratio of lexical items to total running words." See Halliday, *Spoken and Written Language*, 61.
186   Halliday, *Spoken and Written Language*, 76–79.
187   Porter, "Orality and Textuality," 7.
188   Porter, "Orality and Textuality," 10. Here, it seems necessary to define "clause" and "clause complex." Clause is usually related to the presence of "a subject and predicate" (Young, *Greek*, 179); however, unlike English, New Testament Greek contains subjects in the verbs, so even if a separate subject does not appear, if a verb appears in the form of an imperative, interrogative, or indicative, it should be regarded as a single clause. Also, in this study, clause is considered as a unit having a verb part such as participle and infinitive. See, Stanley E. Porter, et al., *Fundamentals of New Testament Greek* (Grand Rapids: Eerdmans, 2010), 374–75. Clause complex is when two or more clauses are included in a sentence ending in a period. There are two cases: (1) combination of two or more main clauses; (2) composition of a main clause and dependant/embedded clause(s). See Porter, et al., *New Testament Greek*, 374–76; John Lyons, *Introduction to Theoretical Linguistics* (Cambridge: Cambridge University Press, 1968), 178; Halliday, *Functional Grammar*, 192–93.

per non-embedded clause; grammatical intricacy is calculated by the non-embedded clauses per clause complex.[189] Particularly, here we need to focus on the two terms: lexical items and grammatical items. For Halliday, lexical items are a sort of content words, and grammatical items are function words. He also explains these words based on the two visual concepts: open and closed. Grammatical items are considered as "those that function in closed systems in the language: in English, determiners, pronouns, most prepositions, conjunctions, some classes of adverb, and finite verbs."[190] In contrast, lexical items are regarded as "lexical" because "they function in lexical sets, not grammatical systems: that is to say, they enter into open not closed contrasts."[191] This study generally follows Halliday's definitions of these concepts, but it is also necessary to set some criteria regarding the orality and textuality of each text. In other words, for this analysis, we need to understand the definitions of the content/lexical item and the grammatical item of Halliday, and when applying the linguistic model of Halliday to the ancient Koine Greek Gospel texts, we should think carefully about the parts that need to be changed or modified. Here are some examples: (1) verbs of εἰμί are to be entered as a grammatical item; (2) the infinitive verb form seems better to be put in the lexical item because it carries specific content(s).

## 5.4 Verbal Aspect[192]

In his doctoral volume, *Verbal Aspect in the Greek of the New Testament*, Porter attempts a more appropriate grammatical model regarding verbal aspect than those offered in previous Greek verbal interpretations.[193] In his monographs, Porter contends that a tense-form of a Greek verb does not indicate *temporal*

---

189 Porter, "Orality and Textuality," 10. Halliday asserts that the range of oral language's lexical density is 1–2 and that of written language's lexical density is 3–6. See Halliday, *Spoken and Written Language*, 80. This study follows these criteria.

190 Halliday, *Spoken and Written Language*, 61.

191 Halliday, *Spoken and Written Language*, 63

192 Some of this section is taken verbatim from my article, Hojoon J. Ahn, "A Textual-Critical Study of Luke and Verbal Aspect," *BAGL* 11 (2022-23): 45–47.

193 This monograph was a revolutionary book because, before Porter's assertion, most scholars believed that Greek's verbal tense-form should be interpreted as tense itself. However, in this volume, Porter argues that their understanding of verbal tense-form has a lot of problems because there are so many examples that do not align with what might be supposed to be their grammatical frame. They have tried to explain these things as exceptions; however, Porter thinks that we should not regard these as exceptions but rather make a new paradigm (aspect-centered form) for understanding the Greek verbal system. These words show us his major assertion: "the category of synthetic verbal aspect—a morphologically-based semantic category which grammaticalizes the author/speaker's reasoned subjective choice of conception of a process—provides a suggestive and workable linguistic model for explaining the range of uses of the tense forms in Greek" (*Verbal*

INTRODUCTION TO MODE REGISTER ANALYSIS 89

TABLE 2.2    Rearrangement of Porter's three verbal aspects

| Aspect type | Tense-form | The language user conceives of the action as ... |
| --- | --- | --- |
| Perfective | Aorist | a complete and undifferentiated process |
| Imperfective | Present/Imperfect | being in progress |
| Stative | Perfect/Pluperfect | reflecting a given (often complex) state of affairs |

meaning, but *aspectual* meaning (perfective aspect, imperfective aspect, and stative aspect); and a selection of a particular tense-form by a New Testament author presents a perspective on an action.[194] Three verbal aspects linked to three major tense-forms are shown in Table 2.2.[195]

Porter elucidates three verbal aspects according to the extent of their markedness: stative aspect is most weighted, the next is imperfective aspect, and the least weighted is perfective aspect.[196] This verbal aspectual framework seems useful to examine the Bible, "to see how the choice of verbal aspect is used by the author to shape the discourse and indicate a number of important features of the text."[197] In this sense, we can say that some aspectual choices contain greater prominence/markedness than others.[198] Due to such usefulness, Porter's verbal aspect theory has since been used effectively for studying the Gospels.[199] Verbal

---

*Aspect*, xi). His results were reflected in his revised grammar book, *Idioms of the Greek New Testament*.

194    Porter, *Verbal Aspect*, 79–108. According to Porter, tense is perceived not by the tense form itself, but by the temporal context studies through deictic indicators and temporal reference analyses. See *Verbal Aspect*, 87–107.

195    Porter, *Idioms*, 21–22.

196    Porter, *Idioms*, 22.

197    Stanley E. Porter, "Verbal Aspect and Discourse Function in Mark 16:1–8: Three Significant Instances," in *Studies in the Greek Bible: Essays in Honor of Francis T. Gignac*, eds. Jeremy Corley and Vincent Skemp (Washington, DC: Catholic Biblical Association of America, 2008), 127.

198    Stanley E. Porter, "Prominence: An Overview," in *The Linguist as Pedagogue: Trends in the Teaching and Linguistic Analysis of the Greek New Testament*, eds. Stanley E. Porter and Matthew B. O'Donnell (NTM 11; Sheffield: Sheffield Phoenix, 2009), 58–59; Cynthia L. Westfall, "A Method for the Analysis of Prominence in Hellenistic Greek," in *The Linguist as Pedagogue: Trends in the Teaching and Linguistic Analysis of the Greek New Testament*, eds. Stanley E. Porter and Matthew B. O'Donnell (NTM 11; Sheffield: Sheffield Phoenix, 2009), 79–80.

199    For example, unlike previous attempts based on methodologies such as form, source, and redaction criticism, Wally V. Cirafesi tries to solve the Synoptic Problem through a

90                                                                    CHAPTER 2

aspect analysis is related to transitivity since it reveals the type of process,[200] thus it can be included in the field analysis. However, this study includes it in the mode analysis for recognizing the prominence of text.

Each designated text will be translated according to verbal aspects, and the following is its criteria: (1) the stative aspect is marked in bold, the imperfective aspect is italic, and there is no specific mark for perfective aspect; (2) each verb will be basically translated as present tense, unless it is specifically marked as future tense or past tense by contextual/deictic information. The translations of the designated texts are shown in Appendix 9, 10, and 11.

## 6      Procedure

With the preceding methodological scheme in mind, this section shows a specific procedure for a comparative mode RA of the Eucharist and its co-texts in the Synoptic Gospels. The procedure for analysis is twofold: (1) mode analysis of each designated text; and (2) comparative mode analysis between the designated texts.

First, mode analysis attempts a textual analysis of the designated passages in terms of each text's thematic structure, cohesion, orality, and textuality, along with verbal aspect. Through the analysis of thematization, the paragraph division and the topic of each paragraph will be revealed. Through the cohesion analysis, each designated text's and its paragraphs' degree of cohesiveness will be observed. Orality and textuality analysis examines each text's lexical density and grammatical intricacy to recognize its degree of orality. Verbal aspect theory is utilized to find prominence of each designated text. Based on the analytic results, we will find implications regarding the construction process of each designated text. This procedure will be applied to each designated text of the Synoptic Gospels in the following chapters 3, 4, and 5.

Second, the comparison and assessment section compares the analytic results. To be specific, this section looks at the similarities and differences between the designated texts in terms of their linguistic features. Through this procedure, we attempt to find a plausible construction process of the Synoptic Gospels. It will be done in chapter 6.

---

linguistic methodology. In the case of the temple cleansing episode (Matt 21:13 // Mark 11:17 // Luke 19:46), Cirafesi analyzes three different verbal tense forms (present/perfect/aorist) of ποιέω by using Porter's verbal aspect theory in the light of SFL. See Wally V. Cirafesi, *Verbal Aspect in Synoptic Parallels: On the Method and Meaning of Divergent Tense-Form Usage in the Synoptic Passion Narratives* (LBS 7; Leiden: Brill, 2013), 89–101.

200    Yoon, *Galatians*, 93–94.

CHAPTER 3

# Mode Register Analysis of Matthew 26:14–35

Chapters 3, 4, and 5 examine the four core elements of the mode RA model based on SFL in each designated text: (1) thematization; (2) cohesion; (3) orality & textuality, and (4) verbal aspect.

## 1 Thematization

### 1.1 *Prime and Subsequent*

The prime-subsequent analysis of Matthew 26:14–35 is given in Appendix 1, and among the findings of this process, Table 3.1 reveals various examples in 26:14–35.

TABLE 3.1    Prime-subsequent examples in Matt 26:14–35

| Verse | Prime | Subsequent |
|---|---|---|
| 26:14–15a | Τότε | πορευθεὶς εἷς τῶν δώδεκα, ὁ λεγόμενος Ἰούδας Ἰσκαριώτης, πρὸς τοὺς ἀρχιερεῖς εἶπεν· |
| 26:15b | τί | θέλετέ μοι δοῦναι, |
| 26:16a | (καὶ) ἀπὸ τότε | ἐζήτει εὐκαιρίαν |
| 26:18a | ὁ (δὲ) | εἶπεν· |
| 26:18b | ὑπάγετε | εἰς τὴν πόλιν πρὸς τὸν δεῖνα |
| 26:18d | ὁ διδάσκαλος | λέγει· |
| 26:19b | (ὡς) συνέταξεν | αὐτοῖς ὁ Ἰησοῦς |
| 26:21a | (καὶ) ἐσθιόντων | αὐτῶν |
| 26:21b | εἶπεν· | |
| 26:22b | μήτι | ἐγώ εἰμι, κύριε; |
| 26:23a | ὁ (δὲ) | ἀποκριθεὶς εἶπεν· |
| 26:24c | οὐαὶ (δὲ) | τῷ ἀνθρώπῳ ἐκείνῳ δι᾽ οὗ ὁ υἱὸς τοῦ ἀνθρώπου παραδίδοται· |
| 26:24d | καλὸν | ἦν αὐτῷ |
| 26:24e | (εἰ) οὐκ | ἐγεννήθη ὁ ἄνθρωπος ἐκεῖνος. |

© HOJOON J. AHN, 2024 | DOI:10.1163/9789004696372_005

92                                                                                                        CHAPTER 3

Among the sixty-six clauses in Matthew 26:14–35, the lexemes placed in prime are classified by type as follows: (1) adverb (26:14–15a), (2) subject (pronoun; 26:15b), (3) prepositional phrase (26:16a), (4) subject (definite article; 26:18a, 23a), (5) verb (implied subject existence; 26:18b), (6) subject (noun; 26:18d), (7) verb (separate subject existence; 26:19b), (8) participle as an adverb (26:21a), (9) verb only (without subsequent; 26:21b), (10) interrogative particle (26:22b), (11) particle of interjection (26:24c), (12) adjective (26:24d), and (13) negation (26:24e). From this analysis, we can recognize the flexibility of the Greek language in terms of the position of each lexeme, and each prime shows what the clause focuses on. For instance, in the case of 6, a verb is located in prime despite a separate subject; the clause was probably constructed in this way to focus on the verbal process, not the actor.[1] In the case of 4, however, the subject Jesus is located in prime and, in that case, the subject is highly focused on. As mentioned in the methodology, such aspects of prime and subsequent are closely related to the theme and rheme analysis.

## 1.2    *Theme and Rheme*

A theme and rheme analysis of Matthew 26:14–35 in light of the principles suggested by Porter and O'Donnell, along with Dvorak and Walton, is found in Appendix 5. There are twelve thematic units: (1) 26:14–15a, (2) 26:15b–16, (3) 26:17, (4) 26:18, (5) 26:19, (6) 26:20–24, (7) 26:25, (8) 26:26–30, (9) 26:31–33, (10) 26:34, (11) 26:35a, (12) 26:35b. The thematic actors, which are revealed by the theme and rheme analyses, are as follows: (1) κἀγὼ (1×; 26:15a [26:14; εἷς τῶν δώδεκα, ὁ λεγόμενος Ἰούδας Ἰσκαριώτης]), (2) οἱ (1×; 26:15b [26:14; τοὺς ἀρχιερεῖς]), (3) οἱ μαθηταί (3×; 26:17, 19, 35b [πάντες οἱ μαθηταί]), (4) ὁ (2×; 26:18 [τῷ Ἰησου], 23), (5) Ἰούδας (1×; 26:25), (6) ὁ Ἰησοῦς (2×; 26:26, 34), (7) ὁ Πέτρος (2×; 26:33, 35a). Thus, the five thematic actors are Judas (2×), high priests (1×), disciples (3×), Jesus (4×), and Peter (2×). From this, Jesus appears most outstanding. Furthermore, in the case of 4 (2×; 26:18a, 23a), the thematic actor Jesus is located in prime. Thus, from the above two analyses (prime-subsequent, theme-rheme), Jesus turns out to be the most marked thematic actor. Considering, however, the circumstances in which Jesus appears as the key figure in the designated text, the above results may be natural.

## 1.3    *Topic and Comment*

### 1.3.1    Paragraph Division

Considering the criteria for paragraph division in chapter 2, this section divides Matthew 26:14–35 into paragraphs and suggests a topic for each paragraph.

---

1    Cf. Porter and O'Donnell, *Discourse Analysis*, 106.

MODE REGISTER ANALYSIS OF MATTHEW 26:14–35    93

The results will be compared with the paragraph divisions and topics provided by UBS[5] which is widely used by anyone reading the New Testament in its original language.

UBS[5] divides Matthew 26:14–35 into four paragraphs as follows: (1) Judas's agreement to betray Jesus (26:14–16), (2) the Passover with the disciples (26:17–25), (3) the institution of the Lord's supper (26:26–30); and (4) Peter's denial foretold (26:31–35). Based on the elements for paragraph division suggested in the methodology (one or more thematic units and thematic participants, temporal/spatial deixis, transition of topic, and lexical cohesion), this section will evaluate the paragraph division and titles offered by UBS[5] and suggest an alternative paragraph division.[2]

The first paragraph suggested by UBS[5] is 26:14–16. There are two thematic units (26:14–15a; 26:15b–16) and two thematic participants (κἀγώ [26:15a; cf. 26:14, εἷς τῶν δώδεκα, ὁ λεγόμενος Ἰούδας Ἰσκαριώτης]; οἱ [26:15b; cf. 26:14, τοὺς ἀρχιερεῖς]). This paragraph includes a temporal deixis (τότε; consecutive conjunction; cf. 26:2, μετὰ δύο ἡμέρας τὸ πάσχα γίνεται) as a boundary marker, and it has a clear transition of the topic, from "the anointing at Bethany" (26:6–13) to "Judas's agreement to betray Jesus."[3] Furthermore, this paragraph consists of Judas's plan to betray Jesus and the high priests' proposal of giving silver; the lexemes in domain 57 (δίδωμι; παραδίδωμι) cohesively tie this paragraph. Considering these aspects, the paragraph division of UBS[5] seems appropriate.

The second paragraph suggested by UBS[5] is 26:17–25. It contains five thematic units (26:17; 26:18; 26:19; 26:20–24; 26:25) and three thematic participants (οἱ μαθηταί [26:17, 19]; ὁ [Jesus; 26:18, 23; cf. 26:17; τῷ Ἰησου]; Ἰούδας [26:25]). However, it has two temporal deixes (Τῇ ... πρώτῃ τῶν ἀζύμων [26:17]; Ὀψίας ... γενομένης [26:20]) and an adversative conjunction (δέ; 26:20) as boundary markers. Also, this paragraph consists of two topics: (1) the preparation for the Passover (26:17–19); (2) a person who will betray Jesus (26:20–25). Considering these aspects, it seems appropriate to divide the paragraph proposed by UBS[5] into two paragraphs: 26:17–19 and 26:20–25.[4]

The third paragraph suggested by UBS[5] is 26:26–30. There are one thematic unit (26:26–30) and one thematic participant (ὁ Ἰησοῦς). It has a temporal deixis (Ἐσθιόντων) with an adversative conjunction δέ as a boundary marker. This paragraph begins with a narrative speech margin (26:26a), continues with

---

2  Lexical cohesion analysis, which will be dealt with later in the cohesion section, is a meaningful basis for paragraph division. Due to this utility, although it is a discussion that will be fully dealt with in the cohesion part, the general reference to lexical cohesion will be mentioned in this section when it is needed.

3  These titles are from the UBS[5].

4  The rationale of this proposal will be further revealed via later lexical cohesion analyses.

94                                                                                                      CHAPTER 3

Jesus' speech on the Eucharist (26:26b–29), and ends with a narrative part in which everyone is singing and moving to the Mount of Olives (26:30). Lexemes belonging to Semantic domains 23 (ἐσθίω; πίνω) and 8 (σῶμα; αἶμα) are related to the theme of the Eucharist and cohesively tie this paragraph. Considering these aspects, the paragraph division of UBS[5] seems appropriate.

The fourth paragraph suggested by UBS[5] is 26:31–35. It has four thematic units (26:31–33; 26:34; 26:35a; 26:35b) and three thematic participants (ὁ Πέτρος; ὁ Ἰησοῦς; πάντες οἱ μαθηταί). Temporal deixis (τότε) appears as a boundary marker in 26:31, which points to a new beginning of a paragraph. This paragraph mainly consists of a dialog between Jesus and Peter (as the representative of the disciples), which starts with Jesus and ends with Peter (Jesus → Peter → Jesus → Peter). At the end of 26:35, the narrative part conveying the disciples' response (except Peter) functions to end the paragraph. This paragraph also forms lexical cohesion around σκανδαλίζω (26:31, 33 [2×]; domain 31). Considering these aspects, the paragraph division of UBS[5] seems appropriate.

By applying thematization, the designated text can be divided into five paragraphs as follows: (1) 26:14–16, (2) 26:17–19, (3) 26:20–25, (4) 26:26–30, and (5) 26:31–35. Each paragraph is well-structured based on thematic units, thematic participants, boundary markers, and lexical cohesion.

## 1.3.2     Finding Topics of Each Paragraph

This section addresses the topic of each paragraph in light of the previous paragraph division. For this, the following provides a thematic participant-process analysis to find the topic of each paragraph according to Porter and O'Donnell's approach.[5] Table 3.2 presents the thematic participants and processes of each thematic unit.

Each paragraph's topic in Matthew 26:14–35 is analyzed by observing the thematic participants and major processes.

The major thematic processes of paragraph 1 (26:14–16) are as follows: (1) Judas's actions (going to the chief priests [26:14] and saying [26:15a; cf. asking a price for his betrayal]); (2) the chief priests' reaction (paying Judas thirty pieces of silver [26:15b]). Judas's action is related to betraying and handing over Jesus, and the reaction of the chief priests is related to paying the price for Judas's treachery. Given these points, the topic of this paragraph is proposed as follows: a deal between Judas and the high priests surrounding the betrayal to Jesus.

The major thematic processes of paragraph 2 (26:17–19) are as follows: (1) the disciples' actions (coming to Jesus [26:17], doing as Jesus had directed them [26:19a], and preparing the Passover [26:19b]), (2) Jesus' action (saying regarding the Passover preparation [26:18]). The center of the disciples' actions

---

5     Porter and O'Donnell, *Discourse Analysis*, 119–22.

# MODE REGISTER ANALYSIS OF MATTHEW 26:14–35                    95

TABLE 3.2    Thematic participants and processes in Matt 26:14–35[a]

| Paragraph | Thematic unit | Verse | Thematic participant | Major process |
|---|---|---|---|---|
| 1 | 1 | 14–15a | one of the twelve (Judas Iscariot) | went to the chief priests said |
| | 2 | 15b–16 | they (the chief priests) | paid him (Judas) thirty pieces of silver |
| 2 | 3 | 17 | the disciples | came to Jesus |
| | 4 | 18 | **he** (Jesus) | said |
| | 5 | 19 | the disciples | did as Jesus had directed them prepared the Passover |
| 3 | 6 | 20–24 | **he** (Jesus) | sat at the table said answered |
| | 7 | 25 | Judas | said |
| 4 | 8 | 26–30 | Jesus | took a bread blessed broke it (bread) gave it to the disciples said took a cup gave it to them (the disciples) said to them (the disciples) |
| 5 | 9 | 31–33 | Peter | declared to him (Jesus) |
| | 10 | 34 | Jesus | said to him (Peter) |
| | 11 | 35a | Peter | said to him (Jesus) |
| | 12 | 35b | all the disciples | said so |

a    The words shown in bold reveals several active processes of the most marked-thematic actor (26:18, 23), that is, Jesus.

is related to the preparation of the Passover meal, and that of Jesus' actions is concerned with the specific instructions regarding the preparation. Given these points, the topic of this paragraph is proposed as follows: disciples' inquiry about Passover preparation and Jesus' guideline.

The major thematic processes of paragraph 3 (26:20–25) are as follows: (1) Jesus' actions (sitting at a table with the disciples [26:20], talking about the betrayal [26:21], and answering the disciples' question [26:23–24]), and (2) Judas's action (saying [26:25]). Jesus' action is related to the prophecy of the future treachery and his reference to the disciples' reaction, and Judas's action has a character of a counter-question to Jesus' prediction. Given these, the topic of this paragraph is proposed as follows: Jesus' foretelling of the betrayal and the disciples' responses.

The major thematic processes of paragraph 4 (26:26–30) are Jesus' actions (taking a loaf of bread [26:26], blessing [26:26], breaking the bread [26:26], giving the bread to the disciples [26:26], saying [26:26], taking a cup [26:27], giving the cup to the disciples [26:27], saying [26:29]). The only thematic participant in this paragraph is Jesus; at the center of the act, there are bread and wine—being blessed, given thanks, and distributed to the disciples—which imply Jesus' death. Given these, this paragraph's topic is proposed as follows: Jesus' institution of the Eucharist.

The major thematic processes paragraph 5 (26:31–35) are done by Peter (declaring to Jesus [26:33], saying to Jesus [26:35a]), Jesus (saying to Peter [26:34]), and all the disciples (saying the same as Peter [26:35b]). Peter's action is related to his willful expression that Jesus' foretelling about the stumbling (scattering) and the denial will not come true, Jesus' action is concerned with Peter's denial as well as his stumbling, and the other disciples' action is related to their sharing of Peter's statement. Given these points, this paragraph's topic is proposed as follows: Jesus' foretelling of the disciples' stumbling and Peter's denial.

In summary, the paragraph division and the topic for each paragraph of Matthew 26:14–35 compared to UBS[5] are summarized in Table 3.3.

TABLE 3.3    Paragraph division & topics of UBS[5] and this study

| Paragraph division & topics of UBS[5] | Paragraph division & topics of this study |
| --- | --- |
| 1. Judas's agreement to betray Jesus (26:14–16) | 1. A deal between Judas and the high priests surrounding the betrayal to Jesus (26:14–16) |
| 2. The Passover with the Disciples (26:17–25) | 2. Disciples' inquiry about Passover preparation and Jesus' guideline (26:17–19) |
| | 3. Jesus' foretelling of the betrayal and the Disciples' responses (26:20–25) |
| 3. The institution of the Lord's Supper (26:26–30) | 4. Jesus' institution of the Eucharist (26:26–30) |
| 4. Peter's denial foretold (26:31–35) | 5. Jesus' foretelling of the Disciples' stumbling and Peter's denial (26:31–35) |

The paragraph division and topics suggested by this study show that the designated text has five paragraphs, and each paragraph has one distinctive topic, while UBS[5]'s second paragraph holds two topics. This analysis shows the well-organized structure of the designated text, from which we can deduce the constructor's significant contribution.

### 1.4 Summary and Implication

This section attempted a thematization analysis of Matthew 26:14–35; the results are as follows. There are twelve thematic units (1. 26:14–15a; 2. 26:15b–16; 3. 26:17; 4. 26:18; 5. 26:19; 6. 26:20–24; 7. 26:25; 8. 26:26–32; 9. 26:33; 10. 26:34; 11. 26:35a; 12. 26:35b), and overlapping positions of prime and theme shows us the most marked-thematic actor as Jesus (2×; 26:18, 23). Unlike the division of UBS[5], this study divided the designated texts into five paragraphs: (1) 26:14–16, (2) 26:17–19, (3) 26:20–25, (4) 26:26–30, and (5) 26:31–35. The topic for each paragraph is suggested as follows: (1) a deal between Judas and the high priests surrounding the betrayal to Jesus (26:14–16), (2) the disciples' inquiry for Passover preparation and Jesus' guideline (26:17–19), (3) Jesus' foretelling of the betrayal and the disciples' responses (26:20–25), (4) Jesus' institution of the Eucharist (26:26–30), and (5) Jesus' foretelling of the disciples' stumbling and Peter's denial (26:31–35). These features reveal the well-organized structure, which may have resulted from the constructor's active contribution.

## 2 Cohesion

### 2.1 Conjunction

Analyzing conjunctions is the first section of cohesion analysis. Table 3.4 shows conjunctions and asyndeton in Matthew 26:14–35 divided into the narrative and direct speech parts.

Conjunctions in the designated text are as follows: (1) καί (16×; 26:15, 16, 18, 19 [2×], 21, 22, 26 [2×], 27 [2×], 30, 31, 35 [2×]); (2) δέ (11×; 26:15, 17, 18, 20, 23, 24, 25, 26, 29, 32, 33); (3) τότε (2×; 26:14, 31);[6] (4) γάρ (2×; 26:28, 31); (5) ὅτι (2×; 26:21, 34); (6) εἰ (2×; 26:24, 33); (7) ἵνα (1×; 26:16); (8) ὡς (1×; 26:19); (9) μέν (1×; 26:24); (10) καθώς (1×; 26:24); (11) ὅταν (1×; 26:29). The conjunctions compounded with other words are two: κἀγώ (26:15), κἄν (26:35).[7] The total number of conjunctions in the designated text is thirty-six, of which twenty-three belong to

---

6  Τότε also appears in 26:16, but here it is used as a noun attached to the preposition ἀπό.

7  Κἀγώ is a compound word of καί and ἐγώ, and κἄν is a compound word of καί and ἐάν. These are considered as unique usages, which are not included in the total number of conjunctions.

98                                                                                            CHAPTER 3

TABLE 3.4    Conjunctions and asyndeton in the narratives and direct speeches of
             Matt 26:14–35 (conjunction is indicated by underline, and asyndeton by ∅)

| Paragraphs | Narrative | Direct speech |
|---|---|---|
| 26:14–16 | ¹⁴ <u>Τότε</u> πορευθεὶς εἷς τῶν δώδεκα, ὁ λεγόμενος Ἰούδας Ἰσκαριώτης, πρὸς τοὺς ἀρχιερεῖς ¹⁵ εἶπεν· | |
| | | ∅ τί θέλετέ μοι δοῦναι, <u>κἀγὼ</u> ὑμῖν παραδώσω αὐτόν; |
| | οἱ <u>δὲ</u> ἔστησαν αὐτῷ τριάκοντα ἀργύρια. ¹⁶ <u>καὶ</u> ἀπὸ τότε ἐζήτει εὐκαιρίαν <u>ἵνα</u> αὐτὸν παραδῷ. | |
| 26:17–19 | ¹⁷ Τῇ <u>δὲ</u> πρώτῃ τῶν ἀζύμων προσῆλθον οἱ μαθηταὶ τῷ Ἰησοῦ λέγοντες· | |
| | | ∅ ποῦ θέλεις ἑτοιμάσωμέν σοι φαγεῖν τὸ πάσχα; |
| | ¹⁸ ὁ <u>δὲ</u> εἶπεν· | |
| | | ∅ ὑπάγετε εἰς τὴν πόλιν πρὸς τὸν δεῖνα <u>καὶ</u> εἴπατε αὐτῷ· |
| | |   ∅ ὁ διδάσκαλος λέγει· |
| | |     ∅ ὁ καιρός μου ἐγγύς ἐστιν, ∅ πρὸς σὲ ποιῶ τὸ πάσχα μετὰ τῶν μαθητῶν μου. |
| | ¹⁹ <u>καὶ</u> ἐποίησαν οἱ μαθηταὶ <u>ὡς</u> συνέταξεν αὐτοῖς ὁ Ἰησοῦς <u>καὶ</u> ἡτοίμασαν τὸ πάσχα. | |
| 26:20–25 | ²⁰ Ὀψίας <u>δὲ</u> γενομένης ἀνέκειτο μετὰ τῶν δώδεκα. ²¹ <u>καὶ</u> ἐσθιόντων αὐτῶν εἶπεν· | |
| | | ∅ ἀμὴν λέγω ὑμῖν <u>ὅτι</u> εἷς ἐξ ὑμῶν παραδώσει με. |
| | ²² <u>καὶ</u> λυπούμενοι σφόδρα ἤρξαντο λέγειν αὐτῷ εἷς ἕκαστος· | |
| | | ∅ μήτι ἐγώ εἰμι, κύριε; |
| | ²³ ὁ <u>δὲ</u> ἀποκριθεὶς εἶπεν· | |

# MODE REGISTER ANALYSIS OF MATTHEW 26:14–35

TABLE 3.4    Conjunctions and asyndeton in the narratives and direct speeches (*cont.*)

| Paragraphs | Narrative | Direct speech |
| --- | --- | --- |
| | | ∅ ὁ ἐμβάψας μετ' ἐμοῦ τὴν χεῖρα ἐν τῷ τρυβλίῳ οὗτός με παραδώσει. [24] ὁ <u>μὲν</u> υἱὸς τοῦ ἀνθρώπου ὑπάγει <u>καθὼς</u> γέγραπται περὶ αὐτοῦ, οὐαὶ <u>δὲ</u> τῷ ἀνθρώπῳ ἐκείνῳ δι' οὗ ὁ υἱὸς τοῦ ἀνθρώπου παραδίδοται· ∅ καλὸν ἦν αὐτῷ <u>εἰ</u> οὐκ ἐγεννήθη ὁ ἄνθρωπος ἐκεῖνος. |
| | [25] ἀποκριθεὶς <u>δὲ</u> Ἰούδας ὁ παραδιδοὺς αὐτὸν εἶπεν· | |
| | | ∅ μήτι ἐγώ εἰμι, ῥαββί; |
| | ∅ λέγει αὐτῷ· | |
| | | ∅ σὺ εἶπας |
| 26:26–30 | [26] Ἐσθιόντων <u>δὲ</u> αὐτῶν λαβὼν ὁ Ἰησοῦς ἄρτον <u>καὶ</u> εὐλογήσας ἔκλασεν <u>καὶ</u> δοὺς τοῖς μαθηταῖς εἶπεν· | |
| | | ∅ λάβετε ∅ φάγετε, ∅ τοῦτό ἐστιν τὸ σῶμά μου. |
| | [27] <u>καὶ</u> λαβὼν ποτήριον <u>καὶ</u> εὐχαριστήσας ἔδωκεν αὐτοῖς λέγων· | |
| | | ∅ πίετε ἐξ αὐτοῦ πάντες, [28] τοῦτο <u>γάρ</u> ἐστιν τὸ αἷμά μου τῆς διαθήκης τὸ περὶ πολλῶν ἐκχυννόμενον εἰς ἄφεσιν ἁμαρτιῶν. [29] λέγω <u>δὲ</u> ὑμῖν, ∅ οὐ μὴ πίω ἀπ' ἄρτι ἐκ τούτου τοῦ γενήματος τῆς ἀμπέλου <u>ἕως</u> τῆς ἡμέρας ἐκείνης <u>ὅταν</u> αὐτὸ πίνω μεθ' ὑμῶν καινὸν ἐν τῇ βασιλείᾳ τοῦ πατρός μου. |
| | [30] <u>Καὶ</u> ὑμνήσαντες ἐξῆλθον εἰς τὸ ὄρος τῶν ἐλαιῶν. | |
| 26:31–35 | [31] <u>Τότε</u> λέγει αὐτοῖς ὁ Ἰησοῦς· | |

# 100                                                           CHAPTER 3

TABLE 3.4    Conjunctions and asyndeton in the narratives and direct speeches (*cont.*)

| Paragraphs | Narrative | Direct speech |
|---|---|---|
| | | ∅ πάντες ὑμεῖς σκανδαλισθήσεσθε ἐν ἐμοὶ ἐν τῇ νυκτὶ ταύτῃ, γέγραπται <u>γάρ</u>· ∅ πατάξω τὸν ποιμένα, <u>καὶ</u> δια-σκορπισθήσονται τὰ πρόβατα τῆς ποίμνης. ³² μετὰ <u>δὲ</u> τὸ ἐγερθῆναί με προάξω ὑμᾶς εἰς τὴν Γαλιλαίαν. |
| | ³³ ἀποκριθεὶς <u>δὲ</u> ὁ Πέτρος εἶπεν αὐτῷ· | |
| | | <u>εἰ</u> πάντες σκανδαλισθήσονται ἐν σοί, ∅ ἐγὼ οὐδέποτε σκανδαλισθήσομαι. |
| | ³⁴ ∅ ἔφη αὐτῷ ὁ Ἰησοῦς· | |
| | | ∅ ἀμὴν λέγω σοι <u>ὅτι</u> ἐν ταύτῃ τῇ νυκτὶ πρὶν ἀλέκτορα φωνῆσαι τρὶς ἀπαρνήσῃ με. |
| | ³⁵ ∅ λέγει αὐτῷ ὁ Πέτρος· | |
| | | <u>κἂν</u> δέῃ με σὺν σοὶ ἀποθανεῖν, ∅ οὐ μή σε ἀπαρνήσομαι. |
| | ὁμοίως <u>καὶ</u> πάντες οἱ μαθηταὶ εἶπαν. | |

the narrative part, and thirteen belong to the direct speech part. There are twenty-three asyndeton cases: three cases in narrative parts and twenty cases in direct speech parts.

Now, we will analyze each appearance of conjunctions in the contextual flow, according to the previously divided paragraphs. First, the conjunction analysis for the first paragraph (26:14–16) is as follows. 26:14 begins with the consecutive conjunction τότε,[8] which relates the paragraph to the context of 26:6–13, and functions as a temporal link to the events in Bethany, the pouring of an expensive ointment on Jesus by a woman. In the first clause of 26:15, a separate conjunction does not appear (asyndeton). According to Stephanie L. Black, "the first sentence in any sequence of exposition or reported

---

8  Τότε appears ninety times in Matthew, which is a significantly higher number compared to six times in Mark and fifteen times in Luke. From this, it can be said that τότε is a unique expression of Matthew.

MODE REGISTER ANALYSIS OF MATTHEW 26:14–35        101

speech is ... asyndetic."[9] Since the first clause of 26:15 is the first part of Judas's speech part which reveals his desire for money, this asyndeton is explicable. In the second clause of 26:15, a compound lexeme κἀγώ appears, which is used in the meaning of "and I"[10] to reveal Judas's will that "I" will betray Jesus.[11] After that, δέ,[12] usually denoting an unmarked discontinuity, appears as a bridge to Judas's speech part with the section dealing with the reaction of the high priests (26:15c). Καί of 26:16 conveys an unmarked continuity of the actions of Judas, who is seeking an opportunity to hand over Jesus after the high priests gave him thirty shekels of silver as a ransom. Cohesion is maintained by the appropriate appearances of conjunctions and explicable asyndeton.

In 26:17, the first verse of the second paragraph (26:17–19), the conjunction δέ is used in the narrative in the sense of transition at the point where the topic shifts to preparing the Passover meal after the previous account of the betrayal of Judas. The following clause is the disciples' speech, a question regarding the place for the Passover, so there is no conjunction (asyndeton; 26:17b). Δέ appears again in the following narrative speech margin, which leads Jesus' speech in 26:18, and it can be translated into "then" (26:18a). Of the four occurrences of asyndeton appearing in the subsequent direct quotation, the first three cases are naturally located at the beginning of the subordinating clause, respectively (26:18b, 18d, 18e), but the case of the fourth asyndeton appears in situations where conjunction such as καί, δέ, or γάρ seems expected (∅ πρὸς σὲ ποιῶ τὸ πάσχα μετὰ τῶν μαθητῶν μου; 26:18f). Καί in the speech part of 26:18 (26:18c) has the function of revealing an unmarked continuity linking Jesus' instruction with his other instruction. After that, καί appearing in the first clause of 26:19 functions to show "causal continuity" in the position of linking Jesus' words with the disciples' responses to them. Subsequent ὡς appears as a resultative conjunction revealing that the disciples did as Jesus instructed. Also, καί in the third clause of 26:19 conveys unmarked continuity. Thus, overall, the appearance of conjunctions conveys cohesion of this paragraph; however, the absence of conjunction in 26:18f may lower the degree of cohesiveness of this paragraph.[13]

---

9    Black, *Conjunctions*, 179.
10   France, *Matthew*, 976.
11   Cf. Alan H. McNeile, *The Gospel according to St. Matthew: The Greek Text with Introduction, Notes, and Indices* (London: Macmillan, 1915), 377.
12   Whereas καί is usually placed first in a sentence, δέ is usually placed after a word like an article, noun, etc.
13   Here, the expression, "lower the degree of cohesiveness," means that a certain factor in a text reduces the degree of cohesiveness, that would have appeared more firmly by other choices, even though the cohesiveness of the text is maintained.

102                                                                                           CHAPTER 3

In the first clause of 26:20, which is the beginning of the third paragraph, there is an adversative/connective conjunction δέ, which indicates a temporal (evening came) and spatial change (a certain one's house), along with the thematic change in terms of the paragraph discourse (from the Passover preparation to one's betrayal). Καί in 26:21 is used to reveal an unmarked continuity in the narrative speech margin of Jesus' words about the betrayal of one of his disciples. At the beginning of the following Jesus' speech, asyndeton appears, and then the main body of his speech is presented with the subordinating conjunction ὅτι. In 26:22, the disciples' responses to Jesus' words are connected by καί implying causal continuity, and the beginning of the disciples' speech part appears as asyndeton. Δέ, which appears in the narrative speech margin of Jesus' response (26:23a), has a discontinuity in that the response is not a direct answer to the disciples' question, and may also function as a conjunction with a connective aspect. After that, the beginning of Jesus' speech in 26:23b appears as asyndeton. In the following part of Jesus' speech, 26:24, four conjunctions (μέν, καθώς, δέ, εἰ) are used to form conjunctive ties to reveal the different destiny between the son of man and the person who hands him over. 26:24 has a case of asyndeton (∅ καλὸν ἦν αὐτῷ). This main clause, which has the following conditional-subordinate clause with εἰ, appears in an inverted form. The asyndeton in 26:24 appears in situation where a conjunction such as γάρ or δέ seems expected. In 26:25, δέ appears in a similar way as in 26:23. Also, there are three cases of asyndeton in the two speech parts and the narrative speech margin of 26:25. Unlike the two cases at the beginning of the speech, the asyndeton (∅ λέγει αὐτῷ) in the narrative seems to be a unique case because it is uncommon that there is no conjunction in a narrative part which is likely to require a conjunction such as δέ. The conjunctions used in the third paragraph thus maintain cohesiveness of the paragraph overall. However, two cases of asyndeton that occur in the narrative speech margin (26:25c) and the direct speech (26:24) may be factors of lowering the degree of cohesiveness of this paragraph.

The fourth paragraph (26:26–30), which recounts the Eucharist, begins with a narrative, in which δέ appears as a transitional conjunction, and the following two occurrences of καί include unmarked continuity. In the second half of 26:26, the speech part has three clauses, with no conjunctions (∅ λάβετε ∅ φάγετε, ∅ τοῦτό ἐστιν τὸ σῶμά μου). The first asyndeton is explicable as it is the beginning of the speech. Also, the second asyndeton, along with the first case, takes the imperative verbal form, which does not need conjunction. In the case of the third asyndeton, there is a possibility that a conjunction with a causal meaning, such as γάρ could be used, but a particular conjunction does not seem to be needed in a situation where the indicative verbal

MODE REGISTER ANALYSIS OF MATTHEW 26:14–35

form appears after the previous two imperative verbs. In 26:27, καί appears to convey an unmarked continuity for the transition from the topic of "bread" to "cup" (26:27a), and another καί is followed to convey the basic continuity in the progress of the narrative (26:27b). Asyndeton appears at the beginning of the speech part (26:27c). After that, 26:28, which begins with the causal conjunction γάρ, reveals that the meaning of the cup given by Jesus is the blood of the covenant, and the purpose is related to the freedom of many people from sin. The following 26:29 begins with the adversative conjunction δέ, implying that Jesus' succeeding words are adversative to the previous one. Whereas Jesus gives order to drink a cup in 26:27–28, he now declares that he will not drink wine *until* he drinks new wine with the disciples in the kingdom of God; in 26:29a, asyndeton appears since it is the beginning of Jesus' speech part, and in the second half of 26:29, an expected temporal conjunction ὅταν appears. After these words, they (possibly Jesus and his disciples) go to the Mount of Olives singing a hymn, which is connected by καί to convey unmarked continuity. In the fourth paragraph, cohesion is maintained by the appropriate appearances of conjunctions and explicable asyndeta.

The fifth paragraph (26:31–35) begins with τότε in the narrative part. It indicates that the following event is happening on the way to the Mount of Olives or on it. After the first clause of 26:31, four additional clauses follow. Asyndeton appears in the two clauses (the second and fourth), which present Jesus' speech and his Old Testament quotation. In the two other clauses (the third and fifth), the causal conjunction γάρ and the connective conjunction καί appears. Here, γάρ is used to reveal the foundation of Jesus' statement that all of his disciples will stumble in him (σκανδαλισθήσεσθε ἐν ἐμοί): a fulfilment of Zechariah 13:7. Καί functions to connect the cause (striking the shepherd) and result (the flock's scattering).[14] In 26:32, the adversative conjunction δέ appears to carry a dramatic reversal: from Jesus' death ("I will strike the shepherd") and the disciples' scattering to Jesus' resurrection and his return to Galilee. After that, in the narrative part of 26:33, the adversative conjunction δέ appears to introduce Peter's words as a rebuttal to Jesus' words, and in the direct speech part, the conditional conjunction εἰ appears where Peter assumes the situation that everyone would stumble in Jesus, to empathize that Peter himself would never stumble in him. Among the remaining two verses (26:34, 35) the narrative speech margins of Jesus and Peter's words do not have conjunctions (∅ ἔφη αὐτῷ ὁ Ἰησοῦς; ∅ λέγει αὐτῷ ὁ Πέτρος). These can be seen as a characteristic

---

14    This Old Testament quotation contains significant allusions to Jesus' arrest—further to his death—as the cause of the disciples' stumbling and scattering. It also functions as the basis for the subsequent 26:32 since resurrection presupposes death.

104 CHAPTER 3

element of the narrative speech margin of Matthew (asyndeton + thematic λέγει + grammatical subject).[15] The following speech parts, 26:34b and 26:35b, appear after these narratives. First, in 26:34b, after the asyndeton at the beginning of Jesus' speech part (∅ ἀμὴν λέγω σοι), it leads to the subordinating conjunction ὅτι, where it is revealed how specifically Peter's denial will be accomplished. After that, Peter's speech part in 26:35b starts with a compound word κἄν, meaning "even if," which functions as the intro of demonstrating Peter's strong will that he will never deny Jesus even if he dies. In the last part of the narrative in 26:35c, Peter and the other disciples share the same will together, and it is expressed by the conjunction καί, conveying unmarked continuity. Overall, the conjunctive ties in this paragraph are well formed, and all asyndeta are explicable. Thus, cohesion of this paragraph is maintained.

## 2.2 *Reference*

Reference is another fundamental element in the cohesion formation of a text. We now look at the formation of reference based on the paragraph division done through the thematization.[16] The participant-referent chains of Matthew 26:14–16 are shown in Figure 3.1.[17]

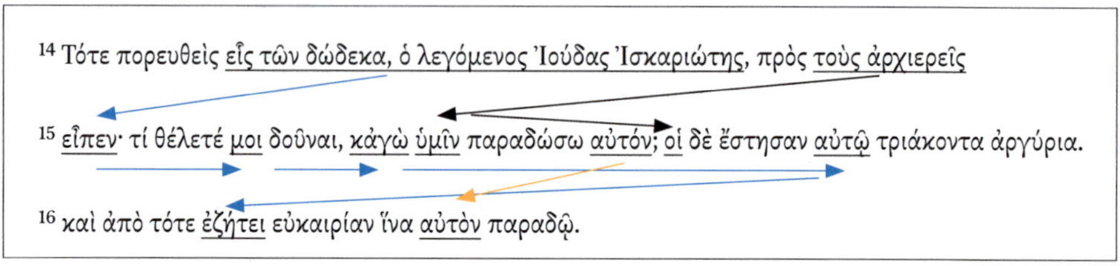

FIGURE 3.1 Participant-referent chains in Matt 26:14–16

---

15 Black, *Conjunctions*, 189–90. Like λέγει, ἔφη tends not to have conjunction when it appears in the narrative speech margin with a grammatical subject (8×; 4:7; 17:26; 19:21; 22:37; 25:21, 23; 26:34; 27:65). This tendency appears three times in Mark (9:38; 10:29; 12:24), and does not appear in Luke, which may be related to Matthew's relatively frequent use of grammatical subjects.

16 Considering the characteristics of New Testament Greek, this study regards the implied subjects in verbs as references. If a grammatical subject (e.g., proper noun, pronoun) appears, it is considered to have replaced the implied subject in the verb part; thus, these are counted as one.

17 In reference analysis, the color of each arrow means as follows: (1) orange: Jesus; (2) blue: disciples; (3) black: the other objects. This is applied to the subsequent participant-referent chains figures.

The participants for which the participant-referent chains are formed are as follows: Judas (6×), the high priests (3×), and Jesus (2×). In the case of Judas, after first appearing as a grammaticalized reference (proper noun), it appears as an implied reference of the verb εἶπεν, the first-person dative case, the first-person subjective case, the third-person dative case, and the implied reference of the verb ἐζήτει. In the case of the high priest, after first appearing as a grammaticalized reference (proper noun), it appears as reduced references (second-person dative and third-person subjective). In the case of Jesus, it appears as reduced references twice (third-person objective), without a grammaticalized reference.[18] Considering the participant referent chains which are well formed, the cohesiveness of this paragraph is overall maintained. However, in the narrative part of 26:16, although it seems more natural to present the identity of Jesus as a proper noun considering the change of topic and thematic participant in this paragraph, he is revealed only by a reduced reference (pronoun). This seemingly unnatural reference may lower the degree of cohesiveness of this paragraph.

The participant-referent chains of Matthew 26:17–19 are shown in Figure 3.2.

The participants for which the participant-referent chains are formed are as follows: the disciples (7×) and Jesus (8×). "A certain one" (2×) can be regarded as a sub-participant. The characteristic of this paragraph is that the name of Jesus as a grammaticalized reference (proper noun) appears two times, and the disciples appear in the form of μαθηταί, as a grammaticalized reference (proper

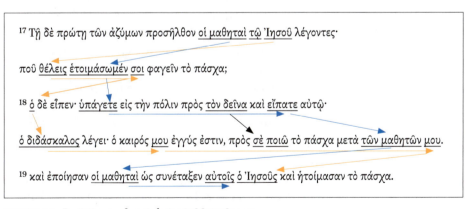

FIGURE 3.2  Participant-referent chains in Matt 26:17–19

18  In the context of change in paragraph and topic, a reduced reference (pronoun) in Judas's speech (26:15) may reveal the intention of Judas himself to hide Jesus' identity in the context of conspiracy situation.

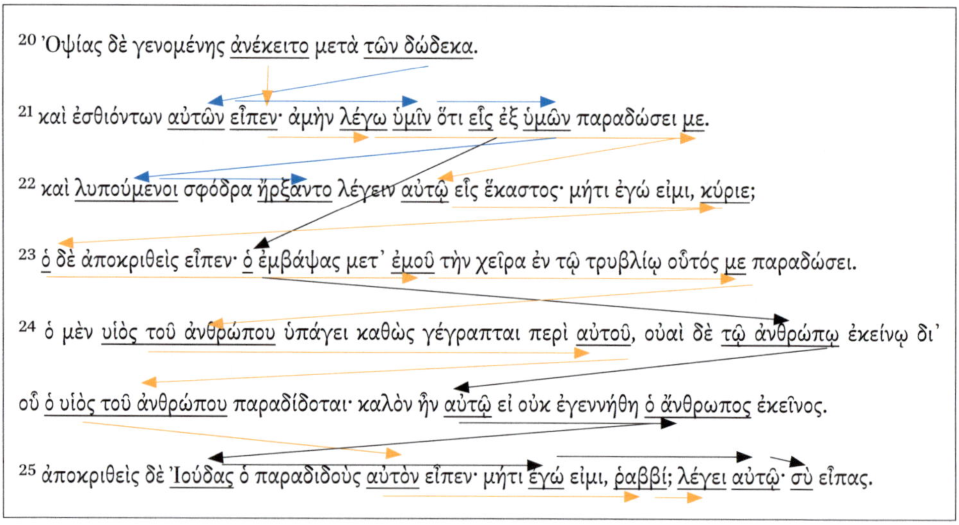

106　　　　　　　　　　　　　　　　　　　　　　　　　　　　　　　　　CHAPTER 3

$^{20}$ Ὀψίας δὲ γενομένης ἀνέκειτο μετὰ τῶν δώδεκα.

$^{21}$ καὶ ἐσθιόντων αὐτῶν εἶπεν· ἀμὴν λέγω ὑμῖν ὅτι εἷς ἐξ ὑμῶν παραδώσει με.

$^{22}$ καὶ λυπούμενοι σφόδρα ἤρξαντο λέγειν αὐτῷ εἷς ἕκαστος· μήτι ἐγώ εἰμι, κύριε;

$^{23}$ ὁ δὲ ἀποκριθεὶς εἶπεν· ὁ ἐμβάψας μετ᾽ ἐμοῦ τὴν χεῖρα ἐν τῷ τρυβλίῳ οὗτός με παραδώσει.

$^{24}$ ὁ μὲν υἱὸς τοῦ ἀνθρώπου ὑπάγει καθὼς γέγραπται περὶ αὐτοῦ, οὐαὶ δὲ τῷ ἀνθρώπῳ ἐκείνῳ δι᾽

οὗ ὁ υἱὸς τοῦ ἀνθρώπου παραδίδοται· καλὸν ἦν αὐτῷ εἰ οὐκ ἐγεννήθη ὁ ἄνθρωπος ἐκεῖνος.

$^{25}$ ἀποκριθεὶς δὲ Ἰούδας ὁ παραδιδοὺς αὐτὸν εἶπεν· μήτι ἐγώ εἰμι, ῥαββί; λέγει αὐτῷ· σὺ εἶπας.

FIGURE 3.3　Participant-referent chains in Matt 26:20–25

noun), three times; these grammaticalized references appear frequently compared to the previous paragraph. Here, a vague expression "a certain one" (τὸν
δεῖνα) appears, which may strengthen the relative ambiguity. Overall, these
participant-referent chains are well formed, thus the cohesiveness of this paragraph is maintained.

The participant-referent chains of Matthew 26:20–25 are shown in Figure 3.3.

The participants for which the participant-referent chains are formed are
as follows: Jesus (15×), the disciples (6×), and the one who will betray Jesus,
that is, Judas (9×). After the appearance of "twelve" as a grammaticalized reference (substitution), disciples appear as reduced references (pronoun) and
implied references. Jesus is mentioned most often in this paragraph as grammaticalized references (common noun and compound noun), reduced references (pronoun and simplified form), and implied references (implied subject
in verb). In this paragraph, Jesus does not appear as a proper noun; however,
the proper noun of Jesus appears in the immediate-preceding passage (26:19).
Thus, based on the close connection between the Passover meal and its preparation, this phenomenon seems explicable. The person who will betray Jesus
appears as a grammaticalized reference (compound noun; εἷς ἐξ ὑμῶν), and it
also appears in reduced references (pronoun), implied references, and a specific grammaticalized reference (proper noun), that is, Judas. Overall, these
participant-referent chains are well formed, thus the cohesiveness of this paragraph is maintained.

The participant-referent chains of Matthew 26:26–30 are shown in Figure 3.4.

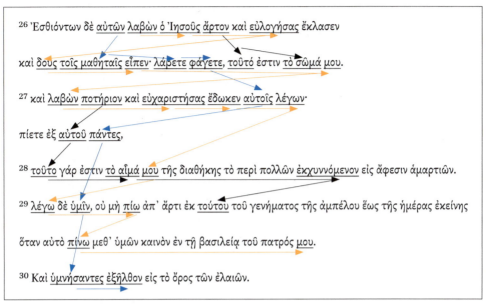

FIGURE 3.4  Participant-referent chains in Matt 26:26–30

The participants for which the participant-referent chains are formed are as follows: Jesus (15×), disciples (9×), bread (3×), and c (6×). In the case of Jesus, it is mentioned once as a grammaticalized reference (proper noun), and the rest are mentioned as implied references (implied subjects of verbs) and reduced references (pronoun). Disciples are also mentioned once as a grammaticalized reference (proper noun), otherwise as reduced references (pronoun) and implied references (implied subjects of verbs). Bread and cup are mentioned as grammaticalized references (proper noun, substitution) and are also referred to in the form of reduced reference (pronoun). In the case of "cup," it is also mentioned once as an implied reference (implied subject of a verb). Overall, these participant-referent chains are well formed, thus the cohesiveness of this paragraph is maintained.

The participant-referent chains of Matthew 26:31–35 are shown in Figure 3.5.

The references in this paragraph are somewhat complicated: Jesus (13×), all disciples (4×), Peter (9×), and all disciples excluding Peter (2×). One of the characteristics of this paragraph is that the grammaticalized references (proper noun) of Jesus and Peter appear frequently. This referential pattern seems to come from the appearance of two third-person singular (Jesus and Peter) in the give-and-take conversation (Peter's two responses to Jesus and Jesus' one response to Peter). Overall, these participant-referent chains are well formed, thus the cohesiveness of this paragraph is maintained.

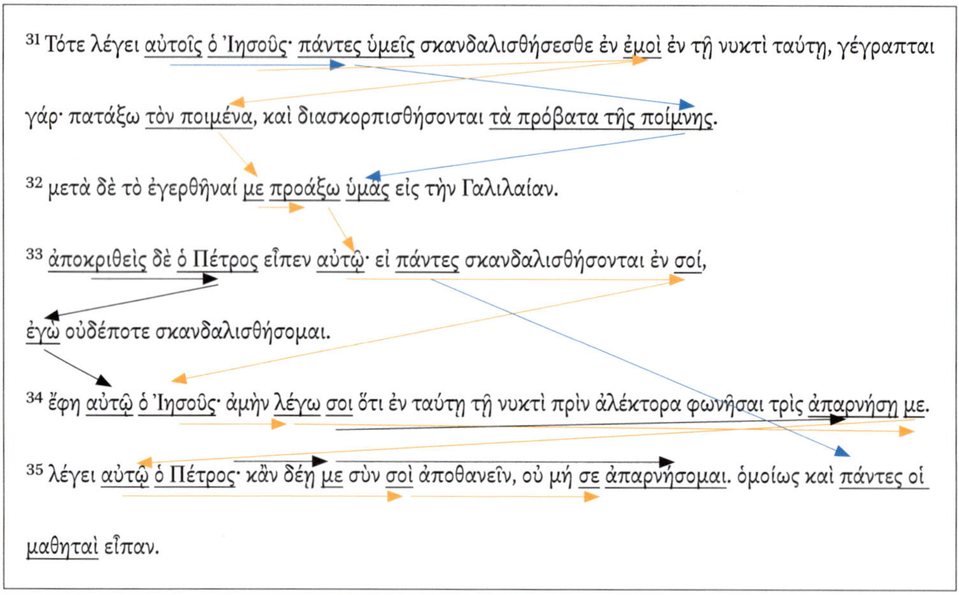

108                                                                                       CHAPTER 3

> $^{31}$ Τότε λέγει αὐτοῖς ὁ Ἰησοῦς· πάντες ὑμεῖς σκανδαλισθήσεσθε ἐν ἐμοὶ ἐν τῇ νυκτὶ ταύτῃ, γέγραπται
>
> γάρ· πατάξω τὸν ποιμένα, καὶ διασκορπισθήσονται τὰ πρόβατα τῆς ποίμνης.
>
> $^{32}$ μετὰ δὲ τὸ ἐγερθῆναί με προάξω ὑμᾶς εἰς τὴν Γαλιλαίαν.
>
> $^{33}$ ἀποκριθεὶς δὲ ὁ Πέτρος εἶπεν αὐτῷ· εἰ πάντες σκανδαλισθήσονται ἐν σοί,
>
> ἐγὼ οὐδέποτε σκανδαλισθήσομαι.
>
> $^{34}$ ἔφη αὐτῷ ὁ Ἰησοῦς· ἀμὴν λέγω σοι ὅτι ἐν ταύτῃ τῇ νυκτὶ πρὶν ἀλέκτορα φωνῆσαι τρὶς ἀπαρνήσῃ με.
>
> $^{35}$ λέγει αὐτῷ ὁ Πέτρος· κἂν δέῃ με σὺν σοὶ ἀποθανεῖν, οὐ μή σε ἀπαρνήσομαι. ὁμοίως καὶ πάντες οἱ
>
> μαθηταὶ εἶπαν.

FIGURE 3.5   Participant-referent chains in Matt 26:31–35

## 2.3   *Substitution and Ellipsis*

First, as mentioned in chapter 2, concerning a reference one needs to go back to the previous context to find a semantic object. But substitution does not need this process because readers get newly added information via substitution, even though it refers to a previous object. The substitutions in Matthew 26:14–35 are as follows. The first is οἱ μαθηταί in 26:17 as a substitution of δώδεκα in 26:14. The second is ὁ διδάσκαλος in 26:18, after Jesus' identity is made clear in 26:17 (τῷ Ἰησοῦ). The third is κύριε in 26:22, a substitution of Jesus, spoken by his disciples. The fourth is ὁ υἱὸς τοῦ ἀνθρώπου, a substitution as a title of Jesus himself, appearing twice in 26:24. The fifth is ῥαββί spoken by Judas to Jesus in 26:25. The sixth is τὸ σῶμά μου in 26:26 as a substitution of bread (ἄρτον).[19]

---

19   In dealing with the sixth case, it is worth looking at some of Jesus' statements in 26:26–29. First of all, in verse 26, when Jesus takes the bread and says it is "my body," is this substitution or metaphor? In fact, it is true that it is difficult to directly connect bread and "body." Nevertheless, after "this" appeared as a reference to bread, Jesus is saying via metaphorical expressions that the bread that Jesus took, blessed, broke, and gave to his disciples is his own body. It seems appropriate to view this as a substitution in terms of definition, that is, adding an additional concept to the previous concept with an ambiguous explanation.

MODE REGISTER ANALYSIS OF MATTHEW 26:14–35          109

The seventh is τὸ αἷμά μου τῆς διαθήκης in 26:26 as a substitution of the cup (ποτήριον).[20] The eighth is τούτου τοῦ γενήματος τῆς ἀμπέλου in 26:29 as a substitution of the cup, Jesus' blood.[21] The ninth and tenth are two concepts revealed in Jesus' words in his Old Testament quotation in 26:31: the shepherd (τὸν ποιμένα) and the flock (τὰ πρόβατα τῆς ποίμνης).[22]

Second, also mentioned in chapter 2, ellipsis is used when the author and reader already know about what has already been said. It can be also used to avoid repeating what has been said previously, or as a device to keep semantic possibilities open by omitting certain information. The ellipsis in Matthew 26:14–35 is μήτι ἐγώ εἰμι, which appears twice (26:22, 25). It is spoken by the disciples in 26:22 (probably excluding Judas) and by Judas in 26:25. What is omitted here is *a person who betrays Jesus* (26:21, εἷς ἐξ ὑμῶν; 26:24, τῷ ἀνθρώπῳ ἐκείνῳ), and it can be regarded as a nominal ellipsis.

Considering these analyses, the distribution of substitution and ellipsis throughout the designated text demonstrates the cohesiveness of this text.

### 2.4    *Lexical Cohesion*
In this section, we will analyze the semantic-lexical ties to examine the cohesiveness of each paragraph in Matthew 26:14–35 and the semantic-lexical chain of the whole designated text.

### 2.4.1    Lexical Cohesion in Each Paragraph
In the first paragraph (26:14–16), Judas plans to hand over Jesus, and the chief priests count thirty pieces of silver to Judas in return. From that time on Judas seeks an opportunity to hand Jesus over. Table 3.5 contains the cases where two or more lexemes in one semantic domain appear in a paragraph.[23]

---

20    Here, "blood" is being modified by two different concepts: "my" and "of the covenant." It may be possible to see "of the covenant" as a substitution connected with "my," but the covenant is the one that directly connects Jesus himself. Since it is difficult to see as a supplementary word, it is not considered as a substitution.

21    In 26:29, "new" (καινὸν) can also be linked to new information about wine, but given the formula that Jesus said is new, "to drink with you in the Father's kingdom," at least what Jesus is saying is different from the wine he was holding; thus, it seems difficult to see it as a substitution.

22    Although these two appear in Old Testament quotations, they are not difficult to connect as concepts that refer to Jesus and his disciples, respectively, so it seems that they should be regarded as a substitution.

23    In Table 3.5, the lexeme with "cf." does not belong to the corresponding semantic domain but indicates a semantically connected lexeme.

110                                                                                  CHAPTER 3

TABLE 3.5    Semantic domains of the lexemes in Matt 26:14–16

| Lexeme | Verse | Semantic domain |
|---|---|---|
| δίδωμι | v. 15 | 57.71 |
| παραδίδωμι | vv. 15, 16 | 57.77/37.111[a] |
| cf. ἵστημι | v. 15 | 85.40 |
| εἷς | v. 14 | 60.10 |
| δώδεκα | v. 14 | 60.21 |
| τριάκοντα | v. 15 | 60.28 |
| τότε | vv. 14, 16 | 67.47 |
| εὐκαιρία | v. 16 | 67.5 |
| λέγω | v. 14 | 33.131 |
|  | v. 15 | 33.69 |
| θέλω | v. 15 | 30.58 |
| cf. ζητέω | v. 16 | 27.41 |

a   Παραδίδωμι has the sense of "to hand over/betray (a person)" (37.111) and "give over (a right or
    authority)" (57.77). See J. P. Louw and E. A. Nida, *Greek-English Lexicon of the New Testament
    Based on Semantic Domains* (2 vols.; 2nd ed.; New York: United Bible Societies, 1989), 485, 567.
    Here domain 57.77/37.111 is written in consideration of the connection with δίδωμι, but it is
    natural to see the actual meaning of this word as 37.111 in the text. All subsequent cases of
    παραδίδωμι are considered as 37.111.

The lexeme δίδωμι ("to give") and the lexical item[24] παραδίδωμι ("to deliver")
belong to domain 57, and ἵστημι, which means "to put/give," can be semantically related to this domain in terms of the "deal" on Jesus, and thus they form
semantic-lexical tie. There are three numbers in domain 60 (εἷς ["one"], δώδεκα
["twelve"], τριάκοντα ["thirty"]), and they are tied around Judas: he was "one"
of the "twelve" and sold Jesus for "thirty" pieces of silver; thus, they form a
semantic-lexical tie. The lexemes τότε (2×; "at that time") and εὐκαιρία ("opportunity") both belong to domain 67. These two lexemes are tied around the time
of Judas's action on betraying Jesus; thus, they form a semantic-lexical tie. The
lexical item λέγω is reiterated two times: the first case in 26:14, which means

---

24   According to Halliday and Hasan, a lexical item is "not bound to a particular grammatical
     category, or to a particular morphological form." It is "not totally clearcut," but "less inde-
     terminate than the folk-linguistic term WORD." See Halliday and Hasan, *Cohesion*, 291–92.
     In this study, when a lexeme appears in two or more forms within a semantic domain, it
     is expressed as a "lexical item."

MODE REGISTER ANALYSIS OF MATTHEW 26:14–35

"to call" (domain 33.131), is used to introduce Judas, and the second case in 26:15, which means "to say" (domain 33.69), is in a narrative speech margin; thus, they are not semantically related, although they both belong to the domain 33. The lexeme θέλω ("to want/wish"; domain 30) and ζητέω ("to seek"; domain 27) can be semantically related since they are tied around the desire of the high priests and Judas; thus, these lexemes form a semantic-lexical tie. From these analyses, we can find four semantic-lexical ties in 26:14–16. Furthermore, among the seventeen content lexemes in the first paragraph, the number of lexemes in the semantic-lexical ties is twelve. The ratio of the lexemes that can be formed into semantic-lexical ties per the number of content lexemes is 70.59%.[25] Thus, these overall results certainly reveal the cohesiveness of this paragraph.

The second paragraph (26:17–19) describes the process of preparing the Passover by Jesus and the disciples. The semantic domains of the lexemes are shown in Table 3.6.

TABLE 3.6    Semantic domains of the lexemes in Matt 26:17–19

| Lexeme | Verse | Semantic domain |
| --- | --- | --- |
| ἑτοιμάζω | vv. 17, 19 | 77.3 |
| μαθητής | vv. 17, 18, 19 | 36.38 |
| διδάσκαλος | v. 18 | 33.243 |
| λέγω | v. 18 | 33.69 |
| συντάσσω | v. 19 | 33.325 |
| πάσχα[a] | vv. 17, 18, 19 | 51.7 |
| cf. ἄζυμος | v. 17 | 5.13 |
| ποιέω | vv. 18, 19 | 90.45 |
| καιρός | v. 18 | 67.78 |
| ἐγγύς | v. 18 | 67.61 |

a    Although this lexeme is a proper noun, it is dealt with here because it forms a semantic-lexical tie by repetition rather than forming a participant-referent tie.

25    The ratio regarding semantic-lexical ties aims to show how strong the cohesiveness is in a target paragraph. Though there is no objective standard to evaluate it, as mentioned earlier, near to or over 50% may well represent strong cohesiveness of the paragraph.

The lexical item ἑτοιμάζω ("to prepare"; domain 77), which is reiterated two times, is tied around the Passover preparation, and these form a semantic-lexical tie. The lexical item μαθητής ("disciple"; domain 36.38) is reiterated three times. The plural forms of μαθητής appear as the preparers (26:17, 19) and participants (26:18) of the Passover; thus, the cases form a semantic-lexical tie.[26] The lexemes διδάσκαλος ("teacher"), λέγω (to say), and συντάσσω ("to direct/order"), which belong to domain 33, are tied around Jesus giving directions for the Passover; thus, they form a semantic-lexical tie. The lexeme πάσχα ("Passover"; domain 51) is reiterated three times and ἄζυμος ("unleavened bread"; domain 5) can be semantically related to πάσχα because of the close connection between the Passover and the feast of Unleavened Bread;[27] thus, they form a semantic-lexical tie. The lexical item ποιέω (domain 90) is reiterated two times, which is semantically tied around the Passover; thus, the cases of ποιέω form a semantic-lexical tie. καιρός ("time") and ἐγγύς ("near") belong to domain 67, which is semantically related to Jesus' death; thus, they form a semantic-lexical tie. From these analyses, we can find six semantic-lexical ties in 26:17–19. Furthermore, among twenty-five content lexemes in the second paragraph, the number of lexemes in the semantic-lexical ties is sixteen. The ratio of the lexemes that can be formed into semantic-lexical ties per the number of content lexemes is 64%. Thus, these overall results clearly reveal the cohesiveness of this paragraph.

The third paragraph (26:20–25) conveys Jesus' foretelling about the betrayer and the disciples' responses (including Judas). The semantic domains of the lexemes in this paragraph are shown in Table 3.7.

There are two numbers in domain 60 (εἷς ["one"], δώδεκα ["twelve"]), and they are tied around the topic of betraying Jesus (one of the twelve); in this sense, they form a semantic-lexical tie. The lexical item παραδίδωμι ("to hand over/betray"; domain 37), which is semantically tied around the main topic of this paragraph, betraying Jesus, is reiterated four times, and these lexical items form a semantic-lexical tie. The lexical item ἄνθρωπος ("man"; domain 9) is reiterated four times; two of them form collocation with υἱός (ὁ υἱὸς τοῦ ἀνθρώπου), which refer to Jesus, and the other two (τῷ ἀνθρώπῳ; ὁ ἄνθρωπος)

---

26    In this paragraph, the disciples (οἱ μαθηταί; the plural form of μαθητής) are closely linked to Jesus in that the disciples come to Jesus (τῷ Ἰησοῦ), are called "my disciples" (τῶν μαθητῶν μου) by him, and obey as Jesus directs them (ὡς συνέταξεν αὐτοῖς ὁ Ἰησοῦς).

27    In the first century, the Passover and the Feast of Unleavened Bread were commonly regarded as an eight-day feast, and there was a tendency to collectively refer to them as the Passover or the Feast of Unleavened Bread. See Rovert H. Gundry, *Matthew: A Commentary on His Handbook for a Mixed Church under Persecution* (2nd ed; Grand Rapids: Eerdmans, 1994), 524.

# MODE REGISTER ANALYSIS OF MATTHEW 26:14–35

TABLE 3.7    Semantic domains of the lexemes in Matt 26:20–25

| Lexeme | Verse | Semantic domain |
|---|---|---|
| δώδεκα | v. 20 | 60.21 |
| εἷς | v. 21 | 60.10 |
| παραδίδωμι | vv. 21, 23, 24, 25 | 37.111 |
| υἱὸς τοῦ ἀνθρώπου[a] | v. 24 (2×) | 9.3 |
| ἄνθρωπος | v. 24 (2×) | 9.1 |
| λέγω | vv. 21 (2×), 22, 23, 25 (3×) | 33.69 |
| γράφω | v. 24 | 33.61 |
| ἀποκρίνομαι | vv. 23, 25 | 33.184[b] |
| ῥαββί | v. 25 | 33.246 |
| μήτι | vv. 22, 25 | 69.16 |
| οὐκ | v. 24 | 69.3 |

a  The phrase υἱὸς τοῦ ἀνθρώπου ("son of man") is a collocation of two lexemes (ἄνθρωπος, υἱός), which refers to Jesus in the Gospel texts. According to Louw and Nida, "son of man" is "a title with Messianic implications used by Jesus concerning himself," so they regard it as a lexeme unit in domain 9.3. See Louw and Nida, *Greek-English Lexicon*, 104. In the lexical cohesion analysis, this is regarded as one content word.

b  In Louw-Nida's lexicon, those with the meaning of "answer" are placed in domain 33.184, and those with the meaning of "speak" are placed in domain 33.28. However, in the cases of verses 22 and 25 in this study, although they do not answer the question directly, they belong to the same category as the "answer" because they contain words corresponding to Jesus' words.

refer to the betrayer (Judas). Thus, each case forms a semantic-lexical tie. The lexical items regarding education and speech (λέγω ["to say"; 26:21b,[28] 26:25c], γράφω ["to write"], ἀποκρίνομαι ["to answer"], ῥαββί ["Rabbi/Master"]) belong to domain 33. In terms of the flow of communication, they can be regarded as a semantic-lexical tie. The lexeme μήτι (domain 69.16), an interrogative article expecting a negative answer, is reiterated two times, which is used for the disciples and Judas's answers; thus, the cases form a semantic-lexical tie. The lexeme οὐκ (domain 69.3) is used to convey Jesus' words to the betrayer ("it would have been better for that man if he had *not* been born"); thus, it seems difficult to find a semantic-lexical connection with μήτι. From these analyses, we can find four semantic-lexical ties in 26:20–25. Furthermore, among

---

28    Here λέγω is used as a collocation with ἀμήν and ὑμῖν (ἀμὴν λέγω ὑμῖν), and it functions as an intro of the following (Jesus' foretelling about the disciples' betrayal). In terms of its function, it can be related to a narrative speech margin.

114 CHAPTER 3

TABLE 3.8    Semantic domains of the lexemes in Matt 26:26–30

| Lexeme | Verse | Semantic domain |
| --- | --- | --- |
| ἐσθίω | v. 26 (2×) | 23.1 |
| πίνω | vv. 27, 29 (2×) | 23.34 |
| λαμβάνω | vv. 26 (2×), 27 | 18.1 |
| ἄρτος | v. 26 | 5.8 |
| cf. ποτήριον | v. 27 | 6.121 |
| εὐλογέω | v. 26 | 33.470 |
| εὐχαριστέω | v. 27 | 33.349 |
| ὑμνέω | v. 30 | 33.113 |
| δίδωμι | vv. 26, 27 | 57.71 |
| σῶμα | v. 26 | 8.1 |
| αἷμα | v. 28 | 8.64 |
| ἄφεσις | v. 28 | 37.132 |
| βασιλεία | v. 29 | 37.64 |
| ἄρτι | v. 29 | 67.38 |
| ἡμέρα | v. 29 | 67.178 |
| ἄμπελος | v. 29 | 3.27 |
| ἐλαία | v. 30 | 3.9 |

thirty-nine content lexemes in the third paragraph, the number of lexemes in the semantic-lexical ties is seventeen. The ratio of the lexemes that can be formed into semantic-lexical ties per the number of content lexemes is 43.59%. Thus, these overall results may reveal the cohesiveness of this paragraph.

The fourth paragraph (26:26–30) is about the Eucharist. The semantic domains of the lexemes in this paragraph are shown in Table 3.8.

The lexical item ἐσθίω ("to eat") is reiterated two times, and the other lexical item πίνω ("to drink") is also reiterated two times. They belong to domain 23, revealing the actions regarding the Passover and Eucharist; thus, they form semantic-lexical ties. The lexical item λαμβάνω ("to take"; domain 18) is reiterated three times, which is tied around Jesus' actions regarding bread and a cup; thus, the three lexemes in λαμβάνω form a semantic-lexical tie. The lexemes εὐλογέω ("to bless"), εὐχαριστέω ("to thank"), and ὑμνέω (sing a hymn) belong to domain 33, and they share common properties as communication towards/from God; thus, they form a semantic-lexical tie. The lexeme ἄρτος ("bread") belongs to domain 5, and ποτήριον ("cup"; domain 6) can be semantically tied with ἄρτος, and the reason is as follows. Considering 26:29 (ἐκ

MODE REGISTER ANALYSIS OF MATTHEW 26:14–35 115

τοῦ γενήματος τῆς ἀμπέλου ["of this fruit of the grapevine"]), what was in the "cup" was probably οἶνος ("wine"; John 2:3).[29] Since bread and a cup (wine) refer to/symbolize Jesus' body and blood, ἄρτος and ποτήριον are semantically tied in the topic of the Eucharist; thus, they form a semantic-lexical tie.[30] The lexical item δίδωμι (domain 57) is reiterated two times, which conveys Jesus' actions of "giving" bread and a cup to the disciples; thus, these two cases form a semantic-lexical tie. The lexemes σῶμα ("body") and αἷμα ("blood") belong to domain 8. They are semantically tied as a case of superordinate; thus, they form a semantic-lexical tie. The lexemes ἄφεσις ("liberty") and βασιλεία ("reign/king-dom") belong to domain 37, which are related to the topic of "control and rule." Semantically, the "liberty" from sin is the result of the "kingdom (reign)" of God; thus, they form a semantic-lexical tie. Two lexemes ἄρτι ("now") and ἡμέρα ("day") belong to domain 67, and they are semantically tied in terms of the period "from" when Jesus does not drink wine "to" when he drinks wine; thus, they form a semantic-lexical tie. The lexemes ἄμπελος (grapevine) and ἐλαία (olive) belong to domain 3; however, it seems hard to find a semantic-lexical tie from this since grapevine is concerned with the Eucharist, and olive is the name of a mountain. From this, we can find eight semantic-lexical ties in 26:26–30. Furthermore, among the thirty-six content lexemes in the fourth paragraph, the number of lexemes in the semantic-lexical ties is twenty-one. The ratio of the lexemes that can be formed into semantic-lexical ties per the number of content lexemes is 58.33%. Thus, these overall results apparently reveal the cohesiveness of this paragraph.

The fifth paragraph (26:31–35) conveys Jesus' prediction of the stumbling of his disciples, along with Peter's denial. The semantic domains of the lexemes in this paragraph are shown in Table 3.9.

The lexical item σκανδαλίζω ("to stumble"; domain 31) is reiterated three times, which conveys the main topic of this paragraph (the disciples' stum-bling); thus, the cases form a semantic-lexical tie. The lexical items (λέγω ["to say"], γράφω ["to write"], ἀπαρνέομαι ["to deny"]) belong to domain 33, which are semantically related to Jesus' foretelling; thus, the cases form a semantic-lexical tie. Two lexemes διασκορπίζω ("to scatter") and προάγω ("go before") belong to domain 15. Here, διασκορπίζω means the scattering of the flock (disciples), and προάγω makes us anticipate the gathering of the dis-ciples by Jesus going to Galilee before them; thus, these two lexemes are

---

29    Interestingly, οἶνος belongs to domain 6 (artifact), not domain 5 (food). See Louw and Nida, *Greek-English Lexicon*, 77.

30    Ποτήριον is an artifact to carry liquids, and such liquids/drinks are included in domain 5 (e.g., πόσις/πόμα ["drink"; domain 5.6]). See Louw and Nida, *Greek-English Lexicon*, 49.

116                                                                                              CHAPTER 3

TABLE 3.9    Semantic domains of the lexemes in Matt 26:31–35

| Lexeme | Verse | Semantic domain |
|---|---|---|
| σκανδαλίζω | vv. 31, 33 (2×) | 31.78[a] |
| λέγω | v. 34 | 33.69 |
| γράφω | v. 31 | 33.61 |
| ἀπαρνέομαι | vv. 34, 35 | 33.277 |
| διασκορπίζω | v. 31 | 15.136 |
| προάγω | v. 32 | 15.142 |
| πρόβατον | v. 31 | 4.22 |
| ποίμνη | v. 31 | 4.28 |
| ἀλέκτωρ | v. 34 | 4.45 |
| τότε | v. 31 | 67.47 |
| νύξ | vv. 31, 34 | 67.192 |
| οὐδέποτε | v. 33 | 67.10 |
| πρίν | v. 34 | 67.17 |
| ἐγείρω | v. 32 | 23.94 |
| ἀποθνῄσκω | v. 35 | 23.99 |

a   Louw-Nida's lexicon interprets this as "cause to no longer believe" (Louw and Nida, *Greek-English Lexicon*, 376), but I doubt whether it is appropriate. It does not reflect the meaning of "stumble" anywhere, unfortunately. It is the part that feels a bit artificial.

semantically intertwined with each other, and they form a semantic-lexical tie. Three lexemes πρόβατον ("sheep"), ποίμνη ("flock"), and ἀλέκτωρ ("cock") belong to domain 4. The first two lexemes are related to the scattering of the disciples, and the last lexeme is related to Peter's denial. Both "scattering" and "denial" belong to the category of "stumbling" (σκανδαλίζω), and thus they form a semantic-lexical tie. Four lexemes, related to time (τότε ["at that time"], νύξ ["night"], οὐδέποτε ["at no time"], πρίν [before]), belong to domain 67. Here, τότε is the temporal deixis of 26:31–35, and νύξ expresses the time of the disciples' stumbling (26:31) and Peter's denial (26:34). Οὐδέποτε appears in Peter's statement that he would deny Jesus "at no time," and πρίν functions to indicate the specific point in time ("before" the cock crows) when Peter denies Jesus. In this respect, the three lexemes (νύξ, οὐδέποτε, πρίν), excluding τότε, are semantically connected and form a semantic-lexical tie. Two lexemes ἐγείρω ("to raise up") and ἀποθνῄσκω ("to die") belong to domain 23. The first lexeme refers to Jesus' "resurrection," and the second is related to Peter's statement that he

MODE REGISTER ANALYSIS OF MATTHEW 26:14–35

would never deny Jesus, which contains the topic of "death." These two concepts, death and resurrection, are semantically connected, and thus they form a semantic-lexical tie. From these analyses, we can find six semantic-lexical ties in 26:31–35. Furthermore, among the twenty-seven content lexemes in the fifth paragraph, the number of lexemes in the semantic-lexical ties is eighteen. The ratio of the lexemes that can be formed into semantic-lexical ties per the number of content lexemes is 66.67%. Thus, these overall results clearly reveal the cohesiveness of this paragraph.

2.4.2 Lexical Cohesion in Matthew 26:14–35

Figure 3.6 reveals the lexical cohesion chains in Matthew 26:14–35.

---

$^{14}$ Τότε πορευθεὶς εἷς τῶν δώδεκα, ὁ λεγόμενος Ἰούδας Ἰσκαριώτης, πρὸς τοὺς ἀρχιερεῖς $^{15}$ εἶπεν· τί θέλετέ μοι δοῦναι, κἀγὼ ὑμῖν <u>παραδώσω</u> αὐτόν; οἱ δὲ ἔστησαν αὐτῷ τριάκοντα ἀργύρια. $^{16}$ καὶ ἀπὸ τότε ἐζήτει εὐκαιρίαν ἵνα αὐτὸν <u>παραδῷ</u>. $^{17}$ Τῇ δὲ πρώτῃ τῶν ἀζύμων προσῆλθον οἱ μαθηταὶ τῷ Ἰησοῦ λέγοντες· ποῦ θέλεις ἑτοιμάσωμέν σοι φαγεῖν τὸ πάσχα; $^{18}$ ὁ δὲ εἶπεν· ὑπάγετε εἰς τὴν πόλιν πρὸς τὸν δεῖνα καὶ εἴπατε αὐτῷ· ὁ διδάσκαλος λέγει· ὁ καιρός μου ἐγγύς ἐστιν, πρὸς σὲ ποιῶ τὸ πάσχα μετὰ τῶν μαθητῶν μου. $^{19}$ καὶ ἐποίησαν οἱ μαθηταὶ ὡς συνέταξεν αὐτοῖς ὁ Ἰησοῦς καὶ ἡτοίμασαν τὸ πάσχα. $^{20}$ Ὀψίας δὲ γενομένης ἀνέκειτο μετὰ τῶν δώδεκα. $^{21}$ καὶ ἐσθιόντων αὐτῶν εἶπεν· ἀμὴν λέγω ὑμῖν ὅτι εἷς ἐξ ὑμῶν <u>παραδώσει</u> με. $^{22}$ καὶ λυπούμενοι σφόδρα ἤρξαντο λέγειν αὐτῷ εἷς ἕκαστος· μήτι ἐγώ εἰμι, κύριε; $^{23}$ ὁ δὲ ἀποκριθεὶς εἶπεν· ὁ ἐμβάψας μετ' ἐμοῦ τὴν χεῖρα ἐν τῷ τρυβλίῳ οὗτός <u>με παραδώσει</u>. $^{24}$ ὁ μὲν υἱὸς τοῦ ἀνθρώπου <u>ὑπάγει</u> καθὼς γέγραπται περὶ αὐτοῦ, οὐαὶ δὲ τῷ ἀνθρώπῳ ἐκείνῳ δι' οὗ ὁ υἱὸς τοῦ ἀνθρώπου <u>παραδίδοται</u>· καλὸν ἦν αὐτῷ εἰ οὐκ ἐγεννήθη ὁ ἄνθρωπος ἐκεῖνος. $^{25}$ ἀποκριθεὶς δὲ Ἰούδας ὁ <u>παραδιδοὺς</u> αὐτὸν εἶπεν· μήτι ἐγώ εἰμι, ῥαββί; λέγει αὐτῷ· σὺ εἶπας. $^{26}$ Ἐσθιόντων δὲ αὐτῶν λαβὼν ὁ Ἰησοῦς ἄρτον καὶ εὐλογήσας ἔκλασεν καὶ δοὺς τοῖς μαθηταῖς εἶπεν· λάβετε φάγετε, τοῦτό ἐστιν <u>τὸ σῶμά μου</u>. $^{27}$ καὶ λαβὼν ποτήριον καὶ εὐχαριστήσας ἔδωκεν αὐτοῖς λέγων· πίετε ἐξ αὐτοῦ πάντες, $^{28}$ τοῦτο γάρ ἐστιν <u>τὸ αἷμά μου</u> τῆς διαθήκης τὸ περὶ πολλῶν ἐκχυννόμενον εἰς ἄφεσιν ἁμαρτιῶν. $^{29}$ λέγω δὲ ὑμῖν, οὐ μὴ πίω ἀπ' ἄρτι ἐκ τούτου τοῦ γενήματος τῆς ἀμπέλου ἕως τῆς ἡμέρας ἐκείνης ὅταν αὐτὸ πίνω μεθ' ὑμῶν καινὸν ἐν τῇ βασιλείᾳ τοῦ πατρός μου. $^{30}$ Καὶ ὑμνήσαντες ἐξῆλθον εἰς τὸ ὄρος τῶν ἐλαιῶν. $^{31}$ Τότε λέγει αὐτοῖς ὁ Ἰησοῦς· πάντες ὑμεῖς <u>σκανδαλισθήσεσθε</u> ἐν ἐμοὶ ἐν τῇ νυκτὶ ταύτῃ, γέγραπται γάρ· πατάξω τὸν ποιμένα, καὶ <u>διασκορπισθήσονται</u> τὰ πρόβατα τῆς ποίμνης. $^{32}$ μετὰ δὲ τὸ ἐγερθῆναί με <u>προάξω ὑμᾶς εἰς τὴν Γαλιλαίαν</u>. $^{33}$ ἀποκριθεὶς δὲ ὁ Πέτρος εἶπεν αὐτῷ· εἰ πάντες σκανδαλισθήσονται ἐν σοί, ἐγὼ οὐδέποτε <u>σκανδαλισθήσομαι</u>. $^{34}$ ἔφη αὐτῷ ὁ Ἰησοῦς· ἀμὴν λέγω σοι ὅτι ἐν ταύτῃ τῇ νυκτὶ πρὶν ἀλέκτορα φωνῆσαι τρὶς <u>ἀπαρνήσῃ</u> με. $^{35}$ λέγει αὐτῷ ὁ Πέτρος· κἂν δέῃ με σὺν σοὶ <u>ἀποθανεῖν</u>, οὐ μή σε <u>ἀπαρνήσομαι</u>. ὁμοίως καὶ πάντες οἱ μαθηταὶ εἶπαν.

---

FIGURE 3.6 Lexical cohesion chains in Matt 26:14–35

118                                                                                                     CHAPTER 3

The lexemes underlined above can be related to Jesus' death.[31] His death is revealed indirectly by ὑπάγει (to depart), τὸ σῶμά μου (my body), and τὸ αἷμά μου (my blood).[32] His death is carried out by the act of handing over (betrayal; παραδίδωμι) of one of the disciples, Judas. After Jesus' arrest as a result of Judas's betrayal, the disciples scatter (διασκορπίζω), and after that, Peter's denial (ἀπαρνέομαι) takes place before Jesus' death. Here, disciples' scattering and Peter's denial can be regarded as their reactions to Jesus' death to come; thus, the actions of scattering and denial can be related to the death of Jesus. The three actions of the disciples including Judas, namely, handing over, denying, and scattering, can be condensed into one concept, "stumbling" (σκανδαλίζω). The notion of "death" itself appears not in the statement of Jesus himself, but in that of Peter (κἂν δέῃ με σὺν σοὶ ἀποθανεῖν, οὐ μή σε ἀπαρνήσομαι). Thus, this discourse maintains cohesiveness around the topic of Jesus' death.

### 2.5    *Summary and Implication*

This section attempted to analyze Matthew 26:14–35 via a fivefold scheme of cohesion: conjunction, reference, substitution, ellipsis, and lexical cohesion. In terms of conjunction analyses, there are some cases of asyndeton (26:18f, 25c, 34a, 35a). Two of them (26:34a, 35a) are explicable as the constructor's style, but the other two cases (26:18f, 25c) seem unnatural. Each paragraph of Matthew 26:14–35 maintains cohesiveness overall, but the two cases of asyndeton in 26:18f and 26:25c may lower the degree of cohesiveness. In terms of reference, the results are as follows: (1) overall, each paragraph forms a participant-reference chain via the main participants; thus, the cohesiveness of each paragraph can be confirmed; (2) the appropriate appearances of the proper noun (grammaticalized reference) for Jesus (×5) seem to secure the cohesiveness; (3) the appearance of the pronoun (reduced reference) for Jesus in the first paragraph seems to lower the degree of cohesiveness (26:16). In terms of substitution and ellipsis, we can recognize the designated text's cohesiveness via the ten cases of substitution and the two cases of ellipsis. In terms of lexical cohesion, we can identify the cohesiveness of each paragraph by semantic-lexical ties. Also, the conceptual flow in the lexemes centering on Jesus' death shows the cohesiveness of the whole designated text.

The implications of this analysis are as follows: the designated text has cohesiveness overall; it primarily reveals the possibility of one constructor's

---

31    In the lexical cohesion chains of the table, the direct relationship between lexemes is indicated by a blue line, and a grey line indicates the indirect relationship. The blue lines are the lexemes carrying Jesus' death more directly.

32    The two elements of the Eucharist, τὸ σῶμά μου (my body) and τὸ αἷμά μου (my blood), convey Jesus' death since Jesus' body was broken (cf. ἔκλασεν; 26:26) and his blood was poured out (ἐκχυννόμενον; 26:28).

formation of this text. However, the existence of features that may lower the degree of cohesiveness may perhaps be an indication that oral tradition(s), along with written sources, were preserved by the constructor.

## 3 Orality and Textuality[33]

This section analyzes the designated text's lexical density and grammatical intricacy according to Porter's methodology based on Halliday's understanding of oral and written language.

### 3.1 *Lexical Density*
Table 3.10 reveals the lexical density of Matthew 26:14–35.

The total number of words in Matthew 26:14–35 is 363, and the total lexical density is 2.849 (151/53). According to Halliday's criteria,[34] this text is close to oral language. The designated text includes the direct speech parts (26:15b, 17b, 18b, 21b, 22b, 23b, 24, 25b, 25d, 26b, 27b, 28, 29, 31b, 32, 33b, 34b, 35b) and narratives (26:14, 15a, 15c, 16, 17a, 18a, 19, 20, 21a, 22a, 23a, 25a, 25c, 26a, 27a, 30, 31a, 33a, 34a, 35a, 35c), so it seems meaningful to observe their lexical density separately. The lexical density of each part is shown in Table 3.11.

TABLE 3.10   Lexical density of Matt 26:14–35

| Lexical density | 26:14–25 | 26:26–30 | 26:31–35 |
| --- | --- | --- | --- |
| Non-embedded clauses | 31 | 11 | 11 |
| Content words | 83 | 36 | 32 |
| Functional words | 107 | 51 | 54 |
| Content words per non-embedded clause | 2.677 | 3.272 | 2.909 |

33   When analyzing lexical density and grammatical intricacy, for convenience, the analysis part for the Eucharistic words is placed in the center, and the rest of the text analysis is placed before and after it respectively. In terms of the clause analysis, this section follows the results of www.opentext.org.

34   As mentioned in chapter 2, according to Halliday, the range of oral language's lexical density is 1–2 and that of written language's lexical density is 3–6 (Halliday, *Spoken and Written Language*, 80). Although the criteria of lexical density presented by Halliday were intended for English, Porter's study "Orality and Textuality" reveals the validity of using these criteria for Greek; this study relies on Porter's study.

TABLE 3.11  Lexical density of the direct speech and narrative in Matt 26:14–35

| Lexical density | Direct speech | Narrative |
| --- | --- | --- |
| Non-embedded clauses | 31 | 22 |
| Content words | 77 | 74 |
| Functional words | 143 | 69 |
| Content words per non-embedded clause | 2.483 | 3.364 |

According to the lexical density analysis above, the direct speech parts are in the category of oral language than the entire discourse, and the narratives are in the category of written language. Nonetheless, the narrative part is close to 3 (3.364). Then in light of Halliday's standard, it can be seen as close to oral language within the category of written language (3–6). This result could lead us to deduce that the constructor may have preserved the oral tradition especially in the direct speech part of the account. Speech part's more oral character than narrative part may surely be natural, considering speech is by nature oral. Overall, however, the average result of 2.849 points to the oral character of the whole designated text. Although it is difficult to determine from whom/which source these oral results originated (e.g., participant or former of oral tradition or constructor), this evidence may be understood as giving weight to oral tradition. Also, if Matthew, one of the twelve, was present in the context of the Eucharist, he surely would have taken part in the conversation and event. He, therefore, would naturally contribute to forming oral tradition of the Eucharist and preserve it in constructing the text. Thus, these phenomena seem to reveal the dual identity of Matthew, the contributor to oral tradition(s) and the preserver of that tradition(s) in the process of constructing the text.

### 3.2    *Grammatical Intricacy*

Table 3.12 reveals the grammatical intricacy of Matthew 26:14–35.

In 26:14–35, the number of non-embedded clauses is 53, the number of clause complexes is 19, and the result of non-embedded clause per clause complex is 2.789 (53/19). Halliday did not reveal his criteria regarding grammatical intricacy; however, at least, Halliday states that in terms of grammatical intricacy, the more oral, the number is higher.[35] Compared to Porter's analysis

---

35    Halliday, *Spoken and Written Language*, 87.

MODE REGISTER ANALYSIS OF MATTHEW 26:14–35 121

TABLE 3.12  Grammatical intricacy of Matt 26:14–35

| Grammatical intricacy | 26:14–25 | 26:26–30 | 26:31–35 |
| --- | --- | --- | --- |
| Non-embedded clauses | 31 | 11 | 11 |
| Total clauses | 50 | 21 | 20 |
| Clause complex | 10 | 4 | 5 |
| Non-embedded clause per clause complex | 3.1 | 2.75 | 2.2 |

of grammatical intricacy of several New Testament texts,[36] the number 2.789 seems high enough; thus, we can say that this text is close to oral language. It is difficult to analyze the grammatical intricacy by dividing the speech and the narrative parts, since a large part of the clause complex in the designated text appears in a merged form of these two parts. For this reason, it is excluded.[37]

### 3.3  Summary and Implication

The analytic results of orality and textuality of Matthew 26:14–35 are as follows. First, the lexical density is 2.849 (151/53); thus, this text as a whole is in the category of oral language. The results of the lexical density of the direct speech parts (2.483) and narrative parts (3.364) show that the direct speech part is more oral than the whole designated discourse, and that the narrative part can be seen as close to oral language within the category of written language. Second, the grammatical intricacy is 2.789 (53/19), and these results show that this text is in the category of oral language. Overall, these results may suggest the possibility that the oral tradition played a significant role in the process of constructing this text.

## 4  Verbal Aspect

### 4.1  Verbal Aspect Analysis

In terms of verbal aspect analysis, the verbs in the designated text can be shown as in Table 3.13.

---

36  Porter, "Orality and Textuality," 13. Here, Porter analyzes the grammatical intricacy of several texts as follows: Acts 12, 18 (2.1); Rom 2 (2.0); Cor 4 (2.3).

37  The same applies to chapters 4 and 5.

## 122 CHAPTER 3

TABLE 3.13 Analysis of verbs in Matt 26:14–35 focusing on verbal aspect[a]

| Perfective aspect (aorist) | Imperfective aspect | Stative aspect | Future |
|---|---|---|---|
| πορευθείς (14), εἶπεν (15), δοῦναι (15), ἔστησαν (15), παραδῷ (16), προσῆλθον (17), ἑτοιμάσωμέν (17), φαγεῖν (17), εἶπεν (18), εἴπατε (18), ἐποίησαν (19), συνέταξεν (19), ἡτοίμασαν (19), γενομένης (20), εἶπεν (21), ἤρξαντο (22), ἀπο-κριθείς (23), εἶπεν (23), ἐμβάψας (23), ἐγεννήθη (24), ἀποκριθείς (25), εἶπεν (25), εἶπας (25), λαβών (26), εὐλογήσας (26), ἔκλασεν (26), δοὺς (26), εἶπεν (26), λάβετε (26), φάγετε (26), λαβών (27), εὐχαριστήσας (27), ἔδωκεν (27), πίετε (27), πίω (29), ὑμνήσαντες (30), ἐξῆλθον (30), ἐγερθῆναί (32), ἀποκριθείς (33), εἶπεν (33), ἔφη (34), φωνῆσαι (34), ἀπο-θανεῖν (35), εἶπαν (35) | **Present** λεγόμενος (14), θέλετέ (15), λέγοντες (17), θέλεις (17), ὑπάγετε (18), λέγει (18), ἐστιν (18), ποιῶ (18), ἐσθιό-ντων (21), λέγω (21), λυπούμενοι (22), λέγειν (22), εἰμι (22), ὑπάγει (24), παραδίδοται (24), παραδιδοὺς (25), εἰμι (25), λέγει (25), ἐσθι-όντων (26), ἐστιν (26), λέγων (27), ἐστιν (28), ἐκχυννόμενον (28), λέγω (29), πίνω (29), λέγει (31), λέγω (34), λέγει (35), δέῃ (35) | **Perfect** γέγραπται (24), γέγραπται (31) | παραδώσω (15), παραδώ-σει (21), παραδώσει (23), σκανδαλισθήσεσθε (31), πατάξω (31), σκανδαλισθή-σονται (31), προάξω (32), σκανδαλισθήσονται (33), σκανδαλισθήσομαι (33), ἀπαρνήσῃ (34), ἀπαρνήσο-μαι (35) |
| | **Imperfective** ἐζήτει (16), ἀνέκειτο (20), ἦν (24) | **Pluperfect** | |

a The number in the bracket indicates the verse of the text that the word was used.

The results can be shown as follows: (1) perfective aspect (aorist): forty-four times; (2) imperfective aspect: nineteen times (present) + three times (imperfective); (3) stative aspect (perfect): two times; and (4) future: eleven times. As mentioned in chapter 2, Porter elucidates three verbal aspects according to the extent of their markedness: stative aspect is most weighted, the next is imperfective aspect, and the least weighted is perfective aspect. Most perfective aspect verbs play a role in forming the background of Jesus' Eucharistic words in the narrative process. Twenty-two usages of imperfective aspects

MODE REGISTER ANALYSIS OF MATTHEW 26:14–35

function as the foregrounded elements in the accounts. Two usages of stative aspects, "it is written" (γέγραπται; indicative perfect), function as the frontgrounded elements of the accounts which have Old Testament text in mind: Jesus' death and the disciples' denial of Jesus (26:24, 31). These results show the varying degree of markedness of the verbs in the designated text, and it is hard to discern from which/whom the markedness came. Three possible origins are as follows: (1) the participant within the text (including Jesus); (2) the eyewitness/former/contributor(s) of traditions; and (3) the constructor (1, 2 and 3 can overlap in the case of Matthew).[38] Comparative analysis in chapter 6 may help us to discern the possible origin(s).

### 4.2 Summary and Implication

The verbal aspect analysis of Matthew 26:14–35 shows us the varying degree of markedness of the verbs in the designated text. There are two frontgrounded parts via stative aspect (26:24, 31; "it is written" [γέγραπται; indicative perfect]), several foregrounded parts via imperfective aspect, and many background parts via perfective aspect. The varying degrees of markedness may have been affected by the oral/written traditions and/or the constructor.

### 5 Conclusion

This chapter identifies the mode (thematization, cohesion, orality & textuality, and verbal aspect) of Matthew 26:14–35. These are some notable features in terms of the designated text's textual characteristics. First, the thematization analysis shows that the designated text has twelve thematic units and five paragraphs, and each paragraph has one distinctive topic, while UBS[5]'s second paragraph holds two topics. The overlapping positions of prime and theme in this text show us the most marked-thematic actor as Jesus (2×). This analysis shows the well-organized structure of the designated text, from which we can deduce the constructor's significant contribution. Second, the results of cohesion analysis reveal that overall, the cohesiveness of each paragraph is maintained via conjunction ties, participant-reference chains (including substitution and ellipsis), and semantic-lexical ties. The cohesiveness of the entire designated text is also observed in lexical cohesion chains. There are several factors, however, that may lower the degree of cohesiveness (e.g., asyndeton

---

38    Among these cases, all the subjects (1, 2, 3) can be applied to direct speeches, and two of them (2, 3) can be applied to narratives.

[26:18f; 26:25c], a reduced reference [26:16]). These overall features may have come from one constructor, Matthew, perhaps along with the oral tradition(s). Third, via the analysis of lexical density and grammatical intricacy, it is revealed that the designated text is close to oral language, and in particular, the direct speech part is more oral than the narrative part, though the narrative part is still close to oral language within the category of written language. The oral properties of this text reveal the possibility that this text is significantly rooted in oral tradition. From these results, it is possible to deduce the dual identity of Matthew, the contributor to oral tradition and the preserver of the tradition in the process of constructing the text. Fourth, the results of verbal aspect analysis reveal the different levels of markedness of the verbs in the designated text. The varying markedness may have been affected by the oral/written traditions and/or the constructor.

CHAPTER 4

# Mode Register Analysis of Mark 14:10–31

## 1 Thematization

### 1.1 *Prime and Subsequent*

The prime-subsequent analysis of Mark 14:10–31 is presented in Appendix 2, and among the findings of this process, Table 4.1 shows various examples in 14:10–31.

Among the sixty-four clauses in Mark 14:10–31, the lexemes posited in prime, which are classified by type, are as follows: (1) subject (noun; 14:10a, 29a), (2) object (pronoun; 14:10b), (3) verb (inherent subject existence; 14:11b), (4) verb only (without subsequent; 14:11c), (5) interrogative adverb (14:11d), (6) prepositional phrase (14:12a), (7) verb (separate subject existence; 14:16a), (8) adverb (14:18d), (9) interrogative particle (14:19b), (10) particle of interjection (14:24c), (11) adjective (14:21e), (12) participle as an adverb (14:22b),

TABLE 4.1    Prime-subsequent examples in Mark 14:10–31

| Verse | Prime | Subsequent |
| --- | --- | --- |
| 14:10a | (Καὶ) Ἰούδας Ἰσκαριὼθ | ὁ εἷς τῶν δώδεκα ἀπῆλθεν πρὸς τοὺς ἀρχιερεῖς |
| 14:10b | (ἵνα) αὐτὸν | παραδοῖ αὐτοῖς. |
| 14:11b | (καὶ) ἐπηγγείλαντο | αὐτῷ ἀργύριον δοῦναι. |
| 14:11c | (καὶ) ἐζήτει | |
| 14:11d | πῶς | αὐτὸν εὐκαίρως παραδοῖ. |
| 14:12a | (Καὶ) τῇ πρώτῃ ἡμέρᾳ τῶν ἀζύμων, | ὅτε τὸ πάσχα ἔθυον, λέγουσιν αὐτῷ οἱ μαθηταὶ αὐτοῦ· |
| 14:16a | (καὶ) ἐξῆλθον | οἱ μαθηταὶ |
| 14:18d | ἀμὴν | λέγω ὑμῖν |
| 14:19b | μήτι | ἐγώ; |
| 14:21c | οὐαὶ (δὲ) | τῷ ἀνθρώπῳ ἐκείνῳ |
| 14:21e | καλὸν | αὐτῷ |
| 14:22b | λαβών | ἄρτον εὐλογήσας ἔκλασεν |
| 14:29a | ὁ (δὲ) Πέτρος | ἔφη αὐτῷ |
| 14:31a | ὁ (δὲ) | ἐκπερισσῶς ἐλάλει· |

© HOJOON J. AHN, 2024 | DOI:10.1163/9789004696372_006

126    CHAPTER 4

and (13) subject (definite article; 14:31a). From this analysis, we can realize the flexibility of New Testament Greek in terms of the position of each lexeme, and each prime shows what the clause focuses on. For example, in the case of 7, a verb is located in prime despite the existence of a separate subject, inferring that the text was constructed here to focus the clause on the process, not the subject. In the case of 1 and 13, however, the subject Peter is located in prime, and in that case, the subject is highly focused on. As mentioned earlier, such aspects of prime and subsequent offer the basis of the following theme-rheme analysis.

## 1.2    *Theme and Rheme*

A theme and rheme analysis of Mark 14:10–31 is found in Appendix 6. There are eight thematic units: (1) 14:10, (2) 14:11, (3) 14:12–17, (4) 14:18–26, (5) 14:27–29, (6) 14:30, (7) 14:31a, (8) 14:31b. The thematic actors, which are revealed by the theme and rheme analysis, are as follows: (1) Ἰούδας Ἰσκαριώθ (1×; 14:10), (2) οἱ (1×; 14:11 [14:10; τοὺς ἀρχιερεῖς]), (3) οἱ μαθηταί (1×; 14:12), (4) ὁ Ἰησοῦς (2×; 14:18, 30), (5) ὁ Πέτρος (1×; 14:29a), (6) ὁ (1×; 14:31a [14:29; ὁ Πέτρος]), and (7) πάντες (1×; 14:31b). Thus, the five thematic actors are Judas (1×), high priests (1×), disciples (2×), Jesus (3×), and Peter (2×). In terms of reiteration, Jesus appears most outstanding here. Furthermore, in the cases of 5 and 6 (14:29a, 31a), the thematic actor Peter is located in prime. Thus, from the above two analyses (prime-subsequent, theme-rheme), Peter turns out to be the most marked thematic actor. It seems a unique aspect of the designated text, which may indicate Peter's influence on the second Gospel.

## 1.3    *Topic and Comment*

### 1.3.1    Paragraph Division

This section divides Mark 14:10–31 into paragraphs and suggests a topic for each paragraph. The results will be compared with the paragraph divisions and topics provided by UBS[5].

UBS[5] divides Mark 14:10–31 into four paragraphs as follows: (1) Judas's agreement to betray Jesus (14:10–11), (2) the Passover with the disciples (14:12–21), (3) the institution of the Lord's supper (14:22–26), and (4) Peter's denial foretold (14:27–31). Based on the elements for paragraph division suggested in the methodology (one or more thematic units and thematic participants, temporal/spatial deixis, transition of topic, and lexical cohesion), this section will evaluate the paragraph division and titles offered by UBS[5] and suggest an alternative paragraph division.

The first paragraph suggested by UBS[5] is 14:10–11. There are two thematic units (14:10; 14:11) and two thematic participants (Ἰούδας Ἰσκαριώθ [14:10]; οἱ

MODE REGISTER ANALYSIS OF MARK 14:10–31

[14:11; cf. 14:10; τοὺς ἀρχιερεῖς]). This paragraph has no temporal deixis,[1] but there is a clear transition of topics, from "the anointing at Bethany" to "Judas's agreement to betray Jesus."[2] Furthermore, this paragraph consists of Judas's plan to betray Jesus and the high priests' proposal of giving silver the lexemes in the semantic domain 57 (δίδωμι; παραδίδωμι) cohesively tie this paragraph. Considering these aspects, the paragraph division of UBS[5] seems appropriate.

The second paragraph suggested by UBS[5] is 14:12–21. It is related to two thematic units (14:12–16; 14:17–26), and it has lexical cohesion in terms of its theme regarding Passover. However, it is not easy to agree with the division of UBS[5]; this study suggests 14:12–16 as one paragraph due to the following. First of all, 14:12–21 includes two temporal deictic phrases (τῇ πρώτῃ ἡμέρᾳ τῶν ἀζύμων [14:12]; ὀψίας γενομένης [14:17]) as boundary markers, so it seems difficult to regard 14:12–21 as one paragraph. Second, 14:12–16 is tied into one topic, the preparation for Passover, and it has one thematic unit as a minimum unit to become a paragraph; thus, it seems natural to regard this as one paragraph. The remaining part of UBS[5]'s second paragraph, 14:17–21, will be dealt with in the next section since it is included in the thematic unit 14:17–26.

The third paragraph suggested by UBS[5] is 14:22–26, which is included in the thematic unit 14:17–26, and its thematic participant is Jesus (ὁ Ἰησοῦς). Although 14:17–21 and 14:22–26 can be divided by topics (the betrayal and the Eucharist), they are in one thematic unit, which is the minimum unit of a paragraph, according to the thematic unit analysis. Furthermore, 14:22–26 has the deictic participle phrase (καὶ ἐσθιόντων αὐτῶν), which is linked to the situational participles of 14:18 (καὶ ἀνακειμένων αὐτῶν καὶ ἐσθιόντων).[3] Thus, in this sense, the third paragraph can be suggested as 14:17–26.

The fourth paragraph suggested by UBS[5] is 14:27–31. It has four thematic units (14:27–29, 30, 31a, 31b) and three thematic participants (ὁ Πέτρος; ὁ Ἰησοῦς; πάντες). There is no temporal deixis but there is a clear transition of topics, from "the institution of the Lord's Supper" to "Peter's Denial Foretold."[4] This paragraph mainly consists of a dialog between Jesus and Peter (as the

---

1 The temporal deixis of 14:1 (Ἦν δὲ τὸ πάσχα καὶ τὰ ἄζυμα μετὰ δύο ἡμέρας) is connected to this paragraph, differentiated with the new temporal deixis in 14:12 (τῇ πρώτῃ ἡμέρᾳ τῶν ἀζύμων).

2 These titles are from the UBS[5].

3 In general, "deixis" and its adjective, "deictic," are related to linguistic functions that indicate certain situational elements, and are primarily classified into personal, temporal, and spatial deixis. See P. H. Matthews, *The Concise Oxford Dictionary of Linguistics* (3rd ed.; Oxford: Oxford University Press, 2014), 97; Reed, *Philippians*, 94–97. Here, the adjective "deictic" is used differently from the general usage since this participle phrase functions as a contextual indication in the text.

4 These titles are from the UBS[5].

128                                                                                    CHAPTER 4

representative of the disciples), which starts with Jesus and ends with Peter
(Jesus → Peter → Jesus → Peter). At the end of 14:31, the narrative part conveying the disciples' response (except Peter) functions to end the paragraph. This
paragraph also forms lexical cohesion around σκανδαλίζω (14:27, 29; domain 31).
Considering these aspects, the paragraph division of UBS⁵ seems appropriate.

By applying thematization, the designated text can be divided into four
paragraphs as follows: (1) 14:10–11, (2) 14:12–16, (3) 14:17–26, and (4) 14:27–31.
The first, second, and fourth paragraphs are well-structured based on thematic
units, thematic participants, boundary markers, and lexical cohesions; however, the third paragraph has one thematic unit with two topics, which may
show the less organized aspect of this paragraph.

### 1.3.2   Finding Topics of Each Paragraph

This section presents the topic of each paragraph in light of the previous paragraph division. For this, the following provides a thematic participant-processes
analysis to find the topic of each paragraph. Table 4.2 presents the thematic
participants and processes of each thematic unit.

Each paragraph's topic in Mark 14:10–31 is analyzed by observing the thematic participants and major processes.

The major thematic processes of paragraph 1 (14:10–11) are as follows:
(1) Judas's action (going to the chief priests [14:10]) and (2) the chief priests'
reaction (promising Judas silver [14:10]). Judas's action is concerned with
betraying and handing over Jesus, and the reaction of the chief priests is concerned with paying the price for Judas's treachery. Given these points, the topic
of this paragraph is proposed as follows: a deal between Judas and the high
priests surrounding the betrayal to Jesus.

The major thematic processes of paragraph 2 (14:12–16) are the disciples'
actions (saying to Jesus [14:12], leaving [14:16], going into the city [14:16], and
preparing for the Passover [14:16]). The center of the disciples' actions is
related to preparing the Passover meal. Only the disciples are described as
thematic participants, excluding Jesus. Given these points, the topic of this
paragraph is proposed as follows: disciples' inquiry about Passover preparation and their obedience.

The major thematic processes of paragraph 3 (14:17–26) are Jesus' actions
(speaking about the betrayal [14:18], speaking about its details [14:20–21], taking bread [14:22], blessing [14:22], breaking the bread [14:22], giving the bread
to the disciples [14:22], speaking [14:22], taking a cup [14:23], giving the cup
to the disciples [14:23], speaking [14:24]). Jesus appears as the only thematic
participant in this paragraph. There are two characteristics of actions done
by Jesus. Firstly, his action relates to the prophecy of the future treachery and

MODE REGISTER ANALYSIS OF MARK 14:10−31          129

TABLE 4.2    Thematic participants and processes in Mark 14:10–31[a]

| Paragraph | Thematic unit | Verse | Thematic participant | Major process |
| --- | --- | --- | --- | --- |
| 1 | 1 | 10 | Judas Iscariot | went to the chief priests |
|   | 2 | 11 | they (the chief priests) | promised to give him (Judas) silver |
| 2 | 3 | 12–16 | the disciples | said to him (Jesus) left went to the city prepared the Passover |
| 3 | 4 | 17–26 | Jesus | said said to them (the disciples) took bread blessed broke it (bread) gave it to the disciples said took a cup gave it to them (the disciples) *said* to them (the disciples) |
| 4 | 5 | 29 | **Peter** | declared to him (Jesus) |
|   | 6 | 30 | Jesus | said to him (Peter) |
|   | 7 | 31a | **he** (Peter) | said to him (Jesus) |
|   | 8 | 31b | all (the disciples) | said so |

a  The words shown in bold reveals several active processes of the most marked-thematic actor (14:29, 31), that is, Peter.

his reference to the disciples' reaction. Secondly, at the center of Jesus' act, there are bread and wine—being blessed, given thanks, and distributed to the disciples—which imply Jesus' death. Given these points, the topic of this paragraph is proposed as follows: Jesus' foretelling of the betrayal and his institution of the Eucharist.

The major thematic processes of paragraph 4 (14:27–31) are carried out by Peter (declaring to Jesus [14:29], talking to Jesus [14:31a]), Jesus (talking to

130

CHAPTER 4

TABLE 4.3    Paragraph division & topics of UBS[5] and this study

| Paragraph division & topics of UBS[5] | Paragraph division & topics of this study |
| --- | --- |
| 1. Judas's agreement to betray Jesus (14:10–11) | 1. A deal between Judas and the high priests surrounding the betrayal to Jesus (14:10–11) |
| 2. The Passover with the disciples (14:12–21) | 2. Disciples' inquiry about Passover preparation and their obedience (14:12–16) |
| 3. The institution of the Lord's Supper (14:22–26) | 3. Jesus' foretelling of the betrayal and His institution of the Eucharist (14:17–26) |
| 4. Foretelling of peter's denial (14:27–31) | 4. Jesus' foretelling of the disciples' stumbling and Peter's denial (14:27–31) |

Peter [14:30]), and all the disciples (speaking the same as Peter [14:31b]). Peter's action is related to his willful expression that Jesus' foretelling about the stumbling (scattering) and the denial will not come true. Jesus' action is related to Peter's denial as well as his stumbling, and the other disciples' action is concerned with their sharing of Peter's statement. Given these points, the topic of this paragraph is proposed as follows: Jesus' foretelling of the disciples' stumbling and Peter's denial.

To summarize, the paragraph division and the topic for each paragraph of Mark 14:10–31 compared to UBS[5] are summarized in Table 4.3.

The paragraph division and topics suggested by this study show that the designated text has four paragraphs. In paragraphs 1, 2, and 4, each has one distinctive topic; however, the third paragraph has two distinctive topics ("Jesus' foretelling of the betrayal" and "Jesus' institution of the Eucharist"). These analytic results show the organized structure of the designated text overall, from which the constructor's role could be deduced. However, the phenomenon in the third paragraph (14:17–26) shows the less organized character of the designated text, which may show us the degree of the constructor's role in the construction process.

## 1.4    *Summary and Implication*

This section attempted an analysis of thematization for Mark 14:10–31; the following are the results. There are eight thematic units (1. 14:10; 2. 14:11; 3. 14:12–17; 4. 14:18–26; 5. 14:27–29; 6. 14:30; 7. 14:31a; 8. 14:31b), and overlapping positions of prime and theme reveals the most marked-thematic actor as Peter (2×; 14:29, 31). Unlike the paragraph division of UBS[5] (14:10–11, 14:12–21, 14:22–26, 14:27–31), this study divided the designated texts into the following four paragraphs: (1) 14:10–11, (2) 14:12–16, (3) 14:17–26, and (4) 14:27–31. The topic for each paragraph is suggested as follows: (1) a deal between Judas and the high priests surrounding the betrayal to Jesus (14:10–11), (2) the disciples' inquiry for Passover preparation and their obedience (14:12–16), (3) Jesus' foretelling of the betrayal and his institution of the Eucharist (14:17–26), and (4) Jesus' foretelling of the disciples' stumbling and Peter's denial (14:27–31).

These results show us the organized structure of the designated text overall, but the third paragraph, which has one thematic unit with two distinctive topics, reveals the less organized aspect. It is notable that the most marked-thematic actor is Peter. Considering these features, we could deduce the possibility of the construction based on the oral tradition, possibly contributed by Peter.

## 2 Cohesion

### 2.1 *Conjunction*

Table 4.4 shows conjunctions and asyndeton in Mark 14:10–31 divided into the narrative and direct speech parts.

TABLE 4.4 Conjunctions and asyndeton in the narratives and direct speeches of Mark 14:10–31

| Paragraphs | Narrative | Direct speech |
|---|---|---|
| 14:10–11 | ¹⁰ Καὶ Ἰούδας Ἰσκαριὼθ ὁ εἷς τῶν δώδεκα ἀπῆλθεν πρὸς τοὺς ἀρχιερεῖς ἵνα αὐτὸν παραδοῖ αὐτοῖς. ¹¹ οἱ δὲ ἀκούσαντες ἐχάρησαν καὶ ἐπηγγείλαντο αὐτῷ ἀργύριον δοῦναι. καὶ ἐζήτει πῶς αὐτὸν εὐκαίρως παραδοῖ. | |
| 14:12–16 | ¹² Καὶ τῇ πρώτῃ ἡμέρᾳ τῶν ἀζύμων, ὅτε τὸ πάσχα ἔθυον, λέγουσιν αὐτῷ οἱ μαθηταὶ αὐτοῦ· | |
| | | ∅ ποῦ θέλεις ἀπελθόντες ἑτοιμάσωμεν ἵνα φάγῃς τὸ πάσχα; |
| | ¹³ καὶ ἀποστέλλει δύο τῶν μαθητῶν αὐτοῦ καὶ λέγει αὐτοῖς· | |

132                                                                                    CHAPTER 4

TABLE 4.4    Conjunctions and asyndeton in the narratives and direct speeches (*cont.*)

| Paragraphs | Narrative | Direct speech |
|---|---|---|
| | | ∅ ὑπάγετε εἰς τὴν πόλιν, <u>καὶ</u> ἀπαντή-σει ὑμῖν ἄνθρωπος κεράμιον ὕδατος βαστάζων· ∅ ἀκολουθήσατε αὐτῷ [14] <u>καὶ</u> <u>ὅπου</u> ἐὰν εἰσέλθῃ εἴπατε τῷ οἰκοδεσπότῃ <u>ὅτι</u> ὁ διδάσκαλος λέγει· ∅ ποῦ ἐστιν τὸ κατάλυμά μου <u>ὅπου</u> τὸ πάσχα μετὰ τῶν μαθη-τῶν μου φάγω; [15] <u>καὶ</u> αὐτὸς ὑμῖν δείξει ἀνάγαιον μέγα ἐστρωμένον ἕτοιμον· <u>καὶ</u> ἐκεῖ ἑτοιμά-σατε ἡμῖν. |
| | [16] <u>καὶ</u> ἐξῆλθον οἱ μαθηταὶ <u>καὶ</u> ἦλθον εἰς τὴν πόλιν <u>καὶ</u> εὗρον <u>καθὼς</u> εἶπεν αὐτοῖς <u>καὶ</u> ἡτοίμασαν τὸ πάσχα. | |
| 14:17–26 | [17] <u>Καὶ</u> ὀψίας γενομένης ἔρχεται μετὰ τῶν δώδεκα. [18] <u>καὶ</u> ἀνακει-μένων αὐτῶν <u>καὶ</u> ἐσθιόντων ὁ Ἰησοῦς εἶπεν· | |
| | | ∅ ἀμὴν λέγω ὑμῖν <u>ὅτι</u> εἷς ἐξ ὑμῶν παραδώσει με ὁ ἐσθίων μετ' ἐμοῦ. |
| | [19] ∅ ἤρξαντο λυπεῖσθαι <u>καὶ</u> λέγειν αὐτῷ εἷς κατὰ εἷς· | |
| | | ∅ μήτι ἐγώ; |
| | [20] ὁ <u>δὲ</u> εἶπεν αὐτοῖς· | |
| | | ∅ εἷς τῶν δώδεκα, ὁ ἐμβαπτόμενος μετ' ἐμοῦ εἰς τὸ τρύβλιον. [21] <u>ὅτι</u> ὁ <u>μὲν</u> υἱὸς τοῦ ἀνθρώπου ὑπάγει <u>καθὼς</u> γέγραπται περὶ αὐτοῦ, οὐαὶ <u>δὲ</u> τῷ ἀνθρώπῳ ἐκείνῳ δι' οὗ ὁ υἱὸς τοῦ ἀνθρώπου παραδίδοται· καλὸν αὐτῷ <u>εἰ</u> οὐκ ἐγεννήθη ὁ ἄνθρωπος ἐκεῖνος. |
| | [22] <u>Καὶ</u> ἐσθιόντων αὐτῶν λαβὼν ἄρτον εὐλογήσας ἔκλασεν <u>καὶ</u> ἔδωκεν αὐτοῖς <u>καὶ</u> εἶπεν· | |

# MODE REGISTER ANALYSIS OF MARK 14:10–31    133

TABLE 4.4    Conjunctions and asyndeton in the narratives and direct speeches (*cont.*)

| Paragraphs | Narrative | Direct speech |
| --- | --- | --- |
| | | ∅ λάβετε, τοῦτό ἐστιν τὸ σῶμά μου. |
| | ²³ <u>καὶ</u> λαβὼν ποτήριον εὐχαριστή-σας ἔδωκεν αὐτοῖς, <u>καὶ</u> ἔπιον ἐξ αὐτοῦ πάντες. ²⁴ <u>καὶ</u> εἶπεν αὐτοῖς· | |
| | | ∅ τοῦτό ἐστιν τὸ αἷμά μου τῆς δια-θήκης τὸ ἐκχυννόμενον ὑπὲρ πολλῶν. ²⁵ ∅ ἀμὴν λέγω ὑμῖν <u>ὅτι</u> οὐκέτι οὐ μὴ πίω ἐκ τοῦ γενήματος τῆς ἀμπέλου <u>ἕως</u> τῆς ἡμέρας ἐκείνης <u>ὅταν</u> αὐτὸ πίνω καινὸν ἐν τῇ βασιλείᾳ τοῦ θεοῦ. |
| | ²⁶ <u>Καὶ</u> ὑμνήσαντες ἐξῆλθον εἰς τὸ ὄρος τῶν ἐλαιῶν. | |
| 14:27–31 | ²⁷ <u>καὶ</u> λέγει αὐτοῖς ὁ Ἰησοῦς ὅτι | |
| | | ∅ πάντες σκανδαλισθήσεσθε, <u>ὅτι</u> γέγραπται· |
| | | ∅ πατάξω τὸν ποιμένα, <u>καὶ</u> τὰ πρόβατα διασκορπισθήσονται. ²⁸ <u>ἀλλὰ</u> μετὰ τὸ ἐγερθῆναί με προάξω ὑμᾶς εἰς τὴν Γαλιλαίαν. |
| | ²⁹ ὁ <u>δὲ</u> Πέτρος ἔφη αὐτῷ· | |
| | | εἰ καὶ πάντες σκανδαλισθήσονται, <u>ἀλλ’</u> οὐκ ἐγώ. |
| | ³⁰ <u>καὶ</u> λέγει αὐτῷ ὁ Ἰησοῦς· | |
| | | ∅ ἀμὴν λέγω σοι <u>ὅτι</u> σὺ σήμερον ταύτῃ τῇ νυκτὶ <u>πρὶν</u> ἢ δὶς ἀλέκτορα φωνῆσαι τρίς με ἀπαρνήσῃ. |
| | ³¹ ὁ <u>δὲ</u> ἐκπερισσῶς ἐλάλει· | |
| | | <u>ἐὰν</u> δέῃ με συναποθανεῖν σοι, οὐ μή σε ἀπαρνήσομαι. |
| | ὡσαύτως <u>δὲ</u> <u>καὶ</u> πάντες ἔλεγον. | |

Conjunctions in the designated text are as follows: (1) καί (29×; 14:10, 11 [2×], 12, 13 [3×], 14, 15 [2×], 16 [4×], 17, 18 [2×], 19, 22 [3×], 23 [2×], 24, 26, 27 [2×], 30, 31); (2) ὅτι (7×; 14:14, 18, 21, 25, 27 [2×], 30); (3) δέ (5×; 14:11, 20, 21, 29, 31); (4) ἀλλά (2×; 14:28, 29); (5) ὅπου (2×; 14:14 [2×]); (6) καθώς (14:16, 21); (7) εἰ (2×;

134                                                                                      CHAPTER 4

14:21, 29), (8) ἵνα (1×; 14:10); (9) μέν (1×; 14:21); (10) ὅταν (1×; 14:25); (11) πρίν (1×; 14:30); (12) ἐάν (1×; 14:31). Synthetic forms of conjunctions do not appear in the designated text of Mark, and there are two consecutive conjunctions, δέ καί (14:31). The total number of conjunctions in the designated text is fifty-three, of which thirty-one of them belong to the narrative part, and twenty-two of them belong to the direct speech part. There are eleven asyndeton cases: ten cases in direct speech parts and one case in narrative parts.[5]

Now, we will analyze each appearance of conjunction in the contextual flow, according to the previous divided paragraphs. First, the conjunction analysis for the first paragraph (14:10–11) is as follows. 14:10 begins with καί. This conjunction is used here to convey continuity and transition in the context of a thematic change to Judas's betrayal after the story of a woman anointing Jesus (14:3–9). It is notable that καί appears rather than other conjunctions, such as τότε or δέ, that may seem more suitable for the transition of the subject.[6] The conjunction of the second clause of 14:10 is the subordinating conjunction ἵνα, which conveys the purpose of Judas: handing over Jesus to the high priests. The clauses in 14:11 are connected with three conjunctions (δέ, καί [2×]) to express the high priests' positive response to Judas's words, their promise to give him money, and Judas's reaction. The conjunctive ties in the second paragraph convey cohesiveness. All cases of asyndeton appearing here are in direct speeches, which seem natural.

The second paragraph also starts with καί (14:12a), containing the functions of continuity and transition, as in 14:10a. The subsequent temporal conjunction ὅτε in the narrative appears as the introduction of a subordinate clause—sacrificing the Passover lamb—that modifies the first day of Unleavened Bread. At the beginning of the subsequent disciples' direct speech part—a question regarding the place for the Passover—asyndeton appears, and the Passover, the object to be prepared, is introduced by ἵνα (14:12b). After that, 14:13 begins with καί, followed by Jesus sending two of his disciples. Given the context, this conjunction seems to mean "so/then" as a link to Jesus' response to the disciples' questions. The next καί connects Jesus' two actions (ἀποστέλλει; λέγει), implying an unmarked continuity (14:13b). After that, the first part of direct speech appears as asyndeton (∅ ἄγετε εἰς τὴν πόλιν; 14:13c), and the connective conjunction καί, which can be translated as "then," links the back and forth

---

5  It is possible that the last clause of 14:11, πῶς αὐτὸν εὐκαίρως παραδοῖ, can be viewed as asyndeton, but it is not regarded as asyndeton since the adverb πῶς acts as a conjunction.

6  It may be a reflection of the linguistic style of the constructor, who uses καί extensively, or it may reflect the oral characteristics of Peter's testimony. It seems that oral text tends to have less variety of conjunctions compared to written text, and that there is a tendency to use conjunctions more widely, which can be used in various contexts, such as "and" or "but."

MODE REGISTER ANALYSIS OF MARK 14:10–31 135

(14:13d). The following command "follow him" in 14:13e appears as asyndeton (∅ ἀκολουθήσατε αὐτῷ). In 14:14, which carries the following words of Jesus, conjunctions (καί; ὅπου; ὅτι; ὅπου) and asyndeton (before ποῦ)[7] coexist. First, 14:14 starts with καί, a coordinating conjunction containing unmarked continuity. Right after this, ὅπου, the subordinating spatial conjunction, functions as "wherever." The third clause of 14:14 is the intro of Jesus' words to the owner of the house, where the subordinating conjunction ὅτι is used. This verse's fourth and fifth clauses are Jesus' words to the house owner. Here, asyndeton appears in the first part of the direct speech, and the following clause uses the spatial subordinating conjunction ὅπου to ask questions about the place to eat the Passover food with Jesus' disciples. The house owner's response is continued in 14:15, which is linked by the connective conjunction καί, which can be translated into "(and) then." In 14:15b, Jesus tells his disciples to prepare the Passover there, and here καί appears again to convey unmarked continuity. Following 14:16, the disciples' response to Jesus' words appears as a narrative, connecting four clauses with four cases of καί. The first καί carries continuity with the meaning of "so/then," and the other cases of καί carry unmarked continuity. The conjunctive ties in the second paragraph convey cohesiveness. All instances of asyndeton in the second paragraph are placed in the direct speeches, which seem natural.

The beginning of 14:17, the introductory part of the third paragraph, is also καί. Here, the connective conjunction καί carries the meaning of "now/then," which implies temporal (it is the evening) and spatial (going to a place for the Passover) change. Subsequently, the two cases of καί used in the narrative part of 14:18 convey unmarked continuity. After the asyndeton of the first part of the direct speech, the subordinating conjunction ὅτι connects Jesus' words about one of the disciples handing over Jesus. In 14:19, asyndeton appears at the narrative speech margin preceding the disciples' reaction to Jesus' words. It is the first asyndeton found in the narrative part of the designated text. It seems more natural to use a conjunction such as δέ or καί to form a conjunctive tie, but there is none. In the middle of 14:19, καί is used to connect two infinitive verbs (λυπεῖσθαι; λέγειν). The abbreviated expression (with the verb and complement omitted), μήτι ἐγώ, is in the direct speech part with no conjunction (asyndeton). Then, in 14:20, the adversative conjunction δέ appears at the narrative speech margin for Jesus' answer. The use of δέ here seems to be that Jesus' answer is not a direct answer to the disciples' questions. After that, asyndeton appears in the following Jesus' words, which have no main verb: "one

---

7  Another example of asyndeton in 14:14 could be found before εἴπατε, but the conjunction of this verb can be viewed as καί, so it is not considered as asyndeton.

136                                                                                     CHAPTER 4

of the twelve, one who dips with me in the bowl" (14:20b). The following 14:21 appears very similar to the parallel verse in Matthew, but it begins with the subordinating conjunction ὅτι, unlike Matthew. Here, μέν, δέ, or καθώς seem natural for 14:21; however, ὅτι, which has the meaning of "for" to convey causality, is used here.[8] Here, ὅτι seems unnatural since there is no particular causal relationship between 14:20 and 14:21. The first half of 14:21 relates to the death of Jesus: on the one hand (μὲν), Jesus, the "son of the man," departs (ὑπάγει) "as it is written" (καθὼς γέγραπται). In this respect, the first half shows the causal relationship between Jesus' departure/death and the Scripture (OT). However, on the other hand (δέ), woe to him who betrays Jesus; here, the emphasis by δέ is revealed. Next, since any conjunction does not appear before καλόν, there is a case of asyndeton; however, it is explicable because it is the main clause followed by a conditional clause with the subordinating conjunction εἰ. In the following clause, the hypothetical situation, "if he had not been born," appears with εἰ, emphasizing how significant the woe would be on one who hands over Jesus.

The latter half of the third paragraph, 14:22–26, conveys the Eucharist, which is a shift from the previous subject. Καί in 14:22 forms a conjunctive tie between the previous treachery notice and Jesus' Eucharistic words, which takes place in the same context, the Passover meal. In this sense, it seems appropriate to understand that καί used here means continuity and transition together. The two cases of καί appearing later function as unmarked continuity to link the following actions of Jesus: (1) breaking the bread—that was taken and blessed, (2) giving it to the disciples, and (3) speaking. After the narrative speech margin, Jesus' words are followed by two appearances of asyndeton: ∅ λάβετε, ∅ τοῦτό ἐστιν τὸ σῶμά μου. It can be understood that the first asyndeton naturally appears as it is the first part of speech, and in the second case, it may have taken some time in the process of sharing the bread with his disciples (αὐτοῖς; plural); thus, here a time gap may be indicated by the absence of conjunction. After this, in 14:23, Jesus' actions with a cup and the disciples' reactions are presented in a short narrative form, that is, without a direct speech part. In this process, two cases of καί are used. The first καί appears as unmarked continuity, linking Jesus' words about the bread with Jesus' actions on the "cup." The second καί appears as unmarked continuity to link the action of Jesus

---

8   Robert H. Gundry, *Mark: A Commentary on His Apology for the Cross* (Grand Rapids: Eerdmans, 1993), 828. Here, we cannot rule out the possibility that ὅτι is used in the meaning of "with regard to the fact that." See H. G. Liddel and R. Scott, *A Greek-English Lexicon* (9th ed.; Oxford: Clarendon, 1996), 1265; however, Gundry's suggestion seems to reveal a more general use of ὅτι.

MODE REGISTER ANALYSIS OF MARK 14:10–31          137

(ἔδωκεν αὐτοῖς) and the reaction of the disciples (ἔπιον ἐξ αὐτοῦ). The meaning of this cup—Jesus' blood of the covenant—is revealed in the following Jesus' words, and its narrative speech margin is initiated by καί (14:24). At the intro of Jesus' speech, there is a case of asyndeton: ∅ τοῦτό ἐστιν τὸ αἷμά μου τῆς διαθήκης τὸ ἐκχυννόμενον ὑπὲρ πολλῶν. Jesus' words, continuing in 14:25, begin with asyndeton (∅ ἀμὴν λέγω ὑμῖν), and the following two clauses are led by two subordinating conjunctions: ὅτι, ὅταν.[9] Here, ὅτι plays the role of receiving the clause of Jesus' subsequent statement, "I will not drink from the fruit of the vine," and ὅταν appears as temporal conjunction to convey that the time to drink new wine in the kingdom of God is coming. After Jesus' Eucharistic speech, their (probably the disciples and Jesus') actions of going to the Mount of Olives (singing a hymn) are linked by καί. This conjunction can be translated as "then," which contains the meaning of some transition with unmarked continuity. The conjunctive ties in the third paragraph maintain cohesiveness. However, there is a case of asyndeton in the narrative (14:19) and an unnatural appearance of ὅτι (14:21) which seem to lower the degree of cohesiveness. All other cases of asyndeton in this paragraph appear in the direct speech sections, which are explicable.

In the fourth paragraph, Jesus foretells that all his disciples will stumble and then mentions Peter's denial. The first clause, the narrative speech margin, is connected by καί (14:27a), which can be understood as "now/then." The following Jesus' words—"all of you will be stumbled" (14:27b)—is linked by a subordinating conjunction ὅτι. Here, the narrative and direct speech parts are connected by ὅτι, which does not need a particular translation, and it functions as a quotation mark.[10] The other case of ὅτι, which appears subsequently, functions as an intro of γέγραπται for the following Old Testament quotation, which provides the ground for what was said previously (πάντες σκανδαλισθή-σεσθε); thus, we can translate it as "for" (14:27c). There is a case of asyndeton at the beginning of the Old Testament quotation (∅ πατάξω τὸν ποιμένα; 14:27d), followed by καί, which indicates a causal continuity between striking the shepherd and the dispersal of the flock (14:27e). The cause of the disciples' stumbling is revealed as "striking the shepherd" by the Old Testament quotation, and is portrayed as the fulfilment of the OT; in this process, ὅτι functions to reveal the causality between Jesus' foretelling and the quotation. After that, a hopeful message appears in 14:28: Jesus' "revival" and "return to Galilee." The conjunction connecting these two clauses is ἀλλά. It is a conjunction that appears only

---

9    Here, ἕως functions as a preposition, not a conjunction.
10   Daniel B. Wallace, *Greek Grammar Beyond the Basics: An Exegetical Syntax of the New Testament* (Grand Rapids: Zondervan, 1996), 454–55.

138                                                                                                                    CHAPTER 4

in Mark among the designated parallel texts, which has both an adversative and emphatic meaning.[11] After this, the narrative speech margin begins with δέ, which carries an adversative meaning, to convey Peter's reaction against Jesus' words about stumbling: *but* Peter says to him (14:29a). His speech starts with εἰ καί, the conditional-connective conjunctions, and end with ἀλλ᾽, an abbreviation of ἀλλά, which connects "all will be stumbled" and "I will not be." It seems that εἰ καί is an emphatic expression carrying the meaning of "even if/though," and ἀλλά has an emphatic adversative sense as in the previous case. By adding these conjunctions conveying emphasis, Peter is asserting that he will not stumble upon Jesus. In 14:30, Jesus' response to Peter's remark is led by καί, which can be understood as "and" or "then."[12] After the narrative speech margin, Jesus' words consist of three clauses, each connected by ὅτι and πρίν. The first part of the speech appears as asyndeton, and ὅτι appears to link Jesus' typical intro (ἀμὴν λέγω σοι) and his specific words; there is no need for a particular translation for it. Πρίν is used as temporal conjunction to indicate that Peter's denials to Jesus will happen that night, "before" the rooster crows twice. This speech directly breaks Peter's strong will in 14:29; so, in 14:31, δέ appears as adversative conjunction followed by ἐκπερισσῶς, which forms more emphasis: *but* he *insistently* says (14:31a). In his speech, Peter intensifies his determination with an assumed situation of death by using the conditional conjunction ἐάν with δέῃ (14:31b); thereafter, he demonstrates that he will never deny Jesus (14:31c).[13] Here, asyndeton appears, which seems to be a natural form of the main clause after the conditional clause introduced by ἐάν. In the last clause, the rest of the disciples react the same as Peter, and two linear conjunctions, δέ καί, connect 14:31c and 14:31d. Here, δέ is used as the causal and connective conjunction, and καί modifies the following πάντες, so it can mean that "everyone *also* says the same thing." The conjunctive ties in the fourth paragraph convey cohesiveness, and all cases of asyndeton in this paragraph appear in the direct speech sections, which are explicable.

## 2.2    *Reference*
We now look at the formation of reference based on the paragraph division done through the thematization. The participant-referent chains of Mark 14:10–11 are shown in Figure 4.1.

---

11     Cf. Porter, *Idioms*, 206.

12     Jesus' words that follow in 14:30 contradict Peter's in subject matter, so δέ seems to be a natural option in this context. However, considering the broad usage of καί in Mark, it seems explicable. Also, such use of καί may reflect Jesus' meek attitude, which may have been experienced by Peter, the eyewitness.

13     Here Peter's words are emphasized by the double negation (οὐ μή).

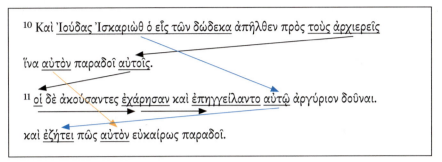

FIGURE 4.1  Participant-referent chains in Mark 14:10–11

The participants for which the participant-referent chains are formed are as follows: Judas (3×), the high priests (5×), and Jesus (2×). In the case of Judas, after first appearing as a grammaticalized reference (proper noun), it is presented as a reduced reference (third-person singular dative) and an implied reference of ἐζήτει. In the case of the high priest, after first appearing as a grammaticalized reference (proper noun), it occurs as reduced references (third-person plural dative and third-person plural subjective) and implied references (implied subject of ἐχάρησαν and ἐπηγγείλαντο). In the case of Jesus, it appears as the reduced reference twice (third-person objective) without a grammaticalized reference. Considering the participant referent chains which are well formed, the cohesiveness of this paragraph is overall maintained. However, in the narrative part of 14:11, although it seems more natural to present the identity of Jesus as a proper noun considering the change of topic and thematic participant in this paragraph, he is revealed only by a reduced reference (pronoun). This seemingly unnatural reference may lower the degree of cohesiveness of this paragraph.

The participant-referent chains of Mark 14:12–16 are shown in Figure 4.2.

The participants for which the participant-referent chains are formed are as follows: Jesus (12×), the disciples (2×), and two of them (13×). Jesus appears as grammaticalized references (common noun), reduced references (pronoun), and implied references (implied subject in verb), but he does not appear as a proper noun. What seems notable in this paragraph is the vagueness of the distinction between "the disciples" (οἱ μαθηταὶ αὐτοῦ) and "two of the disciples" (δύο τῶν μαθητῶν αὐτοῦ). To be more specific, two of the disciples are the ones whom Jesus distinguished from the whole group of disciples, and Jesus told them how to prepare for Passover. However, at the end of this paragraph, where they followed his guideline, they are referred to just as the "disciples." This phenomenon could suggest the roughness of this text, which may show its oral property. Moreover, in the narrative speech margin in 14:12, although it seems

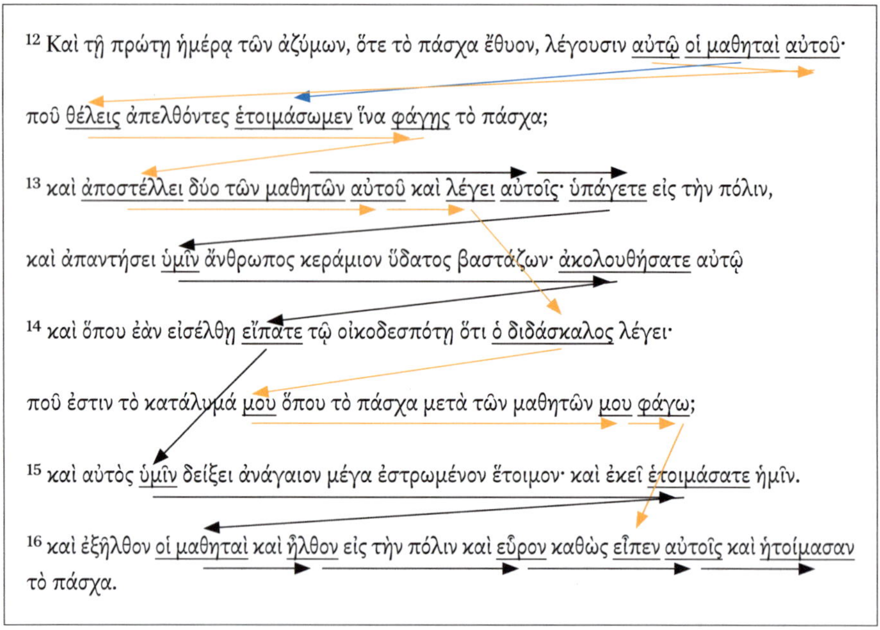

140

CHAPTER 4

> $^{12}$ Καὶ τῇ πρώτῃ ἡμέρᾳ τῶν ἀζύμων, ὅτε τὸ πάσχα ἔθυον, λέγουσιν αὐτῷ οἱ μαθηταὶ αὐτοῦ·
>
> ποῦ θέλεις ἀπελθόντες ἑτοιμάσωμεν ἵνα φάγῃς τὸ πάσχα;
>
> $^{13}$ καὶ ἀποστέλλει δύο τῶν μαθητῶν αὐτοῦ καὶ λέγει αὐτοῖς· ὑπάγετε εἰς τὴν πόλιν,
>
> καὶ ἀπαντήσει ὑμῖν ἄνθρωπος κεράμιον ὕδατος βαστάζων· ἀκολουθήσατε αὐτῷ
>
> $^{14}$ καὶ ὅπου ἐὰν εἰσέλθῃ εἴπατε τῷ οἰκοδεσπότῃ ὅτι ὁ διδάσκαλος λέγει·
>
> ποῦ ἐστιν τὸ κατάλυμά μου ὅπου τὸ πάσχα μετὰ τῶν μαθητῶν μου φάγω;
>
> $^{15}$ καὶ αὐτὸς ὑμῖν δείξει ἀνάγαιον μέγα ἐστρωμένον ἕτοιμον· καὶ ἐκεῖ ἑτοιμάσατε ἡμῖν.
>
> $^{16}$ καὶ ἐξῆλθον οἱ μαθηταὶ καὶ ἦλθον εἰς τὴν πόλιν καὶ εὗρον καθὼς εἶπεν αὐτοῖς καὶ ἡτοίμασαν τὸ πάσχα.

FIGURE 4.2  Participant-referent chains in Mark 14:12–16

appropriate to mark the identity of Jesus as a proper noun, he is revealed as a reduced reference (pronoun). Thus, these seemingly unnatural references may lower the degree of cohesiveness of this paragraph. Overall, however, these participant-referent chains are well formed, thus the cohesiveness of this paragraph is maintained.

The participant-referent chains of Mark 14:17–26 are shown in Figure 4.3.

The participants for which the participant-referent chains are formed are as follows: Jesus (26×), the disciples (15×), one of you (6×), bread (3×), and cup (7×). Although the overall flow of Mark is similar to Matthew, according to the analysis of thematic units, Mark forms just one paragraph, whereas, in Matthew, it is the third and fourth paragraphs of Matthew into one paragraph. Indeed, in the Greek text, quite a few references appear as implied references (implied subjects of verbs). In the case of Jesus, it appears as an implied reference (implied subject of a verb) from the beginning. After appearing as a grammaticalized reference (proper noun), "Jesus," in the second, appears as an implied reference (implied subject of a verb) and reduced reference (pronoun). The case of "one of you" is similar to the pattern of Jesus. In the case of "bread" and "cup," it is similar to Matthew in that it first appears as grammaticalized references (proper noun and substitution) and in the form of a reduced

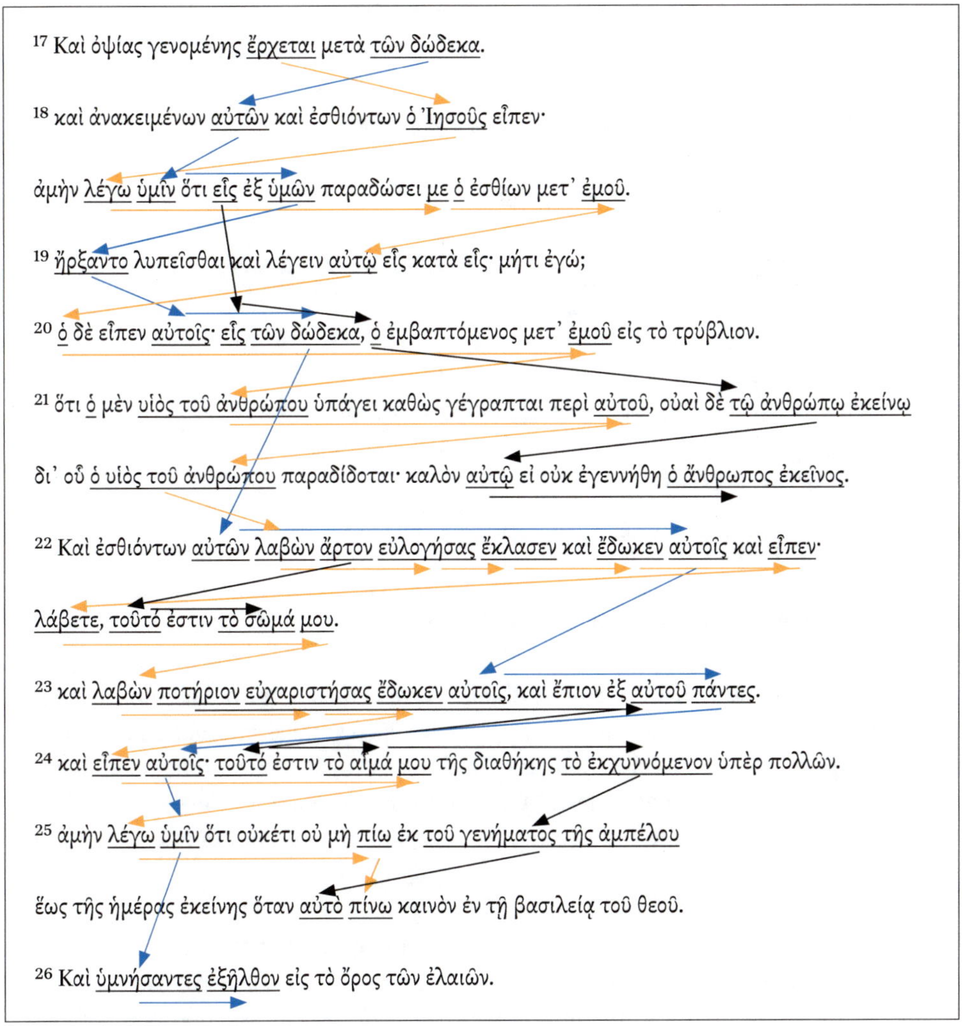

## MODE REGISTER ANALYSIS OF MARK 14:10–31

[17] Καὶ ὀψίας γενομένης ἔρχεται μετὰ τῶν δώδεκα.

[18] καὶ ἀνακειμένων αὐτῶν καὶ ἐσθιόντων ὁ Ἰησοῦς εἶπεν·

ἀμὴν λέγω ὑμῖν ὅτι εἷς ἐξ ὑμῶν παραδώσει με ὁ ἐσθίων μετ' ἐμοῦ.

[19] ἤρξαντο λυπεῖσθαι καὶ λέγειν αὐτῷ εἷς κατὰ εἷς· μήτι ἐγώ;

[20] ὁ δὲ εἶπεν αὐτοῖς· εἷς τῶν δώδεκα, ὁ ἐμβαπτόμενος μετ' ἐμοῦ εἰς τὸ τρύβλιον.

[21] ὅτι ὁ μὲν υἱὸς τοῦ ἀνθρώπου ὑπάγει καθὼς γέγραπται περὶ αὐτοῦ, οὐαὶ δὲ τῷ ἀνθρώπῳ ἐκείνῳ

δι' οὗ ὁ υἱὸς τοῦ ἀνθρώπου παραδίδοται· καλὸν αὐτῷ εἰ οὐκ ἐγεννήθη ὁ ἄνθρωπος ἐκεῖνος.

[22] Καὶ ἐσθιόντων αὐτῶν λαβὼν ἄρτον εὐλογήσας ἔκλασεν καὶ ἔδωκεν αὐτοῖς καὶ εἶπεν·

λάβετε, τοῦτό ἐστιν τὸ σῶμά μου.

[23] καὶ λαβὼν ποτήριον εὐχαριστήσας ἔδωκεν αὐτοῖς, καὶ ἔπιον ἐξ αὐτοῦ πάντες.

[24] καὶ εἶπεν αὐτοῖς· τοῦτό ἐστιν τὸ αἷμά μου τῆς διαθήκης τὸ ἐκχυννόμενον ὑπὲρ πολλῶν.

[25] ἀμὴν λέγω ὑμῖν ὅτι οὐκέτι οὐ μὴ πίω ἐκ τοῦ γενήματος τῆς ἀμπέλου

ἕως τῆς ἡμέρας ἐκείνης ὅταν αὐτὸ πίνω καινὸν ἐν τῇ βασιλείᾳ τοῦ θεοῦ.

[26] Καὶ ὑμνήσαντες ἐξῆλθον εἰς τὸ ὄρος τῶν ἐλαιῶν.

FIGURE 4.3  Participant-referent chains in Mark 14:17–26

reference (pronoun). Overall, the participant-referent chains are well-formed, thus the cohesiveness of the paragraph is maintained.

The participant-referent chains of Mark 14:27–31 are shown in Figure 4.4.

The participants for which the participant-referent chains are formed are as follows: Jesus (9×), all disciples (4×), Peter (8×), and all disciples except Peter (2×). In the case of Jesus, after first appearing as a grammaticalized reference (proper noun), it is mainly referred to as reduced references (pronoun). Also, it is referred to as a word in the Old Testament quotation (τὸν ποιμένα)

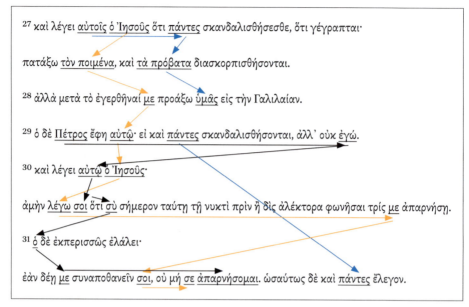

FIGURE 4.4 Participant-referent chains in Mark 14:27–31

in the second half of 14:27 and then referred to as a grammaticalized reference (proper noun) again in 14:30. Also, Jesus appears as an implied reference (implied subject of a verb) in 14:30. In the case of Peter, the reference flow is almost similar to that of Jesus. Overall, these participant-referent chains are well formed, thus the cohesiveness of this paragraph is maintained.

### 2.3   *Substitution and Ellipsis*

This section will analyze the substitution and ellipsis of the designated text. First, the substitutions in Mark 14:10–31 are as follows. The first is ὁ εἷς τῶν δώδεκα in 14:10 as a substitution of Ἰούδας Ἰσκαριώθ. The second is οἱ μαθηταί in 14:12 as a substitution of δώδεκα in 14:10. The third is ἀνάγαιον μέγα in 14:15, which is revealed as an added reference to τὸ κατάλυμα in 14:14. The fourth, fifth, and sixth cases are ὁ ἐσθίων μετ' ἐμοῦ in 14:19, εἷς τῶν δώδεκα and ὁ ἐμβαπτόμενος μετ' ἐμοῦ εἰς τὸ τρύβλιον in 14:20, which are the new information referring εἷς ἐξ ὑμῶν in 14:19. The seventh is ὁ υἱὸς τοῦ ἀνθρώπου in 14:21 (2×) as a substitution of ὁ διδάσκαλος in 14:14, as a title for Jesus himself. The eighth is τῷ ἀνθρώπῳ ἐκείνῳ δι' οὗ ὁ υἱὸς τοῦ ἀνθρώπου παραδίδοται in 14:21, referring εἷς ἐξ ὑμῶν in 14:19. The ninth and tenth cases are τὸ σῶμά μου in 14:22 and τὸ αἷμά μου τῆς διαθήκης in 14:24 as a substitution of the cup (ποτήριον). The eleventh is τοῦ γενήματος τῆς ἀμπέλου in 14:25 as a substitution of the cup, Jesus' blood. The twelfth and thirteenth cases are the two references revealed in Jesus' words in

MODE REGISTER ANALYSIS OF MARK 14:10–31    143

his Old Testament quotation in 14:27: the shepherd (τὸν ποιμένα) and the flock (τὰ πρόβατα τῆς ποίμνης).

Second, the ellipsis which can be found in the designated text is μήτι ἐγώ, which appears in 14:19. It is expressed by Jesus' disciples. What is omitted here is *a person who betrays Jesus* (εἷς ἐξ ὑμῶν παραδώσει με ὁ ἐσθίων μετ' ἐμοῦ, 14:18) and the process part (εἰμι); thus, this case can be considered as a nominal-verbal ellipsis.

Considering these analyses, the distribution of substitution and ellipsis within the designated text demonstrates the cohesiveness of this text.

### 2.4 *Lexical Cohesion*
In this section, we will analyze the semantic-lexical ties to examine the cohesiveness of each paragraph in Mark 14:10–31 and the semantic-lexical chain of the whole designated text.

### 2.4.1 Lexical Cohesion in Each Paragraph
In the first paragraph (14:10–11), Judas plans to hand over Jesus, and the chief priests promise to give him money. From that time on Judas seeks an opportunity to hand Jesus over. Table 4.5 contains the cases where two or more lexemes in one semantic domain appear in a paragraph.

The lexeme δίδωμι ("to give") and the lexical item παραδίδωμι ("to deliver") belong to domain 57; which are semantically related in terms of the "deal" on Jesus; thus they form semantic-lexical tie. There are two numbers in domain 60 (εἷς ["one"], δώδεκα ["twelve"]), and these lexemes are tied around Judas, "one" of the "twelve"; thus, they form a semantic-lexical tie. The lexemes ἀκούω and ἐπαγγέλλομαι belong to domain 33, which are done by the chief priests as their communicative responses to Judas's plan to betray Jesus; thus, they form a semantic-lexical tie. From these analyses, we can identify three

TABLE 4.5    Semantic domains of the lexemes in Mark 14:10–11

| Lexeme | Verse | Semantic domain |
| --- | --- | --- |
| δίδωμι | v. 11 | 57.71 |
| παραδίδωμι | vv. 10, 11 | 57.77/37.111 |
| εἷς | v. 10 | 60.10 |
| δώδεκα | v. 10 | 60.21 |
| ἀκούω | v. 11 | 33.212 |
| ἐπαγγέλλομαι | v. 11 | 33.286 |

144 CHAPTER 4

TABLE 4.6 Semantic domains of the lexemes in Mark 14:12–16

| Lexeme | Verse | Semantic domain |
| --- | --- | --- |
| ἑτοιμάζω | vv. 12, 15 | 77.3 |
| ἕτοιμος | v. 15 | 77.2 |
| πρῶτος | v. 12 | 60.46 |
| δύο | v. 13 | 60.11 |
| πάσχα | vv. 12 (2×), 14, 16 | 51.7 |
| cf. ἄζυμος | v. 12 | 5.13 |
| μαθητής | vv. 12, 13, 14, 16 | 36.38 |
| ἀπέρχομαι | v. 12 | 15.37 |
| ἀποστέλλει | v. 13 | 15.66 |
| ὑπάγω | v. 13 | 15.35 |
| ἀπαντάω | v. 13 | 15.78 |
| βαστάζω | v. 13 | 15.188 |
| ἀκολουθέω | v. 13 | 15.144 |
| εἰσέρχομαι | v. 14 | 15.93 |
| ἐξέρχομαι | v. 16 | 15.40 |
| ἔρχομαι | v. 16 | 15.7 |
| ἐσθίω | vv. 12, 14 | 23.1 |
| κατάλυμα | v. 14 | 7.30 |
| ἀνάγαιον | v. 15 | 7.27 |

semantic-lexical ties in 14:10–11. Furthermore, among the thirteen content lexemes in the first paragraph, the number of lexemes in the semantic-lexical ties is seven. The ratio of the lexemes that can be formed into semantic-lexical ties per the number of content lexemes is 53.85%. Thus, these overall results apparently reveal the cohesiveness of this paragraph.

The second paragraph (14:12–16) describes the process of preparing the Passover by Jesus and his disciples. The semantic domains of the lexemes in this paragraph are shown in Table 4.6.

The lexical item ἑτοιμάζω ("to prepare"), which is reiterated two times, and ἕτοιμος ("prepared") belong to domain 77. They are semantically tied around the preparation of the Passover; thus, these form a semantic-lexical tie. The lexemes of numbers (πρῶτος ["first"], δύο ["two"]) belong to domain 60, but each of them is related to different objects (the day of Unleavened Bread, his disciples), so it seems hard to find a semantic-lexical tie from them. The lexeme πάσχα ("Passover"; domain 51) is reiterated four times and ἄζυμος ("unleavened bread"; domain 5) can be semantically concerned with πάσχα due to the

MODE REGISTER ANALYSIS OF MARK 14:10–31 145

close connection between the Passover and the feast of Unleavened Bread; thus, they form a semantic-lexical tie. The lexical item μαθητής ("disciple"; domain 36.38) is reiterated four times. The plural forms of μαθητής appear as the preparers (14:12, 13, 16) and participants (14:14) of the Passover; thus, the cases form a semantic-lexical tie. Nine lexemes (ἀπέρχομαι ["to go away"], ἀποστέλλω ["to send"], ὑπάγω ["to depart"], ἀπαντάω ["to meet"], βαστάζω ["to carry"], ἀκολουθέω ["to follow"], εἰσέρχομαι ["go into"], ἐξέρχομαι ["to go out"], ἔρχομαι ["to go"]), which belong to domain 15, related to "movements" in terms of the preparation of the Passover; thus, they form a semantic-lexical tie. The lexical item ἐσθίω ("to eat"; domain 23) is reiterated two times in terms of the Passover meal; thus, they form semantic-lexical ties. Two lexemes κατάλυμα ("guest room") and ἀνάγαιον ("upper room") which belong to domain 7, are related to places for the Passover; thus, they form a semantic-lexical tie. From these analyses, we can find four semantic-lexical ties in 14:12–16. Furthermore, among fifty-one content lexemes in the second paragraph, the number of lexemes in the semantic-lexical ties is twenty-nine. The ratio of the lexemes that can be formed into semantic-lexical ties per the number of content lexemes is 56.86%. Thus, these overall results apparently reveal the cohesiveness of this paragraph.

The third paragraph (14:17–26) conveys Jesus' foretelling about the betrayer, the disciples' responses (including Judas), and the Eucharist. The semantic domains of the lexemes in this paragraph are shown in Table 4.7.

TABLE 4.7    Semantic domains of the lexemes in Mark 14:17–26

| Lexeme | Verse | Semantic domain |
|---|---|---|
| παραδίδωμι | vv. 18, 21 | 37.111 |
| εἷς | v. 18, 19 (2×), 20 | 60.10 |
| δώδεκα | v. 20 | 60.21 |
| υἱὸς τοῦ ἀνθρώπου | v. 21 (2×) | 9.3 |
| ἄνθρωπος | v. 21 (2×) | 9.1 |
| λέγω | vv. 18, 25 | 33.69 |
| γράφω | v. 21 | 33.61 |
| εὐλογέω | v. 22 | 33.470 |
| εὐχαριστέω | v. 23 | 33.349 |
| ὑμνέω | v. 26 | 33.113 |
| μήτι | v. 19 | 69.16 |
| οὐκ | v. 21 | 69.3 |
| οὐ | v. 25 | 69.3 |
| μή | v. 25 | 69.3 |

146    CHAPTER 4

TABLE 4.7    Semantic domains of the lexemes in Mark 14:17–26 (*cont.*)

| Lexeme | Verse | Semantic domain |
| --- | --- | --- |
| ἐσθίω | vv. 18 (2×), 22 | 23.1 |
| πίνω | vv. 23, 25 (2×) | 23.34 |
| λαμβάνω | vv. 22 (2×), 23 | 18.1 |
| δίδωμι | vv. 22, 23 | 57.71 |
| ἄρτος | v. 22 | 5.8 |
| cf. ποτήριον | v. 23 | 6.121 |
| σῶμα | v. 22 | 8.1 |
| αἷμα | v. 24 | 8.64 |
| ὀψία | v. 17 | 67.197 |
| οὐκέτι | v. 25 | 67.130 |
| ἡμέρα | v. 25 | 67.178 |
| ἄμπελος | v. 25 | 3.27 |
| ἐλαία | v. 26 | 3.9 |
| τρύβλιον | v. 20 | 6.136 |
| ποτήριον | v. 23 | 6.121 |

The lexical item παραδίδωμι ("to hand over/betray"; domain 37), which is semantically tied around the main topic of this paragraph, betraying Jesus, is reiterated two times, and these lexical items form a semantic-lexical tie. There are two numbers in domain 60 (εἷς ["one"], δώδεκα ["twelve"]). Among the four cases of εἷς, two cases (14:18, 20) are tied around Judas along with δώδεκα: "one of you," that is, "one" of the "twelve"; thus, they form a semantic-lexical tie. The two cases, which are used as "one by one" (2×; 14:19), are not semantically related to them. The lexical item ἄνθρωπος ("man"; domain 9) is reiterated four times; two of them form collocation with υἱός (ὁ υἱὸς τοῦ ἀνθρώπου), which refer to Jesus, and the other two (τῷ ἀνθρώπῳ; ὁ ἄνθρωπος) refer to the betrayer (Judas). Thus, each case forms a semantic-lexical tie. The lexical items (λέγω ["to say"; 14:18, 25[14]], γράφω ["to write"], εὐλογέω ["to bless"], εὐχαριστέω ["to thank"], and ὑμνέω [sing a hymn]) belong to domain 33. These lexemes can be grouped as two according to the two distinctive topics: (1) the betrayal: λέγω (14:18), γράφω; (2) the Eucharist: εὐλογέω, εὐχαριστέω, ὑμνέω, and λέγω (14:25). In this sense, we can say that these lexemes have their own semantic-lexical

---

14    These two cases of λέγω are used as collocations with ἀμήν and ὑμῖν (ἀμὴν λέγω ὑμῖν).

MODE REGISTER ANALYSIS OF MARK 14:10–31

tie; however, considering the two topics can be connected with Jesus' death, it may be possible to say that these lexemes have a semantic-lexical tie. The lexeme μήτι (domain 69.16), an interrogative article expecting a negative answer, is used for the disciples' answer to Jesus' foretelling on the betrayal, and the lexeme οὐκ (domain 69.3) is used to convey Jesus' words to the betrayer ("it would have been better for that man if he had *not* been born"), and the lexemes οὐ and μή (domain 69.3) is used to present Jesus' declaration not to drink of "the fruit of the vine"; thus, it seems difficult to find a semantic-lexical connection between them. The lexical item ἐσθίω ("to eat") is reiterated three times, and the other lexical item πίνω ("to drink") is also reiterated three times. They belong to domain 23, revealing the actions regarding the Passover and Eucharist; thus, they form semantic-lexical ties. The lexical item λαμβάνω ("to take"; domain 18) is reiterated three times, which is tied around Jesus' actions on bread and a cup; thus, the three lexemes in λαμβάνω form a semantic-lexical tie. The lexical item δίδωμι (domain 57) is reiterated two times, which conveys Jesus' actions of "giving" bread and a cup to the disciples; thus, these two cases form a semantic-lexical tie. The lexeme ἄρτος ("bread") belongs to domain 5, and ποτήριον ("cup"; domain 6) can be semantically tied with ἄρτος, and the reason is as follows. Considering 14:25 (ἐκ τοῦ γενήματος τῆς ἀμπέλου ["of this fruit of the grapevine"]), what was in the "cup" was probably οἶνος ("wine"; John 2:3). Since bread and a cup (wine) refer to/symbolize Jesus' body and blood, ἄρτος and ποτήριον are semantically tied in the topic of the Eucharist; thus, they form a semantic-lexical tie. The lexemes σῶμα ("body") and αἷμα ("blood") belong to domain 8. They are semantically tied as a case of superordinate; thus, they form a semantic-lexical tie. Two lexemes οὐκέτι ("no longer") and ἡμέρα ("day") belong to domain 67, which is concerned with time, and they are semantically tied around the period of time Jesus will not drink wine; thus, they form a semantic-lexical tie. The other lexeme ὀψία in domain 67 functions as a temporal deixis of 14:17, so it seems hard to find a semantic-lexical tie with other lexemes in domain 67 here. The lexemes ἄμπελος (grapevine) and ἐλαία (olive) belong to domain 3; however, it seems hard to find a semantic-lexical tie from this since vine is concerned with the Eucharist, but olive is the name of a mountain. Two lexemes (τρύβλιον ["bowl"], ποτήριον ["cup"]) belong to domain 6, and they function to reveal one context of Passover meal as a set for a meal, even though they appear in different topics (τρύβλιον in the betrayal and ποτήριον in the Eucharist); it seems possible to find a semantic-lexical tie between them. From these analyses, we can find nine semantic-lexical ties in 14:17–26. Furthermore, among the sixty-eight content lexemes in the third paragraph, the number of lexemes in the semantic-lexical ties is thirty-three.

148 CHAPTER 4

TABLE 4.8    Semantic domains of the lexemes in Mark 14:27–31

| Lexeme | Verse | Semantic domain |
| --- | --- | --- |
| σκανδαλίζω | vv. 27, 29 | 31.78 |
| λέγω | v. 30 | 33.69 |
| γράφω | v. 27 | 33.61 |
| ἀπαρνέομαι | vv. 30, 31 | 33.277 |
| διασκορπίζω | v. 27 | 15.136 |
| προάγω | v. 28 | 15.142 |
| πρόβατον | v. 27 | 4.22 |
| ἀλέκτωρ | v. 30 | 4.45 |
| ἐγείρω | v. 28 | 23.94 |
| συναποθνῄσκω | v. 31 | 23.118 |
| οὐκ | v. 29 | 69.3 |
| οὐ | v. 31 | 69.3 |
| μή | v. 31 | 69.3 |
| σήμερον | v. 30 | 67.205 |
| νύξ | v. 30 | 67.192 |
| πρίν | v. 30 | 67.17 |
| δίς | v. 30 | 60.69 |
| τρίς | v. 30 | 60.71 |

The ratio of the lexemes that can be formed into semantic-lexical ties per the number of content lexemes is 48.53%. Thus, these overall results may reveal the cohesiveness of this paragraph.

The fourth paragraph (14:27–31) conveys Jesus' foretelling of the stumbling of his disciples, along with Peter's denial. The semantic domains of the lexemes in this paragraph are shown in Table 4.8.

The lexical item σκανδαλίζω ("to stumble"; domain 31) is reiterated two times, which conveys the main topic of this paragraph (the disciples' stumbling); thus, the cases form a semantic-lexical tie. The lexical items (λέγω ["to say"], γράφω ["to write"], ἀπαρνέομαι ["to deny"]) belong to domain 33, which are semantically related to Jesus' foretelling; thus, the cases form a semantic-lexical tie. Two lexemes διασκορπίζω ("to scatter") and προάγω ("go before") belong to domain 15. Here, διασκορπίζω means the scattering of the flock (disciples), and προάγω makes us anticipate the gathering of the disciples by Jesus going to Galilee before them; thus, these two lexemes are semantically intertwined

MODE REGISTER ANALYSIS OF MARK 14:10–31 149

with each other, and they form a semantic-lexical tie. Two lexemes πρόβατον ("sheep") and ἀλέκτωρ ("cock") belong to domain 4; πρόβατον is related to the scattering of the disciples, and ἀλέκτωρ is related to Peter's denial. Both "scattering" and "denial" belong to the category of "stumbling" (σκανδαλίζω), and thus they form a semantic-lexical tie. Two lexemes ἐγείρω ("to raise up") and συναποθνήσκω ("to die together") belong to domain 23. The first lexeme refers to Jesus' "resurrection," and the second is related to Peter's statement that he would never deny Jesus, which contains the topic of "death." These two concepts, death and resurrection, are semantically connected, and thus they form a semantic-lexical tie. The lexemes οὐκ, οὐ, and μή (domain 69; negation) are used for Peter's declarations in 14:29, 31; thus they form a semantic-lexical tie. Three lexemes, related to time (σήμερον ["today"], νύξ ["night"], πρίν [before]), belong to domain 67. These lexemes function to indicate the specific point in time ("today," this "night," "before" the cock crows) when Peter denies Jesus. In this respect, the three lexemes are semantically connected and form a semantic-lexical tie. The two lexemes δίς ("twice") and τρίς ("thrice"), which belong to domain 60, are semantically related to Peter's denial; thus they form a semantic-lexical tie. From these analyses, we can find seven semantic-lexical ties in 14:27–31. Furthermore, among the twenty-nine content lexemes in the fifth paragraph, the number of lexemes in the semantic-lexical ties is twenty. The ratio of the lexemes that can be formed into semantic-lexical ties per the number of content lexemes is 68.97%. Thus, these overall results clearly reveal the cohesiveness of this paragraph.

### 2.4.2    Lexical Cohesion in Mark 14:10–31

Figure 4.5 shows the lexical cohesion chains in Mark 14:10–31.

The lexemes underlined in Figure 4.5 are related to Jesus' death. His death is revealed indirectly by ὑπάγει (to depart), τὸ σῶμά μου (my body), and τὸ αἷμά μου (my blood). His death is carried out by the act of handing over (betrayal; παραδίδωμι) of one of the disciples, Judas. After Jesus' arrest as a result of Judas's betrayal, the disciples scatter (διασκορπίζω). Peter's denial (ἀπαρνέομαι) takes place before Jesus' death. Here, disciples' scattering and Peter's denial can be regarded as their reactions to Jesus' death to come; thus, the actions of scattering and denial can be related to the death of Jesus. The three actions of the disciples including Judas, namely, handing over, denying, and scattering, can be condensed into one concept, "stumbling" (σκανδαλίζω). The notion of "death" itself appears not in the statement of Jesus himself, but in that of Peter (ἐὰν δέῃ με συναποθανεῖν σοι, οὐ μή σε ἀπαρνήσομαι). As with Matthew, thus, this discourse maintains cohesiveness around the topic of Jesus' death.

150 CHAPTER 4

---

¹⁰ Καὶ Ἰούδας Ἰσκαριὼθ ὁ εἷς τῶν δώδεκα ἀπῆλθεν πρὸς τοὺς ἀρχιερεῖς ἵνα αὐτὸν παραδοῖ αὐτοῖς. ¹¹ οἱ δὲ ἀκούσαντες ἐχάρησαν καὶ ἐπηγγείλαντο αὐτῷ ἀργύριον δοῦναι. καὶ ἐζήτει πῶς αὐτὸν εὐκαίρως παραδοῖ. ¹² Καὶ τῇ πρώτῃ ἡμέρᾳ τῶν ἀζύμων, ὅτε τὸ πάσχα ἔθυον, λέγουσιν αὐτῷ οἱ μαθηταὶ αὐτοῦ· ποῦ θέλεις ἀπελθόντες ἑτοιμάσωμεν ἵνα φάγῃς τὸ πάσχα; ¹³ καὶ ἀποστέλλει δύο τῶν μαθητῶν αὐτοῦ καὶ λέγει αὐτοῖς· ὑπάγετε εἰς τὴν πόλιν, καὶ ἀπαντήσει ὑμῖν ἄνθρωπος κεράμιον ὕδατος βαστάζων· ἀκολουθήσατε αὐτῷ ¹⁴ καὶ ὅπου ἐὰν εἰσέλθῃ εἴπατε τῷ οἰκοδεσπότῃ ὅτι ὁ διδάσκαλος λέγει· ποῦ ἐστιν τὸ κατάλυμά μου ὅπου τὸ πάσχα μετὰ τῶν μαθητῶν μου φάγω; ¹⁵ καὶ αὐτὸς ὑμῖν δείξει ἀνάγαιον μέγα ἐστρωμένον ἕτοιμον· καὶ ἐκεῖ ἑτοιμάσατε ἡμῖν. ¹⁶ καὶ ἐξῆλθον οἱ μαθηταὶ καὶ ἦλθον εἰς τὴν πόλιν καὶ εὗρον καθὼς εἶπεν αὐτοῖς καὶ ἡτοίμασαν τὸ πάσχα. ¹⁷ Καὶ ὀψίας γενομένης ἔρχεται μετὰ τῶν δώδεκα. ¹⁸ καὶ ἀνακειμένων αὐτῶν καὶ ἐσθιόντων ὁ Ἰησοῦς εἶπεν· ἀμὴν λέγω ὑμῖν ὅτι εἷς ἐξ ὑμῶν παραδώσει με ὁ ἐσθίων μετ᾽ ἐμοῦ. ¹⁹ ἤρξαντο λυπεῖσθαι καὶ λέγειν αὐτῷ εἷς κατὰ εἷς· μήτι ἐγώ; ²⁰ ὁ δὲ εἶπεν αὐτοῖς· εἷς τῶν δώδεκα, ὁ ἐμβαπτόμενος μετ᾽ ἐμοῦ εἰς τὸ τρύβλιον. ²¹ ὅτι ὁ μὲν υἱὸς τοῦ ἀνθρώπου ὑπάγει καθὼς γέγραπται περὶ αὐτοῦ, οὐαὶ δὲ τῷ ἀνθρώπῳ ἐκείνῳ δι᾽ οὗ ὁ υἱὸς τοῦ ἀνθρώπου παραδίδοται· καλὸν αὐτῷ εἰ οὐκ ἐγεννήθη ὁ ἄνθρωπος ἐκεῖνος. ²² Καὶ ἐσθιόντων αὐτῶν λαβὼν ἄρτον εὐλογήσας ἔκλασεν καὶ ἔδωκεν αὐτοῖς καὶ εἶπεν· λάβετε, τοῦτό ἐστιν τὸ σῶμά μου. ²³ καὶ λαβὼν ποτήριον εὐχαριστήσας ἔδωκεν αὐτοῖς, καὶ ἔπιον ἐξ αὐτοῦ πάντες. ²⁴ καὶ εἶπεν αὐτοῖς· τοῦτό ἐστιν τὸ αἷμά μου τῆς διαθήκης τὸ ἐκχυννόμενον ὑπὲρ πολλῶν. ²⁵ ἀμὴν λέγω ὑμῖν ὅτι οὐκέτι οὐ μὴ πίω ἐκ τοῦ γενήματος τῆς ἀμπέλου ἕως τῆς ἡμέρας ἐκείνης ὅταν αὐτὸ πίνω καινὸν ἐν τῇ βασιλείᾳ τοῦ θεοῦ. ²⁶ Καὶ ὑμνήσαντες ἐξῆλθον εἰς τὸ ὄρος τῶν ἐλαιῶν. ²⁷ καὶ λέγει αὐτοῖς ὁ Ἰησοῦς ὅτι πάντες σκανδαλισθήσεσθε, ὅτι γέγραπται· πατάξω τὸν ποιμένα, καὶ τὰ πρόβατα διασκορπισθήσονται. ²⁸ ἀλλὰ μετὰ τὸ ἐγερθῆναί με προάξω ὑμᾶς εἰς τὴν Γαλιλαίαν. ²⁹ ὁ δὲ Πέτρος ἔφη αὐτῷ· εἰ καὶ πάντες σκανδαλισθήσονται, ἀλλ᾽ οὐκ ἐγώ. ³⁰ καὶ λέγει αὐτῷ ὁ Ἰησοῦς· ἀμὴν λέγω σοι ὅτι σὺ σήμερον ταύτῃ τῇ νυκτὶ πρὶν ἢ δὶς ἀλέκτορα φωνῆσαι τρίς με ἀπαρνήσῃ. ³¹ ὁ δὲ ἐκπερισσῶς ἐλάλει· ἐὰν δέῃ με συναποθανεῖν σοι, οὐ μή σε ἀπαρνήσομαι. ὡσαύτως δὲ καὶ πάντες ἔλεγον.

FIGURE 4.5  Lexical cohesion chains in Mark 14:10–31

## 2.5    *Summary and Implication*

This section attempted to analyze Mark 14:10–31 via a fivefold scheme of cohesion: conjunction, reference, substitution, ellipsis, and lexical cohesion. In terms of conjunctions, there is a case of asyndeton in the narrative, which seems to lower the degree of cohesiveness (14:19). The other cases of asyndeton are explicable as they are located in the speech section. Each paragraph of Mark 14:10–31 maintains cohesiveness overall via appropriate conjunctive ties. In terms of reference, the results are as follows: (1) overall, each paragraph holds a participant-reference chain via the main participants; thus, each paragraph can be considered as having cohesiveness; (2) the several appearances of the proper noun (grammaticalized reference) for Jesus (3×) seem to raise

MODE REGISTER ANALYSIS OF MARK 14:10–31

the degree of cohesiveness; (3) the appearance of the pronoun (reduced reference) for Jesus in the first paragraph (14:11) seems to decrease the degree of cohesiveness. In terms of substitution and ellipsis, we can recognize the designated text's cohesiveness via the thirteen cases of substitution and the one case of ellipsis. In terms of lexical cohesion, we can find the cohesiveness of each paragraph via semantic ties. In addition, the conceptual flow between the lexemes around Jesus' death identifies the cohesiveness of the designated text.

The implications of this analysis are as follows: the designated text has cohesiveness overall; this primarily suggests the possibility of one constructor's formation of this text. However, several features that lower the degree of cohesiveness may indicate that the constructor has tried to preserve the oral tradition from Peter, along with written sources.

## 3 Orality and Textuality

This section analyzes the designated text's lexical density and grammatical intricacy according to Porter's based on Halliday's understanding of oral and written language.

### 3.1 Lexical Density

Table 4.9 shows the lexical density of Mark 14:10–31.

The total number of words in Mark 14:10–31 is 367, and the total lexical density in 14:10–31 is 2.782 (153/55). According to Halliday's criteria, this text can be seen as more of an oral language. The lexical density of the direct speeches (14:12b, 13b, 14, 15, 18b, 19b, 20b, 21, 22b, 24b, 25, 27b, 28, 29b, 30b, 31b) and the narratives (14:10, 11, 12a, 13, 16, 17, 18a, 19a, 20a, 22a, 23, 24a, 26, 27a, 29a, 30a, 31a, 31c) is shown in Table 4.10.

TABLE 4.9   Lexical density of Mark 14:10–31

| Lexical density | 14:10–21 | 14:22–26 | 14:27–31 |
| --- | --- | --- | --- |
| Non-embedded clauses | 32 | 12 | 11 |
| Content words | 95 | 30 | 28 |
| Functional words | 116 | 47 | 51 |
| Content words per non-embedded clause | 2.969 | 2.5 | 2.545 |

TABLE 4.10   Lexical density of the direct speech and narrative in Mark 14:10–31

| Lexical density | Direct speech | Narrative |
| --- | --- | --- |
| Non-embedded clauses | 28 | 27 |
| Content words | 79 | 74 |
| Functional words | 131 | 84 |
| Content words per non-embedded clause | 2.82 | 2.74 |

From this analysis, the lexical density of the speech part is a little bit higher than that of the narrative part (0.08); there is almost no difference in lexical density between the direct speech and the narrative, and the results of the two parts reveal orality in light of Halliday's standard. Although it is difficult to determine from whom/which source these oral results originated (e.g., participant or former of oral tradition or constructor), this result could lead us to deduce that the constructor may have preserved the oral tradition in the construction of both the speech and narrative parts. Considering these results, it seems possible to say that this Gospel is rooted in oral tradition, as many scholars assume.[15]

### 3.2   *Grammatical Intricacy*

Table 4.11 reveals the grammatical intricacy of Mark 14:10–31.

TABLE 4.11   Grammatical intricacy of Mark 14:10–31

| Grammatical intricacy | 14:10–21 | 14:22–26 | 14:27–31 |
| --- | --- | --- | --- |
| Non-embedded clauses | 32 | 12 | 11 |
| Total clauses | 53 | 20 | 19 |
| Clause complex | 12 | 5 | 5 |
| Non-embedded clause per clause complex | 2.666 | 2.4 | 2.2 |

---

15   Burkett, *Origins*, 124; Maurice Casey, *Jesus of Nazareth: An Independent Historian's Account of His Life and Teaching* (London: T&T Clark, 2010), 77; Evans, "Two Source Hypothesis"; David S. Jacobsen, *Mark* (FBPC; Minneapolis: Fortress, 2014), 4; cf. Schuyler Brown, *The Origins of Christianity: A Historical Introduction to the New Testament* (Rev. ed.; Oxford: Oxford University Press, 1993), 43; Marxsen, *Mark*, 16–17.

In 14:10–31, the number of non-embedded clauses is 55, the number of clause complexes is 22, and the result of the non-embedded clause per clause complex is 2.5 (55/22). Considering Porter's analysis of grammatical intricacy,[16] the number 2.5 seems high enough; thus, we can say that this text is close to oral language.

### 3.3 Summary and Implication

The analytic results of the orality and textuality of Mark 14:10–31 are as follows. First, the total lexical density is 2.782 (153/55); thus, this text as a whole is in the category of oral language. The result of the lexical density of the direct speech parts (2.82) and narrative parts (2.74) shows that they are both close to oral language. Second, the grammatical intricacy is 2.5 (55/22), and these results show that this text is in the category of oral language. Overall, these results may suggest the possibility that the oral tradition played a significant role in the process of constructing this text.

## 4 Verbal Aspect

### 4.1 Verbal Aspect Analysis

In terms of verbal aspect analysis, the verbs which were used in Mark 14:10–31 can be revealed as in Table 4.12.

The results can be summarized as follows: (1) perfective aspect (aorist): forty-three times; (2) imperfective aspect: twenty-seven times (present) + five times (imperfective); (3) stative aspect (perfect): three times; and (4) future: ten times. In the cases of the perfective aspect, mainly for the narrative accounts, Mark (43×) seems very much similar to Matthew (44×); but in Mark, more imperfective aspects (32×) were used than in Matthew (22×). The stative aspect usages in Mark share those of Matthew (two cases of γέγραπται), but there is one more stative aspect usage (ἐστρωμένον). In a sense, the emphasis on Mark in terms of verbal aspect usage seems stronger than on Matthew. These analyses reveal the markedness of the designated text, but it is difficult to figure out whether this markedness is from the tradition/source or the constructor. As mentioned in chapter 3, these results show the varying degree of markedness of the verbs in the designated text, and it is hard to discern from which/whom the markedness came. Three possible origins are as follows: (1) participant within the text (including Jesus); (2) the eyewitness/former/contributors(s) of

---

16   Cf. Porter, "Orality and Textuality," 13–14.

## 154                                                    CHAPTER 4

TABLE 4.12   Analysis of verbs in Mark 14:10–31 focusing on verbal aspect

| Perfective aspect (aorist) | Imperfective aspect | Stative aspect | Future |
|---|---|---|---|
| ἀπῆλθεν (10), παραδοῖ (10), ἀκούσαντες (11), ἐχάρησαν (11), ἐπηγγείλαντο (11), παραδοῖ (11), ἀπελθόντες (12), ἑτοιμάσωμεν (12), φάγῃς (12), ἀκολουθήσατε (13), εἰσέλθῃ (14), εἴπατε (14), φάγω (14), ἑτοιμάσατε (15), ἐξῆλθον (16), ἦλθον (16), εὗρον (16), εἶπεν (16), ἡτοίμασαν (16), γενομένης (17), εἶπεν (18), ἤρξαντο (19), εἶπεν (20), ἐγεννήθη (21), λαβών (22), εὐλογή- σας (22), ἔκλασεν (22), ἔδωκεν (22), εἶπεν (22), λάβετε (22), λαβών (23), εὐχαριστήσας (23), ἔδωκεν (23), ἔπιον (23), εἶπεν (24), πίω (25), ὑμνήσαντες (26), ἐξῆλθον (26), ἐγερθῆναί (28), ἔφη (29), φωνῆσαι (30), συναποθανεῖν (31) | **Present** λέγουσιν (12), θέλεις (12), ἀποστέλλει (13), λέγει (13), βαστάζων (13), λέγει (14), ἐστιν (14), ἔρχεται (17), ἀνακει- μένων (18), ἐσθιόντων (18), λέγω (18), ἐσθίων (18), λυπεῖσθαι (19), λέγειν (19), ἐμβαπτό- μενος (20), ὑπάγει (21), παραδίδοται (21), ἐσθι- όντων (22), ἐστιν (22), ἐστιν (24), ἐκχυννόμενον (24), λέγω (25), πίνω (25), λέγει (27), λέγει (30), λέγω (30), δέῃ (31) **Imperfective** ἐζήτει (11), ἔθυον (12), ὑπάγετε (13), ἐλάλει (31), ἔλεγον (31) | **Perfect** ἐστρωμένον (15), γέγραπται (21), γέγραπται (27) **Pluperfect** | ἀπαντήσει (13), δείξει (15), παραδώσει (18), σκανδαλισθήσεσθε (27), πατάξω (27), σκανδαλι- σθήσονται (27), πατάξω (28), σκανδαλισθήσο- νται (29), ἀπαρνήσῃ (30), ἀπαρνήσομα (31) |

traditions; or (3) the constructor. Comparative analysis in chapter 6 may help us to discern the possible origin(s).

### 4.2   *Summary and Implication*

The verbal aspect analysis of Mark 14:10–31 reveals the varying degree of markedness of the verbs in the designated text. There are three frontgrounded prominent parts via stative aspects (ἐστρωμένον; 14:15; γέγραπται; 14:21, 27), several foregrounded parts via imperfective aspect, and many background parts via perfective aspect. The varying degrees of markedness may have been affected by the oral/written traditions and/or the constructor.

## 5 Conclusion

This chapter identifies the mode (thematization, cohesion, orality & textuality, and verbal aspect) of Mark 14:10–31. These are some notable characteristics in terms of the designated text's textual characteristics. First, the thematization analysis reveals that the designated text has eight thematic units and four paragraphs, and the first, second, and fourth paragraph each has one distinctive topic. The third paragraph, however, holds two topics in one thematic unit. The overlapping positions of prime and theme in this text show us the most marked-thematic actor as Peter (2×). These results have the following implications: (1) the overall organized structure of the designated text; (2) the constructor's preservation of traditions, which could be deduced by the less organized aspect in the third paragraph; (3) the connection between this text and Peter, which could be inferred by the most marked-thematic actor of the designated text. Second, the results of cohesion analysis show us that the cohesiveness of each paragraph is maintained via conjunction ties, participant-reference chains (including substitution and ellipsis), and semantic-lexical ties. The cohesiveness of the entire designated text is also recognized in lexical cohesion chains. There are several factors, however, that may lower the degree of cohesiveness (e.g., asyndeton [14:19], a reduced reference [14:11]). These overall features may have come from one constructor, who may have tried to preserve the oral tradition from Peter. Third, the analysis of lexical density and grammatical intricacy reveals that the designated text is close to oral language, and the gap between the narrative part (2.74) and the speech part (2.82) appears to be slight. The oral properties of the designated text show the possibility that this text is significantly rooted in oral tradition. From these results, it is possible to deduce the identity of the constructor as the preserver of the oral tradition. Fourth, the results of verbal aspect analysis reveal the different levels of markedness of the verbs in the designated text. The varying markedness may have been affected by the oral/written traditions and/or the constructor.

CHAPTER 5

# Mode Register Analysis of Luke 22:3–23, 31–34

## 1 Scope of the Text for Analysis

Before the mode register analysis of the designated text of Luke, it seems necessary to mention the object of this analysis in chapter 5 briefly. As mentioned in the introduction, 22:1–2 and 22:24–30, which are not included in the designated texts in Matthew and Mark, are omitted to obtain a similar amount of text for parallel comparative analysis. However, a linguistic analysis of the Gospel according to Luke will be attempted with these omitted parts in mind. They will be referred to and analyzed when deemed necessary.

## 2 Thematization

### 2.1 *Prime and Subsequent*

The prime-subsequent analysis of Luke 22:3–23, 31–34 is given in Appendix 3, and among the findings of this process, Table 5.1 shows various examples in Luke 22:3–23, 31–34.

TABLE 5.1    Prime-subsequent examples in Luke 22:3–23, 31–34

| Verse | Prime | Subsequent |
| --- | --- | --- |
| 22:3 | Εἰσῆλθεν (δὲ) | σατανᾶς εἰς Ἰούδαν τὸν καλούμενον Ἰσκαριώτην, ὄντα ἐκ τοῦ ἀριθμοῦ τῶν δώδεκα· |
| 22:4 | (καὶ) ἀπελθὼν | συνελάλησεν τοῖς ἀρχιερεῦσιν καὶ στρατηγοῖς τὸ πῶς αὐτοῖς παραδῷ αὐτόν. |
| 22:5a | (καὶ) ἐχάρησαν | |
| 22:5b | (καὶ) συνέθεντο | αὐτῷ ἀργύριον δοῦναι. |
| 22:7b | [ἐν] ᾗ | ἔδει θύεσθαι τὸ πάσχα· |
| 22:9b | ποῦ | θέλεις ἑτοιμάσωμεν; |
| 22:10a | ὁ (δὲ) | εἶπεν αὐτοῖς |
| 22:10b | ἰδοὺ | |
| 22:10f | εἰς ἣν | εἰσπορεύεται, |
| 22:12a | (κἀκεῖνος) ὑμῖν | δείξει ἀνάγαιον μέγα ἐστρωμένον· |
| 22:16b | (ὅτι) οὐ μὴ | φάγω αὐτὸ ἕως ὅτου πληρωθῇ ἐν τῇ βασιλείᾳ τοῦ θεοῦ. |

© HOJOON J. AHN, 2024 | DOI:10.1163/9789004696372_007

MODE REGISTER ANALYSIS OF LUKE 22:3–23, 31–34    157

TABLE 5.1    Prime-subsequent examples in Luke 22:3–23, 31–34 (*cont.*)

| Verse | Prime | Subsequent |
| --- | --- | --- |
| 22:31b | ὁ σατανᾶς | ἐξητήσατο ὑμᾶς τοῦ σινιάσαι ὡς τὸν σῖτον· |
| 22:32a | ἐγὼ (δὲ) | ἐδεήθην περὶ σοῦ |
| 22:34a | ὁ (δὲ) | εἶπεν |

Among the sixty-three clauses in Luke 22:3–23, 31–34, the lexemes placed in prime are classified by type as follows: (1) verb (separate subject existence; 22:3), (2) participle as an adverb (22:4), (3) verb only (without subsequent; 22:5a), (4) verb (inherent subject existence; 22:5b), (5) relative pronoun (22:7b), (6) subject (definite article; 22:10a, 34a), (7) interrogative adverb (22:9b), (8) particle of interjection (22:10b), (9) prepositional phrase (22:10f), (10) dative (pronoun; 22:12a), (11) negation (22:16b), (12) subject (noun; 22:31b), and (13) subject (pronoun; 22:32a). From this analysis, we can recognize the flexibility of the Greek language in terms of the position of each lexeme. In particular, in case 1, a verb is located in prime despite the existence of a separate subject, inferring that the text was constructed like this here to focus the clause around the process, not the actor. In the cases of 6 and 13, however, the subject Jesus is located in prime, and in that case, the subject is highly focused on. These elements of prime and subsequent are closely concerned with the theme-rheme analysis.[1]

### 2.2    *Theme and Rheme*

A theme and rheme analysis of Luke 22:3–23, 31–34 in light of the principles suggested by Porter and O'Donnell, along with Dvorak and Walton, is found in Appendix 7.[2] There are ten thematic units (1. 22:3–6; 2. 22:7–8; 3. 22:9; 4. 22:10–13; 5. 22:14a; 6. 22:14b–23; 7. 22:31; 8. 22:32; 9. 22:33; 10. 22:34). The thematic actors, which are revealed by the theme and rheme analyses, are as follows: (1) σατανᾶς (2×; 22:3, 31 [ὁ σατανᾶς]), (2) ἡ ἡμέρα τῶν ἀζύμων (22:7), (3) οἱ (22:9 [cf. 22:8; Πέτρον καὶ Ἰωάννην]), (4) ὁ (22:10; Jesus), (5) ἡ ὥρα (22:14a), (6) οἱ ἀπόστολοι (22:14b), (7) ἐγὼ (22:32; Jesus), (8) ὁ (22:33; Peter), and (9) ὁ (22:34; Jesus). Thus, the seven thematic actors are Jesus (3×), Peter (1×), Satan (1×), the apostles

---

1    A prime-subsequent analysis of Luke 22:24–30, the omitted part of this study, is given in Appendix 4.

2    A theme and rheme analysis of Luke 22:24–30, the omitted part of this study, is given in Appendix 8.

158                                                                                    CHAPTER 5

(1×), Peter and John (1×), the day of Unleavened Bread (1×), and the hour (1×). From this, Jesus appears most outstanding. Furthermore, in the case of 4, 7, 9 (3×; 22:10, 32, 34), the thematic actor Jesus is located in prime. Thus, from the above two analyses (prime-subsequent, theme-rheme), Jesus turns out to be the most marked thematic actor. Considering, however, the circumstances in which Jesus appears as the key figure in the designated text, the above results may be natural.

### 2.3     *Topic and Comment*
#### 2.3.1     Paragraph Division
Considering seven formal/functional criteria for dividing paragraphs suggested by Porter (although not every case in Luke 22:3–23, 31–34 necessitates an alignment of all seven criteria for a paragraph division), this section divides Luke 22:3–23, 31–34 into paragraphs and suggests a topic for each paragraph. The results will be compared with the paragraph divisions and topics provided by UBS[5].

The paragraph division of UBS[5] including the designated text (Luke 22:3–23, 31–34) is as follows: (1) the plot to kill Jesus (22:1–6), (2) the preparation of the Passover (22:7–13), (3) the institution of the Lord's supper (22:14–23); and (4) Peter's denial foretold (22:31–34).[3] Based on the elements for paragraph division suggested in the methodology (one or more thematic units and thematic participants, temporal/spatial deixis, transition of topic, and lexical cohesion), this section will evaluate the paragraph division and titles offered by UBS[5] and suggest an alternative paragraph division.

The overlapping part between the first paragraph suggested by UBS[5] and the designated text is 22:3–6. There are one thematic unit (22:3–6) and one thematic participant (σατανᾶς; 22:3). This part has no temporal deixis, but it could be connected with the temporal deixis of 22:1 (Ἤγγιζεν δὲ ἡ ἑορτὴ τῶν ἀζύμων ἡ λεγομένη πάσχα). However, considering the introduction of a new participant, Satan, and the appearance of adversative conjunction δέ in 22:3, it seems possible to divide 22:1–6 into two paragraphs: 22:1–2 and 22:3–6. This division is also supported by NA[28] and several Bible translations.[4] Based on these points, this study regards 22:3–6 as a paragraph.

The second paragraph divided by UBS[5] is 22:7–13. It contains three thematic units (22:7–8; 22:9; 22:10–13) and three thematic participants (ἡ ἡμέρα

---

3   UBS[5] presents 22:24–30 as the fourth paragraph and 22:31–34 as the fifth paragraph, but 22:24–30 is excluded from the main analysis of this study. Thus, accordingly, 22:31–34 will be referred to as the fourth paragraph in subsequent studies.

4   RSV, NRSV, NKJV, ESV, *etc.*

MODE REGISTER ANALYSIS OF LUKE 22:3–23, 31–34    159

τῶν ἀζύμων; 22:7; οἱ; 22:9 [cf. 22:8; Πέτρον καὶ Ἰωάννην]; ὁ; 22:10 [Jesus]). This paragraph includes a temporal deixis (Ἦλθεν δὲ ἡ ἡμέρα τῶν ἀζύμων) as a boundary marker, which points to a new beginning of a paragraph. It also has a clear transition of the topic ("the plot to kill Jesus" → "the preparation of the Passover"). Furthermore, this paragraph consists of the Passover meal preparation; the reiterative lexical items/lexemes in domain 77 (4×; ἑτοιμάζω) and 51 (3×; πάσχα; cf. ἄζυμος [domain 5]) cohesively tie this paragraph. Considering these aspects, the paragraph division of UBS⁵ seems appropriate.

The third paragraph suggested by UBS⁵ is 22:14–23. There are two thematic units (22:14a; 22:14b–23) and two thematic participants (ἡ ὥρα; 22:14a; οἱ ἀπό-στολοι; 22:14b). This paragraph contains two distinctive topics: the Eucharist (22:14–20) and foreseeing betrayal (22:21–23), so it may seem natural to divide 22:14–23 into two paragraphs in terms of topic: 22:14–20 and 22:21–23. However, the thematic unit 22:14b–23 (along with 22:14a) embraces 22:14–20 and 22:21–23; thus, 22:14–23 can be considered one paragraph. Furthermore, this paragraph has only one temporal deixis (ὅτε ἐγένετο ἡ ὥρα; 22:14) as a boundary marker. Also, this paragraph has three lexemes, ποτήριον ("cup"; 22:17, 20 [2×]), ἄρτος ("bread"; 22:19), τράπεζα ("table"; 22:21), which are semantically tied around the context of Passover meal;[5] thus, they cohesively tie this paragraph. For these reasons, 22:14–23 can be regarded as one paragraph.

Prior to Luke 22:31–34, let us briefly observe the omitted part of this study, 22:24–30. This section has two thematic units (22:24; 22:25–30) and two thematic participants (φιλονεικία; 22:24; ὁ [Jesus]; 22:25). There is no temporal or spatial deixis; however, this paragraph forms a cohesion around the topic of a dispute among the disciples regarding the issue of the greatest and Jesus' words to teach the principle to be the one who serves (ὁ διακονῶν; 22:26, 27 [2×]).

The fourth paragraph suggested by UBS⁵ is 22:31–34. It has four thematic units (22:31; 22:32; 22:33; 22:34) and three thematic participants (ὁ σατανᾶς; 22:31; ὁ Ἰησοῦς [ἐγὼ; 22:32, ὁ; 22:34]; ὁ Πέτρος; 22:33). There is no temporal or spatial deixis; however, there is a distinct transition of topics, from "dispute about greatness" (22:24–30) to "Satan's temptation and Peter's denial foretold" (22:31–34). This paragraph mainly consists of a dialog between Jesus and Peter (as the representative of the disciples), which starts with Jesus and ends with Jesus (Jesus → Peter → Jesus). In terms of lexical cohesion, this paragraph has three lexemes, ἐπιστρέφω ("to return"), ἐκλείπω ("to depart/fail"), πορεύομαι ("to go") belong to domain 15, which are semantically tied around the disciple's

---

5  For the detailed semantic-lexical analysis, see the lexical cohesion analysis of the third paragraph.

160                                                                                        CHAPTER 5

journey of faith; thus, they cohesively tie this paragraph. Considering these aspects, the paragraph division of UBS[5] seems appropriate.

By applying thematization, the designated text can be divided into four paragraphs as follows: (1) 22:3–6, (2) 22:7–13, (3) 22:14–23, and (4) 22:31–34. We will examine the validity of this suggestion in the following discussion. The first, second, and fourth paragraphs are well-structured based on thematic units, thematic participants, boundary markers, and lexical cohesions; however, the third paragraph has one large thematic unit (22:14b–23; including a tiny thematic unit [22:14a]) with two topics, which may show the less organized aspect of this paragraph.

### 2.3.2    Finding Topics of Each Paragraph

This section presents the topic of each paragraph in light of the previous paragraph division. This section provides a thematic participant-processes analysis to find the topic of each paragraph based on Porter and O'Donnell's approach. Table 5.2 presents the thematic participants and processes of each thematic unit.

TABLE 5.2    Thematic participants and processes in Luke 22:3–23, 31–34 (including 22:24–30)

| Paragraph | Thematic unit | Verse | Thematic participant | Major process |
|---|---|---|---|---|
| 1 | 1 | 3–6 | Satan | entered into Judas |
| 2 | 2 | 7–8 | the day of Unleavened Bread | came |
| | 3 | 9 | they (Peter and John) | said to him (Jesus) |
| | 4 | 10–13 | he (Jesus) | said to them (Peter and John) |
| 3 | 5 | 14a | the hour | came |
| | 6 | 14b–23 | the apostles | (were) with him (Jesus) |
| Omitted Part | a | 24 | a dispute | arose among them (apostles) |
| | b | 25–30 | he (Jesus) | said to them (apostles) |
| 4 | 7 | 31 | Satan | demanded to sift you (apostles) |
| | 8 | 32 | I (Jesus) | prayed for you (Peter) |
| | 9 | 33 | he (Peter) | said to him (Jesus) |
| | 10 | 34 | he (Jesus) | said |

MODE REGISTER ANALYSIS OF LUKE 22:3–23, 31–34        161

Each paragraph's topic in Luke 22:3–23, 31–34 is analyzed by observing the thematic participants and major processes.

The major thematic process of paragraph 1 (22:3–6) is Satan's action (entering into Judas). Here, Satan's action as a thematic participant appears in relation to entering Judas and provoking his betrayal against Jesus. Compared to Matthew and Mark, which describe Judas and the high priests as thematic participants, it seems to be a characteristic element of Luke. The topic of this paragraph is proposed as follows: Satan's activity around Judas and the high priests for the betrayal to Jesus.

The major thematic processes of paragraph 2 (22:7–13) are the day of Unleavened Bread's action (coming [22:7]), Peter and John's action (saying to Jesus [22:9]), and Jesus' action (saying to Peter and John [22:10]). Here, like Matthew and Mark, Jesus' action is concerned with the specific instructions regarding the preparation. However, in Luke, the day of Unleavened Bread is added as another actor whose action is characterized as "coming." Also, in Luke, the object of Jesus' words is limited to Peter and John, and their action relates to preparing the Passover meal. Given these points, the topic of this paragraph is proposed as follows: Jesus' words for Passover and the preparation of Peter and John.

The major thematic processes of paragraph 3 (22:14–23) are as follows: 1. the hour's action (coming); 2. the apostles' action (being with Jesus). Unlike Mark, where the only thematic actor is Jesus, and in Matthew, where Jesus and Judas appear together as thematic participants, in Luke, the hour and the apostles appear as thematic participants, and their actions are drawn as "coming" and "being with Jesus." However, their central concept relates to the Eucharist formed by Jesus and the future betrayal by one of his disciples. Given these points, the topic of this paragraph is proposed as follows: the hour of the Eucharist and Jesus' foretelling of the betrayal by one of the apostles.

The major thematic processes of paragraph 4 (22:31–34) comprise Satan (demanding to sift the apostles [22:31]), Jesus (praying for Peter [22:32], speaking [22:34]), and Peter (talking to Jesus [22:33]). Like Matthew and Mark, Jesus and Peter appear as thematic participants in Luke. Their core actions are revealed, in Jesus' case, as a prayer for Peter and his prophecy of Peter's denial. And in Peter's case, the core actions are his confident words that will never happen. Unlike other Gospels, other disciples do not appear as thematic participants here, and Satan reappears as a thematic participant, as in 22:3–6. And Satan's key action seems to be a claim to Jesus to "sift" the apostles (disciples), including Peter, "like wheat." Given these points, the topic of this paragraph is proposed as follows: Satan's demand, Jesus' prayer, and his foretelling of Peter's denial.

162                                                                                                                      CHAPTER 5

TABLE 5.3    Paragraph division & topics of UBS[5] and this study

| Paragraph division & topics of UBS[5] | Paragraph division & topics of this study |
| --- | --- |
| 1. The plot to kill Jesus (22:1–6) | 1. Satan's activity around Judas and the high priests for the betrayal to Jesus (22:3–6) |
| 2. The preparation of the Passover (22:7–13) | 2. Jesus' words for Passover and its preparation of Peter and John (22:7–13) |
| 3. The institution of the Lord's supper (22:14–23) | 3. The hour of the Eucharist and Jesus' foretelling about the betrayal by one of the apostles (22:14–23) |
| 4. Peter's denial foretold (22:31–34) | 4. Satan's demand, Jesus' prayer, and His foretelling of Peter's denial (22:31–34) |

In summary, the paragraph division and the topic for each paragraph of Luke 22:3–23, 31–34, according to the thematic analyses compared to UBS[5], are summarized in Table 5.3.

The paragraph division and topics suggested by this study show that the designated text has four paragraphs. In paragraphs 1, 2, and 4, each has one distinctive topic. However, the third paragraph has two distinctive topics ("Jesus' institution of the Eucharist" and "Jesus' foretelling of the betrayal"). These analytic results show the organized structure of the designated text overall, from which the constructor's role could be deduced. However, the phenomenon in the third paragraph (22:14–23) shows the less organized character of the designated text, which may show us the degree of the constructor's role in the construction process.

## 2.4    *Summary and Implication*

In this section, an analysis of thematization for Luke 22:3–23, 31–34 was conducted: the following elements are the results. There are ten thematic units (1. 22:3–6; 2. 22:7–8; 3. 22:9; 4. 22:10–13; 5. 22:14a; 6. 22:14b–23; 7. 22:31; 8. 22:32; 9. 22:33; 10. 22:34), and overlapping positions of prime and theme show us the most marked-thematic actor as Jesus (3×; 22:10, 32, 34). This study divides the designated texts into four paragraphs: (1) 22:3–6, (2) 22:7–13, (3) 22:14–23, and (4) 22:31–34. The topics for each paragraph are suggested as follows: (1) Satan's activity around Judas and the high priests for the betrayal to Jesus (22:3–6), (2) Jesus' words for Passover and its preparation of Peter and John (22:7–13), (3) the hour of the Eucharist and his foretelling of the betrayal (22:14–23), and (4) Satan's demanding, Jesus' prayer, and his foretelling of Peter's denial (22:31–34).

These results reveal the organized structure of the designated text overall, but the third paragraph, which has one large thematic unit (22:14b–23; including a tiny thematic unit [22:14a]) with two distinctive topics, reveals the less organized aspect. Considering these features, we could deduce the possibility of preserving oral traditions in the construction process.

## 3    Cohesion

### 3.1    *Conjunction*

Table 5.4 shows conjunctions and asyndeton in the designated text (Luke 22:3–23, 31–34) divided into the narrative and direct speech parts.

TABLE 5.4    Conjunctions and asyndeton in the narrative and direct speech of Luke 22:3–23, 31–34

| Paragraphs | Narrative | Direct speech |
| --- | --- | --- |
| 22:3–6 | 3 Εἰσῆλθεν <u>δὲ</u> σατανᾶς εἰς Ἰούδαν τὸν καλούμενον Ἰσκαριώτην, ὄντα ἐκ τοῦ ἀριθμοῦ τῶν δώδεκα· 4 <u>καὶ</u> ἀπελθὼν συνελάλησεν τοῖς ἀρχιερεῦσιν <u>καὶ</u> στρατηγοῖς τὸ πῶς αὐτοῖς παραδῷ αὐτόν. 5 <u>καὶ</u> ἐχάρησαν <u>καὶ</u> συνέθεντο αὐτῷ ἀργύριον δοῦναι. 6 <u>καὶ</u> ἐξωμολόγησεν, <u>καὶ</u> ἐζήτει εὐκαιρίαν τοῦ παραδοῦναι αὐτὸν ἄτερ ὄχλου αὐτοῖς. | |
| 22:7–13 | 7 Ἦλθεν <u>δὲ</u> ἡ ἡμέρα τῶν ἀζύμων, [ἐν] ᾗ ἔδει θύεσθαι τὸ πάσχα· 8 <u>καὶ</u> ἀπέστειλεν Πέτρον <u>καὶ</u> Ἰωάννην εἰπών· | |
| | | ∅ πορευθέντες ἑτοιμάσατε ἡμῖν τὸ πάσχα <u>ἵνα</u> φάγωμεν. |
| | 9 οἱ <u>δὲ</u> εἶπαν αὐτῷ· | |
| | | ∅ ποῦ θέλεις ἑτοιμάσωμεν; |
| | 10 ὁ <u>δὲ</u> εἶπεν αὐτοῖς· | |
| | | ∅ ἰδοὺ ∅ εἰσελθόντων ὑμῶν εἰς τὴν πόλιν συναντήσει ὑμῖν ἄνθρωπος κεράμιον ὕδατος βαστάζων· ∅ ἀκολουθήσατε αὐτῷ εἰς τὴν οἰκίαν εἰς ἣν εἰσπορεύεται, 11 <u>καὶ</u> ἐρεῖτε τῷ οἰκοδεσπότῃ τῆς οἰκίας· |

164                                                                      CHAPTER 5

TABLE 5.4    Conjunctions and asyndeton in the narrative and direct speech (*cont.*)

| Paragraphs | Narrative | Direct speech |
|---|---|---|
| | | ∅ λέγει σοι ὁ διδάσκαλος· |
| | | ∅ ποῦ ἐστιν τὸ κατάλυμα <u>ὅπου</u> τὸ πάσχα μετὰ τῶν μαθητῶν μου φάγω; |
| | | ¹² ∅ <u>κἀκεῖνος</u> ὑμῖν δείξει ἀνάγαιον μέγα ἐστρωμένον· ἐκεῖ ἑτοιμάσατε. |
| | ¹³ ἀπελθόντες <u>δὲ</u> εὗρον καθὼς εἰρήκει αὐτοῖς <u>καὶ</u> ἡτοίμασαν τὸ πάσχα. | |
| 22:14–23 | ¹⁴ <u>Καὶ</u> ὅτε ἐγένετο ἡ ὥρα, ἀνέπεσεν <u>καὶ</u> οἱ ἀπόστολοι σὺν αὐτῷ. ¹⁵ <u>καὶ</u> εἶπεν πρὸς αὐτούς· | |
| | | ∅ ἐπιθυμίᾳ ἐπεθύμησα τοῦτο τὸ πάσχα φαγεῖν μεθ' ὑμῶν πρὸ τοῦ με παθεῖν· ¹⁶ λέγω <u>γὰρ</u> ὑμῖν <u>ὅτι</u> οὐ μὴ φάγω αὐτὸ <u>ἕως</u> ὅτου πληρωθῇ ἐν τῇ βασιλείᾳ τοῦ θεοῦ. |
| | ¹⁷ <u>καὶ</u> δεξάμενος ποτήριον εὐχαριστή-σας εἶπεν· | |
| | | ∅ λάβετε τοῦτο <u>καὶ</u> διαμερίσατε εἰς ἑαυτούς· ¹⁸ λέγω <u>γὰρ</u> ὑμῖν, [ὅτι] οὐ μὴ πίω ἀπὸ τοῦ νῦν ἀπὸ τοῦ γενήμα-τος τῆς ἀμπέλου <u>ἕως</u> οὗ ἡ βασιλεία τοῦ θεοῦ ἔλθῃ. |
| | ¹⁹ <u>Καὶ</u> λαβὼν ἄρτον εὐχαριστήσας ἔκλασεν <u>καὶ</u> ἔδωκεν αὐτοῖς λέγων· | |
| | | ∅ τοῦτό ἐστιν τὸ σῶμά μου τὸ ὑπὲρ ὑμῶν διδόμενον· ∅ τοῦτο ποιεῖτε εἰς τὴν ἐμὴν ἀνάμνησιν. |
| | ²⁰ <u>καὶ</u> τὸ ποτήριον ὡσαύτως μετὰ τὸ δειπνῆσαι, λέγων· | |
| | | ∅ τοῦτο τὸ ποτήριον ἡ καινὴ διαθήκη ἐν τῷ αἵματί μου τὸ ὑπὲρ ὑμῶν ἐκχυννόμενον. ²¹ <u>Πλὴν</u> ἰδοὺ ∅ ἡ χεὶρ τοῦ παραδιδόντος με μετ' ἐμοῦ ἐπὶ τῆς τραπέζης. ²² <u>ὅτι</u> ὁ υἱὸς μὲν τοῦ ἀνθρώπου κατὰ τὸ ὡρισμένον πορεύε-ται, <u>πλὴν</u> οὐαὶ τῷ ἀνθρώπῳ ἐκείνῳ δι' οὗ παραδίδοται. |

MODE REGISTER ANALYSIS OF LUKE 22:3–23, 31–34

TABLE 5.4    Conjunctions and asyndeton in the narrative and direct speech (*cont.*)

| Paragraphs | Narrative | Direct speech |
|---|---|---|
|  | ²³ <u>καὶ</u> αὐτοὶ ἤρξαντο συζητεῖν πρὸς ἑαυτοὺς τὸ τίς ἄρα εἴη ἐξ αὐτῶν ὁ τοῦτο μέλλων πράσσειν. |  |
| 22:31–34 |  | ³¹ ⊘ Σίμων ⊘ Σίμων, ⊘ ἰδοὺ ⊘ ὁ σατανᾶς ἐξῃτήσατο ὑμᾶς τοῦ σινιάσαι <u>ὡς</u> τὸν σῖτον· 32 ἐγὼ <u>δὲ</u> ἐδεήθην περὶ σοῦ <u>ἵνα</u> μὴ ἐκλίπῃ ἡ πίστις σου· <u>καὶ</u> σύ ποτε ἐπιστρέψας στήρισον τοὺς ἀδελφούς σου. |
|  | ³³ ὁ <u>δὲ</u> εἶπεν αὐτῷ· |  |
|  |  | ⊘ κύριε, ⊘ μετὰ σοῦ ἕτοιμός εἰμι <u>καὶ</u> εἰς φυλακὴν <u>καὶ</u> εἰς θάνατον πορεύεσθαι. |
|  | ³⁴ ὁ <u>δὲ</u> εἶπεν· |  |
|  |  | ⊘ λέγω σοι, ⊘ Πέτρε, ⊘ οὐ φωνήσει σήμερον ἀλέκτωρ <u>ἕως</u> τρίς με ἀπαρνήσῃ εἰδέναι. |

Conjunctions in the designated text are as follows: (1) καί (22×; 22:4 [2×], 5 [2×], 6 [2×], 8 [2×], 11, 13, 14 [2×], 15, 17 [2×], 19 [2×], 20, 23, 32, 33 [2×]); (2) δέ (8×; 22:3, 7, 9, 10, 13, 32, 33, 34); (3) γάρ (2×; 22:16, 18); (4) ἵνα (22:8, 32); (5) πλήν (22:21, 22); (6) ὅτι (22:16, 22); (7) ὅπου (22:11); (8) καθώς (22:13); (9) ὅτε (22:14); (10) μέν (22:22); (11) ὡς (22:31); (12) ἕως (22:34).⁶ There is a synthetic form of conjunction and another lexeme: κἀκεῖνος (καί + ἐκεῖνος), but there are no cases of simultaneous appearance of conjunctions in the designated text in Luke. The total number of conjunctions in the designated text is forty-one, of which twenty-five belong to the narrative part and sixteen belong to the direct speech part. There are twenty-four asyndeton cases in direct speech parts; there is no asyndeton for narrative parts.

Now, we will analyze each appearance of conjunctions in the contextual flow, according to the previously divided paragraphs. The first conjunction of the first paragraph (22:3–6) is δέ. It links the story of the high priests and scribes

---

6   The conjunction ἕως also appears in Matthew (26:29) and Mark (14:25), but here it functions as a preposition. In Luke, ἕως appears three times, and it functions as a conjunction only in 22:34, and is used as a proposition to receive the last noun clause in 22:16 and 22:18.

166  CHAPTER 5

looking for a way to get rid of Jesus in the context of the approaching feast of Unleavened Bread in 22:1–2 with the story of Judas in 22:3. In other words, they were seeking a way to kill Jesus, "however," Judas finally solves their problems by Satan's intervention; here δέ seems to be appropriately used as adversative conjunction. Subsequently, καί, which begins 22:4, is used as a conjunction to reveal causal and connective aspects in the passage where Judas visits and discusses with the chief priests and officers after Satan entered Judas. The second occurrence of καί in 22:4 reveals unmarked continuity to connect dative nouns as two objects that Judas visits (ἀρχιερεῦσιν καὶ στρατηγοῖς). The last clause of 22:4 is accusative, requiring no conjunction (τὸ πῶς αὐτοῖς παραδῷ αὐτόν), and reveals the purpose of Judas's visit. Καί, which begins 22:5, links the act of discussing how to hand over Jesus (22:4) and the gladness the chief priest and officers had. In this context, καί is used as the connective and causal conjunction. Their gladness leads to a promise to give silver to Judas, and the conjunction that connects them is καί, which reveals an unmarked continuity. After their agreement, Judas's consent is linked by καί with causal continuity, which can be translated as "so." After this agreement, Judas seeks to hand over "him" to them, also led by καί, containing an unmarked continuity. In the first paragraph, which is purely narrative, all conjunctions are καί except for one case of δέ, which appears at the beginning. Asyndeton is not found here, and the conjunctive ties are formed by the appearances of δέ and καί, which leads to maintaining the cohesiveness of the paragraph.

The second paragraph (22:7–13) deals with the topic related to the preparation for the Passover. The first conjunction appears as δέ, forming a transitive and adversative connection from the previous topic of Judas's betrayal to a new topic. When the day of Unleavened Bread comes (22:7), Jesus sends Peter and John, which are connected by a connective conjunction καί, where the meaning of it can be translated as "so" or "and" (22:8). Thereafter, the conjunction connecting Peter and John, the object of Jesus' sending, is καί, which reveals unmarked continuity. After the narrative part, asyndeton appears at the beginning of the direct speech (∅ πορευθέντες ἑτοιμάσατε ἡμῖν τὸ πάσχα); thus, this asyndeton is explicable. The following conjunction ἵνα leads the primary purpose of preparation for the Passover: "to eat" (ἵνα φάγωμεν). In 22:9, a narrative speech margin of Peter and John's question starts with δέ. Jesus' words may have been abstract (22:8), so 22:9 is connected by the adversative/connective δέ to reveal their need for more specific information. Asyndeton appears in the speech in 22:9, which is at the beginning of the direct speech as a question about where to prepare the Passover (∅ ποῦ θέλεις ἑτοιμάσωμεν;); thus, this asyndeton is explicable. Jesus' answer to their question follows in 22:10–12, and the narrative speech margin starts with the adversative/connective

MODE REGISTER ANALYSIS OF LUKE 22:3–23, 31–34        167

conjunction δέ. After ἰδού, the expression of attention,[7] Jesus gives the two disciples a description of what they will encounter when they enter the city and a command to follow the man (22:10); these all consist of asyndeton, which is explicable because the first case is at the beginning of the speech, and the second case is where a clause begins with the imperative (ἀκολουθήσατε). 22:11 contains the continuation of Jesus' words, starting with καί for an unmarked continuity, which links his words to the previous imperative. The remainder of 22:11 includes two instances of asyndeton (∅ λέγει σοι ὁ διδάσκαλος; ∅ ποῦ ἐστιν τὸ κατάλυμα); these all seem natural since the first asyndeton appears at the beginning of the quotation in Jesus' words (22:11b), and the second asyndeton appears at the beginning of the other quotation within the previous quotation (22:11c). After this, a subordinating conjunction ὅπου follows to reveal the purpose of his order: to prepare the place for the Passover meal. In 22:12, καί is used as a connective conjunction for the following Jesus' words. More specifically, καί is combined with ἐκεῖνος (κἀκεῖνος). When the disciples do what Jesus commands, *then that person* (κἀκεῖνος) will show where to prepare the Passover meal. After that, asyndeton appears in the last clause of 22:12 (∅ ἐκεῖ ἑτοιμάσατε), which is explicable because it is an imperative clause. 22:13 shows the disciples' reactions and the results: everything is accomplished according to the words of Jesus; the conjunction to connect Jesus' words (22:10–12) and its results (22:13) is δέ. It can be understood as "so," basically containing causal connective meaning.[8] The two conjunctions of the remaining clauses in 22:13 are καθώς and καί. Here, καθώς is used as comparative conjunction to reveal that "*as* Jesus said, it had been done," and καί functions as connective conjunctions indicating that "*and/so* the disciples prepared the Passover." Thus, overall, the appearance of conjunctions conveys cohesion of this paragraph, and the appearance of asyndeton is all explicable.

The beginning of the third paragraph (22:14–23) is καί. Here, it is used with ὅτε to convey the meaning of "and when," revealing the meaning of continuity and transition together, which leads to the following topic: "the hour comes." The second καί in 22:14 functions as a coordinating conjunction to carry

---

7   The beginning of the speech in 22:10 is ἰδού, an aorist middle imperative verb form of εἶδον. This expression, ἰδού, is often used as a demonstrative particle. This study does not regard it as a conjunction but as an imperative verb form and particle; thus, the clause including this lexeme has no conjunction (asyndeton), even though ἰδού has a conjunctive function in emphasizing the following content. See Louw and Nida, *Greek-English Lexicon*, 812. It seems to be a characteristic expression that frequently appears in Matthew and Luke, although this expression appears in all Synoptic Gospels (Matthew [62×], Mark [7×], and Luke [57×]).

8   When we think about the adversative characteristic in δέ, it could be used to reveal that, even though Jesus' words seemed difficult to be realized, they were actually accomplished.

168 CHAPTER 5

the meaning of "also": the "apostles" *also* sit with him. In 22:15, the narrative speech margin of Jesus' words starts with καί revealing unmarked continuity, and asyndeton appears in the following Jesus' speech. After Jesus' longing for the Passover meal with his disciples is expressed, the following λέγω ὑμῖν of 22:16 is connected with a causal conjunction γάρ, which can be translated into "for." In 22:16, along with γάρ, a content conveying conjunction ὅτι that leads to the main content of Jesus' words appears. After, a temporal conjunction ἕως appears, which marks the time when he will eat the fulfilled (πληρωθῇ) Passover. After these Passover-related passages, an unmarked continuity of καί follows where Jesus takes a cup and gives thanks to God (22:17a), and asyndeton appears at the first part of his following words: ∅ λάβετε τοῦτο καὶ διαμερίσατε εἰς ἑαυτούς (22:17b). Here, two aorist-imperative verbs (λάβετε, διαμερίσατε), meaning "take this" and "divide it among yourselves," are connected by καί, revealing an unmarked continuity. 22:18 shares a similar structure with 22:16 (λέγω γὰρ ὑμῖν, [ὅτι] οὐ μὴ ... ἕως ... βασιλεία τοῦ θεου). Here, γάρ appears again as a causal conjunction to explain why he gave the cup only to the disciples (22:17): "*for* ... I will not drink again ... until the kingdom of God comes." Subsequently, in 22:19, the topic of bread appears in the narrative, and a conjunctive tie is formed by the connective conjunction καί. The following καί, conveying unmarked continuity, connects Jesus' two actions on bread (ἔκλασεν καὶ ἔδωκεν). After the narrative speech margin, two cases of asyndeton appear in both clauses of Jesus' speech on the meaning of bread and remembrance of Jesus. Since the first clause is the first part of the speech and the second clause is in the imperative form, the appearance of asyndeton is explicable. Subsequently, in 22:20, the scene where Jesus retakes the cup after supper appears, and a conjunctive tie is formed between 22:19–20 via καί, which reveals unmarked continuity. In the first part of the following direct speech, where Jesus explains the meaning of the cup—his sacrificial death, asyndeton appears.

After the first main topic of the third paragraph (the Eucharist), 22:21 begins with πλήν, the adversative conjunction containing strong contrast. In 22:20, Jesus spoke of his blood (death) for "you," that is, for the disciples, *but* (πλήν) in 22:21, what follows is Jesus' utterance about a person who will betray him.[9] In 22:22, an explanation of the future situation appears with the subordinating conjunction ὅτι. Then, πλήν is used again to show the contrast: "the son of man (Jesus) goes as determined (died), *but* woe to that man who betrays him." Hearing these shocking words of Jesus, the connective conjunction καί forms a conjunctive tie between the previous Jesus' words and the disciples'

---

9 The following ἰδού in 22:21 further emphasizes the adversative aspect. Here, the expression appears to be used as an imperative verb that requires an object: "the hand of the one who will deliver me—which is with me on the table."

MODE REGISTER ANALYSIS OF LUKE 22:3–23, 31–34          169

questioning each other as to who will do these things. It seems difficult to imply that καί reveals simple unmarked continuity here; it appears to be used as causal-connective conjunction, which can be translated as "then." Cohesion is maintained by the appropriate appearances of conjunctions and explicable asyndeta. Thus, in the third paragraph, the appearance of various conjunctions forms conjunctive ties to convey the cohesiveness of this text, and all the instances of asyndeton seem natural.

The fourth paragraph is 22:31–34, but 22:24–30 appears between the third and fourth paragraphs of the designated text, and it seems worth mentioning the omitted part (22:24–30) briefly for the study of conjunctions. In the third paragraph, the disciples question each other on who will do such a thing (betraying Jesus). However, after this, in 22:24–30, they dispute who is the greatest. Since the topic of 22:24–30 is quite different from the previous one, δέ is used as expected (22:24). In response to these disciples' arguments, Jesus gives them the message to be the one who serves (22:25–30).[10] After this message, Jesus' words continue without a narrative speech margin in 22:31. It begins with Jesus calling Peter's name "Simon" twice; here, asyndeton appears. After that, ἰδού, which is used as an interjection or particle, leads to another asyndeton, and the content that Satan demanded to sift "you" like wheat appears with another asyndeton. The only conjunction in 22:31 is the comparative conjunction ὡς, used to describe Satan's sifting action. Subsequent speeches and narrative speech margins of Jesus and Peter in 22:33–34 appear with adversative conjunction δέ. In 22:32, δέ is used to connect Satan's request with Jesus' words, "I pray for you." In 22:33, δέ appears at the beginning of Peter's words, expressing his strong will to follow the Lord to prison or even death. Finally, in 22:34, δέ is used in the narrative speech margin of Jesus' words regarding Peter's repeated denial. In addition to this, these three verses contain the following conjunctions. In 22:32, the final conjunction ἵνα and causal-connective conjunction καί are used. In 22:33, there are two appearances of καί, revealing unmarked continuity. In 22:34, the temporal conjunction ἕως conveys the meaning of "until." Also, there are five instances of asyndeton (22:33 [2×], 34 [3×]). The expected use of these conjunctions and the natural occurrence of asyndeton reveal the cohesiveness of this paragraph.

### 3.2  Reference

We now look at the formation of reference based on the paragraph division done through the thematization. The participant-reference chains of Luke 22:3–6 are shown in Figure 5.1.

---

10      This message is also introduced and proceeded by the adversative conjunction δέ (22:25).

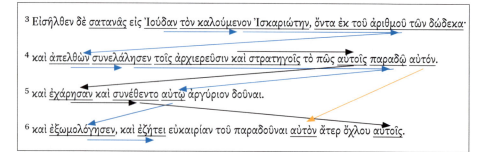

FIGURE 5.1  Participant-referent chains in Luke 22:3–6

The participants for which the participant-referent chains are formed are as follows: Satan (1×), Judas (9×), the chief priests & officers (5×), and Jesus (2×). There are two objects in 22:3: Satan and Judas. However, from 22:4, it appears only as implied references (implied subject of the verbs), so it is unclear whether the third-person singular subject refers to Satan or Judas. It seems natural, however, to understand that Satan entered Judas, and Judas went away to meet and discuss with them, but it is not clear grammatically. Considering the participant referent chains which are well formed, the cohesiveness of this paragraph is overall maintained. However, in the narrative part of 22:4, although it seems more natural to present the identity of Jesus as a proper noun, considering the change of topic and thematic participant in this paragraph, he appears only as a reduced reference (pronoun). This seemingly unnatural reference may lower the degree of cohesiveness of this paragraph.[11]

The participant-referent chains of Luke 22:7–13 are shown in Figure 5.2.

The participants for which the participant-referent chains are formed are as follows: Jesus (9×), Peter and John (16×), us (2×), and the day of Unleavened Bread (2×). Jesus does not appear as a grammatical reference (proper noun) as in the previous paragraph, but mainly appears as implied references (implied subjects of verbs) and reduced references (pronouns and a case of a nominative masculine singular article in 22:10), and a unique use case is a part where a grammatical reference (substitution) is formed by presenting Jesus himself as ὁ διδάσκαλος (22:11). After Peter and John first appear as reduced references (proper noun; 22:8), they form implied references (implied subjects of verbs) and reduced references (pronoun). "Us" spoken by Jesus in 22:8 includes both Jesus and his disciples, and it is mentioned once as an implied reference to

---

11   This phenomenon also appears in the remaining paragraphs, so it will not be referred to in the following analyses.

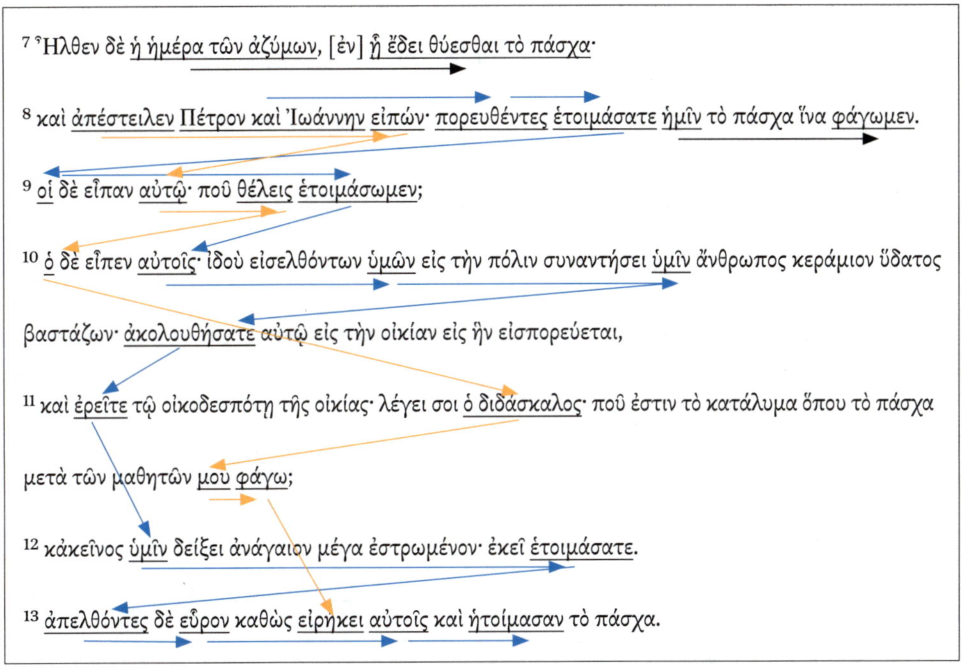

## MODE REGISTER ANALYSIS OF LUKE 22:3–23, 31–34

7 Ἦλθεν δὲ ἡ ἡμέρα τῶν ἀζύμων, [ἐν] ᾗ ἔδει θύεσθαι τὸ πάσχα·

8 καὶ ἀπέστειλεν Πέτρον καὶ Ἰωάννην εἰπών· πορευθέντες ἑτοιμάσατε ἡμῖν τὸ πάσχα ἵνα φάγωμεν.

9 οἱ δὲ εἶπαν αὐτῷ· ποῦ θέλεις ἑτοιμάσωμεν;

10 ὁ δὲ εἶπεν αὐτοῖς· ἰδοὺ εἰσελθόντων ὑμῶν εἰς τὴν πόλιν συναντήσει ὑμῖν ἄνθρωπος κεράμιον ὕδατος

βαστάζων· ἀκολουθήσατε αὐτῷ εἰς τὴν οἰκίαν εἰς ἣν εἰσπορεύεται,

11 καὶ ἐρεῖτε τῷ οἰκοδεσπότῃ τῆς οἰκίας· λέγει σοι ὁ διδάσκαλος· ποῦ ἐστιν τὸ κατάλυμα ὅπου τὸ πάσχα

μετὰ τῶν μαθητῶν μου φάγω;

12 κἀκεῖνος ὑμῖν δείξει ἀνάγαιον μέγα ἐστρωμένον· ἐκεῖ ἑτοιμάσατε.

13 ἀπελθόντες δὲ εὗρον καθὼς εἰρήκει αὐτοῖς καὶ ἡτοίμασαν τὸ πάσχα.

FIGURE 5.2  Participant-referent chains in Luke 22:7–13

φάγωμεν. "The day of Unleavened bread" in 22:7 is referenced once by ᾗ ἔδει θύεσθαι τὸ πάσχα. Like the previous paragraph, the second paragraph has no proper noun of Jesus, which may lower the degree of cohesiveness. Overall, however, these participant-referent chains are well formed, thus the cohesiveness of this paragraph is maintained.

The participant-referent chains of 22:14–23 are shown in Figure 5.3.

The participants for which the participant-referent chains are formed are as follows: Jesus (25×), apostles (14×), this Passover (3×), the first cup (3×), bread (5×), the second cup (3×), Jesus' blood (2×), that person (2×). In the case of Jesus, it appears as implied references (implied subjects of verbs) and reduced references (pronoun) without a grammaticalized reference (proper noun). Nevertheless, Jesus has a reference of ὁ υἱὸς μὲν τοῦ ἀνθρώπου in 22:22. The case of "disciples" is similar to the pattern of Jesus, but it is unique that their first reference is οἱ ἀπόστολοι, as a characteristic expression of Luke. In the case of "bread" and "cup," they are similar to Matthew and Mark in that they first appear as a self-identifying word (grammaticalized reference; proper noun), then in the form of a reduced reference (pronoun) and grammaticalized references (substitutional/alternative words). However, it is only in Luke

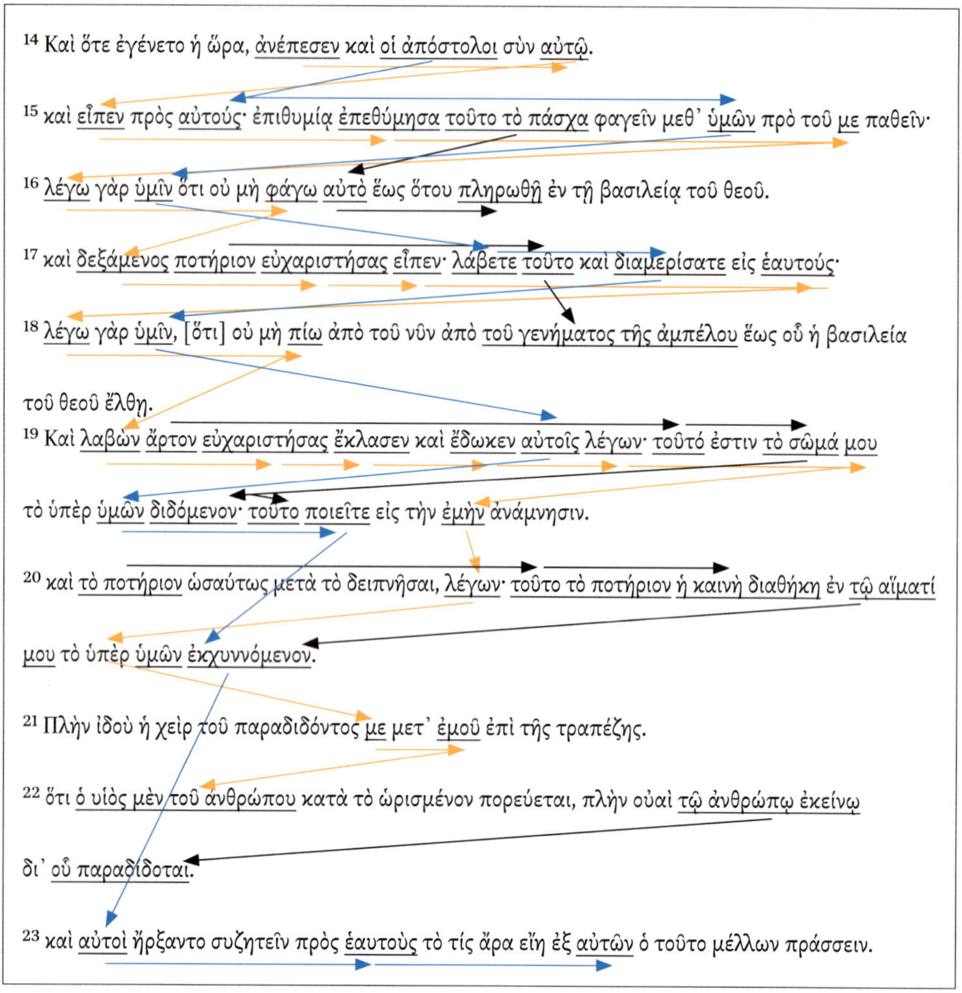

# 172

CHAPTER 5

---

$^{14}$ Καὶ ὅτε ἐγένετο ἡ ὥρα, ἀνέπεσεν καὶ οἱ ἀπόστολοι σὺν αὐτῷ.

$^{15}$ καὶ εἶπεν πρὸς αὐτούς· ἐπιθυμίᾳ ἐπεθύμησα τοῦτο τὸ πάσχα φαγεῖν μεθ' ὑμῶν πρὸ τοῦ με παθεῖν·

$^{16}$ λέγω γὰρ ὑμῖν ὅτι οὐ μὴ φάγω αὐτὸ ἕως ὅτου πληρωθῇ ἐν τῇ βασιλείᾳ τοῦ θεοῦ.

$^{17}$ καὶ δεξάμενος ποτήριον εὐχαριστήσας εἶπεν· λάβετε τοῦτο καὶ διαμερίσατε εἰς ἑαυτούς·

$^{18}$ λέγω γὰρ ὑμῖν, [ὅτι] οὐ μὴ πίω ἀπὸ τοῦ νῦν ἀπὸ τοῦ γενήματος τῆς ἀμπέλου ἕως οὗ ἡ βασιλεία

τοῦ θεοῦ ἔλθῃ.

$^{19}$ Καὶ λαβὼν ἄρτον εὐχαριστήσας ἔκλασεν καὶ ἔδωκεν αὐτοῖς λέγων· τοῦτό ἐστιν τὸ σῶμά μου

τὸ ὑπὲρ ὑμῶν διδόμενον· τοῦτο ποιεῖτε εἰς τὴν ἐμὴν ἀνάμνησιν.

$^{20}$ καὶ τὸ ποτήριον ὡσαύτως μετὰ τὸ δειπνῆσαι, λέγων· τοῦτο τὸ ποτήριον ἡ καινὴ διαθήκη ἐν τῷ αἵματί

μου τὸ ὑπὲρ ὑμῶν ἐκχυννόμενον.

$^{21}$ Πλὴν ἰδοὺ ἡ χεὶρ τοῦ παραδιδόντος με μετ' ἐμοῦ ἐπὶ τῆς τραπέζης.

$^{22}$ ὅτι ὁ υἱὸς μὲν τοῦ ἀνθρώπου κατὰ τὸ ὡρισμένον πορεύεται, πλὴν οὐαὶ τῷ ἀνθρώπῳ ἐκείνῳ

δι' οὗ παραδίδοται.

$^{23}$ καὶ αὐτοὶ ἤρξαντο συζητεῖν πρὸς ἑαυτοὺς τὸ τίς ἄρα εἴη ἐξ αὐτῶν ὁ τοῦτο μέλλων πράσσειν.

---

FIGURE 5.3  Participant-referent chains in Luke 22:14–23

that the cup appears twice.[12] Jesus' blood has an implied reference (implied subject of a verb), and "this Passover" also has a reduced reference (pronoun) and an implied reference (implied subject of a verb). "That person" also has an implied reference (implied subject of a verb). This paragraph does not have a proper noun of Jesus, and it may lower the degree of cohesiveness of this paragraph. Overall, however, these participant-referent chains are well formed, thus the cohesiveness of this paragraph is maintained.

---

12    The cup in 22:20 is τὸ ποτήριον, which appears to be here again holding the cup that Jesus took, compared to the previous one (ποτήριον), which appears without an article in 22:17.

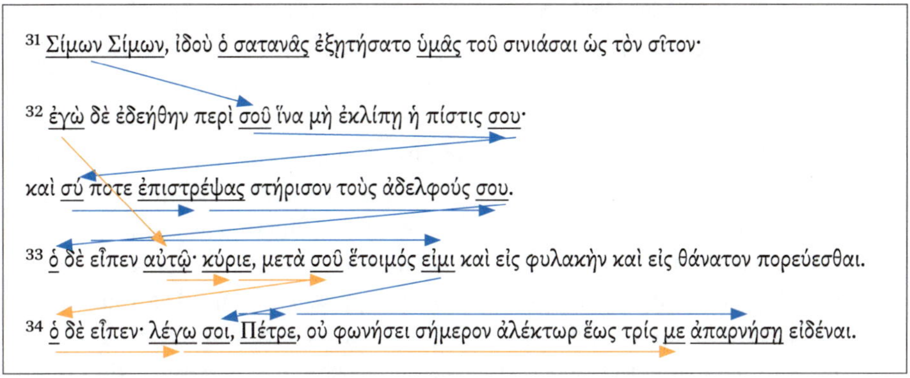

# MODE REGISTER ANALYSIS OF LUKE 22:3–23, 31–34

> [31] <u>Σίμων Σίμων</u>, ἰδοὺ <u>ὁ σατανᾶς</u> ἐξῃτήσατο <u>ὑμᾶς</u> τοῦ σινιάσαι ὡς τὸν σῖτον·
>
> [32] <u>ἐγὼ</u> δὲ ἐδεήθην περὶ <u>σοῦ</u> ἵνα μὴ ἐκλίπῃ ἡ πίστις <u>σου</u>·
>
> καὶ <u>σύ</u> ποτε <u>ἐπιστρέψας</u> στήρισον τοὺς ἀδελφούς <u>σου</u>.
>
> [33] <u>ὁ</u> δὲ εἶπεν <u>αὐτῷ</u>· κύριε, μετὰ <u>σοῦ</u> ἕτοιμός <u>εἰμι</u> καὶ εἰς φυλακὴν καὶ εἰς θάνατον πορεύεσθαι.
>
> [34] <u>ὁ</u> δὲ εἶπεν· <u>λέγω</u> <u>σοι</u>, <u>Πέτρε</u>, οὐ φωνήσει σήμερον ἀλέκτωρ ἕως τρίς <u>με</u> <u>ἀπαρνήσῃ</u> εἰδέναι.

FIGURE 5.4  Participant-referent chains in Luke 22:31–34

The participant-reference chains of 22:31–34 are shown in Figure 5.4.

Before observing the participant-referent chains in 22:31–34, let us consider 22:24–30, which is directly connected with 22:31–34 without a narrative speech margin in between. The participants for which the participant-referent chains are formed in 22:24–30 are apostles (11×) and Jesus (9×). These references form cohesive chains by implied references (implied subjects of verbs) and reduced references (pronoun) without a grammaticalized reference (proper noun). There is a distinct transition of topics between 22:24–30 ("the dispute about greatness") and 22:31–34 ("Peter's Denial Foretold"), but the participants continue with Jesus and the apostles (ὑμᾶς; 22:31).

After 22:24–30, the participants for which the participant-referent chains are formed in Luke 22:31–34 are as follows: Peter (11×) and Jesus (7×). "Satan" and "you" (ὑμᾶς) appear only once each. This paragraph shows a sudden transition from the plural to the singular subject (the apostles → Peter). And after calling Peter twice, Jesus refers to him as the plural "you." After that, it appears again in the singular. One could regard these points as grammatical errors or assume that there must have been some complex theological intent, but this phenomenon seems explicable if we assume that this Gospel was constructed according to tradition. Furthermore, this paragraph does not have a proper noun of Jesus, which may lower the degree of cohesiveness. Overall, however, these participant-referent chains are well formed, thus the cohesiveness of this paragraph is maintained.

## 3.3  *Substitution and Ellipsis*

The substitutions in Luke 22:3–6 are as follows. The first and second substitutions appear to be τὸν καλούμενον Ἰσκαριώτην and ὄντα ἐκ τοῦ ἀριθμοῦ τῶν δώδεκα in 22:3, which function as added information on Ἰούδαν. The third case

174                                                                                              CHAPTER 5

appears to be ᾗ ἔδει θύεσθαι τὸ πάσχα in 22:7, which is considered a substitution of ἡ ἡμέρα τῶν ἀζύμων. The fourth case appears to be ἀνάγαιον in 22:12, which is read as a substitution of κατάλυμα in the immediately preceding verse, as in the case of Mark. The fifth case can be seen as οἱ ἀπόστολοι in 22:14, which appears to function as a substitution of the community of disciples of Jesus, including Peter and John, which has occurred since 22:3. The sixth case appears to be τοῦ γενήματος τῆς ἀμπέλου in 22:18, which seems to function as a substitution of ποτήριον in the previous verse, just like Matthew and Mark. A seventh case, like Matthew and Mark, is τὸ σῶμά μου, which appears to be used as a substitution of ἄρτον in 22:19. The eighth case is ἡ καινὴ διαθήκη ἐν τῷ αἵματί μου, which appears to be a substitution of τὸ ποτήριον in 22:20. It seems to be different from Matthew and Mark, taking as τὸ αἷμά μου τῆς διαθήκης a substitution of τὸ ποτήριον. The ninth example would be τῷ ἀνθρώπῳ ἐκείνῳ in 22:22, referring τοῦ παραδιδόντος με μετ᾽ ἐμοῦ in 22:21. The tenth case is ὁ υἱὸς τοῦ ἀνθρώπου in 22:22, referring Jesus himself. The eleventh case would be κύριε which appears to be a substitution of Jesus at 22:33. The twelfth case seems to be Πέτρε in 22:34, a substitution of Σίμων repeated twice by Jesus in 22:31.

The ellipsis in Luke 22:3–23, 31–34 is found in 22:20b (τοῦτο τὸ ποτήριον ἡ καινὴ διαθήκη ἐν τῷ αἵματί μου τὸ ὑπὲρ ὑμῶν ἐκχυννόμενον), where the verb ἐστιν connecting token and value is omitted. Subsequently, in 22:21b (ἡ χεὶρ τοῦ παραδιδόντος με μετ᾽ ἐμοῦ ἐπὶ τῆς τραπέζης), ἐστιν is omitted again.

Considering these analyses, the distribution of substitution and ellipsis throughout the designated text demonstrates the cohesiveness of this text.

### 3.4    *Lexical Cohesion*

In this section, we will analyze the semantic-lexical ties to examine the cohesiveness of each paragraph in Luke 22:3–23, 31–34, and the semantic-lexical chain of the whole designated text.

### 3.4.1    Lexical Cohesion in Each Paragraph

In the first paragraph (22:3–6), Satan enters Judas, he plans to hand over Jesus, and the chief priests agree to give him money. From that time on Judas seeks an opportunity to hand Jesus over. Table 5.5 contains the cases where two or more lexemes in one semantic domain appear in a paragraph.

The lexeme δίδωμι ("to give") and the lexical item παραδίδωμι ("to deliver") belong to domain 57; which are semantically related in terms of the "deal" on Jesus; thus they form semantic-lexical tie. There are two numbers in domain 60 (ἀριθμός ["number"], δώδεκα ["twelve"]), and these lexemes are tied around Judas, who was one ("number") of the "twelve"; thus, they form

# MODE REGISTER ANALYSIS OF LUKE 22:3–23, 31–34

TABLE 5.5 Semantic domains of the lexemes in Luke 22:3–6

| Lexeme | Verse | Semantic domain |
| --- | --- | --- |
| δίδωμι | v. 5 | 57.71 |
| παραδίδωμι | vv. 4, 6 | 57.77/37.111 |
| ἀριθμός | v. 3 | 60.1 |
| δώδεκα | v. 3 | 60.21 |
| καλέω | v. 3 | 33.131 |
| συλλαλέω | v. 4 | 33.157 |
| ἐξομολογέω | v. 6 | 33.278 |
| εἰσέρχομαι | v. 3 | 15.93 |
| ἀπέρχομαι | v. 4 | 15.37 |

a semantic-lexical tie. The lexemes καλέω ("to call"), συλλαλέω ("to talk with"), and ἐξομολογέω ("agree") belong to domain 33. Συλλαλέω and ἐξομολογέω can be semantically linked around Judas's action and response to the chief priests; thus, they form a semantic-lexical tie. It seems difficult to find a semantic relationship between καλέω and these lexemes. The two lexemes (εἰσέρχομαι ["to go in"], ἀπέρχομαι ["to go away"]), which belong to domain 15 (move), are causally tied as the actions of Satan (going into Judas; cause) and Judas (going away to [the chief priests]; result); thus, these lexemes form a semantic-lexical tie. From these analyses, we can identify four semantic-lexical ties in 22:3–6. Furthermore, among the eighteen content lexemes in the first paragraph, the number of lexemes in the semantic-lexical ties is nine. The ratio of the lexemes that can be formed into semantic-lexical ties per the number of content lexemes is 50%. Thus, these overall results apparently reveal the cohesiveness of this paragraph.

The second paragraph (22:7–13) describes the process of preparing the Passover by Jesus and the disciples. The semantic domains of the lexemes in this paragraph are as follows.

The lexical item ἑτοιμάζω ("to prepare"; domain 77), which is reiterated four times, is tied around the Passover preparation, and these form a semantic-lexical tie. The lexeme πάσχα ("Passover"; domain 51) is reiterated four times and ἄζυμος ("unleavened bread"; domain 5) can be semantically tied with πάσχα due to the close connection between the Passover and the feast of Unleavened Bread; thus, they form a semantic-lexical tie. Eight lexemes (ἔρχομαι ["to go"], ἀποστέλλω ["to send"], πορεύομαι ["to go"], εἰσέρχομαι ["go into"], βαστάζω ["to

176                                                                                                                   CHAPTER 5

TABLE 5.6    Semantic domains of the lexemes in Luke 22:7–13

| Lexeme | Verse | Semantic domain |
| --- | --- | --- |
| ἑτοιμάζω | vv. 8, 9, 12, 13 | 77.3 |
| πάσχα | vv. 7, 11, 13 | 51.7 |
| cf. ἄζυμος | v. 7 | 5.13 |
| ἔρχομαι | v. 7 | 15.81 |
| ἀποστέλλω | v. 8 | 15.66 |
| πορεύομαι | v. 8 | 15.10 |
| εἰσέρχομαι | v. 10 | 15.93 |
| βαστάζω | v. 10 | 15.188 |
| ἀκολουθέω | v. 10 | 15.144 |
| εἰσπορεύομαι | v. 10 | 15.93 |
| ἀπέρχομαι | v. 13 | 15.37 |
| ἐσθίω | vv. 8, 11 | 23.1 |
| οἰκία | vv. 10, 11 | 7.3 |
| κατάλυμα | v. 11 | 7.30 |
| ἀνάγαιον | v. 12 | 7.27 |

carry"], ἀκολουθέω ["to follow"], εἰσπορεύομαι ["to enter"], ἀπέρχομαι ["to go
away"]), which belong to domain 15, are related to "movements" in terms of the
preparation of the Passover; thus, they form a semantic-lexical tie. The lexical
item ἐσθίω ("to eat"; domain 23) is reiterated two times and it is semantically
tied around the Passover meal; thus, they form a semantic-lexical tie. Three
lexemes οἰκία (2×; "house"), κατάλυμα ("guest room"), and ἀνάγαιον ("upper
room"), which belong to domain 7, are related to the places for the Passover;
thus, they form a semantic-lexical tie. From these analyses, we can find five
semantic-lexical ties in 22:7–13. Furthermore, among forty-five content lexemes
in the second paragraph, the number of lexemes in the semantic-lexical ties is
twenty-two. The ratio of the lexemes that can be formed into semantic-lexical
ties per the number of content lexemes is 48.89%. Thus, these overall results
may reveal the cohesiveness of this paragraph.

The third paragraph (22:14–23) conveys Jesus' foretelling about the betrayer,
the disciples' responses (including Judas), and the Eucharist. The semantic
domains of the lexemes in this paragraph are hown in Table 5.7.

The lexical item ἐσθίω (2×; "to eat") and the lexemes πίνω ("to drink") and δει-
πνέω ("to eat") belong to domain 23, revealing the actions regarding the Passover
and Eucharist; thus, they form semantic-lexical ties. The lexical item λαμβάνω
("to take"; domain 18) is reiterated two times, which is tied around Jesus'

# MODE REGISTER ANALYSIS OF LUKE 22:3–23, 31–34

TABLE 5.7    Semantic domains of the lexemes in Luke 22:14–23

| Lexeme | Verse | Semantic domain |
|---|---|---|
| ἐσθίω | vv. 15, 16 | 23.1 |
| πίνω | v. 18 | 23.34 |
| δειπνέω | v. 20 | 23.20 |
| λαμβάνω | vv. 17, 19 | 18.1 |
| εὐχαριστέω | vv. 17, 19 | 33.349 |
| συζητέω | v. 23 | 33.440 |
| διαμερίζω | v. 17 | 57.89 |
| δίδωμι | v. 19 (2×) | 57.71 |
| σῶμα | v. 19 | 8.1 |
| αἷμα | v. 20 | 8.64 |
| χείρ | v. 21 | 8.30 |
| ὥρα | v. 14 | 67.1 |
| νῦν | v. 18 | 67.38 |
| ποτήριον | vv. 17, 20 (2×) | 6.121 |
| τράπεζα | v. 21 | 6.113 |
| cf. ἄρτος | v. 19 | 5.8 |
| ἐπιθυμίᾳ | v. 15 | 25.12 |
| ἐπιθυμέω | v. 15 | 25.12 |
| βασιλεία | vv. 16, 18 | 37.64/1.82[a] |
| οὐ | vv. 16, 18 | 69.3 |
| μή | vv. 16, 18 | 69.3 |
| παραδίδωμι | vv. 21, 22 | 37.111 |
| υἱὸς τοῦ ἀνθρώπου | v. 22 | 9.3 |
| ἄνθρωπος | v. 22 | 9.1 |

a   Βασιλεία has two meanings of "reign" (37.64) and "kingdom" (1.82). See Louw and Nida, *Greek-English Lexicon*, 16, 479–80.

actions on a cup and bread; thus, the cases of λαμβάνω form a semantic-lexical tie. The lexical item εὐχαριστέω ("to thank"), which belongs to domain 33, is reiterated two times in terms of Jesus' giving thanks to God in the context of Eucharist; thus, the cases of εὐχαριστέω form a semantic-lexical tie. Συζητέω ("to dispute/inquire") also belongs to domain 33, but it describes the disciples' discussion on who would betray Jesus; thus, it seems hard to find a semantic connection with εὐχαριστέω. The lexical item δίδωμι (domain 57) is reiterated two times, which conveys Jesus' action of "giving" bread to the disciples and his speech on his body "given" for them. Here, "bread" is a metaphor for his "body,"

178                                                                                    CHAPTER 5

thus, the two cases of δίδωμι are semantically linked. Διαμερίζω ("to divide/distribute") also belongs to domain 57, and it can be semantically linked with δίδωμι in terms of Jesus' giving the Eucharistic materials to the disciples. Thus, these three cases in domain 57 form a semantic-lexical tie. The lexemes σῶμα ("body") and αἷμα ("blood") belong to domain 8. They are semantically tied around the substances of the Eucharistic materials (bread and a cup);[13] thus, they form a semantic-lexical tie. Even though χείρ ("hand") belongs to domain 8, it seems hard to find any connection between the betrayer's hand and Jesus' body and blood. Two lexemes, related to time (ὥρα ["hour"], νῦν ["now"]), belong to domain 67 and are semantically related to the time the Eucharist took place; thus, they form a semantic-lexical tie. Two lexemes (ποτήριον ["cup"], τράπεζα ["table"]) belong to domain 6, and they function to reveal the context of Passover meal as artifacts for a meal, even though they appear in different topics (ποτήριον in the Eucharist and τράπεζα in the betrayal) within the same context. Thus, we can find a semantic-lexical tie between them. Furthermore, ποτήριον can also be semantically tied with ἄρτος since what was in the "cup" was probably οἶνος ("wine"; John 2:3), and bread and a cup (wine) are semantically tied around the topic of the Eucharist; thus, they form a semantic-lexical tie. Two lexemes (ἐπιθυμία ["deep desire"], ἐπιθυμέω ["to desire greatly"]), which belong to domain 25, are semantically tied in which reveals Jesus' longing for the last Passover meal/Eucharist; thus, they form a semantic-lexical tie. The lexeme βασιλεία ("reign/kingdom"; domain 37/1) appears two times and form collocation with τοῦ θεοῦ. This lexeme is connected to Jesus' declarations that he will not eat (the Passover meal) and drink wine until the fulfilment/coming of the "kingdom" of God;[14] thus, the two cases form a semantic-lexical tie. The lexemes οὐ and μή (domain 69; negation) are used for Jesus' declarations above; thus, they form a semantic-lexical tie. The lexical item παραδίδωμι ("to hand over/betray"; domain 37), which is semantically tied around one of the main topics of this paragraph, betraying Jesus, is reiterated two times, and these lexical items form a semantic-lexical tie. The lexical item ἄνθρωπος ("man"; domain 9) is reiterated two times; one of them forms collocation with υἱός (ὁ υἱὸς τοῦ ἀνθρώπου), which refer to Jesus, and the other one (τῷ ἀνθρώπῳ) refer to the betrayer (Judas). It seems difficult to find a semantic-lexical tie between them. From these analyses, we can find nine semantic-lexical ties in 22:14–23. Furthermore, among the sixty-one content lexemes in the third paragraph, the number of lexemes in the semantic-lexical ties is twenty-nine. The ratio of the

---

13    It is also a case of superordinate.
14    Here, the fulfilment of the Kingdom of God may mean the achievement of God's saving plan through Jesus' death and resurrection. See France, *Luke*, 341.

MODE REGISTER ANALYSIS OF LUKE 22:3–23, 31–34                           179

TABLE 5.8     Semantic domains of the lexemes in Luke 22:31–34

| Lexeme | Verse | Semantic domain |
|---|---|---|
| ἐξαιτέω | v. 31 | 33.166 |
| δέομαι | v. 32 | 33.170 |
| λέγω | v. 34 | 33.69 |
| φωνέω | v. 34 | 33.77 |
| ἀπαρνέομαι | v. 34 | 33.70 |
| ἐπιστρέφω | v. 32 | 15.90 |
| ἐκλείπω | v. 32 | 15.58/57.46 |
| πορεύομαι | v. 33 | 15.10 |
| ποτε | v. 32 | 67.30 |
| σήμερον | v. 34 | 67.205 |

lexemes that can be formed into semantic-lexical ties per the number of content lexemes is 47.54%. Thus, these overall results may reveal the cohesiveness
of this paragraph.

The fourth paragraph (22:31–34) conveys Jesus' foretelling of the stumbling
of his disciples, along with Peter's denial. The semantic domains of the lexemes in this paragraph are shown in Table 5.8.

The lexemes (ἐξαιτέω ["to ask"], δέομαι ["to plead/pray"], λέγω ["to say"],
φωνέω ["to cry out"], ἀπαρνέομαι ["to deny"]) belong to domain 33. Among
these, the lexeme ἐξαιτέω conveys Satan's ask to tempt (sift) Peter, and δέομαι conveys Jesus' prayer for Peter, thus they are semantically connected and
form a semantic-lexical tie. The lexemes φωνέω and ἀπαρνέομαι are tied around
Peter's denial; thus, they form a semantic-lexical tie.[15] The three lexemes (ἐπιστρέφω ["to return"], ἐκλείπω ["to depart/fail"], πορεύομαι ["to go"]) belong to
domain 15, and these can be semantically linked around the disciple's journey
of faith; thus, these form a semantic-lexical tie. The lexemes ποτε ("at some
time") and σήμερον ("today") belong to domain 67, and these are semantically
connected around Jesus' foretelling of Peter's denial and return; thus, they form
a semantic-lexical tie. From these analyses, we can find three semantic-lexical
ties in 22:31–34. Furthermore, among the twenty-four content lexemes in the
fourth paragraph, the number of lexemes in the semantic-lexical ties is nine.
The ratio of the lexemes that can be formed into semantic-lexical ties per the

---

15     The lexeme λέγω appears in Jesus' intro; it is not included in the previous two semantic-
       lexical ties.

180                                                                                    CHAPTER 5

number of content lexemes is 37.5%. Thus, these overall results may reveal the cohesiveness of this paragraph.

3.4.2        Lexical Cohesion in Luke 22:3–23, 31–34

Figure 5.5 shows the lexical cohesion chains in Luke 22:3–23, 31–34.

Like the designated text in Matthew and Mark, the lexemes underlined in Figure 5.5 are related to Jesus' death. Like Matthew and Mark, Jesus' death is revealed indirectly by τὸ σῶμά μου ("my body"), τῷ αἵματί μου ("my blood"), and πορεύεται ("to go away"; domain 15.34)—a synonym of ὑπάγει (to depart; domain 15.35). His death is carried out by the act of handing over (betrayal; παραδίδωμι) of one of the disciples, Judas. After Jesus' arrest as a result of Judas's betrayal,

---

³ Εἰσῆλθεν δὲ σατανᾶς εἰς Ἰούδαν τὸν καλούμενον Ἰσκαριώτην, ὄντα ἐκ τοῦ ἀριθμοῦ τῶν δώδεκα· ⁴ καὶ ἀπελθὼν συνελάλησεν τοῖς ἀρχιερεῦσιν καὶ στρατηγοῖς τὸ πῶς αὐτοῖς παραδῷ αὐτόν. ⁵ καὶ ἐχάρησαν καὶ συνέθεντο αὐτῷ ἀργύριον δοῦναι. ⁶ καὶ ἐξωμολόγησεν, καὶ ἐζήτει εὐκαιρίαν τοῦ παραδοῦναι αὐτὸν ἄτερ ὄχλου αὐτοῖς. ⁷ Ἦλθεν δὲ ἡ ἡμέρα τῶν ἀζύμων, [ἐν] ᾗ ἔδει θύεσθαι τὸ πάσχα· ⁸ καὶ ἀπέστειλεν Πέτρον καὶ Ἰωάννην εἰπών· πορευθέντες ἑτοιμάσατε ἡμῖν τὸ πάσχα ἵνα φάγωμεν. ⁹ οἱ δὲ εἶπαν αὐτῷ· ποῦ θέλεις ἑτοιμάσωμεν; ¹⁰ ὁ δὲ εἶπεν αὐτοῖς· ἰδοὺ εἰσελθόντων ὑμῶν εἰς τὴν πόλιν συναντήσει ὑμῖν ἄνθρωπος κεράμιον ὕδατος βαστάζων· ἀκολουθήσατε αὐτῷ εἰς τὴν οἰκίαν εἰς ἣν εἰσπορεύεται, ¹¹ καὶ ἐρεῖτε τῷ οἰκοδεσπότῃ τῆς οἰκίας· λέγει σοι ὁ διδάσκαλος· ποῦ ἐστιν τὸ κατάλυμα ὅπου τὸ πάσχα μετὰ τῶν μαθητῶν μου φάγω; ¹² κἀκεῖνος ὑμῖν δείξει ἀνάγαιον μέγα ἐστρωμένον· ἐκεῖ ἑτοιμάσατε. ¹³ ἀπελθόντες δὲ εὗρον καθὼς εἰρήκει αὐτοῖς καὶ ἡτοίμασαν τὸ πάσχα. ¹⁴ Καὶ ὅτε ἐγένετο ἡ ὥρα, ἀνέπεσεν καὶ οἱ ἀπόστολοι σὺν αὐτῷ. ¹⁵ καὶ εἶπεν πρὸς αὐτούς· ἐπιθυμίᾳ ἐπεθύμησα τοῦτο τὸ πάσχα φαγεῖν μεθ᾽ ὑμῶν πρὸ τοῦ με παθεῖν· ¹⁶ λέγω γὰρ ὑμῖν ὅτι οὐ μὴ φάγω αὐτὸ ἕως ὅτου πληρωθῇ ἐν τῇ βασιλείᾳ τοῦ θεοῦ. ¹⁷ καὶ δεξάμενος ποτήριον εὐχαριστήσας εἶπεν· λάβετε τοῦτο καὶ διαμερίσατε εἰς ἑαυτούς· ¹⁸ λέγω γὰρ ὑμῖν, [ὅτι] οὐ μὴ πίω ἀπὸ τοῦ νῦν ἀπὸ τοῦ γενήματος τῆς ἀμπέλου ἕως οὗ ἡ βασιλεία τοῦ θεοῦ ἔλθῃ. ¹⁹ Καὶ λαβὼν ἄρτον εὐχαριστήσας ἔκλασεν καὶ ἔδωκεν αὐτοῖς λέγων· τοῦτό ἐστιν τὸ σῶμά μου τὸ ὑπὲρ ὑμῶν διδόμενον· τοῦτο ποιεῖτε εἰς τὴν ἐμὴν ἀνάμνησιν. ²⁰ καὶ τὸ ποτήριον ὡσαύτως μετὰ τὸ δειπνῆσαι, λέγων· τοῦτο τὸ ποτήριον ἡ καινὴ διαθήκη ἐν τῷ αἵματί μου τὸ ὑπὲρ ὑμῶν ἐκχυννόμενον. ²¹ Πλὴν ἰδοὺ ἡ χεὶρ τοῦ παραδιδόντος με μετ᾽ ἐμοῦ ἐπὶ τῆς τραπέζης. ²² ὅτι ὁ υἱὸς μὲν τοῦ ἀνθρώπου κατὰ τὸ ὡρισμένον πορεύεται, πλὴν οὐαὶ τῷ ἀνθρώπῳ ἐκείνῳ δι᾽ οὗ παραδίδοται. ²³ καὶ αὐτοὶ ἤρξαντο συζητεῖν πρὸς ἑαυτοὺς τὸ τίς ἄρα εἴη ἐξ αὐτῶν ὁ τοῦτο μέλλων πράσσειν … ³¹ Σίμων Σίμων, ἰδοὺ ὁ σατανᾶς ἐξῃτήσατο ὑμᾶς τοῦ σινιάσαι ὡς τὸν σῖτον· ³² ἐγὼ δὲ ἐδεήθην περὶ σοῦ ἵνα μὴ ἐκλίπῃ ἡ πίστις σου· καὶ σύ ποτε ἐπιστρέψας στήρισον τοὺς ἀδελφούς σου. ³³ ὁ δὲ εἶπεν αὐτῷ· κύριε, μετὰ σοῦ ἕτοιμός εἰμι καὶ εἰς φυλακὴν καὶ εἰς θάνατον πορεύεσθαι. ³⁴ ὁ δὲ εἶπεν· λέγω σοι, Πέτρε, οὐ φωνήσει σήμερον ἀλέκτωρ ἕως τρίς με ἀπαρνήσῃ εἰδέναι.

---

FIGURE 5.5    Lexical cohesion chains in Luke 22:3–23, 31–34

Peter's denial (ἀπαρνέομαι) takes place before Jesus' death. Here, Peter's denial can be regarded as his reaction to Jesus' death to come; thus, the action denial can be related to the death of Jesus. However, in Luke, the topic of death is conveyed via several lexemes that are differentiated from Matthew and Mark. Whereas Matthew and Mark cover this topic with "stumbling" (σκανδαλίζω), in Luke, it appears as Satan's act (σινιάσαι; "to sift"). Both the acts of handing over Jesus and denying him are considered Satan's acts (22:3, 31). Furthermore, in Luke, there are three lexemes (θύω ["to sacrifice/slaughter"; 22:7]; πάσχω ["to suffer"; 22:15]; θάνατος ["death"; 22:33]) revealing the topic of death more specifically/directly. As with Matthew and Mark, thus, this discourse maintains cohesiveness around the topic of Jesus' death.

### 3.5    *Summary and Implication*

This section attempted to analyze Luke 22:3–23, 31–34 via a fivefold scheme of cohesion: conjunction, reference, substitution, ellipsis, and lexical cohesion. In terms of conjunction analyses, all cases of asyndeton are explicable as they are located in the direct speech section. Overall, each paragraph of the designated text maintains cohesiveness via appropriate conjunctive ties. In terms of reference, the results can be summarized as follows: (1) overall, each paragraph forms a participant-reference chain via the main participants; thus, the cohesiveness of each paragraph can be confirmed; (2) there is no proper noun (grammaticalized reference) for Jesus, and it seems to decrease the degree of cohesiveness. Concerning substitution and ellipsis, we can identify the designated text's cohesiveness via the twelve cases of substitution and the two cases of ellipsis. In terms of lexical cohesion, we can find cohesiveness in each paragraph by semantic-lexical ties. Also, the conceptual flow in the lexemes conveying Jesus' death reveals the cohesiveness of the whole designated text.

The implications of this analysis are as follows: the designated text maintains cohesiveness overall; this suggests the possibility of one constructor's construction of this text. However, several elements that lower the degree of cohesiveness may have come in the process of preserving oral traditions along with written sources in constructing the Gospel.

## 4    Orality and Textuality

This section analyzes the designated text's lexical density and grammatical intricacy according to Porter's based on Halliday's understanding of oral and written language.

182                                                                                    CHAPTER 5

TABLE 5.9    Lexical density of Luke 22:3–23, 31–34

| Lexical density | 22:3–13 | 22:14–23 | 22:31–34 |
| --- | --- | --- | --- |
| Non-embedded clauses | 22 | 20 | 9 |
| Content words | 66 | 58 | 27 |
| Functional words | 73 | 106 | 33 |
| Content words per non-embedded clause | 3 | 2.9 | 3.0 |

TABLE 5.10    Lexical density of the speech and narrative in Luke 22:3–23, 31–34

| Lexical density | Direct speech | Narrative |
| --- | --- | --- |
| Non-embedded clauses | 29 | 22 |
| Content words | 92 | 59 |
| Functional words | 136 | 79 |
| Content words per non-embedded clause | 3.172 | 2.682 |

## 4.1    *Lexical Density*

Table 5.9 shows the lexical density of Luke 22:3–23, 31–34.

The total number of words in Luke 22:3–23, 31–34 is 363, and the total lexical density is 2.961 (151/51). According to Halliday's criteria, this text is close to oral language. The lexical density of the direct speech parts (22:8b, 9b, 10b, 11, 12, 15b, 16, 17b, 18, 19b, 20b, 21, 22, 31, 32, 33b, 34b) and narrative parts (22:3, 4, 5, 6, 7, 8a, 9a, 10a, 13, 14, 15a, 17a, 19a, 20a, 23, 33a, 34a) are shown in Table 5.10.

The result of the lexical density in the speech part (3.172) and narrative part (2.682) seems unique. The narrative parts are closer to oral language than the whole designated text, and the speech parts are closer to written language. The lack of orality in the speech part in the designated text in Luke could have come from multiple data that the constructor may have used. From Luke 1:1–4, especially 1:3, we can infer that the constructor may have examined oral traditions and written sources he had in hand as cautiously (ἀκριβῶς) as possible. In this process, it is possible that content words may have increased. As a result, the orality of the speech parts of the designated text in Luke seems to have decreased.[16] In addition, the feature of the narrative part having an oral aspect could be explained via the comparative analysis between 22:3–6, which is a part of the narrative, and the whole narrative part in the designated text. The lexical density of 22:3–6, where only the narrative appears, is 3.5, is higher than that of the whole narrative part (2.682). The reason for the low lexical density of the entire narrative part is probably that most of the narratives of the designated text, excluding 22:3–6, mainly appear as narrative speech margins, which are short intros that tend to have very few content words. Also, the fact that a reference to Jesus in the designated text in Luke never appears as a proper noun can be another reason for this tendency.[17] As in the cases of Matthew and Mark, although it is difficult to determine from whom/which source these oral results originated (e.g., participant or former of oral tradition or constructor), the overall orality in this text may be understood as giving weight to oral tradition.

### 4.2    *Grammatical Intricacy*

Table 5.11 shows the grammatical intricacy of Luke 22:3–23, 31–34.

In 22:3–23, 31–34, the number of non-embedded clauses is 51, the number of clause complexes is 20, and the result of the non-embedded clause per clause complex is 2.55 (51/20). Considering Porter's analysis of grammatical intricacy,[18] the number 2.55 seems high enough; thus, we can say that the designated text is close to oral language.

TABLE 5.11    Grammatical intricacy of Luke 22:3–23, 31–34

| Grammatical intricacy | 22:3–13 | 22:14–23 | 22:31–34 |
| --- | --- | --- | --- |
| Non-embedded clauses | 22 | 20 | 9 |
| Total clauses | 41 | 43 | 16 |
| Clause complex | 8 | 9 | 3 |
| Non-embedded clause per clause complex | 2.75 | 2.222 | 3.0 |

---

16    In particular, the unnatural flow of speech part in 22:31–32 (e.g., inconsistency in number to the object in Jesus' words [Σίμων; ὑμᾶς; σοῦ]) may have come from the process of obtaining and organizing data from various sources.

17    If we change five of ten cases of pronouns and implied nouns of Jesus appearing in the narrative part in Luke into proper nouns like Matthew, the lexical density of the narrative is 2.909.

18    Cf. Porter, "Orality and Textuality," 13–14.

## 4.3 Summary and Implication

The analytic results of orality and textuality of Luke 22:3–23, 31–34 are as follows. First, the total lexical density is 2.961 (151/51); thus, this text as a whole is in the category of oral language.[19] The result of lexical density of the speech parts (3.172) and narrative parts (2.682) shows that the narrative parts are closer to oral language than the whole designated text. These unique results could be explained as follows: (1) the textuality of the speech part could have resulted as content words increased when the constructor utilized multiple data; (2) the orality of the narrative part could have occurred from many speech margins and no occurrence of the proper noun of Jesus. Second, the grammatical intricacy is 2.55 (51/20), and these results show that this text is in the category of oral language. Overall, these results may reveal that the oral tradition played a significant role in the process of constructing this text, along with the identity of the constructor who would have preserved multiple oral and written sources.

## 5 Verbal Aspect

### 5.1 Verbal Aspect Analysis

The verbs in the designated text can be shown according to verbal aspect theory (see Table 5.12).

The results can be arranged as follows: (1) perfective aspect (aorist): fifty-five times; (2) imperfective aspect: twenty-six times (present) + two times (imperfective); (3) stative aspect: three times (perfect) + one time (pluperfect); and (4) future: four times. Although the accounts in Luke are the longest compared to Matthew and Mark, the usage of imperfective aspects (28×) is comparatively fewer than in Mark (32×). The Gospel of Luke contains three distinctive uses of stative aspects (εἰρήκει, ὡρισμένον, εἰδέναι), and it shares one stative aspect with Mark (ἐστρωμένον). Four usages of the future tense also seem unique (cf. Matt [11×], Mark [10×]). These analyses show the markedness of the designated text,

---

19  Scholars have evaluated the third Gospel's constructor, whose writing style is one of the formal and high styles in the NT. See Henry J. Cadbury, *The Style and Literary Method of Luke*. Vol. 1 of *The Diction of the Luke and Acts* (Cambridge, MA: Harvard University Press, 1919), 5; Nolland, *Luke 1:1–9:20*, xxxvii; Mikeal C. Parsons, *Luke: Storyteller, Interpreter, Evangelist* (Peabody: Hendrickson, 2007), 16. This evaluation seems to emphasize the influence of the constructor on the text. However, the possibility that this style in the text came from the characteristics of the multiple data (oral traditions and written sources) used by the constructor should also be considered. Nevertheless, the oral properties shown by the analysis of this designated text should be considered as well.

# MODE REGISTER ANALYSIS OF LUKE 22:3–23, 31–34

TABLE 5.12  Analysis of verbs in Luke 22:3–23, 31–34 focusing on verbal aspect

| Perfective aspect (aorist) | Imperfective aspect | Stative aspect | Future |
|---|---|---|---|
| εἰσῆλθεν (3), ἀπελθών (4), συνελάλησεν (4), παραδῷ (4), ἐχάρησαν (5), συνέθεντο (5), δοῦναι (5), ἐξωμολόγησεν (6), παραδοῦναι (6), ἦλθεν (7), ἀπέστειλεν (8), εἰπών (8), πορευθέντες (8), ἑτοιμάσατε (8), φάγωμεν (8), εἶπαν (9), ἑτοιμάσωμεν (9), εἶπεν (10), εἰσελθόντων (10), ἀκολουθήσατε (10), φάγω (11), ἑτοιμάσατε (12), ἀπελθόντες (13), εὗρον (13), ἡτοίμασαν (13), ἐγένετο (14), ἀνέπεσεν (14), εἶπεν (15), ἐπε- θύμησα (15), φαγεῖν (15), παθεῖν (15), φάγω (16), πληρωθῇ (16), δεξάμενος (17), εὐχαριστήσας (17), εἶπεν (17), λάβετε (17), διαμερίσατε (17), πίω (18), ἔλθῃ (18), λαβών (19), εὐχαριστήσας (19), ἔκλασεν (19), ἔδωκεν (19), δειπνῆσαι (20), ἤρξαντο (23), ... ἐξῃτήσατο (31), σινιάσαι (31), ἐδεήθην (32), ἐκλίπῃ (32), πιστρέψας (32), στήρισον (32), εἶπεν (33), εἶπεν (34), ἀπαρνήσῃ (34) | **Present** καλούμενον (3), ὄντα (3), θύεσθαι (7), θέλεις (9), βαστάζων (10), εἰσπορεύε- ται (10), λέγει (11), ἐστιν (11), λέγω (16), λέγω (18), λέγων (19), ἐστιν (19), διδόμενον (19), ποιεῖτε (19), λέγων (20), ἐκχυννό- μενον (20), παραδιδόντος (21), πορεύεται (22), παραδίδοται (22), συζητεῖν (23), εἴη (23), μέλλων (23), πράσσειν (23), ... εἰμι (33), πορεύεσθαι (33), λέγω (34)<br><br>**Imperfective** ἐζήτει (6), ἔδει (7) | **Perfect** ἐστρωμένον (12), ὡρισμένον (22), εἰδέναι (34)<br><br><br><br><br><br><br><br><br><br><br><br><br><br><br><br><br><br><br><br>**Pluperfect** εἰρήκει (13) | συναντήσει (10), ἐρεῖτε (11), δείξει (12), φωνήσει (34) |

but it is difficult to discern whether this markedness is from the tradition/source or the constructor. These results show the varying degree of markedness of the verbs in the designated text, and it is hard to discern from which/whom the markedness came. Three possible origins are as follows: (1) participant within the text (including Jesus); (2) the eyewitness/former/contributors(s) of traditions; or (3) the constructor. Comparative analysis in chapter 6 may help us to discern the possible origin(s).

186                                                                                    CHAPTER 5

### 5.2    *Summary and Implication*

The verbal aspect analysis of Luke 22:3–23, 31–34 shows us the varying degree of markedness of the verbs in the designated text. There are four frontground prominences via stative aspect (ἐστρωμένον [22:12]; εἰρήκει [22:13]; ὡρισμένον [22:22]; εἰδέναι [22:34]), several foregrounded parts via imperfective aspect, and many background parts via perfective aspect. The varying degrees of markedness may have been affected by the oral/written traditions and/or the constructor.

## 6    Conclusion

This chapter identifies the mode (thematization, cohesion, orality & textuality, and verbal aspect) of Luke 22:3–23, 31–34. These are some notable aspects in terms of the designated text's textual characteristics. First, in the thematization analysis, the designated text has ten thematic units and four paragraphs. In particular, the third paragraph has one large thematic unit (including a tiny thematic unit) with two distinctive topics. The overlapping positions of prime and theme show us the most marked-thematic actor as Jesus (3×). From these results, the following implications could be found: (1) the overall organized structure of the designated text; (2) the constructor's preservation of traditions, which could be inferred by the less organized aspect in the third paragraph. Second, the results of cohesion analysis indicate that each paragraph's overall cohesiveness is sustained via appropriate conjunction ties, participant-reference chains (including substitution and ellipsis), and semantic-lexical ties. The cohesiveness of the entire designated text is also maintained by lexical cohesion chains. There are several factors, however, that may lower the degree of cohesiveness (e.g., absence of the proper nouns for Jesus ['Ιησοῦς]). These overall features may have come from one constructor and his preserving the oral traditions and other sources. Third, by analyzing lexical density and grammatical intricacy, it is revealed that the designated text is close to oral language, and the narrative part seems more oral than the speech part. The oral properties of this text show that this text is significantly rooted in oral tradition. Furthermore, the results of the comparative analysis between speech and narrative could be explained via the identity of the constructor, who may have preserved multiple oral and written sources. Fourth, the results of verbal aspect analysis reveal the different levels of markedness of the verbs in the designated text. The varying markedness may have been affected by the oral/written traditions and/or the constructor.

CHAPTER 6

# Comparison and Implications

This chapter will comparatively analyze the results of chapters 3, 4, and 5 to infer the Synoptic Gospels' construction process.

## 1    Thematization

The critical elements in the thematization analysis of the designated texts are summarized in Table 6.1.

First, regarding the number of thematic units, Matthew is twelve, Mark eight, and Luke ten. To find the implication of these results, we need to identify how finely a chunk of text is fractionized into thematic units. The percentage of thematic units per the total number of lexemes (Matthew: 364; Mark: 368; Luke: 370) in each designated text is as follows: (1) Matthew ($12/364 \times 100$): 3.297%; (2) Mark ($8/368 \times 100$): 2.174%; and (3) Luke ($10/370 \times 100$): 2.703%. Degrees of thematic units' subdivision of each paragraph can be related to the "systematicity" of a text; thus, these results may show the degree of the constructor's influence on each text. More specifically, a higher percentage of thematic units per number of lexemes in the designated text can be regarded as a result of the constructor having more influence on the text, and a lower percentage as relatively less.

Second, regarding the number of paragraphs, Matthew is five, Mark four, and Luke four. The designated text of Matthew is divided into five, and it seems to be the most appropriate paragraph division concerning the thematic flow of the designated text, which consists of five topics. This shows us the well-organized characteristic, which is possibly from the constructor, Matthew. In the case of

TABLE 6.1    Thematization comparison between Matt 26:14–35, Mark 14:10–31, and Luke 22:3–23, 31–34

|  | Matt 26:14–35 | Mark 14:10–31 | Luke 22:3–23, 31–34 |
| --- | --- | --- | --- |
| Thematic units | 12 | 8 | 10 |
| Paragraphs | 5 | 4 | 4 |
| Most marked actor | Jesus (2×) | Peter (2×) | Jesus (3×) |

© HOJOON J. AHN, 2024  |  DOI:10.1163/9789004696372_008

188                                                                              CHAPTER 6

Mark and Luke, however, they both consist of four paragraphs despite the flow
of five topics. These results may indicate that each constructor had a role in
the construction of each text, but there may have been a difference in degree.
Thus, via these two comparative analyses on thematic units and paragraph
division, the degree of the influences of the constructor in terms of each text's
construction can be ranked in the order of Matthew > Luke > Mark.

Third, in Matthew and Luke, Jesus appears as the most marked thematic
actor via the overlapped position of prime and theme (2× in Matthew; 3× in
Luke), and it can be regarded as a natural phenomenon since he is the key
figure in the designated tests. It seems difficult to deduce the construction process of Matthew and Luke from these results. In Mark's case, however, Peter
appears as the most marked thematic actor (2×). This phenomenon may seem
unnatural, considering that Jesus is the core character in the designated text.
A possible explanation for this is that the prominence of Peter in the tradition
may have been the result of Peter's emphasis on his own failure (Mark 14:29,
31), and Mark preserved it without softening such a negative feature of Peter in
the process of the construction of the Gospel.

## 2        Cohesion

### 2.1     *Conjunction*

The analyses of conjunctions and asyndeton in the designated texts reveal
that overall, the texts' cohesiveness is maintained via the conjunctive ties
and natural appearance of asyndeton. Among these analyses, however, there
are appearances of conjunctions that do not seem common, and some cases
where a conjunction seems natural to appear but does not exist (asyndeton).

First, there are several notable cases of asyndeton. Firstly, let us look at
the two cases of asyndeton in the narrative speech margin of the first Gospel
(26:34, 35). These two cases have a distinctive pattern (asyndeton + thematic
λέγει/ἔφη + grammatical subject), which frequently appears in Matthew.[1] These
cases of asyndeton may show the constructor's literary style. The other cases
of asyndeton in Matthew 26:18f and 26:25c, however, may lower the degree of
cohesiveness of the second and third paragraphs (26:17–19; 26:20–25); these elements may show the oral properties within the designated text. In Mark, there
is also a case of asyndeton (14:19), which may lower the degree of cohesiveness

---

1   Black, *Conjunctions*, 189–90.

COMPARISON AND IMPLICATIONS

of the third paragraph, and it also may reveal the oral properties within the designated text. In Luke, all the instances of asyndeton seem natural.

Second, regarding the frequency in the appearance of καί, Mark has the highest frequency (29×). In Mark, this conjunction appears extensively, which could be considered a characteristic of oral language.[2] This may have come from the primary source of Mark, Peter's oral testimony/tradition. In Matthew, καί is used the least (14×). This Gospel tends to use conjunctions that are appropriate for specific situations rather than those with a broader meaning like καί. From this, we can deduce that as an eyewitness, Matthew's own contribution to the constructing process of the text may have been much greater than Mark and Luke. In that process, Matthew may perhaps have used conjunctions more sensitively as the context requires. This phenomenon thus may show the textuality of Matthew. In Luke, the frequency of using καί is relatively high (22×); this phenomenon could be understood as a trace of oral tradition(s) that Luke may have preserved in the construction process. Compared to Mark, however, Luke tends to select more specific conjunctions rather than καί—particularly in the narrative; this may have come from the constructor's own contribution or the multiple sources.

### 2.2 Reference

The cohesiveness of each text was revealed in the analyses of the participant-referent chains in the designated texts. In each paragraph in the designated texts, typically, after the participants appear as a proper noun, the chains are formed as a pronoun or an implied subject in a verb. However, in the case of the reference to Jesus, some paragraphs show the phenomenon that the proper noun Ἰησοῦς does not appear where it is expected. In some cases, this phenomenon occurs despite the confusion to the readers is anticipated. The frequency of such phenomenon differs: Matthew: 1, Mark: 2, Luke: 4. To analyze the references to Jesus in each designated text, this section classifies the cases in which Jesus is referred to as proper nouns, common nouns, pronouns, implied subjects in verbs, simplified article forms, and compound nouns in Table 6.2.

In Matthew's case, among the total of fifty-three references to Jesus, five of the references appear as proper nouns (Ἰησοῦς [5×; 26:17, 19, 26, 31, 34]), in Mark's case, three of forty-nine (Ἰησοῦς; [3×; 14:18, 27, 30]), and in Luke's case, it appears not once out of forty-three references. In order to assess the implications of these occurrences, we may need to calculate the possible cases

---

2    Cf. Halliday, *Spoken and Written Language*, 82–86.

190                                                                    CHAPTER 6

TABLE 6.2   References to Jesus in Matt 26:14–35, Mark 14:10–31, Luke 22:3–23, 31–34

| | Matt 26:14–35 | Mark 14:10–31 | Luke 22:3–23, 31–34 |
|---|---|---|---|
| Proper noun | 5× (Ἰησοῦ [26:17]; Ἰησοῦς [26:19, 26, 31, 34]) | 3× (Ἰησοῦς [14:18, 27, 30]) | – |
| Common noun | 6× (κύριε [26:22]; διδάσκαλος [3×; 26:18, 24*]; ῥαββί [26:25]; ποιμένα [26:31]) | 2× (διδάσκαλος [14:14]; ποιμένα [14:27]) | 2× (διδάσκαλος [22:11]; κύριε [22:33]) |
| Pronoun | 20× (αὐτόν; [3×; 26:15, 16, 25]; σοι [2×; 26:17, 33, 35]; μου [4×; 26:18*, 28, 29]; με [4×; 26:21, 23, 32, 34]; αὐτῷ [3×; 26:22, 33, 35]; ἐμοῦ [26:23]; αὐτοῦ [26:24]; ἐμοί [26:31]; σε [26:35]) | 19× (αὐτόν; [2×; 14:10, 11]; αὐτῷ [3×; 14:12, 19, 29]; αὐτοῦ [3×; 14:12, 13, 21]; μου [4×; 14:14*, 22, 24]; με [3×; 14:18, 28, 30]; ἐμοῦ [2×; 14:18, 20]; σοι [14:31]; σε [14:31]) | 16× (αὐτόν; [2×; 22:4, 6]; αὐτῷ [3×; 22:9, 14, 33]; μου [2×; 22:11, 19, 20]; με [3×; 22:15, 21, 34]; ἑαυτούς [22:17]; ἐμήν [22:19]; ἐμοῦ [22:21]; ἐγὼ [22:32]; σοῦ [22:33]) |
| Implied subject in verbs | 15× (θέλεις [26:17]; ἀνέκειτο [26:20]; εἶπεν [2×; 26:21, 26]; λέγω [3×; 26:21, 29, 34]; λέγει [26:25]; λαβών [2×; 26:26, 27]; εὐλογήσας [26:26]; δοὺς [26:26]; εὐχαριστήσας [26:27]; ἔδωκεν [26:27]; λέγων [26:27]; πίω [26:29]; πίνω [26:29]; προάξω [26:32]) | 22× (θέλεις [14:12]; φάγῃς [14:12]; ἀποστέλλει [14:13]; λέγει [14:13]; φάγω [14:14]; εἶπεν [3×; 14:16, 22, 24]; ἔρχεται [14:17]; λέγω [3×; 14:18, 25, 30]; λαβών [2×; 14:22, 23]; εὐλογήσας [14:22]; ἔκλασεν [14:22]; ἔδωκεν [2×; 14:22, 23]; λάβετε [14:22]; εὐχαριστήσας [14:23]; πίω [14:25]; πίνω [14:25]) | 22× (ἀπέστειλεν [22:8]; εἰπών [22:8]; θέλεις [22:9]; φάγω [2×; 22:11, 16]; εἰρήκει [22:13]; ἀνέπεσεν [22:14], εἶπεν [2×; 22:15, 17], ἐπεθύμησα [22:15]; λέγω [3×; 22:16, 18, 34]; δεξάμενος [22:17]; εὐχαριστήσας [2×; 22:17, 19]; πίω [22:18]; λαβών [22:19]; ἔκλασεν [22:19]; ἔδωκεν [22:19]; λέγων [2×; 22:19, 20]) |
| Simplified form | 2× (ὁ [26:18, 23]) | 1× (ὁ [14:20]) | 2× (ὁ [22:10, 34]) |
| Compound noun | 2× (ὁ υἱὸς τοῦ ἀνθρώπου [26:24*]) | 2× (ὁ υἱὸς τοῦ ἀνθρώπου [14:21*]) | 1× (ὁ υἱὸς τοῦ ἀνθρώπου [22:22]) |
| Total | 53 | 49 | 43 |

COMPARISON AND IMPLICATIONS                                              191

where the non-proper noun references (that is, pronouns, implied subjects in verbs, and simplified article forms) can be replaced by Jesus in each designated text. Obviously, those cases which occur in Jesus' speeches are to be excluded from the calculation. And when a proper noun once occurs in a sentence the other references in the same sentence are also to be excluded. In that case, there are thirteen cases in Matthew (αὐτόν; [3×; 26:15, 16, 25]; ὁ [2×; 26:18, 23]; ἀνέκειτο [26:20]; εἶπεν [2×; 26:21, 26]; αὐτῷ [3×; 26:22, 33, 35]; λέγει [26:25]; ἔδω-κεν [26:27]), sixteen cases in Mark (αὐτόν; [2×; 14:10, 11]; αὐτῷ [3×; 14:12, 19, 29]; αὐτοῦ [14:12, 13]; ἀποστέλλει [14:13]; λέγει [14:13]; εἶπεν [3×; 14:16, 22, 24]; ἔρχεται [14:17]; ὁ [14:20]; ἔκλασεν [14:22]; ἔδωκεν [2×; 14:22, 23]), and fourteen cases in Luke (αὐτόν; [2×; 22:4, 6]; ἀπέστειλεν [22:8]; αὐτῷ [3×; 22:9, 14, 33]; ὁ [2×; 22:10, 34]; εἰρήκει [22:13]; ἀνέπεσεν [22:14], εἶπεν [2×; 22:15, 17], ἔκλασεν [22:19]; ἔδωκεν [22:19]). Among the references to Jesus in the designated text in Matthew, five appear as proper nouns out of eighteen cases (proper nouns + references that can be replaced by proper nouns), accounting for 27.8%. For Mark, it is 15.8%, three out of nineteen cases, and for Luke, 0%, zero out of fourteen cases. The implications of these results can be deduced as follows.

First, let us look at Luke's "zero cases." After appearing as a proper noun ('Ιησοῦς) in 20:34, it does not appear as a proper noun even once until the end of our designated text, and in 22:47, it appears again (τῷ 'Ιησοῦ). Between these proper nouns, there are as many as one hundred sixty-eight verses; this phenomenon seems uncommon. In the designated text, there are four cases where a proper noun Jesus seems much more natural in each paragraph (αὐτόν [22:4]; ἀπέστειλεν [22:8]; ἀνέπεσεν [22:14]; αὐτῷ [22:33]). It seems necessary to contemplate the implications of this. Luke probably used multiple data, as stated in Luke 1:3 that he would "investigate" (παρηκολουθηκότι) "all things" (πᾶσιν)—about Jesus—"carefully" (ἀκριβῶς) for the third Gospel construction. From this, we can deduce that the construction of the third Gospel may have been seriously based on oral traditions as well as written sources. Considering that the frequent use of pronouns is a characteristic of oral language,[3] thus, it is possible that he received the pronoun form of Jesus from oral tradition(s), and reflected it as it is. Also, this tendency of Luke is more pronounced when examining the process of making documents in ancient times. According to Pieter J. J. Botha, in the first century, when publishing a book on papyrus or parchment, it would have been revised and supplemented through at least

---

3   According to a study by Mary B. Mann, oral language has a higher (and sometimes signifi-cantly higher) pronoun inclusion than written language. See Mary B. Mann, "The Quantita-tive Differentiation of Samples of Written Language," *PM* 56 (1944): 63.

192                                                              CHAPTER 6

three steps: (1) note-taking and basic composition; (2) rough draft; and (3) copy for distribution.[4] If Luke followed this process, he could have improved certain awkward references to Jesus by using proper noun. Leaving the pronouns as it is then can be evidence that Luke was keen to preserve oral traditions in his hands as they are regarding the text in question.

Such a noteworthy phenomenon can become more evident through comparison with Acts, which is also known as a book written by Luke.[5] For example, if we look at Acts 9:1–22, which contains both the description of a main character and the direct speech section, which is similar in length to the verses of the designated text in Luke, the proper noun of Paul, Σαῦλος, appears three times (Acts 9:1, 8, 22). In 9:1, Paul's name is revealed as a proper noun, which seems appropriate and needed since it appears to change the central character. However, in 9:8 and 9:22, proper nouns appear even though there are plural participants who are distinct from Paul. In light of the previous tendency of the third Gospel, that is, omitting proper nouns of the main character, Paul could be referred to as a pronoun, but Acts does not follow Luke's pattern. If this were Luke's unique writing style, the use of proper nouns and other references in both texts would have been done similarly. However, if Luke and Acts do not have the same pattern, we can say that this distinctive aspect in the third Gospel does not come from Luke's own style. An appropriate understanding of this phenomenon can be as follows: although Luke writes both the third Gospel and Acts, when he writes the Gospel, he may have been faithful to oral traditions and other collected sources. In summary, when Luke writes the Gospel, he may have tried to follow the tradition, and when he writes Acts, he may have been a more active constructor.

Second, let us observe the five cases of proper noun Ἰησοῦς in the designated text of Matthew. Ἰησοῦς appears in 26:10, which is the closest proper noun before our designated text. The reference to Jesus appears only as pronouns in 26:15–16 two times, despite the complete change of topic—from the story of a woman who poured perfume on Jesus' feet to that of Judas and the high priest: this does not seem common.[6] In 26:1–13, the beginning of chapter 26, Jesus appears as the proper noun four times (26:1, 4, 6, 10). Considering these

---

4   Pieter J. J. Botha, *Orality and Literacy in Early Christianity* (PBCS 5; Eugene, OR: Cascade, 2012), 74–75.

5   Fitzmyer, *Luke*, 1–4; David G. Peterson, *The Acts of the Apostles* (PNTC; Grand Rapids: Eerdmans, 2009), 1–4; Robert C. Tannehill, *The Narrative Unity of Luke-Acts: A Literary Interpretation. Vol. 1: The Gospel according to Luke* (Philadelphia: Fortress, 1986), 1:1.

6   Here, the criteria for it to be "natural" for a character's reference to appear as proper noun are as follows: (1) according to changes in the main participants or topics, a proper noun needs to appear at least once in each paragraph; (2) when two or more references with the same

COMPARISON AND IMPLICATIONS

usages of proper nouns, it seems unnatural that the proper noun does not appear in 26:14–16. In other words, it seems more natural for a proper noun to appear at least once in 26:15 or 26:16. In the context of subject change in 26:14, Judas's identification of Jesus as a reduced reference in 26:15 (αὐτόν) could be explained as an original form of Judas's wording with the intention to hand over Jesus to the high priest secretly. However, αὐτόν appears again in 26:16, even though it seems natural to reveal the identity of Jesus by using a proper noun. A plausible explanation for this phenomenon is that Matthew did not experience this event, so he may have followed a tradition formed by another eyewitness(es). In the second, fourth, and fifth paragraphs, the proper noun Ἰησοῦς appears at least once. And in the third paragraph (26:20–25), Jesus does not appear as a proper noun. It seems, however, explicable because the proper noun of Jesus appearing in the immediate-preceding passage (26:19) may well be closely related to the pronoun, since the Passover meal is closely connected to its preparation. In this sense, it seems that Matthew constructed the Gospel systematically for readers' understanding; however, the appearance of the pronoun (αὐτόν) in 26:16 can be seen as a trace of his attempt to preserve a tradition formed by other eyewitness(es) as it is.[7]

Third, in Mark, Jesus appears as a proper noun, Ἰησοῦς, in 14:6, which is the closest proper noun before 14:10, the beginning of our designated texts; thus, the two pronouns of 14:10–11 (αὐτόν) are to be considered as the references to this. However, as in Matthew, it seems more natural to use a proper noun in 14:10 or 14:11, considering the change of subject. Also, in the second paragraph, there is another case where a proper noun seems more natural (αὐτῷ [14:12]), whereas the third and fourth paragraphs include the proper noun Ἰησοῦς (14:18, 27, 30). How can we understand these aspects? According to Papias, Mark constructed his Gospel based on Peter's testimony. In other words, it can be seen that Mark was formed through the testimony of one person, Peter, that is, one primary source. Due to this, in Mark, proper nouns with respect to Jesus are relatively posited in reasonable places in the text, compared to Luke.

These findings can be the meaningful footmarks that all three Gospels were fundamentally written based on (oral) tradition(s). Nevertheless, the Gospel

---

gender and number appear together, each reference or at least one subject needs to be a proper noun.

7  Since Matthew himself was an eyewitness, it is possible that he tried to organize his Gospel more systematically based on his own experience. In the designated text, except for the first paragraph, Matthew plays a role as an eyewitness for the contents in other paragraphs (from the second to the fifth). However, as mentioned above, Judas's story in the first paragraph must have been received from other witness(es) since Matthew himself did not experience it. Thus, he may have tried to preserve its original form.

194                                                        CHAPTER 6

according to Matthew probably had the most considerable features of influence from its constructor.

### 2.3 *Substitution and Ellipsis*

The substitution and ellipsis of the specified texts of Matthew, Mark, and Luke are organized as shown in Table 6.3.

TABLE 6.3    Substitution and ellipsis comparison between Matt 26:14–35, Mark 14:10–31, and Luke 22:3–23, 31–34[a]

| | Matt 26:14–35 | Mark 14:10–31 | Luke 22:3–23, 31–34 |
|---|---|---|---|
| Substitution | οἱ μαθηταί (26:17) | ὁ εἷς τῶν δώδεκα (14:10) | τὸν καλούμενον Ἰσκαριώτην |
| | ὁ διδάσκαλος (26:18) | οἱ μαθηταί (14:12) | (22:3) |
| | κύριε (26:22) | ἀνάγαιον μέγα (14:15) | ὄντα ἐκ τοῦ ἀριθμοῦ τῶν |
| | ὁ υἱὸς τοῦ ἀνθρώπου | ὁ ἐσθίων μετ᾽ ἐμοῦ (14:19) | δώδεκα (22:3) |
| | (26:24) | εἷς τῶν δώδεκα (14:20) | ἢ ἔδει θύεσθαι τὸ πάσχα |
| | ῥαββί (26:25) | ὁ ἐμβαπτόμενος μετ᾽ ἐμοῦ | (22:7) |
| | τὸ σῶμά μου (26:26) | εἰς τὸ τρύβλιον (14:20) | ἀνάγαιον (22:12) |
| | τὸ αἷμά μου τῆς διαθήκης | ὁ υἱὸς τοῦ ἀνθρώπου (14:21) | οἱ ἀπόστολοι (22:14) |
| | (26:28) | τῷ ἀνθρώπῳ ἐκείνῳ δι᾽ οὗ ὁ | τοῦ γενήματος τῆς ἀμπέλου |
| | τοῦ γενήματος τῆς | υἱὸς τοῦ ἀνθρώπου παραδί- | (22:18) |
| | ἀμπέλου (26:29) | δοται (14:21) | τὸ σῶμά μου (22:19) |
| | τὸν ποιμένα (26:31) | τὸ σῶμά μου (14:22) | ἡ καινὴ διαθήκη ἐν τῷ αἵματί |
| | τὰ πρόβατα τῆς ποίμνης | τὸ αἷμά μου τῆς διαθήκης | μου (22:20) |
| | (26:31) | (14:24) | τῷ ἀνθρώπῳ ἐκείνῳ (22:22) |
| | | τοῦ γενήματος τῆς ἀμπέλου | ὁ υἱὸς τοῦ ἀνθρώπου (22:22) |
| | | (14:25) | κύριε (22:33) |
| | | τὸν ποιμένα (14:27) | Πέτρε (22:34) |
| | | τὰ πρόβατα τῆς ποίμνης | |
| | | (14:27) | |
| Ellipsis | Omission of a person who betrays Jesus (26:22, 25) | Omission of a person who betrays Jesus and the process part (14:19) | Omission of the process part (22:20, 21) |

a  In the comparison table, things that are the same in the three texts are underlined, those that are not identical but similar in the three texts are shown in italics, and things that are consistent between the two texts are written in bold.

COMPARISON AND IMPLICATIONS

In writings written by ordinary authors, substitution and ellipsis can be efficiently utilized for specific purposes. However, in the Synoptic Gospel texts, we need to consider their origin, which has several possibilities: constructors or traditions/sources. As seen from Table 6.3, the analysis of substitution and ellipsis of the designated texts can be divided into four categories: (1) all three texts matching together; (2) not identical but appearing similarly in all three texts; (3) two texts matching together; and (4) unique to each text. One of the characteristic elements of this analysis is that most cases of substitution and ellipsis belong to the direct speech part, except for a few cases. This section looks at several cases in terms of the Gospel construction process.

The first is about the substitutions: μαθηταί and ἀπόστολοι. These lexemes seem to reflect the constructors' understanding of the group. In the designated texts, only Luke has the lexeme ἀπόστολοι. There is a total of six plural references to ἀπόστολος in Luke (6:13; 9:10; 11:49; 17:5; 22:14; 24:10), which shed light on Luke's understanding of Jesus' discipleship. The lexeme ἀπόστολος surely is Luke's characteristic substitution in Luke-Acts.[8] This probably reflects the common term for Jesus' twelve disciples, used by the early church when Luke constructed the third Gospel. In Matthew, ἀπόστολος appears only once in the genitive plural form (ἀποστόλων; 10:2). Here, ἀποστόλων appears to be a one-time expression used when Jesus sent the disciples. It is used in the context of Jesus calling his disciples, giving them power (10:1), and sending (ἀποστέλλω) them (10:5). Thus, it is difficult to regard this as Matthew's general expression referring to the twelve disciples. Even though Matthew was an apostle, it seems clear that Matthew recognized Jesus' twelve selected people, which he himself also belonged to, as "disciples" rather than "apostles." In Mark, the use of ἀπόστολος appears only twice (3:14 [ἀποστόλους], 6:30 [ἀπόστολοι]).[9] These two cases in Mark, as in the cases of Matthew, are used when the disciples were sent by Jesus and in the context of the sent disciples returning and reporting (3:14; 6:30). Thus, these two usages express the role of those sent by Jesus. Other than this, the twelve selected people were recognized as "disciples" rather than "apostles." Then in the second Gospel, it is also difficult to regard ἀπόστολος as a general expression in the second Gospel for Jesus' twelve disciples. Assuming that the second Gospel was constructed on the

---

8  Luke's understanding of the group of disciples is confirmed by the use of ἀπόστολος, which appears twenty-eight times in Acts (7× subjective; 13× genitive; 3× dative; 5× accusative).

9  These two cases in Mark, similar to Matthew, are used when sent by Jesus, and in the context of the sent disciples returning and reporting (3:14; 6:30). As such, these two usages express the role of those sent by Jesus; thus, it is difficult to regard it as Mark's general expression for Jesus' twelve disciples.

basis of Peter's oral testimony, this phenomenon may have come from Peter's self-awareness as a disciple, like Matthew. In this sense, ἀπόστολος in 3:14 and 6:30 seems to be a contextual expression, possibly from Peter. These aspects are more clearly confirmed when we look at the use of μαθηταί as a title for the twelve disciples in the Synoptic Gospels: Matthew (66× [39× subjective plural, 17× dative plural, 1× genitive plural, 9× accusative plural]), Mark (46× [20× subjective plural, 11× dative plural, 8× genitive plural, 7× accusative plural]), and Luke (28× [10× subjective plural, 3× dative plural, 4× genitive plural, 11× accusative plural]).[10] As we can see here, considering the length of each Gospel, the number of appearances of μαθηταί in Luke is considerably low, and in the case of Matthew and Mark, it is relatively high. Thus, each Gospel's unique expressions of Jesus' twelve disciples may be a natural reflection of each constructor's identity (Matthew: eyewitness; Mark: personal relationship with eyewitness; Luke: no personal relationship with eyewitness).[11]

Another significant observation relates to the substitution of the "cup" given by Jesus at the Eucharist. Matthew and Mark refer to the cup as "my (Jesus') blood of the covenant," while Luke calls it "the new covenant in my (Jesus') blood." In other words, the order "blood" and "covenant" is reversed here. Luke seems to share the same tradition with Paul (1 Cor 11:25; ἡ καινὴ διαθήκη ἐστὶν ἐν τῷ ἐμῷ αἵματι) but expresses it in a slightly different form. It seems possible that Luke may be taking an intermediate position between Paul and Matthew-Mark. Table 6.4 shows this.

TABLE 6.4   Comparison between four texts on the substitution of ποτήριον

| Matt 26:28 | τὸ αἷμά μου τῆς διαθήκης |
|---|---|
| Mark 14:24 | τὸ αἷμά μου τῆς διαθήκης |
| Luke 22:20 | ἡ καινὴ διαθήκη ἐν τῷ αἵματί μου |
| 1 Cor 11:25 | ἡ καινὴ διαθήκη ἐστὶν ἐν τῷ ἐμῷ αἵματι |

---

10  Although the use of the nominative singular of μαθητής appears once in Matthew (10:24) and four times in Luke (6:40; 14:26, 27, 33), they do not refer directly to Jesus' twelve disciples, but rather are related to qualifications/conditions to be Jesus' disciple. Since they were used in the relationship with the teacher along with the reference to them, these examples are not included in the number of times. Also, the use of the plural genitive of μαθητής appears as follows: Matt: 3×; Mark: 8×, and Luke: 7×. Besides, the use of the plural accusative of μαθητής appears as follows: Matt: 10×; Mark: 7×, and Luke: 13×. These genitive and accusative cases are also not included in the number of times.

11  Particularly, this point could be a reflection of Luke's characteristic inferred from καθεξῆς (Luke 1:3).

COMPARISON AND IMPLICATIONS

Unlike Matthew and Mark, Luke refers to Jesus' cup as "the new covenant," not "blood." However, the latter part of Luke (ἐν τῷ αἵματί μου) is different from that of 1 Corinthians (ἐστὶν ἐν τῷ ἐμῷ αἵματι). Moreover, it takes μου as a modifier for blood, which follows Matthew and Mark rather than 1 Corinthians' ἐμῷ. Considering this, it seems that the overall form of Luke follows the same tradition as 1 Corinthians while also taking the tradition of Matthew and Mark (Peter) into account. Possible explanations for this phenomenon are as follows. First, the content shared equally in Matthew 26:28, and Mark 14:24 was possibly Jesus' actual words at the Passover, which Matthew and Peter heard directly. However, as Paul reveals in 1 Corinthians 11:23, the Eucharistic words that he "received" (παρέλαβον)[12] were from the Lord (ἀπὸ τοῦ κυρίου). Considering that παραλαμβάνω was a "technical term" for carrying the meaning of "handing over" a tradition, custom, or teaching in Jewish culture at the time,[13] we could understand it as Paul declaring that he received Jesus' Eucharistic words from an oral tradition.[14] There is a possibility of tension between these two traditions of the Eucharist in the early Church era (Matthean-Markan tradition and Pauline tradition); thus, Luke may have accepted the two traditions together. Another possibility is that Luke may have encountered this form of tradition as it is: ἡ καινὴ διαθήκη ἐν τῷ αἵματί μου.

## 2.4    *Lexical Cohesion*
The comparative-analytic results for lexical cohesion are shown in Table 6.5.[15]

As Table 6.5 shows, Matthew, Mark, and Luke share the majority of the semantic domains. Of the twenty-one domains, the three Gospels share sixteen domains. It is worth noting that, in terms of lexemes, Matthew and Luke have unique vocabularies, but Mark does not, at least in the semantic domain analysis of the designated text. It seems to reveal the existence of a tradition shared by all three Gospels and the existence of unique sources and traditions

---

12    Louw and Nida explain that παραλαμβάνω has the nuance of "receiving" tradition in particular. Louw and Nida, *Greek-English Lexicon*, 327.

13    See C. K. Barrett, *The First Epistle to the Corinthians* (BNTC; 2nd ed.; London: A & C Black, 1971), 238–40; Hans Conzelmann, *1 Corinthians: A Commentary on the First Epistle to the Corinthians* (trans. James W. Leitch; Hermeneia; Philadelphia: Fortress, 1975), 195; Richard A. Horsley, *1 Corinthians* (ANTC; Nashville: Abingdon, 1998, 160).

14    Barrett, *Corinthians*, 239–40.

15    The lexical cohesion analyses in chapters 3, 4, and 5 analyzed the cases where two or more lexemes in one semantic domain appear in a paragraph. However, in this comparative analysis, even if a lexeme occurs only once in a designated text, it will be dealt with when it shares the semantic domain with other designated text(s). The order of the semantic domain basically follows the order in which words appear in the Gospel according to Matthew.

198                                                                           CHAPTER 6

TABLE 6.5    Comparative lexical cohesion analysis between Matt 26:14–35, Mark 14:10–31, and
Luke 22:3–23, 31–34

| Semantic domain | Matt 26:14–35 | Mark 14:10–31 | Luke 22:3–23, 31–34 |
|---|---|---|---|
| 57 | δίδωμι; παραδίδωμι | δίδωμι (3×); παραδίδωμι | δίδωμι (3×); παραδίδωμι (4×); διαμερίζω |
| 60 | εἷς; δώδεκα; τριάκοντα | εἷς; δώδεκα | ἀριθμός; δώδεκα |
| 67 | τότε (2×); εὐκαιρία; καιρός; ἐγγύς; ἄρτι; ἡμέρα; νύξ; οὐδέποτε; πρίν | οὐκέτι; ἡμέρα; σήμερον; νύξ; πρίν | ὥρα; ἕως; νῦν; μέλλω |
| 77 | ἑτοιμάζω (2×) | ἑτοιμάζω (2×); ἕτοιμος | ἑτοιμάζω (4×) |
| 36 | μαθητής (3×) | μαθητής (4×) | |
| 51 | πάσχα (3×) | πάσχα (4×) | πάσχα (3×) |
| 90 | ποιέω (2×) | – | – |
| 33 | λέγω (21×); διδάσκαλος; συντάσσω; γράφω (2×); ἀποκρίνομαι; ῥαββί; εὐλογέω; εὐχαριστέω; ὑμνέω; φημί; ἀπαρνέομαι | ἀκούω; ἐπαγγέλλομαι (2×); λέγω (15×); γράφω; εὐλογέω; εὐχαριστέω; ὑμνέω; φημί; ἀπαρνέομαι; λαλέω | συλλαλέω; ἐξομολογέω; ἐξαιτέω; δέομαι; λέγω (14×); ἀπαρνέομαι; φωνέω εὐχαριστέω; συζητέω; |
| 37 | παραδίδωμι (4×); ἄφεσις; σκανδαλίζω (2×) | παραδίδωμι (2×); σκανδαλίζω (2×) | παραδίδωμι (2×) |
| 9 | υἱὸς τοῦ ἀνθρώπου (2×) ἄνθρωπος (2×) | υἱὸς τοῦ ἀνθρώπου (2×) ἄνθρωπος (2×) | υἱὸς τοῦ ἀνθρώπου ἄνθρωπος |
| 69 | μήτι (2×); οὐ (2×); μή (2×) | μήτι; οὐ (3×); μή (2×); οὐκ | οὐ (3×); μή (3×) |
| 23 | ἐσθίω; πίνω; ἐγείρω; ἀποθνήσκω | ἐσθίω (3×); πίνω (3×); ἐγείρω; συναποθνήσκω | ἐσθίω (2×); πίνω; δειπνέω |
| 8 | χεὶρ; σῶμα; αἷμα | σῶμα; αἷμα | σῶμα; αἷμα; χεὶρ |
| 3 | ἄμπελος; ἐλαία | ἄμπελος; ἐλαία | ἄμπελος |
| 15 | διασκορπίζω; προάγω | ἀπέρχομαι; ὑπάγω; ἀπαντάω; βαστάζω; ἀκολουθέω; εἰσέρχομαι; ἐξέρχομαι; ἔρχομαι; διασκορπίζω; προάγω | ἔρχομαι; ἀποστέλλω; πορεύομαι (2×); εἰσέρχομαι; βαστάζω; ἀκολουθέω; εἰσπορεύομαι; ἀπέρχομαι; ἐπιστρέφω |
| 4 | πρόβατον; ποίμνη; ἀλέκτωρ | πρόβατον; ἀλέκτωρ | – |
| 7 | – | κατάλυμα; ἀνάγαιον | οἰκία (3×); κατάλυμα; ἀνάγαιον |

COMPARISON AND IMPLICATIONS

TABLE 6.5 Comparative lexical cohesion analysis (*cont.*)

| Semantic domain | Matt 26:14–35 | Mark 14:10–31 | Luke 22:3–23, 31–34 |
|---|---|---|---|
| 18 | λαμβάνω (2×) | λαμβάνω (3×) | λαμβάνω (2×) |
| 6 | τρύβλιο | τρύβλιον; ποτήριον | ποτήριον (2×); τράπεζα |
| 25 | – | – | ἐπιθυμίᾳ; ἐπιθυμέω |
| 1/37 | βασιλεία | βασιλεία | βασιλεία (2×) |

that Matthew and Luke had independently. There are domains shared by Matthew-Mark and those shared by Mark-Luke, but it is also a characteristic that there is no domain shared only by Matthew-Luke. This could be seen as a meaningful ground for the theory of Markan priority. Nevertheless, this analysis alone does not ascertain whether Matthew and/or Luke depended on Mark to construct their Gospels.

Some specific observations on the lexical cohesion analysis in terms of the Gospel construction process are as follows. Lexemes related to spatial movement belonging to domain 15 appear in Matthew, Mark, and Luke, but Mark and Luke have many more lexemes in this domain compared to Matthew (Matt: 2×; Mark: 10×; and Luke: 10×). And the vocabulary related to "place" belonging to domain 7 appears only in Mark and Luke. This phenomenon seems related to the recipients of Jesus' instruction to prepare for the Passover. Matthew identifies them simply as "disciples," but Mark as "two" of the disciples, and Luke more specifically identifies them as "Peter" and "John." Although all three have different expressions, they may all refer to the two of Jesus' disciples, Peter and John. If Mark constructed his Gospel based on Peter's tradition, it is likely that Peter added more detail as a person with actual experience, and Luke may have shared these traditions formed by Peter (or possibly John; cf. 22:8). Matthew may have constructed this part in a simple version since he may not attach any significance to the identities of the participants.

Lexemes in domain 4 are specifically related to the Old Testament quotation of Jesus, belonging to Matthew and Mark, but not appearing in Luke. Given that Luke is the only evangelist who quotes Isaiah 61:1–2a in Luke 4:18–19, for example, it seems unlikely to conceive that he deliberately excluded the quotation from the tradition. It would be more plausible to say that this quotation is missing from the traditions or sources that Luke had.

## 3 Orality and Textuality

The lexical density and grammatical intricacy of the three designated texts are shown comparatively in Table 6.6.

Considering the overall lexical density and grammatical intricacy of the three designated texts, they are overall closer to oral texts than written texts. In the case of lexical density, the rank of the orality appears as Mark > Matthew > Luke. In the case of grammatical intricacy, however, the rank of the orality appears Matthew > Luke > Mark. Having said this, however, there is little difference between their orality, and it is not easy to say which is more oral, considering both analyses of lexical density and grammatical intricacy. When looking at the results on lexical density, it can be said that all three texts are close to oral language because the results are under three, but the fact that their results are close to three makes us hard to deny that they also have written aspects.[16]

The comparison table of the lexical density analysis of the designated texts can be classified into two categories of direct speech and narrative parts (see Table 6.7).

TABLE 6.6    Lexical density and grammatical intricacy comparison between Matt 26:14–35, Mark 14:10–31, and Luke 22:3–23, 31–34

|  | Matt 26:14–35 | Mark 14:10–31 | Luke 22:3–23, 31–34 |
| --- | --- | --- | --- |
| Lexical density | 2.849 (151/53) | 2.782 (153/55) | 2.961 (151/51) |
| Grammatical intricacy | 2.789 (53/19) | 2.5 (55/22) | 2.55 (51/20) |

TABLE 6.7    Lexical density of direct speech and narrative parts in Matt 26:14–35, Mark 14:10–31, and Luke 22:3–23, 31–34

|  | Direct speech | Narrative |
| --- | --- | --- |
| Matt 26:14–35 | 2.483 | 3.364 |
| Mark 14:10–31 | 2.82 | 2.74 |
| Luke 22:3–23, 31–34 | 3.172 | 2.682 |

---

16    Cf. Porter, "Orality and Textuality," 8.

COMPARISON AND IMPLICATIONS 201

Each result shown in Table 6.7 seems interesting. From these different results, we can infer the characteristics of each Gospel's construction process as follows. First, from the result of the lexical density in Matthew's speech part (2.483) and narrative part (3.364), we can infer that the oral tradition of the speech part to which he contributed may have been preserved by Matthew himself, since he was one of the first-hand audience of the speech; however, in the case of the narrative part, Matthew may have written basically on his own, mainly based on his own experience. Second, the results of the lexical density in Mark's speech part (2.82) and narrative part (2.74) are almost the same; thus, we can deduce that Mark may have consistently constructed the Gospel from one primary oral source, Peter. Third, the result of the lexical density in Luke's speech part (3.172) and narrative part (2.682) is considerably unique: it is rather an unexpected result. In Luke, the speech part has more written aspect, and the narrative part has more oral aspect. The less orality in the speech part in the designated text in Luke suggests that Luke may have constructed the text based on written as well as oral sources. From Luke 1:1–4 (esp. 1:3), we can infer that the constructor, Luke, gave careful (ἀκριβῶς) attention to all the traditions and sources he collected, and he preserved them. In this process, it is possible that content words may have increased. As a result, the orality of the speech parts of the designated text in Luke seems to have decreased. In addition, as mentioned before, the narrative part's oral aspect can be explained via the comparative analysis between 22:3–6, and the whole narrative part in the designated text. The lexical density of 22:3–6 is 3.5, higher than that of the whole narrative part (2.682). The reason for the low lexical density of the whole narrative part is probably because most of the narratives of the designated text, excluding 22:3–6, mostly appear as narrative speech margins, which are short intros that tend to have few content words. This may explain the comparatively lower lexical density than Matthew and Mark.

## 4 Verbal Aspect

The verbal aspect analysis discussed in the previous chapters 3, 4, and 5 is useful in understanding the prominence of each text. This section will compare the appearances of stative aspect in the designated texts.

As shown in Table 6.8, these stative aspect verbs overlap each other as follows: (1) Matthew and Mark's common stative aspect verb: γέγραπται (Matt 26:24, 31; Mark 14:21, 27); (2) Stative aspect verb common to Mark and Luke: ἐστρωμένον (Mark 14:15; Luke 22:12). The stative aspect verbs that appear only in Luke are as follows: εἰρήκει (22:13), ὡρισμένον (22:22), and εἰδέναι (22:34). Based on these observations, we can deduce the following.

202                                                                                                    CHAPTER 6

TABLE 6.8    Stative aspects in the designated texts

| Matt 26:14–35 | Mark 14:10–31 | Luke 22:3–23, 31–34 |
|---|---|---|
| γέγραπται (24), γέγραπται (31) | ἐστρωμένον (15), γέγραπται (21), γέγραπται (27) | ἐστρωμένον (12), ὡρισμένον (22), εἰδέναι (34), εἰρήκει (13) |

First, γέγραπται in Matthew 26:31 and Mark 14:27 shows that Matthew and Mark share the same prominence.[17] Similarly, ἐστρωμένον in Mark and Luke (Mark 14:15; Luke 22:12) reveals that Mark and Luke share the same prominence.[18] These aspects may have come from the shared oral tradition/written source or the process of literary dependence.

Second, εἰρήκει (22:13; stative aspect), which appears in Luke, has a distinct difference in terms of verbal aspect when compared to εἶπεν (perfective aspect), which appears in Mark 14:16. Furthermore, εἰδέναι (22:34), which appears in Luke, is not included in the parallel texts of Matthew and Mark. These two cases—even though they have different phenomena—may have come from either deference of oral tradition/written sources or the constructor.

Third, γέγραπται in Matthew 26:24 and Mark 14:21 does not appear in Luke, but in Luke 22:22, the corresponding word appears as ὡρισμένον in the same context. From the perspective of literary dependence, Luke may have chosen ὡρισμένον after looking at γέγραπται in Mark or Matthew. To be more specific, in this perspective, Luke may have changed γέγραπται, the word which implies the "fulfilment" of the OT, into ὡρισμένον, which has the meaning of "determined."[19] However, given that, throughout the third Gospel, γέγραπται appears in Luke (9×) the same number of times as Matthew (9×) and even more than Mark (7×),[20] it seems that Luke also shared the perspective of "fulfilment."[21] Also, considering the case where γέγραπται is used in Luke 24:46 in a context that does not quote any specific Old Testament text (in a context

---

17    Luke does not have the parallel passages of Matthew and Mark (Matt 26:31–32; Mark 14:27–28) that contain γέγραπται.

18    ἐστρωμένον in Mark and Luke does not appear in the abbreviated parallel text of Matthew.

19    Considering that the three Gospels share the same stative aspect, it is possible that Luke expressed the stative aspect through another verb, after encountering the text of Mark or Matthew.

20    Matt 2:5; 4:4, 6, 7, 10; 11:10; 21:13; 26:24, 31; Mark 1:2; 7:6; 9:12, 13; 11:17; 14:21, 27; Luke 2:23; 3:4; 4:4, 8, 10; 7:27; 10:26; 19:46; 24:46.

21    Cf. In Luke 10:26, γέγραπται appears in the context where Jesus asks on what is written in the law.

COMPARISON AND IMPLICATIONS 203

similar to 22:22), it seems difficult to find the reason for such change by Luke himself. Instead, a more natural explanation of this phenomenon may be that ὡρισμένον in Luke came from a different oral/written source.

## 5  Summary

This chapter compared and analyzed the significant findings of chapters 4, 5, and 6 with respect to the Gospel construction process. First, the thematization study shows us the following: (1) given the thematic units and paragraph divisions of each Gospel, the degree of each constructor's influence in each Gospel can be inferred as follows: Matthew > Luke > Mark; (2) the most prominent actor in each Gospel revealed through the theme-rheme structure appears to be Jesus in Matthew and Luke, whereas Peter in Mark; we can deduce that in Mark the prominence of Peter may have been the result of Peter's emphasis on his own failure.

Second, cohesion analysis reveals the following: (1) in conjunction analysis, the unusual appearances of asyndeton in Matthew (26:18f, 25c) and Mark (14:19) may reveal the oral properties of these designated texts (Luke does not have a such case), and the frequency of appearance of καί (Mark [29×], Luke [22×], Matthew [14×]) could indicate Mark's oral characteristic which has probably originated from Peter's oral testimony/tradition, Luke's construction based on multiple oral/written sources, and Matthew's construction as an eyewitness; (2) in reference analysis, the absence of a proper noun of Jesus in Luke may show oral properties which may have come from oral traditions, and the different pattern of references in Acts makes it clearer; the referential phenomenon of Matthew, in which the proper noun of Jesus appears most often, may have occurred from the constructor's organized description of the context in a written form as an eyewitness, and yet the part where he did not directly experience, the pronoun form other tradition may have been preserved; the frequency of the proper noun Ἰησοῦς in Mark is intermediate between Matthew and Luke, and it may have been originated from Peter's oral tradition/testimony; (3) among the substitution and ellipsis analysis, the observation of μαθηταί and ἀπόστολοι reveals Peter (the primary source of Mark) and Matthew's self-awareness as the "disciple" of Jesus, and shows the characteristic of Luke's lexeme choice, who may have recognized Jesus' disciples as the apostles; regarding the substitution the "cup" in the Eucharist, Luke's clause may have two possibilities: Luke may have attempted to contain the two traditions of the Eucharist (Matthean-Markan tradition and Pauline tradition) or Luke may have encountered another tradition; (4) in the lexical cohesion analysis, Mark and Luke have the specific details of the "place" for the Passover, which may have been originated from the oral tradition contributed by Peter (or John), who experienced it firsthand, whereas Matthew, who had not, may have constructed the Gospel in a more abbreviated form, or he may have received that form from the other tradition. Unlike the Old Testament quotations in Matthew and Mark, Luke does not have it, and it seems possible that this part is missing from the oral traditions and the other sources that Luke had.

Third, the orality and textuality analysis shows us the following: (1) analysis of the lexical density and grammatical intricacy of each designated text reveals that all three Gospels retain the properties of oral language; (2) the lexical density analysis of the designated texts divided into direct speech and narrative parts leads to inferring the following aspects about the construction process of each Gospel. Matthew may have preserved the direct speech part of the oral tradition as it is, and the narrative part may have been written based on his own experience and/or oral/written sources. Mark may have received both direct speech and narrative parts in oral form through Peter and preserved them. The less oral aspects of the direct speech part may be the result of the high number of content words since Luke may have constructed the Gospel via multiple sources. The high oral aspects of the narrative part seem to have resulted from the few content words since the narrative speech margin and pronoun (especially for Jesus) appear a lot in the narrative part.

Fourth, the comparative verbal aspect analysis focusing on stative aspect in the designated texts reveals the following: (1) the stative aspects in Matthew 26:31, Mark 14:15, 27, and Luke 22:12 may have come from the shared oral tradition/written source or the process of literary dependence; the stative aspects in Luke 22:13, 34 may have come from either deference of oral tradition/written sources or the constructor; (2) it seems more natural to say that ὡρισμένον in Luke 22:22, the corresponding word of γέγραπται in Matthew 26:24 and Mark 14:21, may have come from a different oral/written sources, though it cannot be denied that it comes from the result of literary dependence.

CHAPTER 7

# Conclusion and Further Research

## 1     Conclusions

A recapitulation of the conclusions that have been reached thus far is as follows.

In Chapter 1, the history of discussions surrounding the so-called Synoptic Problem was briefly examined, and the question of literary dependence between the Synoptic Gospels was raised. Subsequently, a position for the study of the Synoptic Gospels was proposed based on discussions regarding the constructor of each Gospel, known as the "Oral Tradition(s) and Constructor's Identity Hypothesis."

In Chapter 2, a model of RA based on SFL was presented. The model includes four main components: thematization, cohesion (conjunction, reference, substitution, ellipsis, lexical cohesion), orality & textuality, and verbal aspect. Before this main discussion, however, brief observations on the genre and oral tradition were made, regarding their relevance to the study of the Synoptic Gospels.

In Chapter 3, Matthew 26:14–35 was analyzed according to the model of mode RA. Its results are as follows: (1) according to the thematization analysis, the designated text contains twelve thematic units and is organized into five paragraphs. The most marked-thematic actor in the text is Jesus. These results demonstrate the well-organized structure of the text, which may have come from the constructor; (2) cohesion analysis shows conjunctive ties, participant-referent chains, appropriate substitutions & ellipsis, semantic-lexical ties, and semantic-lexical chain of the whole designate text; all these factors consistently reveals each paragraph and that of entire designated text's cohesiveness which may reveal *one constructor*'s formation of this text, although it reveals several factors (two cases of asyndeton and one case of reduced reference) which may lower the degree of cohesiveness; (3) orality and textuality analysis shows that the designated text is close to oral language, and particularly, the direct speech part is more oral than the narrative part; these results may show that the designated text is rooted in *oral tradition*, and Matthew may have the dual identity as the contributor to and preserver of oral tradition; and (4) verbal aspect analysis reveals the different levels of markedness of the designated text; the possible origins of these markedness are as follows: (a) the participant within the text; (b) the eyewitness/contributor(s) to traditions; and (c) the constructor.

© HOJOON J. AHN, 2024 | DOI:10.1163/9789004696372_009

206                                                                          CHAPTER 7

In chapter 4, Mark 14:10–31 was investigated according to the model of mode RA. Its results are as follows: (1) thematization analysis reveals that the designated text has eight thematic units and four paragraphs, that the most marked-thematic actor in the text is Peter, and that the third paragraph has one thematic unit with two topics; these results may demonstrate the constructor's contribution to the *organized structure* along with his preservation of Peter's *oral testimony/tradition*; (2) by analyzing the cohesion of the designated text, we can identify conjunctive ties, participant-referent chains, appropriate substitutions & ellipsis, semantic-lexical ties, and semantic-lexical chain of the whole designate text; all these factors consistently maintain cohesiveness of each paragraph and that of the entire designated text, which may reveal *one constructor's* formation of the designated text, although there are several factors (one case of asyndeton and one case of reduced reference), which may lower the degree of cohesiveness; (3) orality and textuality analysis reveals that the designated text is close to oral language, and the gap between its narrative part and direct speech part appears to be slight; these results convey that the designated text is probably rooted in *oral tradition*; and (4) verbal aspect analysis shows the different levels of markedness of the designated text; the possible origins of these markedness are the same as Matthew.

In Chapter 5, Luke 22:3–23, 31–34 were examined according to the model of mode RA. Its results are as follows: (1) thematization analysis shows that the designated text has ten thematic units and four paragraphs, that the most marked-thematic actor is Jesus, and that the third paragraph has one large thematic unit (including a tiny thematic unit) with two distinctive topics; these results may demonstrate the constructor's contribution to the *organized* structure along with his preservation of *oral traditions*; (2) the cohesive analysis indicates that the designated text has conjunctive ties, participant-referent chains, appropriate substitutions & ellipsis, semantic-lexical ties, and semantic-lexical chain of the whole designate text; these cohesive factors demonstrate the cohesiveness of each paragraph and that of the entire designated text, which may reveal *one constructor's* formation of the text, although there are several factors (absence of the proper nouns for Jesus), which may lower the degree of cohesiveness; (3) orality and textuality analysis shows that the designated text is close to oral language, and the narrative part is more oral than the direct speech part probably due to many speech margins and no occurrence of the proper noun of Jesus; these results may indicate that this text is rooted in *oral traditions*, with the identity of the constructor who would have preserved multiple oral and written sources; and (4) verbal aspect analysis reveals the different levels of markedness of the designated text; the possible origins of these markedness are the same as Matthew and Mark.

CONCLUSION AND FURTHER RESEARCH 207

Chapter 6 employs a comparative analysis of the designated texts of the Synoptic Gospels, building upon the analytical findings presented in chapters 3, 4, and 5, in order to unveil the construction process behind the formation of those texts. From these analyses, we were able to detect the footprints in each text in relation to the construction process of the Gospels. These results can be summarized as follows.

First, thematization study reveals the following: (1) considering the thematic units and paragraph divisions of each Gospel, the ranking according to the degree of constructor's influence is described as follows: Matthew > Luke > Mark; (2) in Matthew and Luke, the most marked thematic actor is Jesus, but Peter in Mark; Matthew and Luke's results seem natural, but Mark's result shows the possibility that Mark's preservation of Peter's oral testimony/tradition.

Second, cohesion study shows the following: (1) in conjunction analysis, the unusual cases of asyndeton in Matthew and Mark may show the oral properties within them, and the varying frequency of καί in each designated text could indicate (a) Mark's oral characteristic, derived from Peter's oral testimony/tradition, (b) Luke's construction from multiple oral/written sources, and (c) Matthew's construction from the viewpoint of the eyewitness; (2) in reference analysis, the absence of a proper noun of Jesus in Luke could indicate oral properties from oral traditions, and the comparison with Acts makes it clearer; the proper noun of Jesus appears most often in Matthew, which may show the well-organized construction by the eyewitness; Mark is intermediate between Matthew and Luke concerning the proper noun of Jesus, which may have been originated from Peter's oral tradition/testimony; (3) in the substitution and ellipsis analysis, the analysis of μαθηταί and ἀπόστολοι reveals Peter (the primary source of Mark) and Matthew's self-awareness as the "disciple" of Jesus, and reveals Luke's recognition of the disciples as the "apostles"; regarding the substitution the "cup" in the Eucharist, Luke may have contained two kinds of Eucharistic traditions or a different form of tradition; (4) in the lexical cohesion analysis, Mark and Luke's specific details of the "place" for the Passover may have come from Peter's (or John's) oral testimony/tradition, whereas Matthew may have constructed the Gospel in an abbreviated form or preserved the other tradition.

Third, the analysis of orality and textuality reveals the following: (1) examination of the lexical density and grammatical intricacy of each text demonstrates that all three Gospels retain the oral properties; (2) the lexical density analysis of the designated texts, broken down into direct speech and narrative sections, reveals the following; Matthew may have preserved the direct speech part of the oral tradition and written the narrative part based on his experience and/or tradition. Mark may have preserved both the speech and narrative parts from one source, Peter. Assuming that Luke has constructed the Gospel via multiple sources, the written property in the direct speech part seems to have increased as the number of content words increased in the process. Also, the high orality of the narrative part in Luke seems to have resulted from the few content words since there are a lot of narrative speech margins and pronouns (especially for Jesus) in the narrative part.

Fourth, the comparative verbal aspect analysis reveals that ὡρισμένον in Luke 22:22, the corresponding word of γέγραπται in Matthew 26:24 and Mark 14:21, may have come from different oral/written sources; other six stative cases may have been originated from the shared oral tradition/written source or the literary dependence.

Based on these analyses, this study suggests each Gospel's characteristics concerning its construction process.

First, the construction process of the first Gospel can be inferred as follows. Matthew, the eyewitness who had direct experience with Jesus' words and life as his disciple and apostle, was probably a contributor to the formation of oral tradition. As regards Matthew's construction of the Gospel, four features are to be observed: (1) Matthew, as a contributor and preserver of oral tradition, seems to have reflected oral tradition to construct the Gospel, which can be revealed by (a) lexical density in the orality and textuality analysis, especially the high orality of its direct speech part, and (b) the factors which lower the degree of cohesiveness, revealed by cohesion analysis; (2) in terms of the parts that Matthew did not experience directly, he may have reflected other oral/written sources, which is revealed by the omission of a proper noun of Jesus in the first paragraph; (3) Matthew, as a person with organized and literary abilities, appears to have constructed the Gospel systematically, which can be confirmed by (a) well-organized thematic units and paragraphs, (b) diverse and appropriate use of conjunctions, (c) his unique writing style revealed from the observation of asyndeton, (d) appropriate use of proper noun of Jesus, and (e) overall cohesiveness revealed via cohesion analysis; (4) Matthew may have elaborately described what he experienced as an eyewitness, and it may have particularly influenced the formation of the narrative part, which can be revealed by the written properties of narrative part in the orality and textuality analysis.

Second, based on the above discussions, it can be inferred that the construction process of the second Gospel involved John Mark, who had a close relationship with Peter. While it is unlikely that Mark was a direct contributor to the oral tradition, he appears to have acted as a preserver of Peter's testimony/tradition. As regards Mark's construction of the Gospel, two features are to be observed: (1) Mark appears to have constructed the Gospel based on

CONCLUSION AND FURTHER RESEARCH

one primary source, Peter's oral testimony/tradition, considering the following features: (a) Peter, the most marked thematic actor revealed through thematization analysis; (b) the less organized aspect in the third paragraph revealed from paragraph division analysis; (c) the factors which lower the degree of cohesiveness, revealed by cohesion analysis; (d) frequent use of the conjunction καί; (e) the analytic result of the proper noun of Jesus; (f) the result of lexical density, which is the lowest among the three Gospels; and (g) consistency of orality between the direct speech part and the narrative part; (2) Mark's own role as a constructor seems to have moderate influence in constructing the Gospel, which can be inferred by the organized thematic units and paragraphs (first, second, and fourth paragraphs) and the overall cohesiveness revealed from cohesion analysis.

Third, the construction process of the third Gospel can be inferred as follows. Luke, a companion of the apostle Paul, was not an eyewitness nor a contributor to oral traditions, but a sincere preserver of the oral/written sources (Luke 1:1–4). As regards Luke's construction of the Gospel, three features are to be observed: (1) Luke may have constructed the Gospel based on the oral traditions, which can be revealed by (a) the less organized aspect in the third paragraph revealed from paragraph division analysis; (b) the factors which lower the degree of cohesiveness, revealed by cohesion analysis; (c) the analytic result of the proper noun of Jesus (zero cases); (d) the result of lexical density which reveals the orality of the text; (2) in the process of constructing the third Gospel, Luke may have used multiple sources (oral traditions along with written sources), which is revealed by the large proportion of contents words in the direct speech part; (3) Luke seems to play his own influence in constructing the Gospel, which can be inferred by the organized thematic units and paragraphs (first, second, and fourth paragraphs) and the overall cohesiveness revealed from cohesion analysis.

Finally, what implications the above analyses and results may bring to the so-called Synoptic Problem? The study above provides significant support for the literary independence hypothesis, though there is still the possibility of the literary dependence hypothesis. As such, it is crucial to consider the role of the sources seriously, both oral and written, as well as the Gospel constructor, when studying the Synoptic Gospels. By adopting a balanced approach that takes into account these various factors, researchers can move towards a more comprehensive understanding of what traditionally has been called the synoptic problem. Overall, this study serves as a considerable contribution to the field, filling in some of the gaps left by previous major proposals regarding the so-called Synoptic Problem.

210                                                                                                    CHAPTER 7

## 2      Further Possible Research

This monograph attempted to explore the implications of the construction process of the Synoptic Gospels by analyzing the Eucharist and the adjacent texts from a linguistic perspective. Readers who have reached this point may naturally wonder how effectively this approach can be applied to ascertain the implications of the formation process of the other texts in the Synoptic Gospels. As a matter of fact, in order to comprehensively examine the construction process of the Synoptic Gospels, it is essential to apply the present methodology to the teachings and miracle narratives of Jesus, which predominantly occupy the Synoptic Gospels. This constitutes a vast undertaking, and it is my expectation that not only myself but also numerous scholars engaged in this research may have the opportunity to apply this methodology to various passages in the future. The accumulation of such research endeavors will afford the opportunity to infer the construction processes of each Synoptic Gospel with greater objectivity. I aim to undertake the future research, focusing on specific passages, such as the parable of the Sower among the parables and the narrative of the healing of the Gadarene demoniacs among the miracle stories, both of which are present in all three Synoptic Gospels. I intend to apply my methodology to these two passages, particularly utilizing the thematic unit and lexical density analyses. The outcomes of these analyses are expected to shed light on, albeit tentatively, the construction processes of the two texts, and this may engender insights that will orient the future comprehensive and in-depth research.

Let us first examine the parable of the Sower (Matt 13:1–23 // Mark 4:1–20 // Luke 8:4–15). The following is a preliminary application of the methodology utilizing the thematic unit and lexical density analyses to the parable.

Firstly, let us analyze the thematic unit. In a situation where there is a clear thematic shift, only Matthew uses the proper noun ὁ Ἰησοῦς (Matt 13:1). Mark and Luke only have implicit subjects in their verbs (Mark 4:1; Luke 8:4). The three texts all share the subject "crowd" in slightly different ways. In the section where the disciples ask questions, οἱ μαθηταί appears in Matthew and Luke but not in Mark. In the subsequent section where Jesus responds, Matthew and Luke have a separate subject form, ὁ, referring to Jesus, while Mark does not. When dividing the thematic units based on the emergence of the new subject, Matthew has four (ὁ Ἰησοῦς, crowd, οἱ μαθηταί, ὁ), Mark has one (crowd [οἱ περὶ αὐτὸν σὺν]), and Luke has three (crowd, οἱ μαθηταί, ὁ) thematic units.

The percentage of thematic units per the total number of lexemes (Matthew: 414; Mark: 348; Luke: 235) in each designated text is as follows: (1) Matthew (4/414 × 100): 0.966%; (2) Mark (1/348 × 100): 0.287%; and

CONCLUSION AND FURTHER RESEARCH

(3) Luke ($3/235 \times 100$): 1.276%. As mentioned above, degrees of thematic units' subdivision of each paragraph can be related to the "systematicity" of a text; thus, these results may show the degree of the constructor's influence on each text. More specifically, a higher percentage of thematic units per number of lexemes in the designated text can be regarded as a result of the constructor having more influence on the text, and a lower percentage as relatively less influence. From the perspective of thematic units, even though there are limitations due to the difference of textual length, the designated text of Luke seems the most systematically structured, followed by Matthew, and then Mark. However, considering the difference between Matthew, Mark, and Luke in terms of their length and the small amount of details in Luke, such an implication is subject to certain limitations. A modeling to set the criteria to discern implications through analyses of such texts which have difference in length and details would be a remaining task for future studies.

Secondly, let us analyze the lexical density. To calculate the lexical density of the three texts, the ratio of content words to the number of non-embedded clauses in each designated text is as follows: Matthew: 2.686 ($188/70$); Mark: 3.0 ($156/52$); Luke: 2.86 ($103/36$). The rank of the orality appears Matthew > Luke > Mark. According to Halliday's criteria, these values reflect characteristics of oral-driven written documents. Even though we do not have the full analyses including grammatical intricacy, it can be said that these results could imply the presence of oral tradition within these texts.

Although not all aspects have been analyzed, based on the results examined above, it can be inferred that oral tradition influenced the construction process of each text. The constructor of each text may have used oral tradition as contributor, preserver, and transmitter, and constructed each text in drawing on oral tradition along with other multiple sources.

Additionally, it is essential to consider the differences in length among the texts. The length difference can lead to different inferences depending on the hypothesis adopted. If we consider the priority of Mark, one might infer that Matthew expanded on Mark, while Luke shortened it. However, it is crucial to ponder whether such inferences are definite. If the intention of the constructors was to preserve oral tradition(s) in the formation process of the text, the differences in length and content could be due to variations in the transmission and materials each constructor possessed. This aspect can be applied to the subsequent text as well.

Next, let us examine the healing narrative of the Gadarene demoniacs (Matt 8:28–34 // Mark 5:1–20 // Luke 8:26–39). The following is the preliminary application of the methodology utilizing the thematic unit and lexical density analyses to the narrative. The story of the healing of the Gadarene demoniacs is a case where the length and content differences among Matthew and the other two Gospels are significant. However, we will conduct a comparative analysis while keeping in mind the potential differences in characters and places due to the possibility of literary dependence and/or variations in the materials each constructor may have used.

Firstly, let us analyze the thematic unit. The occurrence of the proper noun ὁ Ἰησοῦς is different among Matthew, Mark, and Luke, with Matthew having it once, Mark four times, and Luke three times. However, due to the substantial difference in narrative length, it is not easy to make a straightforward comparison. Matthew, despite its shorter length (7 verses/135 lexemes compared to Mark's 20 verses/326 lexemes and Luke's 14 verses/294 lexemes), displays a systematic structure in revealing information about Jesus, suggesting the role of the constructor as a systematic organizer. In contrast, Mark and Luke, with their more frequent appearances of ὁ Ἰησοῦς, might have been constructed by materials not preserved by Matthew.

The percentage of thematic units per the total number of lexemes (Matthew: 135; Mark: 326; Luke: 294) in each designated text is as follows: (1) Matthew (5/135 × 100): 3.704%; (2) Mark (7/326 × 100): 2.147%; and (3) Luke (11/294 × 100): 3.741%. As mentioned above, degrees of thematic units' subdivision of each paragraph can be related to the "systematicity" of a text; thus, these results may show the degree of the constructor's influence on each text. More specifically, a higher percentage of thematic units per number of lexemes in the designated text can be regarded as a result of the constructor having more influence on the text, and a lower percentage as relatively less influence. From the perspective of thematic units, even though there are limitations due to the difference of textual length, the designated text of Luke seems the most structured, followed by Matthew, and then Mark. However, when confronted with significant disparities in both length and content across the three texts, drawing premature inferences from the outcomes of the analysis appears hasty. This aspect underscores the need for further research in the future.

Secondly, let us analyze the lexical density. The lexical density values for the specified texts are as follows: Matthew: 3.2 (64/20); Mark: 3.286 (138/42); Luke: 3.35 (134/40). In accordance with Halliday's criteria, these metrics delineate attributes consistent with written documents exhibiting oral qualities. The hierarchical order of orality discerned from these values is Matthew > Mark > Luke. Even though a comprehensive analysis encompassing grammatical intricacy has not been conducted and the lexical density exceeds 3.0, it is still considered possible that each text may contain elements of oral tradition considering that the lexical density values are still close to 3.0.

CONCLUSION AND FURTHER RESEARCH

Drawing from these findings, tentatively discernible implications are as follows: the imprint of oral tradition played a substantive role in the formative trajectory of each textual composition, although the possibility of literary dependence cannot be ruled out. The constructors, in their capacities as a contributor, preserver, and transmitter, conceivably composed their respective texts by using oral tradition. This process likely entailed a synthesis of oral tradition alongside diverse multiple sources.

In conclusion, the analysis of "the Parable of the Sower" and "Healing of the Gadarene Demoniacs" in Matthew, Mark, and Luke tentatively suggests the influence of oral tradition in the formation process of each Gospel. The differences in length, content, and thematic units among the texts can be attributed to the transmission, preservation, and reference to oral tradition by the respective constructors. The occurrence of the proper noun ὁ Ἰησοῦς also varies, and the unique features in each Gospel may more or less reflect the constructors' efforts to faithfully preserve the original transmission and materials.

The above proposed textual analyses of "the Parable of the Sower" and "Healing of the Gadarene Demoniacs" are preliminary, and predicting the outcomes of more detailed research of these passages is difficult. Nevertheless, this will serve as an agenda for the subsequent phases of my individual scholarly investigation. It is my aspiration that this present monograph, by stimulating research on other significant texts, not only by myself but also by other scholars, will contribute to shaping the outcomes towards a more balanced conclusion in comprehending the construction processes of the Synoptic Gospels.

*Appendices*

APPENDIX 1

# Prime and Subsequent Analysis of Matthew 26:14–35

| Verse | Clause | Prime | Subsequent |
|---|---|---|---|
| 26:14–15a | c26_41 | Τότε | πορευθεὶς εἷς τῶν δώδεκα, ὁ λεγόμενος Ἰούδας Ἰσκαριώτης, πρὸς τοὺς ἀρχιερεῖς εἶπεν· |
| 26:15b | c26_44 | τί | θέλετέ μοι δοῦναι, |
| 26:15c | c26_46 | κἀγὼ | ὑμῖν παραδώσω αὐτόν; |
| 26:15d | c26_47 | οἱ (δὲ) | ἔστησαν αὐτῷ τριάκοντα ἀργύρια. |
| 26:16a | c26_48 | (καὶ) ἀπὸ τότε | ἐζήτει εὐκαιρίαν |
| 26:16b | c26_49 | ἵνα αὐτὸν | παραδῷ. |
| 26:17a | c26_50 | Τῇ (δὲ) πρώτῃ τῶν ἀζύμων | προσῆλθον οἱ μαθηταὶ τῷ Ἰησοῦ λέγοντες· |
| 26:17b | c26_52 | ποῦ | θέλεις ἑτοιμάσωμέν σοι φαγεῖν τὸ πάσχα; |
| 26:18a | c26_55 | ὁ (δὲ) | εἶπεν· |
| 26:18b | c26_56 | ὑπάγετε | εἰς τὴν πόλιν πρὸς τὸν δεῖνα |
| 26:18c | c26_57 | (καὶ) εἴπατε | αὐτῷ· |
| 26:18d | c26_58 | ὁ διδάσκαλος | λέγει· |
| 26:18e | c26_59 | ὁ καιρός μου | ἐγγύς ἐστιν, |
| 26:18f | c26_60 | πρὸς σὲ | ποιῶ τὸ πάσχα μετὰ τῶν μαθη- τῶν μου. |
| 26:19a | c26_61 | (καὶ) ἐποίησαν | οἱ μαθηταὶ |
| 26:19b | c26_62 | (ὡς) συνέταξεν | αὐτοῖς ὁ Ἰησοῦς |
| 26:19c | c26_63 | (καὶ) ἡτοίμασαν | τὸ πάσχα. |
| 26:20a | c26_64 | Ὀψίας (δὲ) | γενομένης |
| 26:20b | c26_65 | ἀνέκειτο | μετὰ τῶν δώδεκα. |
| 26:21a | c26_66 | (καὶ) ἐσθιόντων | αὐτῶν |
| 26:21b | c26_67 | εἶπεν· | |
| 26:21c | c26_68 | ἀμὴν | λέγω ὑμῖν |
| 26:21d | c26_69 | (ὅτι) εἷς ἐξ ὑμῶν | παραδώσει με. |

218                                                                APPENDIX 1

(*cont.*)

| | | | |
|---|---|---|---|
| 26:22a | c26_70 | (καὶ) λυπούμενοι σφόδρα | ἤρξαντο λέγειν αὐτῷ εἷς ἕκαστος· |
| 26:22b | c26_73 | μήτι | ἐγώ εἰμι, κύριε; |
| 26:23a | c26_74 | ὁ (δὲ) | ἀποκριθεὶς εἶπεν· |
| 26:23b | c26_76 | ὁ ἐμβάψας | μετ᾽ ἐμοῦ τὴν χεῖρα ἐν τῷ τρυβλίῳ |
| 26:23c | c26_78 | οὗτός | με παραδώσει. |
| 26:24a | c26_79 | ὁ (μὲν) υἱὸς τοῦ ἀνθρώπου | ὑπάγει |
| 26:24b | c26_80 | (καθὼς) γέγραπται | περὶ αὐτοῦ, |
| 26:24c | c26_81 | οὐαὶ (δὲ) | τῷ ἀνθρώπῳ ἐκείνῳ δι᾽ οὗ ὁ υἱὸς τοῦ ἀνθρώπου παραδίδοται· |
| 26:24d | c26_83 | καλὸν | ἦν αὐτῷ |
| 26:24e | c26_84 | (εἰ) οὐκ | ἐγεννήθη ὁ ἄνθρωπος ἐκεῖνος. |
| 26:25a | c26_85 | ἀποκριθεὶς (δὲ) | Ἰούδας ὁ παραδιδοὺς αὐτὸν εἶπεν· |
| 26:25b | c26_88 | μήτι | ἐγώ εἰμι, ῥαββί; |
| 26:25c | c26_89 | λέγει | αὐτῷ· |
| 26:25d | c26_90 | σὺ | εἶπας. |
| 26:26a | c26_91 | Ἐσθιόντων (δὲ) | αὐτῶν |
| 26:26b | c26_92 | λαβὼν | ὁ Ἰησοῦς ἄρτον καὶ εὐλογήσας ἔκλασεν |
| 26:26c | c26_95 | (καὶ) δοὺς | τοῖς μαθηταῖς εἶπεν· |
| 26:26d | c26_97 | λάβετε | |
| 26:26e | c26_98 | φάγετε, | |
| 26:26f | c26_99 | τοῦτό | ἐστιν τὸ σῶμά μου. |
| 26:27a | c26_100 | (καὶ) λαβὼν | ποτήριον καὶ εὐχαριστήσας ἔδωκεν αὐτοῖς λέγων· |
| 26:27b | c26_104 | πίετε | ἐξ αὐτοῦ πάντες, |
| 26:28 | c26_105 | τοῦτο (γάρ) | ἐστιν τὸ αἷμά μου τῆς διαθήκης τὸ περὶ πολλῶν ἐκχυννόμενον εἰς ἄφεσιν ἁμαρτιῶν. |
| 26:29a | c26_107 | λέγω (δὲ) | ὑμῖν, |
| 26:29b | c26_108 | οὐ μὴ | πίω ἀπ᾽ ἄρτι ἐκ τούτου τοῦ γενήματος τῆς ἀμπέλου ἕως τῆς ἡμέρας ἐκείνης |
| 26:29c | c26_109 | (ὅταν) αὐτὸ | πίνω μεθ᾽ ὑμῶν καινὸν ἐν τῇ βασιλείᾳ τοῦ πατρός μου. |

# PRIME AND SUBSEQUENT ANALYSIS OF MATTHEW 26:14–35    219

(*cont.*)

| | | | |
|---|---|---|---|
| 26:30 | c26_110 | (Καὶ) ὑμνήσαντες | ἐξῆλθον εἰς τὸ ὄρος τῶν ἐλαιῶν. |
| 26:31a | c26_112 | Τότε | λέγει αὐτοῖς ὁ Ἰησοῦς· |
| 26:31b | c26_113 | πάντες ὑμεῖς | σκανδαλισθήσεσθε ἐν ἐμοὶ ἐν τῇ νυκτὶ ταύτῃ, |
| 26:31c | c26_114 | γέγραπται (γάρ)· | |
| 26:31d | c26_115 | πατάξω | τὸν ποιμένα, |
| 26:31e | c26_116 | (καὶ) διασκορπισθήσονται | τὰ πρόβατα τῆς ποίμνης. |
| 26:32 | c26_117 | μετὰ (δὲ) τὸ ἐγερθῆναί με | προάξω ὑμᾶς εἰς τὴν Γαλιλαίαν. |
| 26:33a | c26_119 | ἀποκριθεὶς (δὲ) | ὁ Πέτρος εἶπεν αὐτῷ· |
| 26:33b | c26_121 | (εἰ) πάντες | σκανδαλισθήσονται ἐν σοί, |
| 26:33c | c26_122 | ἐγὼ | οὐδέποτε σκανδαλισθήσομαι. |
| 26:34a | c26_123 | ἔφη | αὐτῷ ὁ Ἰησοῦς· |
| 26:34b | c26_124 | ἀμὴν | λέγω σοι |
| 26:34c | c26_125 | (ὅτι) ἐν ταύτῃ τῇ νυκτὶ | πρὶν ἀλέκτορα φωνῆσαι τρὶς ἀπαρνήσῃ με. |
| 26:35a | c26_127 | λέγει | αὐτῷ ὁ Πέτρος· |
| 26:35b | c26_128 | (κἂν) δέῃ | με σὺν σοὶ ἀποθανεῖν, |
| 26:35c | c26_130 | οὐ μή | σε ἀπαρνήσομαι. |
| 26:35d | c26_131 | ὁμοίως (καὶ) | πάντες οἱ μαθηταὶ εἶπαν. |

Total Clauses: 66

APPENDIX 2

# Prime and Subsequent Analysis of Mark 14:10–31

| Verse | Clause | Prime | Subsequent |
|---|---|---|---|
| 14:10a | c14_38 | (Καὶ) Ἰούδας Ἰσκαριὼθ | ὁ εἷς τῶν δώδεκα ἀπῆλθεν πρὸς τοὺς ἀρχιερεῖς |
| 14:10b | c14_39 | (ἵνα) αὐτὸν | παραδοῖ αὐτοῖς. |
| 14:11a | c14_40 | οἱ (δὲ) | ἀκούσαντες ἐχάρησαν |
| 14:11b | c14_42 | (καὶ) ἐπηγγείλαντο | αὐτῷ ἀργύριον δοῦναι. |
| 14:11c | c14_44 | (καὶ) ἐζήτει | |
| 14:11d | c14_45 | πῶς | αὐτὸν εὐκαίρως παραδοῖ. |
| 14:12a | c14_46 | (Καὶ) τῇ πρώτῃ ἡμέρᾳ τῶν ἀζύμων, | ὅτε τὸ πάσχα ἔθυον, λέγουσιν αὐτῷ οἱ μαθηταὶ αὐτοῦ· |
| 14:12b | c14_48 | ποῦ | θέλεις ἀπελθόντες ἑτοιμάσωμεν |
| 14:12c | c14_51 | (ἵνα) φάγῃς | τὸ πάσχα; |
| 14:13a | c14_52 | (καὶ) ἀποστέλλει | δύο τῶν μαθητῶν αὐτοῦ |
| 14:13b | c14_53 | (καὶ) λέγει | αὐτοῖς· |
| 14:13c | c14_54 | ὑπάγετε | εἰς τὴν πόλιν, |
| 14:13d | c14_55 | (καὶ) ἀπαντήσει | ὑμῖν ἄνθρωπος κεράμιον ὕδατος βαστάζων· |
| 14:13e | c14_57 | ἀκολουθήσατε | αὐτῷ |
| 14:14a | c14_58 | (καὶ) ὅπου | ἐὰν εἰσέλθῃ |
| 14:14b | c14_59 | εἴπατε | τῷ οἰκοδεσπότῃ |
| 14:14c | c14_60 | (ὅτι) ὁ ιδάσκαλος | λέγει· |
| 14:14d | c14_61 | ποῦ | ἐστιν τὸ κατάλυμά μου |
| 14:14e | c14_62 | ὅπου | τὸ πάσχα μετὰ τῶν μαθητῶν μου φάγω; |
| 14:15a | c14_63 | (καὶ) αὐτὸς· | ὑμῖν δείξει ἀνάγαιον μέγα ἐστρωμένον ἕτοιμον |
| 14:15b | c14_65 | (καὶ) ἐκεῖ | ἑτοιμάσατε ἡμῖν. |
| 14:16a | c14_66 | (καὶ) ἐξῆλθον | οἱ μαθηταὶ |
| 14:16b | c14_67 | (καὶ) ἦλθον | εἰς τὴν πόλιν |
| 14:16c | c14_68 | (καὶ) εὗρον | |
| 14:16d | c14_69 | (καθὼς) εἶπεν | αὐτοῖς |
| 14:16e | c14_70 | (καὶ) ἡτοίμασαν | τὸ πάσχα. |
| 14:17a | c14_71 | (Καὶ) ὀψίας | γενομένης |

PRIME AND SUBSEQUENT ANALYSIS OF MARK 14:10–31      221

(*cont.*)

| | | | |
|---|---|---|---|
| 14:17b | c14_72 | ἔρχεται | μετὰ τῶν δώδεκα. |
| 14:18a | c14_73 | (καὶ) ἀνακειμένων | αὐτῶν |
| 14:18b | c14_74 | (καὶ) ἐσθιόντων | |
| 14:18c | c14_75 | ὁ Ἰησοῦς | εἶπεν· |
| 14:18d | c14_76 | ἀμὴν | λέγω ὑμῖν |
| 14:18e | c14_77 | (ὅτι) εἷς ἐξ ὑμῶν | παραδώσει με |
| 14:18f | c14_78 | ὁ ἐσθίων | μετ' ἐμοῦ. |
| 14:19a | c14_80 | ἤρξαντο | λυπεῖσθαι καὶ λέγειν αὐτῷ εἷς κατὰ εἷς· |
| 14:19b | c14_83 | μήτι | ἐγώ; |
| 14:20a | c14_84 | ὁ (δὲ) | εἶπεν αὐτοῖς· |
| 14:20b | c14_85 | εἷς τῶν δώδεκα, | ὁ ἐμβαπτόμενος μετ' ἐμοῦ εἰς τὸ τρύβλιον. |
| 14:21a | c14_87 | (ὅτι) ὁ (μὲν) υἱὸς τοῦ ἀνθρώπου | ὑπάγει |
| 14:21b | c14_88 | (καθὼς) γέγραπται | περὶ αὐτοῦ, |
| 14:21c | c14_89 | οὐαὶ (δὲ) | τῷ ἀνθρώπῳ ἐκείνῳ |
| 14:21d | c14_90 | δι' οὗ | ὁ υἱὸς τοῦ ἀνθρώπου παραδίδοται· |
| 14:21e | c14_91 | καλὸν | αὐτῷ |
| 14:21f | c14_92 | (εἰ) οὐκ | ἐγεννήθη ὁ ἄνθρωπος ἐκεῖνος. |
| 14:22a | c14_93 | (Καὶ) ἐσθιόντων | αὐτῶν |
| 14:22b | c14_94 | λαβὼν | ἄρτον εὐλογήσας ἔκλασεν |
| 14:22e | c14_97 | (καὶ) ἔδωκεν | αὐτοῖς |
| 14:22f | c14_98 | (καὶ) εἶπεν· | |
| 14:22g | c14_99 | λάβετε, | |
| 14:22h | c14_100 | τοῦτό | ἐστιν τὸ σῶμά μου. |
| 14:23a | c14_101 | (καὶ) λαβὼν | ποτήριον εὐχαριστήσας ἔδωκεν αὐτοῖς, |
| 14:23d | c14_104 | (καὶ) ἔπιον | ἐξ αὐτοῦ πάντες. |
| 14:24a | c14_105 | (καὶ) εἶπεν | αὐτοῖς· |
| 14:24b | c14_106 | τοῦτό | ἐστιν τὸ αἷμά μου τῆς διαθήκης τὸ ἐκχυννόμενον ὑπὲρ πολλῶν. |
| 14:25a | c14_108 | ἀμὴν | λέγω ὑμῖν |
| 14:25b | c14_109 | (ὅτι) οὐκέτι | οὐ μὴ πίω ἐκ τοῦ γενήματος τῆς ἀμπέλου ἕως τῆς ἡμέρας ἐκείνης |
| 14:25c | c14_110 | (ὅταν) αὐτὸ | πίνω καινὸν ἐν τῇ βασιλείᾳ τοῦ θεοῦ. |
| 14:26a | c14_111 | (Καὶ) ὑμνήσαντες | ἐξῆλθον εἰς τὸ ὄρος τῶν ἐλαιῶν. |
| 14:27a | c14_113 | (καὶ) λέγει | αὐτοῖς ὁ Ἰησοῦς |

222  APPENDIX 2

*(cont.)*

| | | | |
|---|---|---|---|
| 14:27b | c14_114 | (ὅτι) πάντες | σκανδαλισθήσεσθε, |
| 14:27c | c14_115 | (ὅτι) γέγραπται· | |
| 14:27d | c14_116 | πατάξω | τὸν ποιμένα, |
| 14:27e | c14_117 | (καὶ) τὰ πρόβατα | διασκορπισθήσονται. |
| 14:28 | c14_118 | (ἀλλὰ) μετὰ τὸ ἐγερθῆ-ναί με | προάξω ὑμᾶς εἰς τὴν Γαλιλαίαν. |
| 14:29a | c14_120 | ὁ (δὲ) Πέτρος | ἔφη αὐτῷ· |
| 14:29b | c14_121 | (εἰ καὶ) πάντες | σκανδαλισθήσονται, |
| 14:29c | c14_122 | (ἀλλ᾽) οὐκ | ἐγώ. |
| 14:30a | c14_123 | (καὶ) λέγει | αὐτῷ ὁ Ἰησοῦς· |
| 14:30b | c14_124 | ἀμὴν | λέγω σοι |
| 14:30c | c14_125 | (ὅτι) σὺ | σήμερον ταύτῃ τῇ νυκτὶ πρὶν ἢ δὶς ἀλέκτορα φωνῆσαι τρίς με ἀπαρνήσῃ. |
| 14:31a | c14_127 | ὁ (δὲ) | ἐκπερισσῶς ἐλάλει· |
| 14:31b | c14_128 | (ἐὰν) δέῃ | με συναποθανεῖν σοι, |
| 14:31c | c14_130 | οὐ μή | σε ἀπαρνήσομαι. |
| 14:31d | c14_131 | ὡσαύτως (δὲ) (καὶ) | πάντες ἔλεγον. |

Total Clauses: 64

APPENDIX 3

# Prime and Subsequent Analysis of Luke 22:3–23, 31–34

| Verse | Clause | Prime | Subsequent |
|---|---|---|---|
| 22:3 | c22_6 | Εἰσῆλθεν (δὲ) | σατανᾶς εἰς Ἰούδαν τὸν καλούμενον Ἰσκαριώτην, ὄντα ἐκ τοῦ ἀριθμοῦ τῶν δώδεκα· |
| 22:4 | c22_9 | (καὶ) ἀπελθὼν | συνελάλησεν τοῖς ἀρχιερεῦσιν καὶ στρατηγοῖς τὸ πῶς αὐτοῖς παραδῷ αὐτόν. |
| 22:5a | c22_12 | (καὶ) ἐχάρησαν | |
| 22:5b | c22_13 | (καὶ) συνέθεντο | αὐτῷ ἀργύριον δοῦναι. |
| 22:6a | c22_15 | (καὶ) ἐξωμολόγησεν, | |
| 22:6b | c22_16 | (καὶ) ἐζήτει | εὐκαιρίαν τοῦ παραδοῦναι αὐτὸν ἄτερ ὄχλου αὐτοῖς. |
| 22:7a | c22_18 | Ἦλθεν (δὲ) | ἡ ἡμέρα τῶν ἀζύμων, |
| 22:7b | c22_19 | [ἐν] ᾗ ἔδει | θύεσθαι τὸ πάσχα· |
| 22:8a | c22_21 | (καὶ) ἀπέστειλεν | Πέτρον καὶ Ἰωάννην εἰπών· |
| 22:8b | c22_23 | πορευθέντες | ἑτοιμάσατε ἡμῖν τὸ πάσχα |
| 22:8c | c22_25 | (ἵνα) φάγωμεν. | |
| 22:9a | c22_26 | οἱ (δὲ) | εἶπαν αὐτῷ· |
| 22:9b | c22_27 | ποῦ | θέλεις ἑτοιμάσωμεν; |
| 22:10a | c22_29 | ὁ (δὲ) | εἶπεν αὐτοῖς· |
| 22:10b | c22_30 | ἰδοὺ | |
| 22:10c | c22_31 | εἰσελθόντων | ὑμῶν εἰς τὴν πόλιν |
| 22:10d | c22_32 | συναντήσει | ὑμῖν ἄνθρωπος κεράμιον ὕδατος βαστάζων· |
| 22:10e | c22_34 | ἀκολουθήσατε | αὐτῷ εἰς τὴν οἰκίαν |
| 22:10f | c22_35 | εἰς ἣν | εἰσπορεύεται, |
| 22:11a | c22_36 | (καὶ) ἐρεῖτε | τῷ οἰκοδεσπότῃ τῆς οἰκίας· |
| 22:11b | c22_37 | λέγει | σοι ὁ διδάσκαλος· |
| 22:11c | c22_38 | ποῦ | ἐστιν τὸ κατάλυμα |

224                                                            APPENDIX 3

(*cont.*)

| | | | |
|---|---|---|---|
| 22:11d | c22_39 | ὅπου | τὸ πάσχα μετὰ τῶν μαθητῶν μου φάγω; |
| 22:12a | c22_40 | (κἀκεῖνος) ὑμῖν | δείξει ἀνάγαιον μέγα ἐστρωμένον· |
| 22:12b | c22_42 | ἐκεῖ | ἑτοιμάσατε. |
| 22:13a | c22_43 | ἀπελθόντες (δὲ) | εὗρον |
| 22:13b | c22_45 | (καθὼς) εἰρήκει | αὐτοῖς |
| 22:13c | c22_46 | (καὶ) ἡτοίμασαν | τὸ πάσχα. |
| 22:14a | c22_47 | (Καὶ) (ὅτε) ἐγένετο | ἡ ὥρα, |
| 22:14b | c22_48 | ἀνέπεσεν | |
| 22:14c | c22_49 | (καὶ)ᵃ | οἱ ἀπόστολοι σὺν αὐτῷ. |
| 22:15a | c22_50 | (καὶ) εἶπεν | πρὸς αὐτούς· |
| 22:15b | c22_51 | ἐπιθυμίᾳ | ἐπεθύμησα τοῦτο τὸ πάσχα φαγεῖν μεθ᾽ ὑμῶν πρὸ τοῦ με παθεῖν· |
| 22:16a | c22_54 | λέγω (γὰρ) | ὑμῖν |
| 22:16b | c22_55 | (ὅτι) οὐ μὴ | φάγω αὐτὸ ἕως ὅτου πληρωθῇ ἐν τῇ βασιλείᾳ τοῦ θεοῦ. |
| 22:17a | c22_57 | (καὶ) δεξάμενος· | ποτήριον εὐχαριστήσας εἶπεν |
| 22:17b | c22_60 | λάβετε | τοῦτο |
| 22:17c | c22_61 | (καὶ) διαμερίσατε | εἰς ἑαυτούς· |
| 22:18a | c22_62 | λέγω (γὰρ) | ὑμῖν, |
| 22:18b | c22_63 | [ὅτι] οὐ μὴ | πίω ἀπὸ τοῦ νῦν ἀπὸ τοῦ γενήματος τῆς ἀμπέλου ἕως οὗ ἡ βασιλεία τοῦ θεοῦ ἔλθῃ. |
| 22:19a | c22_65 | (Καὶ) λαβὼν | ἄρτον εὐχαριστήσας ἔκλασεν |
| 22:19b | c22_68 | (καὶ) ἔδωκεν | αὐτοῖς λέγων· |
| 22:19c | c22_70 | τοῦτό | ἐστιν τὸ σῶμά μου τὸ ὑπὲρ ὑμῶν διδόμενον· |
| 22:19d | c22_72 | τοῦτο | ποιεῖτε εἰς τὴν ἐμὴν ἀνάμνησιν. |
| 22:20a | c22_73 | (καὶ) τὸ ποτήριον | ὡσαύτως μετὰ τὸ δειπνῆσαι, λέγων· |
| 22:20b | c22_76 | τοῦτο | τὸ ποτήριον ἡ καινὴ διαθήκη ἐν τῷ αἵματί μου τὸ ὑπὲρ ὑμῶν ἐκχυννόμενον. |
| 22:21a | c22_78 | (Πλὴν) ἰδοὺ | |
| 22:21b | c22_79 | ἡ χεὶρ τοῦ παραδιδόντος με | μετ᾽ ἐμοῦ ἐπὶ τῆς τραπέζης. |

a  Here, a verb, ἀνέπεσαν, is omitted, but it functions in this clause, so I only included "(καὶ)" here in the prime section.

## PRIME AND SUBSEQUENT ANALYSIS OF LUKE 22:3–23, 31–34

*(cont.)*

| | | | |
|---|---|---|---|
| 22:22a | c22_81 | (ὅτι) ὁ υἱὸς (μὲν) τοῦ ἀνθρώπου | κατὰ τὸ ὡρισμένον πορεύεται, |
| 22:22b | c22_83 | (πλὴν) οὐαὶ | τῷ ἀνθρώπῳ ἐκείνῳ |
| 22:22c | c22_84 | δι᾽ οὗ | παραδίδοται. |
| 22:23 | c22_85 | (καὶ) αὐτοὶ | ἤρξαντο συζητεῖν πρὸς ἑαυτοὺς τὸ τίς ἄρα εἴη ἐξ αὐτῶν ὁ τοῦτο μέλλων πράσσειν. |
| ... | ... | ... | ... |
| 22:31a | c22_118 | Σίμων Σίμων, | ἰδοὺ |
| 22:31b | c22_119 | ὁ σατανᾶς | ἐξητήσατο ὑμᾶς τοῦ σινιάσαι ὡς τὸν σῖτον· |
| 22:32a | c22_121 | ἐγὼ (δὲ) | ἐδεήθην περὶ σοῦ |
| 22:32b | c22_122 | (ἵνα) μὴ | ἐκλίπῃ ἡ πίστις σου· |
| 22:32c | c22_123 | (καὶ) σύ | ποτε ἐπιστρέψας στήρισον τοὺς ἀδελφούς σου. |
| 22:33a | c22_125 | ὁ (δὲ) | εἶπεν αὐτῷ· |
| 22:33b | c22_126 | κύριε, | μετὰ σοῦ ἕτοιμός εἰμι καὶ εἰς φυλακὴν καὶ εἰς θάνατον πορεύεσθαι. |
| 22:34a | c22_128 | ὁ (δὲ) | εἶπεν· |
| 22:34b | c22_129 | λέγω | σοι, Πέτρε, |
| 22:34c | c22_130 | οὐ | φωνήσει σήμερον ἀλέκτωρ |
| 22:34d | c22_131 | ἕως τρίς | με ἀπαρνήσῃ εἰδέναι. |

Total Clauses: 63

APPENDIX 4

# Prime and Subsequent Analysis of Luke 22:24–30

| Verse | Clause | Prime | Subsequent |
|---|---|---|---|
| 22:24 | c22_90 | Ἐγένετο (δὲ καὶ) | φιλονεικία ἐν αὐτοῖς, τὸ τίς αὐτῶν δοκεῖ εἶναι μείζων. |
| 22:25a | c22_93 | ὁ (δὲ) | εἶπεν αὐτοῖς· |
| 22:25b | c22_94 | οἱ βασιλεῖς τῶν ἐθνῶν | κυριεύουσιν αὐτῶν |
| 22:25c | c22_95 | καὶ οἱ ἐξουσιάζοντες αὐτῶν | εὐεργέται καλοῦνται. |
| 22:26a | c22_97 | ὑμεῖς δὲ | οὐχ οὕτως, |
| 22:26b | c22_98 | ἀλλ' ὁ μείζων ἐν ὑμῖν | γινέσθω ὡς ὁ νεώτερος |
| 22:26c | c22_99 | καὶ ὁ ἡγούμενος | ὡς ὁ διακονῶν. |
| 22:27a | c22_102 | τίς γὰρ | μείζων, |
| 22:27b | c22_103 | ὁ ἀνακείμενος | ἢ ὁ διακονῶν; |
| 22:27c | c22_106 | οὐχὶ | ὁ ἀνακείμενος; |
| 22:27d | c22_108 | ἐγὼ δὲ | ἐν μέσῳ ὑμῶν εἰμι ὡς ὁ διακονῶν. |
| 22:28 | c22_110 | Ὑμεῖς δέ | ἐστε οἱ διαμεμενηκότες μετ' ἐμοῦ ἐν τοῖς πειρασμοῖς μου· |
| 22:29a | c22_112 | κἀγὼ | διατίθεμαι ὑμῖν |
| 22:29b | c22_113 | καθὼς διέθετό | μοι ὁ πατήρ μου βασιλείαν, |
| 22:30a | c22_114 | ἵνα ἔσθητε | |
| 22:30b | c22_115 | καὶ πίνητε | ἐπὶ τῆς τραπέζης μου ἐν τῇ βασιλείᾳ μου, |
| 22:30c | c22_116 | καὶ καθήσεσθε | ἐπὶ θρόνων τὰς δώδεκα φυλὰς κρίνοντες τοῦ Ἰσραήλ. |

Total Clauses: 17

© HOJOON J. AHN, 2024 | DOI:10.1163/9789004696372_013

APPENDIX 5

# Theme and Rheme Analysis of Matthew 26:14–35

### Thematic Unit$_1$

| Rheme$_1$ | Theme$_1$ | | Rheme$_1$ |
|---|---|---|---|
| Τότε | πορευθεὶς εἷς τῶν δώδεκα, ὁ λεγόμενος Ἰούδας Ἰσκαριώτης, πρὸς τοὺς ἀρχιερεῖς εἶπεν· | | |
| Prime$_a$ | Subsequent$_a$ | | |

| Rheme$_1$ | | | |
|---|---|---|---|
| τί | θέλετέ μοι δοῦναι, | κἀγὼ | ὑμῖν παραδώσω αὐτόν; |
| Prime$_b$ | Subsequent$_b$ | Prime$_c$ | Subsequent$_c$ |

### Thematic Unit$_2$

| Theme$_2$ | Rheme$_2$ | | |
|---|---|---|---|
| οἱ (δὲ) | ἔστησαν αὐτῷ τριάκοντα ἀργύρια. | (καὶ) ἀπὸ τότε | ἐζήτει εὐκαιρίαν |
| Prime$_a$ | Subsequent$_a$ | Prime$_b$ | Subsequent$_b$ |

| Rheme$_2$ | |
|---|---|
| (ἵνα) αὐτὸν | παραδῷ. |
| Prime$_c$ | Subsequent$_c$ |

## Thematic Unit₃

| Rheme₃ | Theme₃ |
|---|---|
| Τῇ (δὲ) πρώτῃ τῶν ἀζύμων <br> Prime$_a$ | προσῆλθον οἱ μαθηταὶ τῷ Ἰησοῦ λέγοντες· <br> Subsequent$_a$ |

| Rheme₃ | |
|---|---|
| ποῦ <br> Prime$_c$ | θέλεις ἑτοιμάσωμέν σοι φαγεῖν τὸ πάσχα; <br> Subsequent$_c$ |

## Thematic Unit₄

| Theme₄ | Rheme₄ | | | | |
|---|---|---|---|---|---|
| ὁ (δὲ) <br> Prime$_a$ | εἶπεν· <br> Subsequent$_a$ | ὑπάγετε <br> Prime$_b$ | εἰς τὴν πόλιν πρὸς τὸν δεῖνα <br> Subsequent$_b$ | (καὶ) εἴπατε <br> Prime$_c$ | αὐτῷ· <br> Subsequent$_c$ |

| Rheme₄ | | | | | |
|---|---|---|---|---|---|
| ὁ διδάσκαλος <br> Prime$_d$ | λέγει· <br> Subsequent$_d$ | ὁ καιρός μου <br> Prime$_e$ | ἐγγύς ἐστιν, <br> Subsequent$_e$ | πρὸς σὲ <br> Prime$_f$ | ποιῶ τὸ πάσχα μετὰ τῶν μαθητῶν μου. <br> Subsequent$_f$ |

# THEME AND RHEME ANALYSIS OF MATTHEW 26:14–35

### Thematic Unit₅

| Rheme₅ | Theme₅ | Rheme₅ | | | |
|---|---|---|---|---|---|
| (καὶ) ἐποίησαν | οἱ μαθηταὶ | (ὡς) συνέταξεν | αὐτοῖς ὁ Ἰησοῦς | (καὶ) ἡτοίμασαν | τὸ πάσχα. |
| Prime$_a$ | Subsequent$_a$ | Prime$_b$ | Subsequent$_b$ | Prime$_c$ | Subsequent$_c$ |

### Thematic Unit₆

| Rheme₆ | | | | | |
|---|---|---|---|---|---|
| Ὀψίας (δὲ) | γενομένης | ἀνέκειτο | μετὰ τῶν δώδεκα. | (καὶ) ἐσθιόντων | αὐτῶν |
| Prime$_a$ | Subsequent$_a$ | Prime$_b$ | Subsequent$_b$ | Prime$_c$ | Subsequent$_c$ |

| Rheme₆ | | | | |
|---|---|---|---|---|
| εἶπεν· | ἀμὴν | λέγω ὑμῖν | (ὅτι) εἷς ἐξ ὑμῶν | παραδώσει με. |
| Prime$_d$ | Prime$_e$ | Subsequent$_e$ | Prime$_f$ | Subsequent$_f$ |

| Rheme₆ | | | |
|---|---|---|---|
| (καὶ) λυπούμενοι σφόδρα | ἤρξαντο λέγειν αὐτῷ εἷς ἕκαστος· | μήτι | ἐγώ εἰμι, κύριε; |
| Prime$_g$ | Subsequent$_g$ | Prime$_h$ | Subsequent$_h$ |

## Theme$_6$ Rheme$_6$

| ὁ (δὲ) | ἀποκριθεὶς εἶπεν· | ὁ ἐμβάψας | μετ᾽ ἐμοῦ τὴν χεῖρα ἐν τῷ τρυβλίῳ | οὗτός | με παραδώσει. |
|---|---|---|---|---|---|
| Prime$_i$ | Subsequent$_i$ | Prime$_j$ | Subsequent$_j$ | Prime$_k$ | Subsequent$_k$ |

## Rheme$_6$

| ὁ (μὲν) υἱὸς τοῦ ἀνθρώπου | ὑπάγει | (καθὼς) γέγραπται | περὶ αὐτοῦ, |
|---|---|---|---|
| Prime$_l$ | Subsequent$_l$ | Prime$_m$ | Subsequent$_m$ |

## Rheme$_6$

| οὐαὶ (δὲ) | τῷ ἀνθρώπῳ ἐκείνῳ δι᾽ οὗ ὁ υἱὸς τοῦ ἀνθρώπου παραδίδοται· |
|---|---|
| Prime$_n$ | Subsequent$_n$ |

## Rheme$_6$

| ὁ (μὲν) υἱὸς τοῦ ἀνθρώπου | ὑπάγει | (καθὼς) γέγραπται | περὶ αὐτοῦ, |
|---|---|---|---|
| Prime$_o$ | Subsequent$_o$ | Prime$_p$ | Subsequent$_p$ |

## Rheme$_6$

| οὐαὶ (δὲ) | τῷ ἀνθρώπῳ ἐκείνῳ δι᾽ οὗ ὁ υἱὸς τοῦ ἀνθρώπου παραδίδοται· | | καλὸν | ἦν αὐτῷ |
|---|---|---|---|---|
| Prime$_q$ | Subsequent$_q$ | | Prime$_r$ | Subsequent$_r$ |

## THEME AND RHEME ANALYSIS OF MATTHEW 26:14–35

**Rheme$_6$**

| (εἰ) οὐκ | ἐγεννήθη ὁ ἄνθρωπος ἐκεῖνος. |
|---|---|
| Prime$_s$ | Subsequent$_s$ |

### Thematic Unit$_7$

**Rheme$_7$** **Theme$_7$** **Rheme$_7$**

| ἀποκριθεὶς (δὲ) | Ἰούδας ὁ παραδιδοὺς αὐτὸν εἶπεν· | μήτι | ἐγώ εἰμι, ῥαββί; |
|---|---|---|---|
| Prime$_a$ | Subsequent$_a$ | Prime$_b$ | Subsequent$_b$ |

**Rheme$_7$**

| λέγει | αὐτῷ· | σὺ | εἶπας. |
|---|---|---|---|
| Prime$_c$ | Subsequent$_c$ | Prime$_d$ | Subsequent$_d$ |

### Thematic Unit$_8$

**Rheme$_8$** **Theme$_8$**

| Ἐσθιόντων (δὲ) | αὐτῶν | λαβὼν | ὁ Ἰησοῦς ἄρτον καὶ εὐλογήσας ἔκλασεν |
|---|---|---|---|
| Prime$_a$ | Subsequent$_a$ | Prime$_b$ | Subsequent$_b$ |

**Rheme$_8$**

| (καὶ) δοὺς | τοῖς μαθηταῖς εἶπεν· | λάβετε | φάγετε, | τοῦτό | ἐστιν τὸ σῶμά μου. |
|---|---|---|---|---|---|
| Prime$_c$ | Subsequent$_c$ | Prime$_d$ | Prime$_e$ | Prime$_f$ | Subsequent$_f$ |

**Rheme₈**

| (καὶ) λαβὼν | ποτήριον καὶ εὐχαριστήσας ἔδωκεν αὐτοῖς λέγων· | πίετε | ἐξ αὐτοῦ πάντες, |
|---|---|---|---|
| Prime$_g$ | Subsequent$_g$ | Prime$_h$ | Subsequent$_h$ |

**Rheme₈**

| τοῦτο (γάρ) | ἐστιν τὸ αἷμά μου τῆς διαθήκης τὸ περὶ πολλῶν ἐκχυννόμενον εἰς ἄφεσιν ἁμαρτιῶν. |
|---|---|
| Prime$_i$ | Subsequent$_i$ |

**Rheme₈**

| λέγω (δὲ) | ὑμῖν, | οὐ μὴ | πίω ἀπ᾽ ἄρτι ἐκ τούτου τοῦ γενήματος τῆς ἀμπέλου ἕως τῆς ἡμέρας ἐκείνης |
|---|---|---|---|
| Prime$_j$ | Subsequent$_j$ | Prime$_k$ | Subsequent$_k$ |

**Rheme₈**

| (ὅταν) αὐτὸ | πίνω εθ᾽ ὑμῶν καινὸν ἐν τῇ βασιλείᾳ τοῦ πατρός μου. | (Καὶ) ὑμνήσαντες | ἐξῆλθον εἰς τὸ ὄρος τῶν ἐλαιῶν. |
|---|---|---|---|
| Prime$_l$ | Subsequent$_l$ | Prime$_m$ | Subsequent$_m$ |

# THEME AND RHEME ANALYSIS OF MATTHEW 26:14–35

## Thematic Unit$_9$

**Rheme$_9$**

| Τότε | λέγει αὐτοῖς ὁ Ἰησοῦς· | πάντες ὑμεῖς | σκανδαλισθήσεσθε ἐν ἐμοὶ ἐν τῇ νυκτὶ ταύτῃ, |
|---|---|---|---|
| Prime$_a$ | Subsequent$_a$ | Prime$_b$ | Subsequent$_b$ |

**Rheme$_9$**

| γέγραπται (γάρ)· | πατάξω | τὸν ποιμένα, | (καὶ) διασκορπισθήσονται | τὰ πρόβατα τῆς ποίμνης. |
|---|---|---|---|---|
| Prime$_c$ | Prime$_d$ | Subsequent$_d$ | Prime$_e$ | Subsequent$_e$ |

**Rheme$_9$** | | | | **Theme$_9$**

| μετὰ (δὲ) τὸ ἐγερθῆναί με | προάξω ὑμᾶς εἰς τὴν Γαλιλαίαν. | ἀποκριθεὶς (δὲ) | ὁ Πέτρος εἶπεν αὐτῷ· |
|---|---|---|---|
| Prime$_f$ | Prime$_f$ | Subsequent$_g$ | Prime$_g$ |

**Rheme$_9$**

| (εἰ) πάντες | σκανδαλισθήσονται ἐν σοί, | ἐγὼ | οὐδέποτε σκανδαλισθήσομαι. |
|---|---|---|---|
| Prime$_h$ | Subsequent$_h$ | Prime$_i$ | Subsequent$_i$ |

234 APPENDIX 5

### Thematic Unit$_{10}$

| Rheme$_{10}$ | Theme$_{10}$ | Rheme$_{10}$ | | | |
|---|---|---|---|---|---|
| ἔφη | αὐτῷ ὁ Ἰησοῦς· | ἀμὴν | λέγω σοι | ἐγὼ | οὐδέποτε σκανδαλισθήσομαι. |
| Prime$_a$ | Subsequent$_a$ | Prime$_b$ | Subsequent$_b$ | Prime$_c$ | Subsequent$_c$ |

### Thematic Unit$_{11}$

| Rheme$_{11}$ | Theme$_{11}$ | Rheme$_{11}$ | | | |
|---|---|---|---|---|---|
| λέγει | αὐτῷ ὁ Πέτρος· | (κἂν) δέῃ | με σὺν σοὶ ἀποθανεῖν, | οὐ μή | σε ἀπαρνήσομαι. |
| Prime$_a$ | Subsequent$_a$ | Prime$_b$ | Subsequent$_b$ | Prime$_c$ | Subsequent$_c$ |

### Thematic Unit$_{12}$

| Rheme$_{12}$ | Theme$_{11}$ |
|---|---|
| ὁμοίως (καὶ) | πάντες οἱ μαθηταὶ εἶπαν. |
| Prime$_a$ | Subsequent$_a$ |

APPENDIX 6

# Theme and Rheme Analysis of Mark 14:10–31

### Thematic Unit$_1$

| Theme$_1$ | Rheme$_1$ | | |
|---|---|---|---|
| (Καὶ) Ἰούδας Ἰσκαριὼθ | ὁ εἷς τῶν δώδεκα ἀπῆλθεν πρὸς τοὺς ἀρχιερεῖς | (ἵνα) αὐτὸν | παραδοῖ αὐτοῖς. |
| Prime$_a$ | Subsequent$_a$ | Prime$_b$ | Subsequent$_b$ |

### Thematic Unit$_2$

| Theme$_2$ | Rheme$_2$ | | |
|---|---|---|---|
| οἱ (δὲ) | ἀκούσαντες ἐχάρησαν | (καὶ) ἐπηγγείλαντο | αὐτῷ ἀργύριον δοῦναι. |
| Prime$_a$ | Subsequent$_a$ | Prime$_b$ | Subsequent$_b$ |

| Rheme$_2$ | | |
|---|---|---|
| (καὶ) ἐζήτει | πῶς | αὐτὸν εὐκαίρως παραδοῖ. |
| Prime$_c$ | Prime$_d$ | Subsequent$_d$ |

© HOJOON J. AHN, 2024 | DOI:10.1163/9789004696372_015

## Thematic Unit$_3$

| **Rheme$_3$** | **Theme$_3$ Rheme$_3$** |
|---|---|
| (Καὶ) τῇ πρώτῃ ἡμέρᾳ τῶν ἀζύμων, | (ὅτε) τὸ πάσχα ἔθυον, λέγουσιν αὐτῷ οἱ μαθηταὶ αὐτοῦ· |
| Prime$_a$ | Subsequent$_a$ |

| **Rheme$_3$** | | | | | |
|---|---|---|---|---|---|
| ποῦ | θέλεις ἀπελθόντες ἑτοιμάσωμεν | (ἵνα) φάγῃς | τὸ πάσχα; | (καὶ) ἀποστέλλει | δύο τῶν μαθητῶν αὐτοῦ |
| Prime$_b$ | Subsequent$_b$ | Prime$_c$ | Subsequentc | Prime$_d$ | Subsequent$_d$ |

| **Rheme$_3$** | | | | | |
|---|---|---|---|---|---|
| (καὶ) λέγει | αὐτοῖς· | ὑπάγετε | εἰς τὴν πόλιν, | (καὶ) ἀπαντήσει | ὑμῖν ἄνθρωπος κεράμιον ὕδατος βαστάζων· |
| Prime$_e$ | Subsequent$_e$ | Prime$_f$ | Subsequent$_f$ | Prime$_g$ | Subsequent$_g$ |

| **Rheme$_3$** | | | | | | | |
|---|---|---|---|---|---|---|---|
| (καὶ) ὅπου | ἐὰν εἰσέλθῃ | εἴπατε | τῷ οἰκοδεσπότῃ | (ὅτι) ὁ διδάσκαλος | λέγει· | ποῦ | ἐστιντὸ κατάλυμά μου |
| Prime$_h$ | Subsequent$_h$ | Prime$_i$ | Subsequent$_i$ | Prime$_j$ | Subsequent$_j$ | Prime$_k$ | Subsequent$_k$ |

# THEME AND RHEME ANALYSIS OF MARK 14:10–31

### Rheme₃

| ὅπου | τὸ πάσχα μετὰ τῶν μαθητῶν μου φάγω; | (καὶ) αὐτὸς· | ὑμῖν δείξει ἀνάγαιον μέγα ἐστρωμένον ἕτοιμον |
|---|---|---|---|
| Prime$_l$ | Subsequent$_l$ | Prime$_m$ | Subsequent$_m$ |

### Rheme₃

| (καὶ) ἐκεῖ | ἑτοιμάσατε ἡμῖν. | (καὶ) ἐξῆλθον | οἱ μαθηταὶ | (καὶ) ἦλθον | εἰς τὴν πόλιν | (καὶ) εὗρον |
|---|---|---|---|---|---|---|
| Prime$_n$ | Subsequent$_n$ | Prime$_o$ | Subsequent$_o$ | Prime$_p$ | Subsequent$_p$ | Prime$_q$ |

### Rheme₃

| (καθὼς) εἶπεν | αὐτοῖς | (καὶ) ἡτοίμασαν | τὸ πάσχα. |
|---|---|---|---|
| Prime$_r$ | Subsequent$_r$ | Prime$_s$ | Subsequent$_s$ |

## Thematic Unit₄

### Rheme₄

| (Καὶ) ὀψίας γενομένης | ἔρχεται μετὰ τῶν δώδεκα. |
|---|---|
| Primea | Subsequenta |

### Rheme₄ / Theme₄

| (καὶ) ἀνακειμένων | αὐτῶν | (καὶ) ἐσθιόντων | ὁ Ἰησοῦς | εἶπεν· |
|---|---|---|---|---|
| Prime$_b$ | Subsequent$_b$ | Prime$_c$ | Prime$_d$ | Subsequent$_d$ |

## Rheme$_4$

| ἀμὴν | λέγω ὑμῖν | (ὅτι) εἷς ἐξ ὑμῶν | παραδώσει με | ὁ ἐσθίων | μετ᾽ ἐμοῦ. |
|---|---|---|---|---|---|
| Prime$_e$ | Subsequent$_e$ | Prime$_f$ | Subsequent$_f$ | Prime$_g$ | Subsequent$_g$ |

## Rheme$_4$

| ἤρξαντο | λυπεῖσθαι καὶ λέγειν αὐτῷ εἷς κατὰ εἷς· | μήτι | ἐγώ; | ὁ (δὲ) | εἶπεν αὐτοῖς· |
|---|---|---|---|---|---|
| Prime$_h$ | Subsequent$_h$ | Prime$_i$ | Subsequent$_i$ | Prime$_j$ | Subsequent$_j$ |

## Rheme$_4$

| εἷς τῶν δώδεκα, | ὁ ἐμβαπτόμενος μετ᾽ ἐμοῦ εἰς τὸ τρύβλιον. | (ὅτι) ὁ (μὲν) υἱὸς τοῦ ἀνθρώπου | ὑπάγει |
|---|---|---|---|
| Prime$_k$ | Subsequent$_k$ | Prime$_l$ | Subsequent$_l$ |

## Rheme$_4$

| (καθὼς) γέγραπται | περὶ αὐτοῦ, | οὐαὶ (δὲ) | τῷ ἀνθρώπῳ ἐκείνῳ | δι᾽ οὗ | ὁ υἱὸς τοῦ ἀνθρώπου παραδίδοται· |
|---|---|---|---|---|---|
| Prime$_m$ | Subsequent$_m$ | Prime$_n$ | Subsequent$_n$ | Prime$_o$ | Subsequent$_o$ |

## Rheme$_4$

| καλὸν | αὐτῷ | (εἰ) οὐκ | ἐγεννήθη ὁ ἄνθρωπος ἐκεῖνος. | (Καὶ) ἐσθιόντων | αὐτῶν |
|---|---|---|---|---|---|
| Prime$_p$ | Subsequent$_p$ | Prime$_q$ | Subsequent$_q$ | Prime$_r$ | Subsequent$_r$ |

# THEME AND RHEME ANALYSIS OF MARK 14:10–31

**Rheme₄**

| λαβὼν | ἄρτον εὐλογήσας ἔκλασεν | (καὶ) ἔδωκεν | αὐτοῖς | (καὶ) εἶπεν· | λάβετε, |
|---|---|---|---|---|---|
| Prime$_s$ | Subsequent$_s$ | Prime$_t$ | Subsequent$_t$ | Prime$_u$ | Prime$_v$ |

**Rheme₄**

| τοῦτό | ἐστιν τὸ σῶμά μου. | (καὶ) λαβὼν | ποτήριον εὐχαριστή- σας ἔδωκεν αὐτοῖς, | (καὶ) ἔπιον | ἐξ αὐτοῦ πάντες. |
|---|---|---|---|---|---|
| Prime$_w$ | Subsequent$_w$ | Prime$_x$ | Subsequent$_x$ | Prime$_y$ | Subsequent$_y$ |

**Rheme₄**

| (καὶ) εἶπεν | αὐτοῖς· | τοῦτό | ἐστιν τὸ αἷμά μου τῆς διαθήκης τὸ ἐκχυννόμενον ὑπὲρ πολλῶν. |
|---|---|---|---|
| Prime$_z$ | Subsequent$_z$ | Prime$_{a'}$ | Subsequent$_{a'}$ |

**Rheme₄**

| ἀμὴν | λέγω ὑμῖν | (ὅτι) οὐκέτι | οὐ μὴ πίω ἐκ τοῦ γενήματος τῆς ἀμπέλου ἕως τῆς ἡμέρας ἐκείνης |
|---|---|---|---|
| Prime$_{b'}$ | Subsequent $_{b'}$ | Prime$_{c'}$ | Subsequent$_{c'}$ |

**Rheme₄**

| (ὅταν) αὐτὸ | πίνω καινὸν ἐν τῇ βασιλείᾳ τοῦ θεοῦ. | (Καὶ) ὑμνήσαντες | ἐξῆλθον εἰς τὸ ὄρος τῶν ἐλαιῶν. |
|---|---|---|---|
| Prime$_{d'}$ | Subsequent$_{d'}$ | Prime$_{e'}$ | Subsequent$_{e'}$ |

240 APPENDIX 6

## Thematic Unit$_5$

### Rheme$_5$

| (καὶ) λέγει | αὐτοῖς ὁ Ἰησοῦς | (ὅτι) πάντες | σκανδαλισθήσεσθε, | (ὅτι) γέγραπται· |
|---|---|---|---|---|
| Prime$_a$ | Subsequent$_a$ | Prime$_b$ | Subsequent$_b$ | Prime$_c$ |

### Rheme$_5$

| πατάξω | τὸν ποιμένα, | (καὶ) τὰ πρόβατα | διασκορπισθήσονται. | (ἀλλὰ) μετὰ τὸ ἐγερθῆναί με | προάξω ὑμᾶς εἰς τὴν Γαλιλαίαν. |
|---|---|---|---|---|---|
| Prime$_d$ | Subsequent$_d$ | Prime$_e$ | Subsequent$_e$ | Prime$_f$ | Subsequent$_f$ |

### Theme$_5$ — Rheme$_5$

| ὁ (δὲ) Πέτρος | ἔφη αὐτῷ· | εἰ καὶ πάντες | σκανδαλισθήσονται, | ἀλλ᾽ οὐκ | ἐγώ. |
|---|---|---|---|---|---|
| Prime$_g$ | Subsequent$_g$ | Prime$_h$ | Subsequent$_h$ | Prime$_i$ | Subsequent$_i$ |

## Thematic Unit$_6$

### Rheme$_6$ — Theme$_6$ — Rheme$_6$

| (καὶ) λέγει | αὐτῷ ὁ Ἰησοῦς | ἀμὴν | λέγω σοι |
|---|---|---|---|
| Prime$_a$ | Subsequent$_a$ | Prime$_b$ | Subsequent$_b$ |

# Rheme₆

| (ὅτι) σύ | σήμερον ταύτῃ τῇ νυκτὶ πρὶν ἢ δὶς ἀλέκτορα φωνῆσαι τρίς με ἀπαρνήσῃ. |
|---|---|
| Prime_c | Subsequent_c |

## Thematic Unit₇

| Theme₇ | Rheme₇ | | | | |
|---|---|---|---|---|---|
| ὁ | (δὲ) ἐκπερισσῶς ἐλάλει | (ἐὰν) δέῃ με | συναποθανεῖν σοι, | οὐ μή | σε ἀπαρνήσομαι. |
| Prime_a | Subsequent_a | Prime_b | Subsequent_b | Prime_c | Subsequent_c |

## Thematic Unit₈

| Rheme₈ | Theme₈ Rheme₈ |
|---|---|
| ὡσαύτως | (δὲ) (καὶ) πάντες ἔλεγον. |
| Prime_a | Subsequent_a |

APPENDIX 7

# Theme and Rheme Analysis of Luke 22:3–23, 31–34

## Thematic Unit₁

| Rheme₁ | Theme₁ Rheme₁ |
|---|---|
| Εἰσῆλθεν | (δὲ) σατανᾶς εἰς Ἰούδαν τὸν καλούμενον Ἰσκαριώτην, ὄντα ἐκ τοῦ ἀριθμοῦ τῶν δώδεκα· |
| Primeₐ | Subsequentₐ |

### Rheme₁

| (καὶ) ἀπελθὼν | συνελάλησεν τοῖς ἀρχιερεῦσιν καὶ στρατηγοῖς | τὸ πῶς | αὐτοῖς παραδῷ αὐτόν. |
|---|---|---|---|
| Primeᵦ | Subsequentᵦ | Primeᵪ | Subsequentᵪ |

### Rheme₁

| (καὶ) ἐχάρησαν | (καὶ) συνέθεντο | αὐτῷ ἀργύριον δοῦναι. | (καὶ) ἐξωμολόγησεν, |
|---|---|---|---|
| Primeₔ | Primeₑ | Subsequentₑ | Primef |

### Rheme₁

| (καὶ) ἐζήτει | εὐκαιρίαν τοῦ παραδοῦναι αὐτὸν ἄτερ ὄχλου αὐτοῖς. |
|---|---|
| Primeₘ | Subsequentₘ |

© HOJOON J. AHN, 2024 | DOI:10.1163/9789004696372_016

# THEME AND RHEME ANALYSIS OF LUKE 22:3–23, 31–34

### Thematic Unit₂

| Rheme₂ | Theme₂ | Rheme₂ | |
|---|---|---|---|
| ῟Ηλθεν | (δὲ) ἡ ἡμέρα τῶν ἀζύμων, | [ἐν] ᾗ ἔδει θύεσθαι | τὸ πάσχα· |
| Primeₐ | Subsequentₐ | Prime_b | Subsequent_b |

| Rheme₂ | | | |
|---|---|---|---|
| (καὶ) ἀπέστειλεν | Πέτρον καὶ Ἰωάννην εἰπών· | πορευθέντες | ἑτοιμάσατε ἡμῖν τὸ πάσχα ἵνα φάγωμεν. |
| Prime_c | Subsequent_c | Prime_d | Subsequent_d |

### Thematic Unit₃

| Theme₃ | Rheme₃ | | |
|---|---|---|---|
| οἱ | (δὲ) εἶπαν αὐτῷ· | ποῦ | θέλεις ἑτοιμάσωμεν; |
| Primeₐ | Subsequentₐ | Prime_b | Subsequent_b |

### Thematic Unit₄

| Theme₄ | Rheme₄ | | | |
|---|---|---|---|---|
| ὁ | (δὲ) εἶπεν αὐτοῖς· | ἰδοὺ | εἰσελθόντων | ὑμῶν εἰς τὴν πόλιν συναντήσει ὑμῖν ἄνθρωπος κεράμιον ὕδατος βαστάζων· |
| Primeₐ | Subsequentₐ | Prime_b | Prime_c | Subsequent_c |

**Rheme$_4$**

| ἀκολουθήσατε | αὐτῷ εἰς τὴν οἰκίαν εἰς ἣν εἰσπορεύεται, | (καὶ) ἐρεῖτε | τῷ οἰκοδεσπότῃ τῆς οἰκίας· |
|---|---|---|---|
| Prime$_d$ | Subsequent$_d$ | Prime$_e$ | Subsequent$_e$ |

**Rheme$_4$**

| λέγει | σοι ὁ διδάσκαλος· | ποῦ | ἐστιν τὸ κατάλυμα ὅπου τὸ πάσχα μετὰ τῶν μαθητῶν μου φάγω; |
|---|---|---|---|
| Prime$_f$ | Subsequent$_f$ | Prime$_g$ | Subsequent$_g$ |

**Rheme$_4$**

| κἀκεῖνος ὑμῖν | δείξει ἀνάγαιον μέγα ἐστρωμένον· | ἐκεῖ | ἑτοιμάσατε. |
|---|---|---|---|
| Prime$_h$ | Subsequent$_h$ | Prime$_i$ | Subsequent$_i$ |

**Rheme$_4$**

| ἀπελθόντες | (δὲ) εὗρον καθὼς εἰρήκει αὐτοῖς | (καὶ) ἡτοίμασαν | τὸ πάσχα. |
|---|---|---|---|
| Prime$_j$ | Subsequent$_j$ | Prime$_k$ | Subsequent$_k$ |

## Thematic Unit$_5$

**Rheme$_5$** | **Theme$_5$**

| (Καὶ) ὅτε | ἐγένετο ἡ ὥρα, |
|---|---|
| Prime$_a$ | Subsequent$_a$ |

# THEME AND RHEME ANALYSIS OF LUKE 22:3–23, 31–34

## Thematic Unit$_6$

| Rheme$_6$ | Theme$_6$ | Rheme$_6$ | |
|---|---|---|---|
| ἀνέπεσεν | (καὶ) οἱ ἀπόστολοι σὺν αὐτῷ. | (καὶ) εἶπεν | πρὸς αὐτούς· |
| Prime$_a$ | Subsequent$_a$ | Prime$_b$ | Subsequent$_b$ |

| Rheme$_6$ | |
|---|---|
| ἐπιθυμίᾳ | ἐπεθύμησα τοῦτο τὸ πάσχα φαγεῖν μεθ᾽ ὑμῶν πρὸ τοῦ με παθεῖν· |
| Prime$_c$ | Subsequent$_c$ |

| Rheme$_6$ | | | |
|---|---|---|---|
| λέγω | (γὰρ) ὑμῖν | (ὅτι) οὐ μὴ | φάγω αὐτὸ ἕως ὅτου πληρωθῇ ἐν τῇ βασιλείᾳ τοῦ θεοῦ. |
| Prime$_d$ | Subsequent$_d$ | Prime$_e$ | Subsequent$_e$ |

| Rheme$_6$ | | | | | |
|---|---|---|---|---|---|
| (καὶ) δεξάμενος | ποτήριον | εὐχαριστήσας | εἶπεν· | λάβετε | τοῦτο |
| Prime$_f$ | Subsequent$_f$ | Prime$_g$ | Subsequent$_g$ | Prime$_h$ | Subsequent$_h$ |

| Rheme$_6$ | | | |
|---|---|---|---|
| (καὶ) διαμερίσατε | εἰς ἑαυτούς· | λέγω | (γὰρ) ὑμῖν, |
| Prime$_i$ | Subsequent$_i$ | Prime$_j$ | Subsequent$_j$ |

**Rheme6**

| [ὅτι] οὐ μὴ | πίω ἀπὸ τοῦ νῦν ἀπὸ τοῦ γενήματος τῆς ἀμπέλου ἕως οὗ ἡ βασιλεία τοῦ θεοῦ ἔλθῃ. |
|---|---|
| Prime$_k$ | Subsequent$_k$ |

**Rheme6**

| (Καὶ) λαβὼν | ἄρτον εὐχαριστήσας ἔκλασεν | (καὶ) ἔδωκεν | αὐτοῖς λέγων· |
|---|---|---|---|
| Prime$_l$ | Subsequent$_l$ | Prime$_m$ | Subsequent$_m$ |

**Rheme6**

| τοῦτό | ἐστιν τὸ σῶμά μου τὸ ὑπὲρ ὑμῶν διδόμενον· | τοῦτο | ποιεῖτε εἰς τὴν ἐμὴν ἀνάμνησιν. |
|---|---|---|---|
| Prime$_n$ | Subsequent$_n$ | Prime$_o$ | Subsequent$_o$ |

**Rheme6**

| (καὶ) τὸ ποτήριον | ὡσαύτως μετὰ τὸ δει- πνῆσαι, λέγων· | τοῦτο | τὸ ποτήριον ἡ καινὴ διαθήκη ἐν τῷ αἵματί μου τὸ ὑπὲρ ὑμῶν ἐκχυννόμενον. |
|---|---|---|---|
| Prime$_n$ | Subsequent$_n$ | Prime | Subsequent$_o$ |

**Rheme6**

| Πλὴν | ἰδοὺ | ἡ χεὶρ τοῦ παραδιδόντος με μετ᾽ ἐμοῦ | ἐπὶ τῆς τραπέζης. |
|---|---|---|---|
| Prime$_n$ | Subsequent$_n$ | Prime$_o$ | Subsequent$_o$ |

# THEME AND RHEME ANALYSIS OF LUKE 22:3–23, 31–34

## Rheme$_6$

| (ὅτι) ὁ υἱὸς μὲν τοῦ ἀνθρώπου | κατὰ τὸ ὡρισμένον πορεύεται, | πλὴν οὐαὶ | τῷ ἀνθρώπῳ ἐκείνῳ δι' οὗ παραδίδοται. |
|---|---|---|---|
| Prime$_n$ | Subsequent$_n$ | Prime$_o$ | Subsequent$_o$ |

## Rheme$_6$

| (καὶ) αὐτοὶ | ἤρξαντο συζητεῖν πρὸς ἑαυτοὺς τὸ τίς ἄρα εἴη ἐξ αὐτῶν ὁ τοῦτο μέλλων πράσσειν. |
|---|---|
| Prime$_p$ | Subsequent$_p$ |

## Thematic Unit$_7$

| Rheme$_7$ | | Theme$_7$ | Rheme$_7$ |
|---|---|---|---|
| Σίμων Σίμων, | | ἰδοὺ | ὁ σατανᾶς ἐξητήσατο ὑμᾶς τοῦ σινιάσαι ὡς τὸν σῖτον· |
| Prime$_a$ | | Prime$_b$ | Subsequent$_b$ |

## Thematic Unit$_8$

| Theme$_8$ | Rheme$_8$ |
|---|---|
| ἐγὼ | (δὲ) ἐδεήθην περὶ σοῦ ἵνα μὴ ἐκλίπῃ ἡ πίστις σου· |
| Prime$_a$ | Subsequent$_a$ |

### Rheme$_8$

| | |
|---|---|
| (καὶ) σύ | ποτε ἐπιστρέψας στήρισον τοὺς ἀδελφούς σου. |
| Prime$_b$ | Subsequent$_b$ |

## Thematic Unit$_9$

| Theme$_9$ | Rheme$_9$ | | |
|---|---|---|---|
| ὁ | (δὲ) εἶπεν αὐτῷ· | κύριε, | μετὰ σοῦ ἕτοιμός εἰμι καὶ εἰς φυλακὴν καὶ εἰς θάνατον πορεύεσθαι. |
| Prime$_a$ | Subsequent$_a$ | Prime$_b$ | Subsequent$_b$ |

## Thematic Unit$_{10}$

| Theme$_{10}$ | Rheme$_{10}$ | | |
|---|---|---|---|
| ὁ | (δὲ) εἶπεν· | λέγω | σοι, |
| Prime$_a$ | Subsequent$_a$ | Prime$_b$ | Subsequent$_b$ |

### Rheme$_{10}$

| | |
|---|---|
| Πέτρε, | οὐ φωνήσει σήμερον ἀλέκτωρ ἕως τρίς με ἀπαρνήσῃ εἰδέναι. |
| Prime$_c$ | Subsequent$_c$ |

APPENDIX 8

# Theme and Rheme Analysis of Luke 22:24–30

### Thematic Unit₁

| Rheme₁ | Theme₁ | Rheme₁ |
|---|---|---|
| Ἐγένετο (δὲ καὶ) | φιλονεικία ἐν αὐτοῖς, τὸ τίς αὐτῶν δοκεῖ εἶναι μείζων. | |
| Primeₐ | Subsequentₐ | |

### Thematic Unit₂

| Theme₂ | Rheme₂ | | |
|---|---|---|---|
| ὁ (δὲ) | εἶπεν αὐτοῖς· | οἱ βασιλεῖς τῶν ἐθνῶν | κυριεύουσιν αὐτῶν |
| Primeₐ | Subsequentₐ | Primeᵦ | Subsequentᵦ |

**Rheme₂**

| καὶ οἱ ἐξουσιάζοντες αὐτῶν | εὐεργέται καλοῦνται. | ὑμεῖς δὲ | οὐχ οὕτως, | ἀλλ᾽ ὁ μείζων ἐν ὑμῖν | γινέσθω ὡς ὁ νεώτερος |
|---|---|---|---|---|---|
| Primec | Subsequentc | Primed | Subsequentd | Primee | Subsequente |

**Rheme₂**

| καὶ ὁ ἡγούμενος | ὡς ὁ διακονῶν. | τίς γὰρ | μείζων, | ὁ ἀνακείμενος | ἢ ὁ διακονῶν; | οὐχὶ | ὁ ἀνακείμενος; |
|---|---|---|---|---|---|---|---|
| Primef | Subsequentf | Primeg | Subsequentg | Primeh | Subsequenth | Primei | Subsequenti |

© HOJOON J. AHN, 2024 | DOI:10.1163/9789004696372_017

**Rheme₂**

| ἐγὼ δὲ | ἐν μέσῳ ὑμῶν εἰμι ὡς ὁ διακονῶν. | Ὑμεῖς δέ | ἐστε οἱ διαμεμενηκότες μετ' ἐμοῦ ἐν τοῖς πειρασμοῖς μου· |
|---|---|---|---|
| Primeⱼ | Subsequentⱼ | Primeₖ | Subsequentₖ |

**Rheme₂**

| κἀγὼ | διατίθεμαι ὑμῖν | καθὼς διέθετό | μοι ὁ πατήρ μου βασιλείαν, | ἵνα ἔσθητε |
|---|---|---|---|---|
| Primeₗ | Subsequentₗ | Primeₘ | Subsequentₘ | Primeₙ |

**Rheme₂**

| καὶ πίνητε | ἐπὶ τῆς τραπέζης μου ἐν τῇ βασιλείᾳ μου, | καὶ καθήσεσθε | ἐπὶ θρόνων τὰς δώδεκα φυλὰς κρίνοντες τοῦ Ἰσραήλ. |
|---|---|---|---|
| Primeₒ | Subsequentₒ | Primeₚ | Subsequentₚ |

APPENDIX 9

# Translation of Matthew 26:14–35 Based on Conjunction and Verbal Aspect Analysis

The imperfective aspect in verbs will be marked as italic, and the stative aspect as bold. In this translation, the paragraph division and the meaning of conjunctions are expressed together.

---

[14] At that time, one of the twelve, who *is called* (λεγόμενος) Judas Iscariot, goes to the chief priests,
[15] (and) says,
  "What *are* you *willing* (θέλετε) to give me, if I hand him over to you?"
Then they weigh out to him thirty pieces of silver. [16] So, from that moment, he *seeks* (ἐζήτει) an opportunity to hand him over.

[17] On the first day of Unleavened Bread, the disciples come to Jesus, *saying* (λέγοντες),
  "Where do you *want* (θέλεις) us to prepare for you to eat the Passover?"
[18] Then he says,
  "*Go* (ὑπάγετε) into the city to a certain one, and say to him,
    'The teacher *says* (λέγει),
      "My time *is* (ἐστιν) at hand; I *will keep* (ποιῶ) the Passover at your house[a]
      with my disciples."'
[19] So the disciples do as Jesus orders them, and they prepare the Passover.

[20] Now, when evening comes, he *lays down* (ἀνέκειτο)[b] at the table with the twelve disciples. [21] And as they *are eating* (ἐσθιόντων), he says,
  "Truly, I *say* (λέγω) to you,[c] one of you will hand over me."

---

a   It is a non-literary translation of πρὸς σέ, considering its context. Literally translated, it could be "with you/to you."

b   Ἀνάκειμαι, which appears here, is an indicative imperfect middle third-person singular form of ἀνάκειμαι, and it is a vocabulary that reflects the culture of lying down and eating at an angle.

c   This phrase (ἀμὴν λέγω ὑμῖν) appears thirty-one times in Matthew (in 5:26 and 26:34, it appears as ἀμὴν λέγω σοι; in 18:19, ἀμήν is enclosed in parentheses due to the textual variant, but this was also counted here), thirteen times in Mark, six times in Luke, and twenty-five times in John (for John, in the form of ἀμὴν ἀμὴν λέγω ὑμῖν). It is an authentic teaching style of Jesus to reveal important facts. See Joachim Jeremias, *The Prayers of Jesus* (trans. John Reumann; London: SCM, 1967), 112–15; France, *Matthew*, 184.

© HOJOON J. AHN, 2024 | DOI:10.1163/9789004696372_018

252 APPENDIX 9

(*cont.*)

---

[22] So they *become* deeply *grieved* (λυπούμενοι) and begin to *say* (λέγειν) to him one by one,

> "Surely not *am* (εἰμι) I, Lord?"

[23] Then he answers,

> "He, who dips his hand in this vessel with me, will hand me over. [24] The son of man *departs* (ὑπάγει) as it **is written** (γέγραπται) of him, but woe to that man by whom the son of man is handed over! It would have been better for that man if he had not been born."

[25] Then Judas, who *betrays* (παραδιδοὺς) him, says,

> "Surely not *am* (εἰμι) I, Rabbi?"

He *says* (λέγει) to him,

> "You speak."

[26] Now while they *were eating* (ἐσθιόντων), taking a bread,[d] praising,[e] Jesus breaks it, and distributing it to the disciples, he says,

> "Receive, eat; this *is* (ἐστιν) my body."

[27] And taking a cup, giving thanks, he gives it to them, saying,

> "Drink from it, all of you, [28] for this *is* (ἐστιν) my blood of the covenant, which *is poured out* (ἐκχυννόμενον) for many for the liberation[f] from sins. [29] But I *say* (λέγω) to you, I will never drink from the fruit of the vine until the day I *drink* (πίνω) new one with you in the kingdom[g] of my father."

[30] And singing hymns, they go out to the Mount of Olives.

[31] At that time, Jesus says to them,

> "All of you will stumble in me this night, for it **is written** (γέγραπται),
>> 'I will strike the shepherd, and the flock will be scattered.'[h]

[32] But after I have been raised, I will go before you into Galilee."

[33] But Peter says (or replies),

> "Even if they all stumble in you, I will not stumble."

---

d  Here "bread" (goal) is singular, which shows one bread. The emphasis on the "one bread" is also found in 1 Cor 10:17.

e  The basic meaning of εὐλογέω seems twofold: 1. Bless; 2. Praise. See Louw and Nida, *Greek-English Lexicon*, 429–30, 442; Thyer, *Greek-English Lexicon*, 259.

f  The lexeme ἄφεσις basically means liberation; thus, 26:28 reveals the purpose of Jesus' death: freedom from sin for many. The possibility of having the individual sin forgiven and free from the sin itself, but also the concept of freedom from sin as a power.

g  This passage may show the end of Jesus' earthly life ("no more drinking of wine") and the future triumph in the Kingdom of God, which has the image of Messianic banquet. See France, *Matthew*, 995.

h  Zech 13:7.

# TRANSLATION OF MATTHEW 26:14–35

(*cont.*)

---

[34] Jesus says to him,

"Truly, I *say* (λέγει) to you, this night, before the rooster crows, you will deny me three times."

[35] Peter *says* (λέγει) to him,

"Even if I *have to* (δέη) die with you, I will not deny you."

And likewise say all the disciples.

---

APPENDIX 10

# Translation of Mark 14:10–31 Based on Conjunction and Verbal Aspect Analysis

[10] Now, Judas Iscariot, who is one of the twelve, departs to the chief priests in order to hand him over to them. [11] Then, when hearing it, they are glad and promise to give him silver. So, he *seeks* (ἐζήτει) an opportunity to hand him over to them.

[12] Now, on the first day of Unleavened bread, when they *sacrifice* (ἔθυον) the Passover lamb, his disciples *say* (λέγουσιν) to him,

"Where do you *want* (θέλεις) us go and prepare for you to eat the Passover?"

[13] So he *sends* (ἀποστέλλει) two of his disciples, and *says* (λέγει) to them:

"*Go* (ὑπάγετε) into the city, and a man *carrying* (βαστάζων) a jar of water will meet you; follow him.

[14] And wherever he enters, say to the householder,

'The teacher *says* (λέγει),

"Where *is* (ἐστιν) my guest room, where I may eat the Passover with my disciples?.'"

[15] and he will show you a large upper room **furnished** (ἐστρωμένον) and ready; there prepare for us."

[16] So the disciples go out, come to the city, and find it as he told them; and they prepare the Passover.

[17] Now, when evening comes, he *comes* (ἔρχεται) with the twelve. [18] As they *are reclining* (ναχειμένων) at the table and *eating* (ἐσθιόντων), Jesus says,

"Truly, I *say* (λέγω) to you, one of you will hand me over, one who *is eating* (ἐσθίων) with me."

[19] They become to *be grieved* (λυπεῖσθαι), and to *say* (λέγειν) to him one by one,

"Not I?"

[20] Then he says to them,

"One of the twelve, one who *is dipping* (ἐμβαπτόμενος) with me into the bowl. [21] For the son of man *departs* (ὑπάγει) as it **is written** (γέγραπται) of him, but woe to that man by whom the son of man *is handed over* (παραδίδοται)! It would have been better for that man if he had not been born."

© HOJOON J. AHN, 2024 | DOI:10.1163/9789004696372_019

# TRANSLATION OF MARK 14:10–31

255

(*cont.*)

---

22 As they *are eating* (ἐσθιόντων), taking a bread, blessing (it), he breaks it and gives it to them. And he says,

"Receive, this *is* (ἐστιν) my body."

23 And taking a cup, giving thanks, he gives it to them, and they all drink from it.

24 And he says to them,

"This *is* (ἐστιν) my blood of the covenant, which *is poured out* (ἐκχυννόμενον) for many. 25 Truly, I *say* (λέγω) to you, I will never drink from the fruit of the vine until the day I *drink* (πίνω) new one in the kingdom of God."

26 Then while singing a hymn, they go out to the Mount of Olives.

27 Now, he *says* (λέγει) to his disciples,

"All of you will stumble, for it **is written** (γέγραπται),

'I will strike the shepherd, and the sheep will be scattered.'

28 But after I am raised up, I will go before you to Galilee."

29 But Peter says to him,

"Even if everyone stumbles, but I do not."

30 And Jesus *says* (λέγει) to him,

"Truly, I *say* (λέγω) to you, this night, before a cock crows twice, you will deny me three times."

31 But he *says* (ἐλάλει) insistently,

"Even if I have to die with you, I will not deny you."

And they *say* (ἔλεγον) likewise.

---

APPENDIX 11

# Translation of Luke 22:3–23, 31–34 Based on Conjunction and Verbal Aspect Analysis

3 However, Satan enters into Judas, *called* (καλούμενον) Iscariot, who is one of the twelve; 4 then he departs and discusses with the chief priests and the officers how he may hand him over to them. 5 So they rejoice and agree to give him silver. 6 Then he consents and *seeks* (ἐζήτει) an opportunity to hand him over to them apart from the multitude.

7 Then the day of Unleavened Bread, on which the Passover lamb *has to be sacrificed* (ἔδει θύεσθαι), comes. 8 And/so he sends Peter and John, saying,
"Go and prepare the Passover for us so that we may eat."
9 Then they say to him,
"Where do you *want* (θέλεις) us to prepare?"
10 And then he says to them,
"Behold, when you have entered the city, a man *carrying* (βαστάζων) a jar of water will meet you; follow him into the house that he *enters* (εἰσπορεύεται). 11 And tell the householder,
'The teacher *says* (λέγει) to you,
"Where *is* (ἐστιν) the guest room in which I may eat the Passover with my disciples?"'
12 and he will show you a large upper room **furnished** (ἐστρωμένον); there, prepare."
13 So they depart and find (it) as he **told** (εἰρήκει) them; and they prepare the Passover.

14 And when the hour has come, he is reclining at the table, and the apostles with him. 15 And he says to them,
"I have eagerly desired to eat this Passover with you before I suffer; 16 for I *say* (λέγω) to you, I shall never eat it until it is fulfilled in the kingdom of God."
17 And taking a cup, giving thanks, he says,
"Take this and divide it among (into) yourselves; 18 for I *say* (λέγω) to you that from now on I will not drink of the fruit of vine until the kingdom of God comes."
19 And taking a bread, giving thanks, he breaks it and gives it to them, *saying* (λέγων),
"This *is* (ἐστιν) my body, which is *given* (διδόμενον) for you. *Do* (ποιεῖτε) this in remembrance of me."

© HOJOON J. AHN, 2024 | DOI:10.1163/9789004696372_020

TRANSLATION OF LUKE 22:3–23, 31–34

(cont.)

---

20 And likewise, (he takes) the cup after supper, *saying* (λέγων),

"This cup (is)ᵃ the new covenant in my blood, which *is poured out* (ἐκχυννόμενον) for you.

21 But behold the hand of the one who *hands* me *over* (παραδιδόντος) (is)ᵇ with me on the table.

22 For the son of man *goes* (πορεύεται) as it **has been determined** (ὡρισμένον); but woe to that man by whom he *is handed over* (παραδίδοται)."

23 Then they begin to *discuss* (συζητεῖν) among themselves, which one of them *is* (εἴη) that *is going to do* (μέλλων πράσσειν) this.

------------------------------- Luke 22:24–30 (omitted) -------------------------------

31 "Simon, Simon, behold, Satan demands to sift you (ὑμᾶς) like wheat; 32 but I pray for you (σοῦ) that your faith (ἡ πίστις σου) may not fail; and when you turn again, strengthen your brothers."

33 Then he says to him,

"Lord, I *am* (εἰμι) ready to *go* (πορεύεσθαι) with you to prison and to death."

34 Then he says,

"I *say* (λέγω) to you, Peter, the cock will not crow today, until you deny three times that you **know** (εἰδέναι) me."

---

a  Here, ἐστιν is omitted.
b  Here, ἐστιν is omitted.

# Bibliography

Abakuks, Andris. *The Synoptic Problem and Statistics*. Boca Raton, FL: CRC, 2015.

Abbott-Smith, G. *A Manual Greek Lexicon of the New Testament*. New York: Charles Scribner's Sons, 1922.

Ahn, Hojoon J. Review of *A Defense for the Chronological Order of Luke's Gospel: The Meaning of 'Orderly' (καθεξῆς) Account in Luke 1:3*, by Benjamin W. W. Fung. *AJ* 13 (2021) 57–58.

Ahn, Hojoon J. "Exploration of the Appropriateness of the Expression 'Author' and 'Author's Intention' in the Synoptic Gospels." *KNTS* 31 (2024) 1–34.

Ahn, Hojoon J. *Fundamental Foundations for the New Testament Gospel Studies*. 2023. Kindle edition.

Ahn, Hojoon J. *History of Interpretation of the Eucharist and Joachim Jeremias*. 2023. Kindle edition.

Ahn, Hojoon J. "Rainer Riesner: A Synthetic-Historical Researcher on the Historical Jesus and Gospel Tradition Studies." In *Pillars in the History of Biblical Interpretation*, edited by Stanley E. Porter and Zachary K. Dawson. Eugene, OR: Wipf & Stock. Forthcoming.

Ahn, Hojoon J. "A Textual-Critical Study of Luke and Verbal Aspect." *BAGL* 11 (2022–23) 37–67.

Ahn, Hojoon J. "Thematization in Luke 4: A Discourse-Thematic Analysis of Luke 4 in Light of the Models of V. Mathesius, M. A. K. Halliday, and S. E. Porter & M. B. O'Donnell." In *The Literary-Linguistic Analysis of the Bible: The Enduring Legacy of Russian Formalism and the Prague Linguistic Circle*, edited by Stanley E. Porter, et al. Leiden: Brill, Forthcoming.

Alexander, Loveday. *The Preface to Luke's Gospel: Literary Convention and Social Context in Luke 1.1–4 and Acts 1.1*. SNTSMS 78. Cambridge: Cambridge University Press, 1993.

Allen, O. Wesley. *Reading the Synoptic Gospels: Basic Methods for Interpreting Matthew, Mark, and Luke*. Saint Louis: Chalice, 2000.

Augustine. *The Harmony of the Gospels*. Translated by S. D. F. Salmond. Bolton: Aeterna, 2014.

Aune, David E. "Greco-Roman Biography." In *Greco-Roman Literature and the New Testament: Selected Forms and Genres*, edited by David E. Aune, 107–26. Atlanta: Scholars, 1988.

Barnes, Timothy D. *Constantine and Eusebius*. Cambridge, MA: Harvard University Press, 1981.

Barrett, C. K. *The First Epistle to the Corinthians*. BNTC. 2nd ed. London: A & C Black, 1971.

BIBLIOGRAPHY

Bauckham, Richard. *Jesus and the Eyewitnesses: The Gospels as Eyewitness Testimony*. 2nd ed. Grand Rapids: Eerdmans, 2017.

Baur, Ferdinand C. *Kritische Untersuchungen über die kanonische Evangelien*. Tübingen: Fues, 1847.

Baum, A. D. "Synoptic Problem." In *Dictionary of Jesus and the Gospels*, edited by Joel B. Green, et al., 911–19. 2nd ed. Nottingham: InterVarsity, 2013.

Beare, Francis W. *The Earliest Records of Jesus: A Companion to the Synopsis of the First Three Gospels by Albert Huck*. New York: Abingdon, 1962.

Beare, Francis W. *The Gospel according to Matthew: Translation, Introduction and Commentary*. New York: Harper & Row, 1981.

Beaugrande, R. de. "'Register' in Discourse Studies: A Concept in Search of a Theory." In *Register Analysis: Theory and Practice*, edited by Mohsen Ghadessy, 7–25. London: Pinter, 1993.

Benoit, Pierre, and Marie-Emile Boismard. *Synopse des quatres Évangiles en français*. Tome II. Paris: Les Éditions du Cerf, 1972.

Biber, Douglas, and Susan Conrad. *Register, Genre, and Style*. CTL. Cambridge: Cambridge University Press, 2009.

Black, Stephanie L. *Sentence Conjunctions in the Gospel of Matthew: καί, δέ, τότε, γάρ, οὖν and Asyndeton in Narrative Discourse*. JSNTSup 216. Sheffield: Sheffield Academic, 2002.

Blass, F., and A. Debrunner. *A Greek Grammar of the New Testament and Other Early Christian Literature*. Translated by Robert W. Funk. Chicago: University of Chicago Press, 1961.

Bock, Darrell L. *Luke 1:1–9:50*. BECNT 3A. Grand Rapids: Baker Academic, 1994.

Bockmuehl, Markus. *Simon Peter in Scripture and Memory: The New Testament Apostle in the Early Church*. Grand Rapids: Baker Academic, 2012.

Botha, Pieter J. J. *Orality and Literacy in Early Christianity*. PBCS 5. Eugene, OR: Cascade, 2012.

Bovon, François. *Luke 1: A Commentary on the Gospel of Luke 1:1–9:50*. Hermeneia. Minneapolis: Fortress, 2002.

Brown, Gillian, and George Yule. *Discourse Analysis*. CTL. Cambridge: Cambridge University Press, 1983.

Brown, Schuyler. *The Origins of Christianity: A Historical Introduction to the New Testament*. Rev. ed. Oxford: Oxford University Press, 1993.

Bultmann, Rudolf. *History of the Synoptic Tradition*. Translated by John Marsh. New York: Harper & Row, 1963.

Burkett, R. Delbert. *An Introduction to the New Testament and the Origins of Christianity*. 2nd ed. Cambridge: Cambridge University Press, 2019.

Burridge, Richard A. "Gospel: Genre." In *Dictionary of Biblical Criticism and Interpretation*, edited by Stanley E. Porter, 129–31. London: Routledge, 2007.

Burridge, Richard A. "Gospel: Genre." In *Dictionary of Jesus and the Gospels*, edited by Joel B. Green, et al., 335–42. 2nd ed. Nottingham: InterVarsity, 2013.

Burridge, Richard A. *What Are the Gospels? A Comparison with Graeco-Roman Biography*. 2nd ed. Grand Rapids: Eerdmans, 2004.

Byrskog, Samuel. *Story as History—History as Story: The Gospel Tradition in the Context of Ancient Oral History*. WUNT 123. Tübingen: Mohr Siebeck, 2000.

Cadbury, Henry J. *The Style and Literary Method of Luke*. Vol. 1 of *The Diction of the Luke and Acts*. Cambridge, MA: Harvard University Press, 1919.

Calvin, John. *Commentary on a Harmony of the Evangelists, Matthew, Mark, and Luke*. Translated by William Pringle. 3 vols. Edinburgh: Calvin Translation Society, 1845.

Casey, Maurice. *Jesus of Nazareth: An Independent Historian's Account of His Life and Teaching*. London: T&T Clark, 2010.

Catford, John C. *A Linguistic Theory of Translation*. London: Oxford University Press, 1965.

Chen, Diane G. *Luke: A New Covenant Commentary*. NCC. Eugene: Cascade, 2017.

Chilton, Bruce. *Profiles of a Rabbi: Synoptic Opportunities in Reading About Jesus*. BJS 177. Atlanta: Scholars, 1989.

Cirafesi, Wally V. *Verbal Aspect in Synoptic Parallels: On the Method and Meaning of Divergent Tense-Form Usage in the Synoptic Passion Narratives*. LBS 7. Leiden: Brill, 2013.

Clements, R. E. "Wellhausen, Julius." In *Dictionary of Major Biblical Interpreters*, edited by Donald K. McKim, 1030–34. Downers Grove: InterVarsity, 2007.

Collins, Adela Y. *Mark: A Commentary*. Hermeneia. Minneapolis: Fortress, 2007.

Conzelmann, Hans. *1 Corinthians: A Commentary on the First Epistle to the Corinthians*. Hermeneia. Translated by James W. Leitch. Philadelphia: Fortress, 1975.

Cotterell, Peter, and Max Turner. *Linguistics and Biblical Interpretation*. Downers Grove: InterVarsity, 1989.

Dahl, Nils A. "Wellhausen on the New Testament." *Semeia* 25 (1983) 89–110.

Davies, W. D., and Dale C. Allison. *The Gospel according to Saint Matthew*. Vol. 1. ICC. Edinburgh: T&T Clark, 1988.

Dawson, Zachary K. "The Problem of Gospel: Unmasking a Flawed Consensus and Providing a Fresh Way Forward with Systemic Functional Linguistics Genre Theory." *BAGL* 8 (2019) 33–77.

Derico, T. M. *Oral Tradition and Synoptic Verbal Agreement: Evaluating the Empirical Evidence for Literary Dependence*. Eugene, OR: Pickwick, 2016.

DeVries, D. "Schleiermacher, Friedrich Daniel Ernst (*1768–1834*)." In *Dictionary of Major Biblical Interpreters*, edited by Donald K. McKim, 885–91. Downers Grove: InterVarsity, 2007.

Dibelius, Martin. *From Tradition to Gospel*. Translated by Bertram L. Woolf. 2nd ed. London: Ivor Nicholson & Watson, 1934.

Dungan, David L. *A History of the Synoptic Problem: The Canon, the Text, the Composition, and the Interpretation of the Gospels*. New York: Doubleday, 1999.

Dunn, James D. G. *The Evidence for Jesus: The Impact of Scholarship on Our Understanding of How Christianity Began*. London: SCM, 1985.

Dunn, James D. G. *The Living Word*. 2nd ed. Philadelphia: Fortress, 2009.

Dunn, James D. G. *The Oral Gospel Tradition*. Grand Rapids: Eerdmans, 2013.

Dvorak, James D. "Thematization, Topic, and Information Flow." *JLIABG* 1 (2008) 17–37.

Dvorak, James D., and Ryder D. Walton. "Clause as Message: Theme, Topic, and Information Flow in Mark 2:1–12 and Jude." *BAGL* 3 (2014) 31–85.

Eggins, Suzanne. *An Introduction to Systemic Functional Linguistics*. London: Pinter, 1994.

Eichhorn, Johann G. *Einleitung in das Neue Testament*. Vol. 1. Leipzig: Weidmannischen Buchhandlung, 1820.

Elder, Nicholas A. "New Testament Media Criticism." *CBR* 15 (2017) 315–37.

Eusebius of Caesarea. *The History of the Church*. Translated by G. A. Williamson. New York: Penguin Books, 1965.

Eusebius of Caesarea. *The History of the Church: A New Translation*. Translated by Jeremy M. Schott. Oakland: University of California Press, 2019.

Evans, Craig A. *Matthew*. NCBC. Cambridge: Cambridge University Press, 2012.

Evans, Craig A. "The Two Source Hypothesis." In *The Synoptic Problem: Four Views*, edited by Stanley E. Porter and Bryan R. Dyer, 27–45. Grand Rapids: Baker Academic, 2016.

Evans, Craig A. "Two Source Hypothesis Response." In *The Synoptic Problem: Four Views*, edited by Stanley E. Porter and Bryan R. Dyer, 113–25. Grand Rapids: Baker Academic, 2016.

Evans, Craig A., ed. *The Historical Jesus: Critical Concepts in Religious Studies. Vol. 1: The History of the Quest: Classical Studies and Critical Questions*. London: Routledge, 2004.

Farmer, William R. *The Synoptic Problem: A Critical Analysis*. New York: Macmillan, 1964.

Farrer, Austin. "Dispensing with Q." In *Studies in the Gospels: Essays in Memory of R. H. Lightfoot*, edited by Dennis E. Nineham, 55–88. Oxford: Blackwell, 1955.

Fawcett, R. P. *Invitation to Systemic Functional Linguistics through the Cardiff Grammar: An Extension and Simplification of Halliday's Systemic Functional Grammar*. 3rd ed. London: Equinox, 2008.

Fee, Gordon D. *The First Epistle to the Corinthians*. Rev. ed. Grand Rapids: Eerdmans, 2014.

Fergusson, D. "Bultmann, Rudolf." In *Dictionary of Major Biblical Interpreters*, edited by Donald K. McKim, 261–67. Downers Grove: InterVarsity, 2007.

Finch, Geoffrey. *Key Concepts in Language and Linguistics*. New York: Palgrave Macmillan, 2005.

Firbas, Jan. "On Defining the Theme in Functional Sentence Analysis." In *Travaux Linguistiques de Prague 1*, edited by Josef Vachek, 267–80. Tuscaloosa: University of Alabama Press, 1966.

Fitzmyer, Joseph A. *Luke the Theologian: Aspects of His Teaching*. Eugene, OR: Wipf & Stock, 1989.

Ford, Coleman M. "Able to Convince Only the Foolish: Anti-Christian Polemic as Social Scrutiny in Celsus's *On the True Doctrine*." *Chu* 133 (2019) 21–33.

Foster, Paul. "Marcion: His Life, Works, Beliefs, and Impact." *ExpT* 121 (2010) 269–80.

France, R. T. *The Gospel of Mark*. NIGTC 2. Grand Rapids: Eerdmans, 2002.

France, R. T. *The Gospel of Matthew*. NICNT 1. Grand Rapids: Eerdmans, 2007.

France, R. T. *Matthew: Evangelist and Teacher*. Downers Grove: InterVarsity, 1998.

Fung, Benjamin W. W. *A Defense for the Chronological Order of Luke's Gospel: The Meaning of "Orderly" (καθεξῆς) Account in Luke 1:3*. AMS 3. Eugene, OR: Wipe & Stock, 2019.

Gamble, Harry Y. *Books and Readers in the Early Church: A History of Early Christian Texts*. New Haven: Yale University Press, 1995.

Garland, David E. *Luke*. ZECNT 3. Grand Rapids: Zondervan, 2011.

Gathercole, Simon. "The Alleged Anonymity of the Canonical Gospels." *JTS* 69 (2018) 447–76.

Gathercole, Simon. "The Earliest Manuscript Title of Matthew's Gospel (BnF Suppl. gr. 1120 ii 3 / Π⁴)." *NT* 54 (2012) 209–35.

Gerhardsson, Birger. *Memory and Manuscript: Oral Tradition and Written Transmission in Rabbinic Judaism and Early Christianity*. Translated by Eric J. Sharpe. Grand Rapids: Eerdmans, 1998.

Gerhardsson, Birger. *The Origins of the Gospel Traditions*. Translated by Gene J. Lund. Philadelphia: Fortress, 1979.

Gieseler, Johann K. L. *Historisch-kritischer Versuch über die Entstehung und die frühesten Schicksale der schriftlichen Evangelien*. Leipzig: Wilhelm Engelmann, 1818.

Gignilliat, Mark S. *Old Testament Criticism: From Benedict Spinoza to Brevard Childs*. Grand Rapids: Zondervan, 2012.

Goodacre, Mark. *The Case Against Q: Studies in Markan Priority and the Synoptic Problem*. Harrisburg, PA: Trinity Press International, 2002.

Goodacre, Mark. "The Farrer Hypothesis." In *The Synoptic Problem: Four Views*, edited by Stanley E. Porter and Bryan R. Dyer, 47–66. Grand Rapids: Baker Academic, 2016.

Green, Joel B. *The Gospel of Luke*. NICNT. Grand Rapids: Eerdmans, 1997.

Griesbach, Johann J. "Commentatio qua Marci evangelium totum e Matthaei et Lucae commentariis decerptum esse monstratur." In *Opuscula academica*, edited by J. P. Gabler, 358–425. Vol. 2. Jena: Fr. Frommanni, 1825.

BIBLIOGRAPHY

Griesbach, Johann J. "A Demonstration that Mark Was Written after Matthew and Luke." In *J. J. Griesbach: Synoptic and Text-Critical Studies 1776–1976*, edited by Bernard Orchard and Thomas R. W. Longstaff, 103–35. Translated by Bernard Orchard. SNTSMS 34. Cambridge: Cambridge University Press, 1978.

Griesbach, Johann J. "Inquiritur in fontes, unde evangelistae suas de resurrectione Domini narrationes hauserint." In *Opuscula academica*, edited by J. P. Gabler, 241–56. Vol. 2. Jena: Fr. Frommanni, 1825.

Gundry, Robert H. *Mark: A Commentary on His Apology for the Cross*. Grand Rapids: Eerdmans, 1993.

Gundry, Robert H. *Matthew: A Commentary on His Handbook for a Mixed Church under Persecution*. 2nd ed. Grand Rapids: Eerdmans, 1994.

Halliday, M. A. K. "The Gloosy Ganoderm: Systemic Functional Linguistics and Translation." In *Halliday in the 21st Century*, edited by Jonathan J. Webster, 105–25. Collected Works of M. A. K. Halliday 11. London: Bloomsbury, 2013.

Halliday, M. A. K. "Grammar and Daily Life: Concurrence and Complementarity." In *On Grammar*, edited by Jonathan J. Webster, 369–83. Collected Works of M. A. K. Halliday 1. London: Continuum, 2002.

Halliday, M. A. K. *Halliday: System and Function in Language*. Edited by Gunther R. Kress. Oxford: Oxford University Press, 1976.

Halliday, M. A. K. *Halliday's Introduction to Functional Grammar*. Revised by Christian M. I. M. Matthiessen. 4th ed. Abingdon: Routledge, 2014.

Halliday, M. A. K. *An Introduction to Functional Grammar*. London: Edward Arnold, 1985.

Halliday, M. A. K. *Language as Social Semiotic: The Social Interpretation of Language and Meaning*. Baltimore: University Park Press, 1978.

Halliday, M. A. K. "Language Structure and Language Function." In *New Horizons in Linguistics*, edited by John Lyons, 140–65. Harmondsworth: Penguin, 1970.

Halliday, M. A. K. *Learning How to Mean: Explorations in the Development of Language*. ELS 2. London: Edward Arnold, 1975.

Halliday, M. A. K. *Spoken and Written Language*. 2nd ed. Oxford: Oxford University Press, 1989.

Halliday, M. A. K. "Text Semantics and Clause Grammar." In *On Grammar*, edited by Jonathan J. Webster, 219–60. Collected Works of M. A. K. Halliday 1. London: Continuum, 2002.

Halliday, M. A. K., and Ruqaiya Hasan. *Cohesion in English*. London: Routledge, 1976.

Halliday, M. A. K., and Ruqaiya Hasan. *Language, Context, and Text: Aspects of Language in a Social-semiotic Perspective*. 2nd ed. Oxford: Oxford University Press, 1989.

Halliday, M. A. K., et al., *The Linguistic Sciences and Language Teaching*. Bloomington: Indiana University Press, 1964.

Henaut, Barry W. *Oral Tradition and the Gospels: The Problem of Mark 4*. JSNTSup 82. Sheffield: Sheffield Academic, 1993.

Hengel, Martin. *The Four Gospels and the One Gospel of Jesus Christ: An Investigation of the Collection and Origin of the Canonical Gospels*. Translated by John Bowden. Harrisburg: Trinity Press International, 2000.

Hengel, Martin. *Studies in the Gospel of Mark*. Philadelphia: Fortress, 1985.

Herder, Johann G. von. *Against Pure Reason: Writings on Religion, Language, and History*. Edited and translated by Marcia Bunge. Minneapolis: Fortress, 1993.

Holton, David, et al., *Greek: An Essential Grammar*. 2nd ed. New York: Routledge, 2016.

Holtzmann, Heinlich J. *Die synoptischen Evangelien: Ihr Ursprung und geschichtlicher Charakter*. Leipzig: Wilhelm Engelmann, 1863.

Horsley, Richard A. *1 Corinthians*. ANTC. Nashville: Abingdon, 1998.

Hug, Johann L. *Hug's Introduction to the New Testament*. Translated by David Fosdick Jr. Andover: Gould & Newman, 1836.

Hunt, Emily J. *Christianity in the Second Century: The Case of Tatian*. London: Routledge, 2003.

Jacobsen, David S. *Mark*. FBPC. Minneapolis: Fortress, 2014.

Jeffrey, David L. *Luke*. BTCB. Grand Rapids: Brazos, 2012.

Jeremias, Joachim. *The Eucharistic Words of Jesus*. Translated by Norman Perrin. Philadelphia: Fortress, 1981.

Jeremias, Joachim. *The Prayers of Jesus*. Translated by John Reumann. London: SCM, 1967.

Johnson, Luke T. *The Gospel of Luke*. SPS 3. Collegeville: Liturgical, 1991.

Justin. "The First Apology." In *The Fathers of the Church: Saint Justin Martyr*, edited by Hermigild Dressler, et al., 33–111. Translated by Thomas B. Falls. Washington, DC: Catholic University of America Press, 1948.

Karamanolis, George. *The Philosophy of Early Christianity*. 2nd ed. London: Routledge, 2021.

Keener, Craig S. *Christobiography: Memory, History, and the Reliability of the Gospels*. Grand Rapids: Eerdmans, 2019.

Keith, Chris, et al., "Introduction." In *The Reception of Jesus in the First Three Centuries*, edited by Helen K. Bond, 1:xv–xxvii. London: T&T Clark, 2020.

Kelber, Werner H. *Imprints, Voiceprints, and Footprints of Memory*. Atlanta: Society of Biblical Literature, 2013.

Kelber, Werner H. "Mark and Oral Tradition." *Semeia* 16 (1979) 7–55.

Kelber, Werner H. *The Oral Tradition and the Written Gospel: The Hermeneutics of Speaking and Writing in the Synoptic Tradition, Mark, Paul, and Q*. Bloomington: Indiana University Press, 1983.

Kim, Ji Hoe. "A Hallidayan Approach to Orality and Textuality and Some Implications for Synoptic Gospel Studies." *BAGL* 8 (2019) 111–38.

BIBLIOGRAPHY

Kirk, Alan. "The Memory-Tradition Nexus in the Synoptic Tradition: Memory, Media, and Symbolic Representation." In *Memory and Identity*, edited by Tom Thatcher, 131–59. Atlanta: SBL, 2014.

Köhler, Wolf-Dietrich. *Die Rezeption des Matthäusevangeliums in der Zeit vor Irenäus.* Tübingen: Mohr Siebeck, 1987.

Kümmel, Werner G. *The New Testament: The History of the Investigation of Its Problems.* Nashville: Abingdon, 1972.

Lachmann, Karl. "De ordine narrationum in evangeliis synopticis." *ThStK* 8 (1935) 570–90.

Land, Christopher D. *The Integrity of 2 Corinthians and Paul's Aggravating Absence.* NTM 36. Sheffield: Sheffield Phoenix, 2015.

Lane, William L. *The Gospel According to Mark: The English Text with Introduction, Exposition and Notes.* NICNT 2. Grand Rapids: Eerdmans, 1974.

Leckie-Tarry, Helen. *Language and Context: A Functional Linguistic Theory of Register.* Edited by David Birch. London: Pinter, 1995.

Lee, Sang-Il. *Jesus and Gospel Traditions in Bilingual Context: A Study in the Interdirectionality of Language.* BZNW 186. Berlin: de Gruyter, 2012.

Lessing, Gotthold E. "New Hypothesis on the Evangelists as Merely Human Historians." In *Philosophical and Theological Writings*, edited by Hugh B. Nisbet, 148–71. Cambridge: Cambridge University Press, 2012.

Levinsohn, Stephen H. *Discourse Features of New Testament Greek: A Coursebook on the Information Structure of New Testament Greek.* 2nd ed. Dallas: SIL International, 2000.

Liddel, H. G., and R. Scott. *A Greek-English Lexicon.* 9th ed. Oxford: Clarendon, 1996.

Linden, Philip van. *The Gospel according to Mark.* CBC 2. Collegeville: Liturgical, 1983.

Linnemann, Eta. *Is There a Synoptic Problem?: Rethinking the Literary Dependence of the First Three Gospels.* Translated by Robert W. Yarbrough. Grand Rapids: Baker, 1992.

Löhr, Winrich. "Justin Martyr." In *The Reception of Jesus in the First Three Centuries. Vol. 2: From Thomas to Tertullian: Christian Literary Receptions of Jesus in the Second and Third Centuries CE*, edited by Jens Schröter and Christine Jacobi, 433–48. London: T&T Clark, 2020.

Louw, J. P., and E. A. Nida. *Greek-English Lexicon of the New Testament Based on Semantic Domains.* 2 vols. 2nd ed. New York: United Bible Societies, 1989.

Luther, Martin. *Luther's Works: Sermons on the Gospel of St. John Chapter 1–4*, edited by Jaroslav Pelikan. Vol. 22. Saint Louis: Concordia, 1957.

Lyons, John. *Introduction to Theoretical Linguistics.* Cambridge: Cambridge University Press, 1968.

Malinowski, Bronislaw. *Coral Gardens and Their Magic: A Study of the Methods of Tilling the Soil and of Agricultural Rites in the Trobriand Islands.* Vol. 1. 1935. Reprint, London: Routledge, 2002.

Mann, Mary B. "The Quantitative Differentiation of Samples of Written Language." *PM* 56 (1944) 41–74.

Marcion. *The Gospel of the Lord: An Early Version Which Was Circulated by Marcion of Sinope as the Original Gospel.* Translated by James H. Hill. New York: Guernsey, 1891.

Marshall, I. Howard. *The Gospel of Luke.* NIGTC 3. Grand Rapids: Eerdmans, 1978.

Martin, J. R. *English Text: System and Structure.* Philadelphia: Benjamins, 1992.

Martin, J. R., and David Rose. *Working with Discourse: Meaning Beyond the Clause.* 2nd ed. London: Continuum, 2007.

Marxsen, Willi. *Mark the Evangelist.* Translated by Roy A. Harrisville. Nashville: Abingdon, 1969.

Mathesius, Vilém. *A Functional Analysis of Present Day English on a General Linguistic Basis.* Translated by Libuše Dušková. Paris: Mouton, 1975.

Mathesius, Vilém. "Functional Linguistics." In *Praguiana: Some Basic and Less Known Aspects of the Prague Linguistic School,* edited and translated by Josef Vachek and Libuše Dušková, 121–42. Amsterdam: John Benjamins, 1983.

Mathesius, Vilém. "Zum Problem der Belastungs—und Kombinations—fähigkeit der Phoneme?" In *A Prague School Reader in Linguistics,* edited by Josef Vachek, 177–82. Bloomington: Indiana University Press, 1964.

Mathesius, Vilém. "Řeč a sloh." In *Čtení o jazyce a poezii,* edited by B. Havránek and J. Mukařovský, 11–102. Prague: Melantrich, 1942.

Mathesius, Vilém. "La Structure Phonologique du Lexique du Tchéque Moderne." In *A Prague School Reader in Linguistics,* edited by Josef Vachek, 156–76. Bloomington: Indiana University Press, 1964.

Matthews, P. H. *The Concise Oxford Dictionary of Linguistics.* 3rd ed. Oxford: Oxford University Press, 2014.

Mathewson, David L., and Elodie B. Emig. *Intermediate Greek Grammar: Syntax for Students of the New Testament.* Grand Rapids: Baker Academic, 2016.

McNeile, Alan H. *The Gospel according to St. Matthew: The Greek Text with Introduction, Notes, and Indices.* London: Macmillan, 1915.

Meyer, F. B. *Peter: Fisherman, Disciple, Apostle.* London: Morgan & Scott, 1919.

Moessner, D. P. "Reicke, Bo." In *Dictionary of Major Biblical Interpreters,* edited by Donald K. McKim, 853–58. Downers Grove: InterVarsity, 2007.

Most, Glenn W. "Karl Lachmann (1793–1851): Reconstructing the Transmission of a Classical Latin Author." *HistH* 4 (2019) 269–73.

Mounce, W. D. *Greek-Dictionary.* http://www.billmounce.com/greek-dictionary /hermeneutes.

Mournet, Terence C. *Oral Tradition and Literary Dependency: Variability and Stability in the Synoptic Tradition and Q.* WUNT 195. Tübingen: Mohr Siebeck, 2005.

Niederwimmer, Kurt. "Johannes Markus und die Frage nach dem Verfasser des zweiten Evangeliums." *ZNW* 58 (1967) 172–88.

BIBLIOGRAPHY

Nolland, John. *Luke 1:1–9:20.* WBC 35A. Grand Rapids: Zondervan, 2000.

Ong, Walter J. *Orality and Literacy: The Technologizing of the Word.* 3rd ed. London: Routledge, 2012.

Origen. *Contra Celsum.* Translated with an introduction and notes by Henry Chadwick. Cambridge: Cambridge University Press, 1965.

Parker, Pierson. "The Posteriority of Mark." In *New Synoptic Studies: The Cambridge Gospel Conference and Beyond,* edited by William R. Farmer, 67–142. Macon, GA: Mercer University Press, 1983.

Parsons, Mikeal C. *Luke: Storyteller, Interpreter, Evangelist.* Peabody: Hendrickson, 2007.

Parvis, Sara, and Paul Foster, eds. *Justin Martyr and His Worlds.* Minneapolis: Fortress, 2007.

Peabody, David B. "Farmer, William Reuben." In *Dictionary of Major Biblical Interpreters,* edited by Donald K. McKim, 432–38. Downers Grove: InterVarsity, 2007.

Peabody, David B. "The Two Gospel Hypothesis." In *The Synoptic Problem: Four Views,* edited by Stanley E. Porter and Bryan R. Dyer, 67–88. Grand Rapids: Baker Academic, 2016.

Peabody, David B. "Two Gospel Hypothesis Response." In *The Synoptic Problem: Four Views,* edited by Stanley E. Porter and Bryan R. Dyer, 139–50. Grand Rapids: Baker Academic, 2016.

Perrin, Nicholas. "Diatessaron." In *The Reception of Jesus in the First Three Centuries. Vol. 2: From Thomas to Tertullian: Christian Literary Receptions of Jesus in the Second and Third Centuries CE,* edited by Jens Schröter and Christine Jacobi, 141–60. London: T&T Clark, 2020.

Perumalil, A. C. "Papias." *ExpT* 85 (1974) 361–66.

Peterson, David G. *The Acts of the Apostles.* PNTC. Grand Rapids: Eerdmans, 2009.

Petrie, Stewart. "The Authorship of 'The Gospel according to Matthew': A Reconsideration of His External Evidence." *NTS* 14 (1967) 15–32.

Porter, Stanley E. *The Criteria for Authenticity in Historical-Jesus Research: Previous Discussion and New Proposals.* JSNTSup 191. Sheffield: Sheffield Academic, 2000.

Porter, Stanley E. "Dialect and Register in the Greek of the New Testament: Theory." In *Rethinking Contexts, Rereading Texts: Contributions from the Social Sciences to Biblical Interpretation,* edited by M. D. Carroll R., 190–208. JSOTSup 299. Sheffield: Sheffield Academic, 2000.

Porter, Stanley E. *Idioms of the Greek New Testament.* 2nd ed. BLG 2. Sheffield: Sheffield Academic, 1994.

Porter, Stanley E. "The Legacy of B. F. Westcott and Oral Gospel Tradition." In *Earliest Christianity within the Boundaries of Judaism: Essays in Honor of Bruce Chilton,* edited by Alan J. Avery-Peck, et al., 326–45. Leiden: Brill, 2016.

Porter, Stanley E. *The Letter to the Romans: A Linguistic and Literary Commentary.* NTM 37. Sheffield: Sheffield Phoenix, 2015.

Porter, Stanley E. "Orality and Textuality and Implications for Description of the Greek New Testament from a Systemic Function Linguistics Perspective." Forthcoming.

Porter, Stanley E. "Pericope Markers and the Paragraph." In *The Impact of Unit Delimitation on Exegesis*, edited by Raymond de Hoop, et al., 175–95. Leiden: Brill, 2008.

Porter, Stanley E. "Prominence: An Overview." In *The Linguist as Pedagogue: Trends in the Teaching and Linguistic Analysis of the Greek New Testament*, edited by Stanley E. Porter and Matthew B. O'Donnell, 45–74. NTM 11. Sheffield: Sheffield Phoenix, 2009.

Porter, Stanley E. "The Synoptic Problem: The State of the Question." *JGRChJ* 12 (2016) 73–98.

Porter, Stanley E. "Systemic Functional Linguistics and the Greek Language: The Need for Further Modeling." In *Modeling Biblical Language: Selected Papers from the McMaster Divinity College Linguistics Circle*, edited by Stanley E. Porter, et al., 9–47. LBS 13. Leiden: Brill, 2016.

Porter, Stanley E. "Verbal Aspect and Discourse Function in Mark 16:1–8: Three Significant Instances." In *Studies in the Greek Bible: Essays in Honor of Francis T. Gignac*, edited by Jeremy Corley and Vincent Skemp, 123–37. Washington, DC: Catholic Biblical Association of America, 2008.

Porter, Stanley E. *Verbal Aspect in the Greek of the New Testament, with Reference to Tense and Mood*. SBG 1. New York: Peter Lang, 1989.

Porter, Stanley E. "Word Order and Clause Structure in New Testament Greek: An Unexplored Area of Greek Linguistics Using Philippians as a Test Case." *Filologia Neotestamentaria* 6 (1993) 177–205.

Porter, Stanley E., and Bryan R. Dyer. "The Synoptic Problem: An Introduction to Its Key Terms, Concepts, Figures, and Hypotheses." In *The Synoptic Problem: Four Views*, edited by Stanley E. Porter and Bryan R. Dyer, 1–26. Grand Rapids: Baker Academic, 2016.

Porter, Stanley E., and Matthew B. O'Donnell. *Discourse Analysis and the Greek New Testament. Text-Generating Resources*. LNTG 2. London: T&T Clark, 2024.

Porter, Stanley E., et al., *Fundamentals of New Testament Greek*. Grand Rapids: Eerdmans, 2010.

Reed, Jeffrey T. *A Discourse Analysis of Philippians: Method and Rhetoric in the Debate over Literary Integrity*. JSNTSup 136. Sheffield: Sheffield Academic, 1997.

Reicke, Bo. "Griesbach's Answer to the Synoptic Question." In *J. J. Griesbach: Synoptic and Text-Critical Studies 1776–1976*, edited by Bernard Orchard and Thomas R. W. Longstaff, 50–67. SNTSMS 34. Cambridge: Cambridge University Press, 1978.

Reicke, Bo. *The Roots of the Synoptic Gospels*. Philadelphia: Fortress, 1986.

Renan, Ernest. *Life of Jesus*. New York: Howard Wilford Bell, 1904.

Rhoads, David, et al., *Mark as Story: An Introduction to the Narrative of a Gospel*. 3rd ed. Minneapolis: Fortress, 2012.

Riesenfeld, Harald. *The Gospel Tradition*. Philadelphia: Fortress, 1970.

BIBLIOGRAPHY

Riesner, Rainer. "From the Messianic Teacher to the Gospels of Jesus Christ." In *Handbook for the Study of the Historical Jesus. Vol. 1: How to Study the Historical Jesus*, edited by Tom Holmén and Stanley E. Porter, 405–46. Leiden: Brill, 2011.

Riesner, Rainer. *Jesus als Lehrer: Eine Untersuchung zum Ursprung der Evangelien-Überlieferung.* WUNT 2/7. 3rd ed. Tübingen: Mohr Siebeck, 1988.

Riesner, Rainer. "Jesus as Preacher and Teacher." In *Jesus and the Oral Gospel Tradition*, edited by Henry Wansbrough, 185–210. JSNTSup 64. Sheffield: Sheffield Academic, 1991.

Riesner, Rainer. "The Orality and Memory Hypothesis." In *The Synoptic Problem: Four Views*, edited by Stanley E. Porter and Bryan R. Dyer, 89–111. Grand Rapids: Baker Academic, 2016.

Robertson, A. T. *A Grammar of the Greek New Testament in the Light of Historical Research.* 4th ed. Nashville: Broadman, 1923.

Robertson, A. T., and W. H. Davis. *A New Short Grammar of the Greek Testament: For Students Familiar with the Elements of Greek.* 10th ed. Grand Rapids: Baker, 1977.

Runge, Steven E. *Discourse Grammar of the Greek New Testament: A Practical Introduction for Teaching and Exegesis.* Peabody: Hendrickson, 2010.

Sampson, G. *Schools of Linguistics.* Stanford: Stanford University Press, 1980.

Sanday, William. "The Conditions under which the Gospels Were Written, in Their Bearing upon Some Difficulties of the Synoptic Problem." In *Studies in the Synoptic Problem: By Members of the University of Oxford*, edited by William Sanday, 3–26. Oxford: Clarendon, 1911.

Sanday, William. *Essays in Biblical Criticism and Exegesis.* Selected and edited by Craig A. Evans and Stanley E. Porter. JSNTSup 225. Sheffield: Sheffield Academic, 2001.

Sandys-Wunsch, John. "Eichhorn, J(ohann) G(ottefried) (1752–1827)." In *Dictionary of Major Biblical Interpreters*, edited by Donald K. McKim, 400–404. Downers Grove: InterVarsity, 2007.

Saussure, Ferdinand de. *Course in General Linguistics.* Translated by Roy Harris. London: Bloomsbury, 1983.

Schleiermacher, Frederick. *A Critical Essay on the Gospel of St. Luke.* London: John Taylor, 1825.

Schmidt, Karl L. *The Place of the Gospels in the General History of Literature.* Translated by Byron R. McCane. Columbia: University of South California Press, 2002.

Schuler, Philip L. *A Genre for the Gospels: The Biographical Character of Matthew.* Philadelphia: Fortress, 1982.

Spinoza, Baruch. *Theological-Political Treatise.* Translated by Samuel Shirley. 2nd ed. Indianapolis: Hackett, 2001.

Stein, Robert H. *Mark.* BECNT. Grand Rapids: Baker, 2008.

Stein, Robert H. *Studying the Synoptic Gospels: Origin and Interpretation.* 2nd ed. Grand Rapids: Baker Academic, 2001.

Storr, Gottlob C. *Über den Zweck der evangelischen Geschichte, und der Briefe Johannes.* Tübingen: Jacob Friedrich Heerbrandt, 1789.

Storr, Gottlob C., and Carl C. Flatt. *An Elementary Course of Biblical Theology.* 2nd ed. Translated by Samuel S. Schmucker. New York: Gould and Newman, 1836.

Strauss, Mark L. *Four Portraits, One Jesus: An Introduction to Jesus and the Gospels.* Grand Rapids: Zondervan, 2007.

Streeter, Burnett H. *The Four Gospels: A Study of Origins.* London: Macmillan, 1924.

Strickland, Michael. "Evangelicals and the Synoptic Problem." PhD diss., University of Birmingham, 2011.

Talbert, Charles H. *What Is a Gospel? The Genre of the Canonical Gospels.* Philadelphia: Fortress, 1977.

Tannehill, Robert C. *The Narrative Unity of Luke-Acts: A Literary Interpretation. Vol. 1: The Gospel according to Luke.* Philadelphia: Fortress, 1986.

Thayer, J. H. *A Greek-English Lexicon of the New Testament Being Grimm's Wilke's Clavis Novi Testamenti.* Grand Rapids: Baker, 1977.

Thiselton, Anthony C. *1 Corinthians: A Shorter Exegetical & Pastoral Commentary.* Grand Rapids: Eerdmans, 2006.

Tiede, David L. *Luke.* ACNT. Minneapolis: Augsburg, 1988.

Tuckett, Christopher M. *Luke.* TCSG. London: T&T Clark, 1996.

Tzamalikos, Panayiotis. *Origen: New Fragments from the Commentary on Matthew.* Leiden: Brill, 2020.

Vansina, Jan. *Oral Tradition: A Study in Historical Methodology.* Translated by H. M. Wright. Chicago: Aldine, 1965.

Votaw, Clyde W. "The Gospels and Contemporary Biographies." *AJT* 19 (1915) 45–73.

Wallace, Daniel B. *Greek Grammar Beyond the Basics: An Exegetical Syntax of the New Testament.* Grand Rapids: Zondervan, 1996.

Walton, Steve. "What Are the Gospels? Richard Burridge's Impact on Scholarly Understanding of the Genre of the Gospels." *CBR* 14 (2015) 81–93.

Weiss, Johannes. *Paul and Jesus.* Translated by H. J. Chaytor. London: Harper and Brothers, 1909.

Weiße, Christian H. *Die evangelische Geschichte, kritisch und philosophisch bearbeitet.* 2 vols. Leipzig: Breitkopf und Härtel, 1838.

Wellhausen, Julius. *Einleitung in die drei ersten Evangelien.* Berlin: Georg Reimer, 1905.

Wenham, David. *From Good News to Gospels: What Did the First Christians Say about Jesus?* Grand Rapids: Eerdmans, 2018.

Westcott, B. F. *Introduction to the Study of the Gospels.* 3rd ed. London: Macmillan, 1867.

Westfall, Cynthia L. "Blessed Be the Ties that Bind: Semantic Domains and Cohesive Chains in Hebrews 1.1–2.4 and 12.5–8." *JGRChJ* 6 (2009) 199–216.

Westfall, Cynthia L. *A Discourse Analysis of the Letter to the Hebrews: The Relationship between Form and Meaning.* LNTS 297. London: T&T Clark, 2005.

Westfall, Cynthia L. "Goulder, Michael D. (1927–)." In *Dictionary of Biblical Criticism and Interpretation*, edited by Stanley E. Porter, 136. New York: Routledge, 2007.

Westfall, Cynthia L. "Mapping the Text: How Discourse Analysis Helps Reveal the Way through James." In *The Epistle of James: Linguistic Exegesis of an Early Christian Letter*, edited by James D. Dvorak and Zachary K. Dawson, 11–44. LENT 1. Eugene, OR: Wipf & Stock, 2019.

Westfall, Cynthia L. "A Method for the Analysis of Prominence in Hellenistic Greek." In *The Linguist as Pedagogue: Trends in the Teaching and Linguistic Analysis of the Greek New Testament*, edited by Stanley E. Porter and Matthew B. O'Donnell, 75–94. NTM 11. Sheffield: Sheffield Phoenix, 2009.

Westfall, Cynthia L. "A Moral Dilemma? The Epistolary Body of 2 Timothy." In *Paul and the Ancient Letter Form*, edited by Stanley E. Porter and Sean A. Adams, 213–52. Leiden: Brill, 2010.

Westfall, Cynthia L. "The Relationship Between the Resurrection, the Proclamation to the Spirits in Prison and Baptismal Regeneration: 1 Peter 3.19–22." In *Resurrection*, edited by Stanley E. Porter, et al., 106–35. JSNTSup 186. Sheffield: Sheffield Academic, 1999.

Wilke, Christian G. *Der Urevangelist oder exegetisch kritische Untersuchung über das Verwandtschaftsverhältniß der drei ersten Evangelien.* Dresden: Gerhard Fleischer, 1838.

Winer, G. B. *A Treatise on the Grammar of New Testament Greek, Regarded as a Sure Basis for New Testament Exegesis.* Translated by W. F. Moulton. 3rd ed. Edinburgh: T&T Clark, 1882.

Yoon, David I. *A Discourse Analysis of Galatians and the New Perspective on Paul.* LBS 17. Leiden: Brill, 2019.

Young, Richard A. *Intermediate New Testament Greek: A Linguistic and Exegetical Approach.* Nashville: Broadman & Homan, 1994.

Zahn, Theodor. *Introduction to the New Testament.* Translated by John M. Trout, et al., Vol. 2. New York: Charles Scribner's Sons, 1909.

Zimmern, Helen. *Gotthold Ephraim Lessing: His Life and His Works.* London: Longmans, 1878.

# Index of Modern Authors

Abakuks, Andris   $2n7$
Abbott-Smith, G.   $9n14$
Ahn, Hojoon J.   $5n28, 10n16, 40n221, 51n264, 67n76$
Alexander, Loveday   $51n265$
Allen, O. Wesley   $31n168$
Allison, Dale C.   $48n239$
Aune, David E.   54, 55

Barnes, Timothy D.   $14n43$
Barrett, C. K.   $197n13, 197n14$
Bauckham, Richard   4
Baur, Ferdinand C.   23, 29, 30
Baum. A. D.   $3n13, 7n3, 24n127$
Beare, Francis W.   $47n235, 47n239, 48n243, 50n254$
Beaugrande, R. de   $64n58$
Benoit, Pierre   27, 28
Biber, Douglas   $64n61$
Black, Stephanie L.   $81n154, 81n155, 81n156, 100, 101n9, 104n15, 188n1, 197n13$
Blass, F.   $80n151$
Bock, Darrell L.   $31n168, 50n256, 51n263, 51n264$
Bockmuehl, Markus   $49n251$
Boismard, Marie-Emile   27, 28, 29, 30
Botha, Pieter J. J.   191
Bovon, François   50
Brown, Gillian   $70n91$
Brown, Schuyler   152
Bultmann, Rudolf   $3, 7n1, 25n135, 26, 27, 29, 30, 54, 55, 56$
Burkett, R. Delbert   $45n230, 58n29, 152n15$
Burridge, Richard A.   $7n1, 7n2, 54, 56$
Byrskog, Samuel   4

Cadbury, Henry J.   $184n19$
Casey, Maurice   $152n15$
Catford, John C.   $65n62$
Chen, Diane G.   $50n255, 50n259$
Chilton, Bruce   1
Cirafesi, Wally V.   $89n199$
Clements, R. E.   $25n132, 25n135$
Collins, Adela Y.   $49n248$

Conrad, Susan   $64n61$
Conzelmann, Hans.   $7n1, 197n13$
Cotterell, Peter   $70n91$

Dahl, Nils A.   $25n133$
Davies, W. D.   $48n239$
Davis, W. H.   $81n155$
Dawson, Zachary K.   $40n221, 54, 56, 61n46$
Debrunner, A.   $80n151$
Derico, T. M.   $57n27$
DeVries, D.   $22n107, 22n108$
Dibelius, Martin   54, 55
Dungan, David L.   $10, 11n28, 12n34, 12n35, 13n37, 13n38, 13n41, 13n42, 14n44, 14n46, 14n47, 15, 16n60, 17n68$
Dunn, James D. G.   28, 29, 30
Dvorak, James D.   $61n46, 67n75, 75, 92, 157$
Dyer, Bryan R.   $1, 2n8, 5n22, 7n4, 8n9, 42na, 44n223, 44n224, 44n225$

Eggins, Suzanne   $60n39$
Eichhorn, Johann G.   19, 21, 29, 30
Elder, Nicholas A.   $4n20$
Emig, Elodie B.   $80n152$
Evans, Craig A.   $2, 3n9, 8n6, 31, 32, 40, 42, 43, 152n15$

Farmer, William R.   $2n6, 17n71, 27, 29, 30, 46n246$
Farrer, Austin   $2n7, 26, 27n153, 29, 30$
Fawcett, R. P.   60
Fee, Gordon D.   $57n26$
Fergusson, D.   $26n143, 26n144$
Finch, Geoffrey   $66n70$
Firbas, Jan   $70n89$
Fitzmyer, Joseph A.   $50n256, 192n5$
Flatt, Carl C.   19
Ford, Coleman M.   $11n30$
Foster, Paul   $10n17, 11n27$
France, R. T.   $9n15, 47n237, 48n240, 48n241, 48n243, 49n247, 51n266, 51n267, 101n10, 178n14, 249nc, 250ng$
Fung, Benjamin W. W.   $51n264$

# INDEX OF MODERN AUTHORS

Gamble, Harry Y.   47$n$239, 48$n$243
Garland, David E.   50$n$256
Gathercole, Simon   47$n$238
Gerhardsson, Birger   3$n$15, 4$n$15, 27, 29, 30
Gieseler, Johann K. L.   3$n$13, 21, 29, 30
Gignilliat, Mark S.   16$n$68
Goodacre, Mark   2, 3$n$9, 33, 34$n$187, 34$n$188, 34$n$189, 34$n$190, 40, 42, 43
Green, Joel B.   47$n$239, 50$n$256
Griesbach, Johann J.   2$n$6, 15$n$53, 18, 29, 30
Gundry, Robert H.   47$n$239, 112$n$27, 136$n$8

Halliday, M. A. K.   58, 59, 60, 61, 63, 64, 65, 66, 67, 70, 71, 72, 74, 76, 77, 78, 79, 80, 82, 85, 86, 87, 88, 110, 119, 120, 151, 189$n$2
Hasan, Ruqaiya   65$n$63, 65$n$68, 66$n$71, 67$n$72, 77, 78, 79, 80, 82, 110$n$24
Henaut, Barry W.   45$n$229, 58$n$28
Hengel, Martin   38$n$218, 49$n$248
Herder, Johann G. von   19, 20, 29, 30
Holton, David   80$n$150
Holtzmann, Heinlich J.   1$n$5, 24, 29, 30, 31$n$169, 47$n$239
Horsley, Richard A.   197$n$13
Hug, Johann L.   20, 21$n$98, 21$n$99, 21$n$100, 29, 30
Hunt, Emily J.   10$n$23, 10$n$25

Jacobsen, David S.   152$n$15
Jeffrey, David L.   50$n$260
Jeremias, Joachim   8$n$7, 249$n$c
Johnson, Luke T.   51$n$265

Karamanolis, George   13$n$40
Keener, Craig S.   55, 56
Keith, Chris   3$n$12
Kelber, Werner H.   4
Kim, Ji Hoe   85, 86
Kirk, Alan   46$n$233
Köhler, Wolf-Dietrich   10$n$22
Kümmel, Werner G.   2$n$5, 18$n$79, 18$n$80, 20$n$93, 20$n$95, 22$n$110, 22$n$114, 23$n$116, 24$n$125, 24$n$126, 47$n$239

Lachmann, Karl   22, 29, 30
Land, Christopher D.   65$n$69, 77$n$126
Lane, William L.   48$n$243, 49$n$249, 49$n$250
Leckie-Tarry, Helen   64$n$60

Lee, Sang-Il   3$n$11
Lessing, Gotthold E.   17, 18, 29, 30
Levinsohn, Stephen H.   81$n$155
Liddel, H. G.   136$n$8
Linden, Philip van   48$n$243
Linnemann, Eta   19$n$88, 21$n$104, 23$n$123
Löhr, Winrich   10$n$19
Louw, J. P.   82, 110$n$a, 113$n$a, 113$n$b, 115$n$29, 115$n$30, 116$n$a, 167$n$7, 177$n$a, 197$n$12, 250$n$e
Lyons, John   87$n$188

Malinowski, Bronislaw   65$n$64
Mann, Mary B.   191$n$3
Marshall, I. Howard   50$n$156
Martin, J. R.   60, 63$n$51, 76$n$119
Marxsen, Willi   46$n$232, 152$n$15
Mathesius, Vilém   59, 67, 68, 69, 70, 71, 72
Matthews, P. H.   127$n$3
Mathewson, David L.   80$n$152
McNeile, Alan H.   101$n$11
Meyer, F. B.   49$n$251
Moessner, D. P.   28$n$161
Most, Glenn W.   22$n$109
Mounce, W. D.   9$n$14
Mournet, Terence C.   44, 45

Nida, E. A.   82, 110$n$a, 113$n$a, 113$n$b, 115$n$29, 115$n$30, 116$n$a, 167$n$7, 177$n$a, 197$n$12, 250$n$e
Niederwimmer, Kurt   48$n$246
Nolland, John   31$n$168, 50$n$254, 50$n$256, 50$n$258, 50$n$259, 50$n$261, 184$n$19

O'Donnell, Matthew B.   67, 71, 72, 73, 74, 75, 76, 77, 78, 79, 80$n$146, 83$n$166, 92, 94, 157, 160
Ong, Walter J.   84, 85$n$181

Parker, Pierson   48$n$246
Parsons, Mikeal C.   184$n$19
Parvis, Sara   10$n$17
Peabody, David B.   2, 3$n$9, 4$n$22, 27$n$153, 35, 36, 40, 42, 43, 44
Perrin, Nicholas   11$n$26
Perumalil, A. C.   8$n$10
Peterson, David G.   192$n$5
Petrie, Stewart   48$n$240

Porter, Stanley E.   1*n*1, 2*n*6, 2*n*8, 5*n*22, 7*n*4, 8*n*7, 8*n*9, 24n129, 30, 34, 42*n*a, 44*n*223, 44*n*224, 44*n*225, 45, 58*n*32, 59, 67, 69*n*88, 70*n*88, 71, 72, 73, 74, 75, 76, 77, 78, 79, 80*n*146, 80*n*150, 80*n*151, 80*n*151, 81*n*154, 83*n*166, 85, 87, 88, 89, 90*n*199, 92, 94, 119, 120, 121*n*36, 122, 138*n*11, 151, 153, 157, 158, 160, 181, 183

Reed, Jeffrey T.   77*n*126, 127*n*3
Reicke, Bo   17*n*71, 18*n*75, 18*n*76, 18*n*79, 28, 29, 30
Renan, Ernest   54
Rhoads, David   4*n*20
Riesenfeld, Harald   46*n*232
Riesner, Rainer   4, 5*n*23, 5*n*24, 37, 38, 39, 40, 44, 45, 46
Robertson, A. T.   81*n*154, 81*n*155
Rose, David   76*n*119
Runge, Steven E.   81*n*155

Sampson, G.   68*n*81, 68*n*82, 69*n*84
Sanday, William   1*n*5, 24, 29, 30
Sandys-Wunsch, John   19*n*86, 19*n*88
Saussure, Ferdinand de   84
Schleiermacher, Frederick   21, 22, 29, 30, 84*n*171
Schmidt, Karl L.   7*n*1, 54, 55*n*8, 55*n*9, 56, 84*n*171
Schuler, Philip L.   54, 55, 56*n*23
Scott, R.   136*n*8
Stein, Robert H.   7*n*5, 48*n*243, 48*n*245
Storr, Gottlob C.   18, 19, 29, 30
Strauss, Mark L.   47*n*236
Streeter, Burnett H.   1*n*5, 25, 26*n*140, 26*n*141, 26*n*142, 29, 30
Strickland, Michael   15*n*54, 16*n*67

Talbert, Charles H.   54, 55
Tannehill, Robert C.   192*n*5
Thayer, J. H.   9*n*14
Thiselton, Anthony C.   57*n*26
Tiede, David L.   50*n*256
Tuckett, Christopher M.   2*n*5, 50*n*254, 51*n*268
Turner, Max   70*n*91
Tzamalikos, Panayiotis   1*n*3

Vansina, Jan   57
Votaw, Clyde W.   54

Wallace, Daniel B.   137*n*10
Walton, Ryder D.   75, 92, 157
Walton, Steve   56*n*18
Weiss, Johannes   25*n*134, 47*n*239
Weiße, Christian H.   23, 29, 30
Wellhausen, Julius   24, 25*n*133, 29, 30
Wenham, David   4
Westcott, B. F.   3, 24, 29, 30
Westfall, Cynthia L.   2*n*7, 61*n*46, 65*n*61, 65*n*66, 65*n*67, 72*n*100, 77*n*125, 79*n*136, 82*n*166, 89*n*198
Wilke, Christian G.   22, 23*n*116, 29, 30
Winer, G. B.   81*n*154

Yoon, David I.   63, 67*n*75, 78*n*133, 82, 90*n*200
Young, Richard A.   81*n*154, 87*n*188
Yule, George   70*n*91

Zahn, Theodor   23*n*118, 23*n*121, 23*n*122, 24*n*124, 47*n*239
Zimmern, Helen   17*n*70

# Index of Biblical References

**Old Testament**

*Isaiah*

| | |
|---|---|
| 61:1–2a | 199 |

*Zechariah*

| | |
|---|---|
| 13:7 | 103 |

**New Testament**

*Matthew*

| | |
|---|---|
| 2:5 | 202 |
| 3:7b–10 | 35 |
| 3:11–12 | 34 |
| 3:12 | 34 |
| 4:1 | 31 |
| 4:4 | 202n20 |
| 4:6 | 202n20 |
| 4:7 | 104n15 |
| 4:10 | 202n20 |
| 4:18–20 | 49n251 |
| 5:1–7:29 | 5n27 |
| 5:3–6 | 82 |
| 5:26 | 249nc |
| 8:5–13 | 32 |
| 8:28–34 | 211 |
| 9:9 | 47 |
| 9:38 | 104n15 |
| 10:3 | 47 |
| 10:16–23 | 32 |
| 10:24 | 196n10 |
| 10:29 | 104n15 |
| 11:10 | 202n20 |
| 12:24 | 104n15, 196n10 |
| 13:1–23 | 210 |
| 13:1 | 210 |
| 13:54–58 | 51n264 |
| 14:1–12 | 33 |
| 14:9 | 33 |
| 16:18 | 49n251 |
| 17:26 | 104n15 |
| 19:21 | 104n15 |
| 21:13 | 89n199, 202n20 |
| 22:37 | 104n15 |
| 25:14–30 | 34 |
| 25:21, 23 | 104n15 |
| 26:1–13 | 192 |
| 26:2 | 93 |
| 26:6–13 | 93, 100 |
| 26:6 | 192 |
| 26:10 | 192 |
| 26:14–35 | 5, 91, 92, 93, 94, 95, 96, 97, 98, 108, 109, 117, 118, 119, 120, 121, 122, 123, 151, 187, 190, 194, 198, 199, 200, 202, 205, 217, 227, 249 |
| 26:14–25 | 119, 121 |
| 26:14–16 | 93, 94, 96, 97, 98, 100, 104, 109, 110, 111, 193 |
| 26:14a–15a | 91, 92, 93, 95, 97 |
| 26:14 | 92, 93, 94, 97, 100, 108, 110, 119, 119, 193 |
| 26:15–16 | 192 |
| 26:15 | 81, 97, 100, 101, 105n18, 110, 111, 191, 193 |
| 26:15a | 92, 93, 94, 119 |
| 26:15b–16 | 92, 93, 95, 97 |
| 26:15b | 91, 92, 93, 94, 119 |
| 26:15c | 101, 119 |
| 26:16 | 97, 101, 105, 110, 118, 119, 124, 191, 193 |
| 26:16a | 91, 92 |
| 26:17–25 | 93, 96 |
| 26:17–19 | 93, 94, 96, 97, 98, 101, 105, 111 |
| 26:17 | 92, 93, 94, 95, 97, 101, 108, 111, 112, 189 |
| 26:17a | 119 |
| 26:17b | 101, 119 |
| 26:18 | 92, 93, 94, 95, 97, 101, 108, 111, 112, 191 |
| 26:18a | 91, 92, 101, 119 |
| 26:18b | 91, 92, 101, 119 |
| 26:18c | 101 |
| 26:18d | 74, 91, 92, 101 |
| 26:18e | 101 |
| 26:18f | 101, 118, 124, 188, 203 |
| 26:19 | 92, 93, 95, 97, 101, 106, 111, 119, 189, 193 |

# INDEX OF BIBLICAL REFERENCES

*Matthew (cont.)*

| | |
|---|---|
| 26:19a | 94 |
| 26:19b | 91, 92, 94 |
| 26:20–25 | 93, 94, 95, 96, 97, 98, 106, 112, 113, 188, 193 |
| 26:20–24 | 92, 93, 95, 97 |
| 26:20 | 93, 95, 97, 102, 113, 119, 191 |
| 26:21 | 96, 97, 102, 109, 113, 191 |
| 26:21a | 91, 92, 119 |
| 26:21b | 91, 92, 113, 119 |
| 26:22 | 97, 102, 108, 109, 191 |
| 26:22a | 119, 191 |
| 26:22b | 91, 92, 119 |
| 26:23–24 | 96 |
| 26:23 | 93, 95, 97, 102, 113, 191 |
| 26:23a | 91, 92, 102, 119 |
| 26:23b | 102, 119 |
| 26:24 | 97, 102, 108, 109, 113, 119, 123, 201, 202, 204, 208 |
| 26:24c | 91, 92 |
| 26:24d | 91, 92 |
| 26:24e | 91, 92 |
| 26:25 | 37, 92, 93, 95, 96, 97, 102, 108, 109, 113, 191 |
| 26:25a | 119 |
| 26:25b | 119 |
| 26:25c | 102, 113, 118, 119, 124, 188, 203 |
| 26:25d | 119 |
| 26:26–32 | 97 |
| 26:26–30 | 92, 93, 94, 95, 96, 97, 99, 102, 106, 107, 114, 115, 119, 121, 147, 178 |
| 26:26–29 | 108n19 |
| 26:26 | 92, 95, 96, 97, 102, 108, 109, 114, 119n32, 189, 191 |
| 26:26a | 93, 119 |
| 26:26b–29 | 94 |
| 26:26b | 119 |
| 26:27–28 | 103 |
| 26:27 | 96, 97, 103, 114, 191 |
| 26:27a | 103, 119 |
| 26:27b | 103, 119 |
| 26:27c | 103 |
| 26:28 | 97, 103, 118n32, 114, 119, 196, 197, 250nf |
| 26:29 | 96, 97, 103, 109n21, 114, 119, 165n6 |
| 26:29a | 103 |
| 26:30 | 94, 97, 114, 119 |
| 26:31–35 | 93, 94, 96, 97, 99, 103, 107, 108, 115, 116, 117, 119, 121 |
| 26:31–33 | 92, 94, 95 |
| 26:31–32 | 202n17 |
| 26:31 | 94, 97, 103, 109, 116, 123, 189, 201, 202, 204 |
| 26:31a | 119 |
| 26 :31b | 119 |
| 26:32 | 97, 103, 116, 119 |
| 26:33 | 92, 94, 96, 97, 103, 116, 191 |
| 26:33a | 119 |
| 26:33b | 119 |
| 26:34 | 92, 94, 95, 96, 97, 103, 104n15, 116, 188, 189, 249nc |
| 26:34a | 118, 119 |
| 26:34b | 104, 119 |
| 26:35 | 81, 94, 97, 103, 116, 188, 191 |
| 26:35a | 92, 94, 95, 96, 97, 118, 119 |
| 26:35b | 92, 94, 95, 96, 97, 104, 119 |
| 26:35c | 104, 119 |
| 26:49 | 37 |
| 26:51 | 31 |
| 26:67–68 | 34 |
| 26:67b | 34 |
| 26:68 | 3n9, 36, 41, 43 |
| 26:68b | 34n188 |
| 27:65 | 104n15 |
| 28:19–20 | 32 |

*Mark*

| | |
|---|---|
| 1:1 | 31 |
| 1:2 | 202n20 |
| 1:7–8 | 34 |
| 1:12 | 31 |
| 1:16–18 | 49n251 |
| 2:1 | 35n192 |
| 2:13–14 | 35n192 |
| 2:27 | 31 |
| 3:1 | 35n192 |
| 3:14 | 195, 196 |
| 3:20–21 | 31 |
| 3:20 | 35n192 |
| 4:1–20 | 210 |
| 4:1–2 | 35n192 |
| 4:1 | 210 |

# INDEX OF BIBLICAL REFERENCES

277

*Mark (cont.)*

| | |
|---|---|
| 4:26–29 | 31 |
| 4:35–41 | 31 |
| 5:1–20 | 211 |
| 5:21 | 35n192 |
| 6:1–6a | 51n264 |
| 6:14–29 | 33 |
| 6:30–44 | 33 |
| 6:30 | 195, 196 |
| 6:47–52 | 31 |
| 7:2–4 | 31 |
| 7:6 | 202n20 |
| 7:14 | 35n192 |
| 7:24–30 | 31 |
| 7:31 | 35n192 |
| 7:32–37 | 31 |
| 7:33–36 | 33 |
| 8:1 | 35n192 |
| 8:13 | 35n192 |
| 8:14–21 | 31 |
| 8:22–26 | 31 |
| 9:5 | 37 |
| 9:12 | 202n20 |
| 9:13 | 202n20 |
| 9:29 | 31 |
| 9:48–49 | 31 |
| 10:1 | 35n192 |
| 10:10 | 35n192 |
| 10:32 | 35n192 |
| 11:17 | 89n199, 202n20 |
| 11:27 | 35n192 |
| 13:33–37 | 31 |
| 14:1 | 127n1 |
| 14:3–9 | 134 |
| 14:6 | 193 |
| 14:10–31 | 5, 125, 126, 128, 129, 130, 131, 142, 143, 149, 150, 151, 152, 153, 154, 155, 187, 190, 194, 198, 199, 200, 202, 206 |
| 14:10–21 | 151, 152 |
| 14:10–11 | 126, 128, 130, 131, 134, 138, 139, 143, 144, 193 |
| 14:10 | 126, 127, 128, 129, 130, 133, 134, 142, 143, 151, 191, 193 |
| 14:10a | 125, 134 |
| 14:10b | 125 |
| 14:11 | 126, 127, 129, 130, 133, 134, 143, 151, 155, 191, 193 |

| | |
|---|---|
| 14:11b | 125 |
| 14:11c | 125 |
| 14:11d | 125 |
| 14:12–21 | 126, 127, 130 |
| 14:12–17 | 126, 130 |
| 14:12–16 | 127, 128, 129, 130, 131, 139, 140, 144, 145 |
| 14:12 | 126, 127, 128, 133, 139, 142, 144, 145, 191, 193 |
| 14:12a | 125, 134, 151 |
| 14:12b | 134, 151 |
| 14:13 | 133, 134, 144, 145, 151, 191 |
| 14:13b | 134, 151 |
| 14:13c | 134 |
| 14:13d | 135 |
| 14:13e | 135 |
| 14:14 | 133, 135, 142, 144, 145, 151 |
| 14:15 | 133, 135, 142, 144, 151, 154, 201, 202, 204 |
| 14:15b | 135 |
| 14:16 | 128, 133, 135, 144, 145, 151, 191, 202 |
| 14:16a | 125 |
| 14:17–26 | 127, 128, 129, 130, 131, 132, 140, 141, 145 |
| 14:17–21 | 127 |
| 14:17 | 127, 133, 135, 146, 147, 151, 191 |
| 14:18–26 | 126, 130 |
| 14:18 | 126, 127, 128, 133, 135, 143, 145, 146, 189, 193 |
| 14:18a | 151 |
| 14:18b | 151 |
| 14:18d | 125 |
| 14:19 | 133, 135, 137, 142, 143, 145, 146, 150, 155, 188, 191, 203 |
| 14:19a | 151 |
| 14:19b | 125 |
| 14:20–21 | 128 |
| 14:20 | 133, 135, 136, 142, 145, 146, 191 |
| 14:20a | 151 |
| 14:20b | 136, 151 |
| 14:21 | 133, 134, 136, 137, 142, 145, 151, 154, 201, 202, 204, 208 |
| 14:21c | 125 |
| 14:21e | 125 |
| 14:22–26 | 126, 127, 130, 136, 151, 152 |

*Mark (cont.)*

| | |
|---|---|
| 14:22 | 128, 133, 136, 142, 145, 146, 191 |
| 14:22a | 151 |
| 14:22b | 125, 151 |
| 14:23 | 128, 133, 136, 145, 146, 151, 191 |
| 14:24 | 128, 133, 137, 142, 146, 191, 196, 197 |
| 14:24a | 151 |
| 14:24b | 151 |
| 14:25 | 133, 134, 137, 142, 145, 146, 147, 151, 165$n$6 |
| 14:26 | 133, 151 |
| 14:27–31 | 126, 127, 128, 129, 130, 131, 133, 141, 142, 145, 146, 148, 149, 151, 152 |
| 14:27–29 | 126, 127, 130 |
| 14:27–28 | 202$n$17 |
| 14:27 | 128, 133, 142, 143, 148, 154, 189, 193, 201, 202, 204 |
| 14:27a | 137, 151 |
| 14:27b | 137, 151 |
| 14:27c | 137 |
| 14:27d | 137 |
| 14:27e | 137 |
| 14:28 | 133, 137, 148, 151 |
| 14:29 | 75, 126, 128, 129, 130, 133, 134, 138, 148, 149, 188, 191 |
| 14:29a | 125, 126, 138, 151 |
| 14:29b | 151 |
| 14:30 | 81$n$153, 126, 127, 129, 130, 133, 134, 138, 142, 148, 189, 193 |
| 14:30a | 151 |
| 14:30b | 151 |
| 14:31 | 128, 130, 133, 134, 138, 148, 149, 188 |
| 14:31a | 125, 126, 127, 129, 130, 138, 151 |
| 14:31b | 126, 127, 129, 130, 138, 151 |
| 14:31c | 138, 151 |
| 14:31d | 138 |
| 14:47 | 31 |
| 14:51–52 | 31 |
| 14:53–65 | 36 |
| 14:65 | 3$n$9, 34, 43 |
| 16:1–8 | 89$n$196 |

*Luke*

| | |
|---|---|
| 1:1–4 | 50, 51, 52, 57, 182, 201, 209 |
| 1:1 | 51 |
| 1:1–2 | 51 |
| 1:2–4 | 50 |
| 1:3 | 50, 51, 182, 191, 196$n$11, 201 |
| 2:23 | 202$n$20 |
| 3:4 | 202$n$20 |
| 3:7b–9 | 35 |
| 3:15–17 | 34 |
| 3:17 | 34 |
| 4:1 | 31 |
| 4:4 | 202$n$20 |
| 4:8 | 202$n$20 |
| 4:10 | 202$n$20 |
| 4:16–30 | 51$n$264 |
| 4:18–19 | 199 |
| 5:1–11 | 49$n$251 |
| 6:13 | 195 |
| 6:20–49 | 5$n$27 |
| 6:40 | 196$n$10 |
| 7:1–10 | 32 |
| 7:27 | 202$n$20 |
| 7:40 | 74 |
| 8:4–15 | 210 |
| 8:4 | 204 |
| 8:26–39 | 211 |
| 9:10–17 | 33 |
| 9:10 | 33, 195 |
| 9:12 | 33 |
| 10:26 | 202$n$20, 202$n$21 |
| 11:49 | 195 |
| 13:28–30 | 32 |
| 14:26 | 196$n$10 |
| 14:27 | 196$n$10 |
| 14:33 | 196$n$10 |
| 17:5 | 195 |
| 19:11–27 | 34 |
| 19:46 | 89$n$199, 202$n$20 |
| 20:34 | 191 |
| 22:1–6 | 158, 162 |
| 22:1–2 | 5$n$26, 156, 158, 166 |
| 22:1 | 158 |
| 22:3–23, 31–34 | 5, 156, 157, 158, 162, 163, 174, 180, 181, 182, 183, 184, 185, 186, 187, 190, 194, 198, 199, 200, 202, 206 |
| 22:3–13 | 182, 183 |

# INDEX OF BIBLICAL REFERENCES

279

*Luke (cont.)*

| | |
|---|---|
| 22:3–6 | 157, 158, 160, 161, 162, 163, 165, 170, 173, 174, 175, 183, 201 |
| 22:3 | 156, 157, 158, 165, 166, 170, 173, 174, 181, 182 |
| 22:4 | 156, 157, 165, 166, 170, 182, 191 |
| 22:5 | 165, 166, 182 |
| 22:5a | 156, 157 |
| 22:5b | 156, 157 |
| 22:6 | 165, 182, 191 |
| 22:7–13 | 158, 160, 161, 162, 163, 164, 166, 170, 171, 175, 176 |
| 22:7–8 | 157, 158, 160, 162 |
| 22:7 | 157, 159, 161, 165, 166, 171, 174, 175, 182 |
| 22:7b | 156, 157 |
| 22:8 | 157, 159, 165, 166, 170, 191, 199 |
| 22:8a | 182 |
| 22:8b | 182 |
| 22:9 | 157, 158, 159, 160, 161, 162, 165, 166, 191 |
| 22:9a | 182 |
| 22:9b | 156, 157, 182 |
| 22:10–13 | 157, 158, 160, 162 |
| 22:10–12 | 166, 167 |
| 22:10 | 157, 158, 159, 161, 162, 165, 167, 170, 191 |
| 22:10a | 156, 157, 182 |
| 22:10b | 156, 157, 182 |
| 22:10f | 156, 157 |
| 22:11 | 165, 167, 170, 182 |
| 22:11b | 167 |
| 22:11c | 167 |
| 22:12 | 167, 174, 182, 186, 201, 202 |
| 22:12a | 156, 157 |
| 22:13 | 165, 167, 182, 186, 191, 201, 202, 204 |
| 22:14–23 | 158, 159, 160, 161, 162, 164, 165, 167, 171, 172, 176, 177, 182, 183 |
| 22:14–20 | 159 |
| 22:14 | 159, 165, 167, 174, 182, 191, 195 |
| 22:14a | 157, 159, 160, 162, 163 |
| 22:14b–23 | 157, 159, 160, 162, 163 |
| 22:14b | 157, 159 |

| | |
|---|---|
| 22:15 | 165, 168, 181, 191 |
| 22:15a | 182 |
| 22:15b | 182 |
| 22:16 | 165, 168, 182 |
| 22:16b | 156, 157 |
| 22:17 | 159, 165, 168, 172*n*12, 191 |
| 22:17a | 168, 182 |
| 22:17b | 168, 182 |
| 22:18 | 165, 174, 182 |
| 22:19–20 | 168 |
| 22:19 | 159, 165, 174, 191 |
| 22:19a | 182 |
| 22:19b | 182 |
| 22:20 | 159, 165, 168, 172*n*12, 174, 196, 197 |
| 22:20a | 182 |
| 22:20b | 174, 182 |
| 22:21–23 | 159 |
| 22:21 | 159, 165, 168, 174, 182 |
| 22:21b | 174 |
| 22:22 | 165, 168, 171, 174, 182, 186, 201, 202, 203, 204, 208 |
| 22:23 | 165, 182 |
| 22:24–30 | 5*n*26, 156, 157*n*1, 158*n*3, 159, 169, 173 |
| 22:24 | 44, 159, 160, 169, 208 |
| 22:25–30 | 159, 160, 169 |
| 22:25 | 159, 169*n*10 |
| 22:26 | 159 |
| 22:27 | 159 |
| 22:31–34 | 158, 159, 160, 161, 162, 162, 165, 169, 173, 179, 182, 183 |
| 22:31–32 | 183*n*16 |
| 22:31 | 157, 159, 160, 161, 165, 169, 174, 181, 182 |
| 22:31b | 157 |
| 22:32 | 157, 158, 159, 160, 161, 162, 165, 165, 169, 182 |
| 22:32a | 157 |
| 22:32b | 157 |
| 22:33–34 | 169 |
| 22:33 | 157, 159, 160, 161, 162, 165, 169, 174, 181, 191 |
| 22:33a | 182 |
| 22:33b | 182 |
| 22:34 | 157, 158, 159, 160, 161, 162, 165, 169, 186, 191, 201, 202, 204 |
| 22:34a | 157, 182 |

## INDEX OF BIBLICAL REFERENCES

*Luke (cont.)*

| | |
|---|---|
| 22:34b | 182 |
| 22:47 | 191 |
| 22:50 | 31 |
| 22:63–64 | 34 |
| 22:64 | 3$n$9, 36, 41, 43 |
| 22:64b | 34 |
| 24:10 | 195 |
| 24:46 | 202 |

*John*

| | |
|---|---|
| 1:9 | 82 |
| 1:49 | 37 |
| 2:3 | 115, 147, 178 |
| 6:51–58 | 5$n$26 |
| 6:54 | 13 |
| 19:34 | 5$n$26 |

*Acts*

| | |
|---|---|
| 1:1 | 51 |
| 1:15–22 | 49$n$251 |
| 2:14 | 49$n$251 |
| 2:37 | 49$n$251 |
| 2:38 | 49$n$251 |
| 9:1–22 | 192 |
| 9:1 | 192 |
| 9:8 | 192 |
| 9:22 | 192 |
| 12:12 | 49 |

| | |
|---|---|
| 12:25 | 49 |
| 13:4 | 49 |
| 15:36–41 | 49 |
| 22:3 | 37 |
| 24:5 | 17 |

*1 Corinthians*

| | |
|---|---|
| 10:17 | 250$nd$ |
| 11:17–34 | 5$n$26 |
| 11:23 | 57, 197 |
| 11:25 | 196 |
| 11:25b | 5$n$26 |
| 15:1–3 | 37 |

*Colossians*

| | |
|---|---|
| 4:10 | 49 |
| 4:14 | 50 |

*2 Timothy*

| | |
|---|---|
| 4:11 | 49, 50 |

*Philemon*

| | |
|---|---|
| 24 | 49, 50 |

*1 Peter*

| | |
|---|---|
| 5:13 | 49 |

*1 John*

| | |
|---|---|
| 1:9 | 82 |

Printed in the United States
by Baker & Taylor Publisher Services